ASBOs

A practitioner's guide to defending anti-social behaviour orders

Maya Sikand is a barrister at Garden Court Chambers in London. She specialises in criminal defence work and crime-related civil work. She approaches all areas of her practice in the context of human rights jurisprudence. She has written articles for *Archbold News, New Law Journal* and *Legal Action.*

The Legal Action Group is a national, independent charity which campaigns for equal access to justice for all members of society. Legal Action Group:

- provides support to the practice of lawyers and advisers
- inspires developments in that practice
- campaigns for improvements in the law and the administration of justice
- stimulates debate on how services should be delivered.

ASBOs

A practitioner's guide to defending anti-social behaviour orders

Maya Sikand

Legal Action Group
2006

This edition published in Great Britain 2006
by LAG Education and Service Trust Limited
242 Pentonville Road, London N1 9UN
www.lag.org.uk

While every effort has been made to ensure that the details in this text and correct, readers must be aware that the law changes and that the accuracy of the material cannot be guaranteed and the author and the publisher accept no responsibility for any losses or damage sustained.

British Library Cataloguing in Publication Data
a CIP catalogue record for this book is available from the British Library.

ISBN 10: 1 903307 41 4
ISBN 13: 978 1 903307 41 4

Typeset by Regent Typesetting, London
Printed and bound in Great Britain by William Clowes Ltd, Beccles, Suffolk

Foreword

From its introductory overview, this book makes clear why a study of ASBO law is important. The ASBO regime is of course a key element of this government's social policy. And it was intended to address the real misery and distress caused by conduct involving harassment and intimidation. But the ASBO regime has its dangers. Anti-social behaviour orders can be triggered by a frighteningly wide range of 'anti-social' behaviour; the contents of ASBOs can themselves be frighteningly wide in their prohibitions; and the consequences of breach can be draconian – frequently involving immediate custody and further extending the state's powers of imprisonment. So ASBOs can easily be misused: by excessive deployment against the young and mentally disordered, by their use against conduct that is disturbed or dysfunctional rather than serious and threatening, by resort to over-wide prohibitions, and by an over-readiness to impose custodial terms for breaches. Maya Sikand's book exposes all this. It eloquently answers the question 'so what's wrong with ASBOs?' with the statistics for 2003. In that year 42 per cent of ASBOs were breached, 55 per cent of breaches were punished with a custodial term, and 46 per cent of young people received immediate custody for breach of an ASBO.

From the point of view of the practitioner, this book has it all: detailed exposition of the statutory tests; masterful analysis of the developing case law and its conflicting trends; helpful guidance on tactics – for example in dealing with hearsay and representing juveniles. Above all there is a sympathetic engagement with the great variety of people and behaviour that are affected by the coercive effects of ASBOs – not just threatening gangs of youths on council estates, but also compulsive loners, the young and mentally disturbed, persistent petty criminals, graffiti-writers, street prostitutes and shoplifters.

This book goes through all aspects of the law and practice of ASBOs. It starts with the social and political context, and takes the reader through all the key issues: what should be considered before an ASBO is applied for; the difference between 'stand-alone' and post-conviction ASBOs; the procedural safeguards, and the admissibility of hearsay. It analyses in detail the types of conduct that *should* be covered, and those that some courts wrongly permit to be covered by the concept of 'anti-social behaviour'. In chapter 7 the book provides a profound critique of the proper scope of ASBO prohibitions. It then deals with the range of punishments for breach and the over-readiness to resort to custody. Finally, the book addresses the special problems of juveniles subject to ASBOs – with full reference to the general legal principles that should govern the treatment of children, and extent to which those principles are, in fact, respected by the courts.

Of particular value is the in-depth treatment of the 'human rights' issues raised by resort to ASBOs; the analysis of issues such as the use of ASBOs to make general prohibitions of all criminal offences; and the need to apply Convention principles of proportionality to restrict the alarming scope of certain ASBO prohibitions.

But this book is not just scholarly and comprehensive. It is above all practical, clear and helpful. I came to the issue with little prior knowledge of ASBOs. Having read it, I feel equipped to represent people on ASBOs at all levels, and sufficiently informed to engage in the wider debate as to the fair and civilised legal response to the real life issues of anti-social behaviour.

Edward Fitzgerald QC
August 2006

Preface

The writing of this book has coincided with an intensity of focus by our current Government on anti-social behaviour. The Respect Action Plan was launched early this year amidst much publicity, after I began writing, and only two years after the Together Campaign was launched. Both campaigns focus on the vast array of available tools to tackle anti-social behaviour and both promote community enforcement. ASBOs are just one of the many tools recently introduced by the Government to tackle what it sees as the one of the biggest problems in local communities. Since ASBOs were added to the anti-social behaviour armoury in 1999, the number of orders applied for has escalated dramatically. In 1999 only 104 orders were applied for but in 2005 that figure had increased to 2,679. In August this year, just as this book was going to press, the Home Office published a new guide to anti-social behaviour orders. Additionally, the Government passed a statutory instrument on the 1 August 2006, giving Transport for London and the Environment Agency the power to apply for stand-alone and county court ASBOs as of 1 September 2006. It remains to be seen what impact this will have on the number and type of ASBOs applied for.

This book aims to guide lawyers and other advisers through the law and practice relating to the application and imposition of ASBOs. It also aims to consider ASBO practice in the context of human rights law. Its focus is on defending ASBOs, both in the criminal courts and in the county court. There is growing ASBO expertise amongst local authority and CPS lawyers – indeed the very recent Home Office guide to ASBOs makes mention of a team of 14 'anti-social behaviour expert prosecutors'. Given the growth and popularity of ASBOs, and the common perception that the lower courts will simply 'rubber stamp' an application, I decided to write a book on how to defend the making of an ASBO. It is not a political treatise: it is simply an attempt to redress the balance.

Given that the majority of ASBOs are imposed in the criminal courts, that is where the focus of the book lies although readers will see that Chapter 8 is devoted to the county court. That chapter is authored by Rajeev Thacker (Garden Court Chambers), who brings his experience of civil practise to bear on the ASBO question. I owe him a huge debt of gratitude for agreeing to write that chapter as well as sharing his expertise on costs and appeals in the civil arena in Chapters 11 and 12. I am also extremely grateful to him for being the first reader of a number of other chapters.

I owe an extra special thank you to Jan Luba QC (Garden Court Chambers) for the mass of material on ASBOs he shared with me (law reports, press cuttings, TV programmes) as well as his personal contribution to ASBO case law, in particular the now well known case of *Moat Housing Group-South v Harris*. I am terribly grateful to Edward Fitzgerald QC (Doughty Street Chambers) for writing the foreword – particularly as it interfered with his summer break and therefore his Article 8 rights!

I want to pay tribute to the youth department at Lawrence & Co. Solicitors, in particular Shauneen Lambe and Aika Stephenson, as their tireless commitment to young people in the criminal justice system and those faced with ASBO proceedings has been a real inspiration to me.

I am also grateful to those pupils and law students who helped me with legal research, in particular Gabrielle Guillemin, who spent hours analysing Home Office statistics when she should have been preparing for her Bar exams and Morayo Fagborun who trawled through Hansard for me and taught me how to cite parliamentary debates properly (although if I've still got them wrong, it's my fault). Thank you also to Vikram Dodd at the *Guardian* for sending me all those ASBO stories from the Press Association.

I would like to thank my colleagues and the staff at Garden Court for their support and enthusiasm and this beautiful building (which almost makes it bearable to be here on a Saturday night or Sunday morning). As always, Owen Davies QC has been utterly supportive of this project. My clerks have exhibited incredible patience waiting for me to finish writing and I must thank them for that – in particular Bob Archer and my senior clerk, Colin Cook.

My greatest debt of all is to LAG, especially Esther Pilger. Esther has the patience of a saint and has been a pillar of support throughout the writing of this book. I was introduced to Esther by Alison Hannah (the Director of LAG) – this book was born out of a conversation with Alison – so my first thank you is to her.

Lastly, thank you to Richard Spencer (Powell Spencer & Partners) for Pedras D'el Rei which is where I spent a wonderful week correcting the proofs – and to Bela for putting up with my boring outbursts about citations and paragraphs while on holiday.

Maya Sikand
Garden Court Chambers
August 2006

Contents

Table of cases

References in the right-hand column are to paragraph numbers.

Table of statutes

References in the right-hand column are to paragraph numbers.

Table of statutory instruments

References in the right-hand column are to paragraph numbers.

Table of European legislation

References in the right-hand column are to paragraph numbers.

Abbreviations

ABC	Acceptable Behaviour Contract
ASBA 2003	Anti-social Behaviour Act 2003
ASBO	Anti-social Behaviour Order
BTP	British Transport Police
CA 2003	Courts Act 2003
CAA 1968	Criminal Appeals Act 1968
CDA 1998	Crime and Disorder Act 1998
CDRP	Crime and Disorder Reduction Partnership
CDS	Criminal Defence Service
CEA 1995	Civil Evidence Act 1995
CJA 2003	Criminal Justice Act 2003
CLS	Community Legal Service
CPR	Civil Procedure Rules
CPS	Crown Prosecution Service
CRASBO	Post-conviction ASBO
CRIMINT	Criminal Intelligence
CRIS	Crime Report Information System
CSP	Community Safety Partnership
CYPA 1933	Children and Young Persons Act 1933
DDA 1995	Disability Discrimination Act 1995
DPA 1998	Data Protection Act 1998
ECHR	European Convention on the Protection of Human Rights and Fundamental Freedoms
HA 1996	Housing Act 1996
HAT	Housing Action Trust
HRA 1998	Human Rights Act 1998
ISO	Individual Support Order
LSC	Legal Services Commission
MCA 1980	Magistrates' Court Act 1980
MC(ASBO)R 2002	Magistrates' Courts (Anti-Social Behaviour Orders) Rules 2002
MC(H)R 1999	Magistrates' Court (Hearsay Evidence in Civil Proceedings) Rules 1999
PHCT	Primary Health Care Trust
PII	public interest immunity
POA 1986	Public Order Act 1986
PRA 2002	Police Reform Act 2002

RSL	Registered social landlord
SCA 1981	Supreme Court Act 1981
SOCPA 2005	Serious Organised Crime and Police Act 2005
YJCEA 1999	Youth Justice and Criminal Evidence Act 1999
YOT	Youth Offending Team

Introduction: an overview of the social and political landscape

The Government's perspective

The language employed by the Government's 'Together' campaign reflects its prevailing view that there has been a recent increase in anti-social behaviour as a result of the decline in moral standards and family values and hence the need for tougher powers to control it.[1] The Prime Minister's decision to enter into the ASBO debate by writing a newspaper piece demonstrates that he feels the need to publicly justify anti-social behaviour measures such as ASBOs, some six years after their introduction. He suggests in his commentary that, as he unveils new measures to tackle anti-social behaviour and crime, his government will once more 'be under attack for eroding essential civil liberties' and that it is incumbent upon him to explain the importance of such powers 'within a more coherent intellectual and political framework'.[2] Effectively, he reasserts the 'Together' language of moral decline and resultant increase in anti-social behaviour, and points out the importance of communities not living in fear. Measures, such as ASBOs, are an attempt, he says, 'to protect the most fundamental liberty of all – freedom from harm by others'.[3]

It is outside the remit of this book to investigate whether there has indeed been a decline in morality and/or an increase in anti-social behaviour and, if both those propositions were found to be true, whether there is in fact a correlation between them.

1 See www.together.gov.uk. See also www.respect.gov.uk

2 Tony Blair, 'Our citizens should not live in fear', *The Observer*, 11 December 2005.

3 Ibid.

The public's perception

A recent study commissioned by the Joseph Rowntree Foundation (JRF)[4] found that there were three main strands of thought among communities about the causes of anti-social behaviour, a decline in moral standards and family values being just one of them. There was also a belief not only that a significant minority of children and young people (and, in many cases, their families) was increasingly disengaged from wider society, but also that young people have always challenged boundaries and antagonised their elders ('kids will be kids').

Significantly, the study found that for *most* people in Britain, anti-social behaviour is not a major concern.[5] It is of acute concern however for a significant minority of people, mainly those living in deprived urban areas.[6] Perhaps more significantly, the JRF study reveals that when asked about tackling anti-social behaviour, people were more likely to opt for preventative action to deal with the causes than tough action against perpetrators. This is in stark contrast to the populist language and message of the 'Together' campaign.

So what's wrong with ASBOs?

It has often been said by the Government that civil liberties organisations or individuals that campaign against ASBOs are out of touch with or unaware of the plight of those whose lives are deeply affected by anti-social behaviour. The Government points to the fact that there is a wide range of behaviour that cannot be effectively policed or prosecuted in the criminal courts for evidential reasons. There are indeed those who are affected by the unacceptable behaviour of others, and who are entitled to protection from this persistent interference with their right to private life. But the ASBO regime has not always focused on the plight of those people and has often been misused by those who have the power to make applications. The overuse, and sometimes abuse, of ASBO powers has meant that the orders have been ridiculed by the media and considered a 'badge of honour' by some

4 A Millie, J Jacobson, E McDonald and M Hough, *Anti-social behaviour strategies: finding a balance*, Policy Press, 2005.

5 Ibid, chapter 2, p13. To be contrasted with the Government's assertion on www.together.gov.uk: 'Many people across England and Wales believe that anti-social behaviour is a problem where they live. One in five say that there is a high level of disorder in their area.'

6 Ibid.

disaffected youth. Some of the ways in which ASBOs are perceived to be misused are discussed below.

ASBOs 'made to be breached'

A glance at the BBC News website[7] as well as the *ASBO Concern* website[8] discloses the arguably irresponsible use that has been made of this power to date. There is a spectrum of behaviour in society which can be defined as dysfunctional, obsessive-compulsive, and/or disordered: for example, calling 999 repeatedly and pretending to faint when ambulance staff turn up; faking a heart attack to get into an operating theatre; having a fetish for medical supplies and hanging around hospitals; pretending to be a werewolf and howling loudly. These are all real examples of behaviour that has been subject to ASBOs.[9] There is no doubt that some of this behaviour is alarming, perhaps even distressing, but one thing it ought not to lead to is a 'two-stop criminal offence'.[10]

The British Institute for Brain Injured Children (BIBIC) and the National Autistic Society have been highlighting the plight of those with autism, ADHD and other disorders against whom ASBOs have been obtained.[11] In fact BIBIC has been so concerned about the use of ASBOs against children with conditions that affect their learning ability, it launched a campaign in 2003 called 'Ain't Misbehavin''.[12]

Obtaining ASBOs against people with behavioural difficulties and/or obsessive-compulsive disorders is unlikely to make them desist from this behaviour. Indeed breach is almost guaranteed and all it does is catapult vulnerable people into the criminal justice system and eventually into already overflowing prisons. This is where governmentspeak about rights and responsibilities breaks down. People in this category are not always able to take responsibility for their actions precisely because they suffer from a disorder that may need psychiatric or other specialist treatment or support. It may well be that the disorder is untreatable or has gone undiagnosed. This

7 See http://news.bbc.co.uk.

8 See www.asboconcern.org.uk.

9 See 'Asbowatch 2005: Look back at anger', http://news.bbc.co.uk.

10 To use a phrase coined by Gil-Robles, *Report by Mr Alvaro Gil-Robles, Commissioner for Human Rights, on his visit to the UK 4–12 November 2004*, CommDH(2005)6, Strasbourg: Council of Europe, para 112.

11 Martin Bright, 'Charity pleads for tolerance as autistic youngsters face ASBOs', *The Guardian*, 22 May 2005.

12 See www.bibic.org.uk.

is why those who defend ASBOs must ensure that they are properly equipped with medical and other expert evidence so that they can challenge the imposition of a 'made to be breached' ASBO. The argument that can be deployed in these circumstances is that an ASBO is not 'necessary' within the meaning of the second limb of the statutory test for imposing ASBOs (discussed in full in chapter 5).

Geographical inconsistencies

There is no doubt that the use of ASBOs varies across Britain. There is a perception that if you live in a particular part of the country, you are more likely to have an ASBO imposed upon you for behaviour which in another part of the country would be dealt with by some other means, if at all. A glance at the Home Office statistics[13] reveals that Greater Manchester had by far the largest number of applications in the April 1999 to September 2005 period (1,045),[14] followed by Greater London (749),[15] the West Midlands (554)[16] and West Yorkshire (550).[17] This could suggest that inner-city areas are the most troubled by anti-social behaviour and therefore most receptive to ASBOs. However, in Greater London, the London Borough of Camden has had by far and away the highest number of ASBO applications to date (107), followed by Westminster (46), whereas traditionally troubled London boroughs such as Brent and Hackney have made only 19 and 14 applications respectively. This is a clear indication that the use of ASBOs is directly related to the political priorities and resources of a particular local authority and not necessarily to the level of anti-social behaviour. This could lead to the criminalisation of certain communities as well as a risk that the problem is just shifted out of one area and into another.

A fast track to prison?

Whatever the geographical inconsistencies, the most worrying government statistics in 2004/5 were that 42 per cent of ASBOs are breached, 55 per cent of breaches are punished with a custodial term and 46 per cent of young people receive immediate custody for breach

13 See www.crimereduction.gov.uk/asbos2.htm.
14 Only 5 were refused.
15 10 refused.
16 1 refused.
17 1 refused.

of an ASBO.[18] A closer look at the statistics shows that in 2003 almost half of all ASBOs applied for were against 10–17-year-olds, and in 2004/5, this figure reduces to about 40 per cent.[19] Young people are most likely to breach ASBO terms which involve geographical restrictions and restrictions on association with others (the terms most commonly imposed on youths) and most will breach in the first quarter of their ASBO term.[20] As the number of ASBOs applied for increases, given the high success rate in obtaining them (see below), it follows that more ASBOs will be breached, and that in turn will continue to have an impact on our prison system and, ultimately, the society we live in. Hence the importance of ensuring that ASBOs are only imposed when strictly necessary and that they are appealed when they are too wide and/or unnecessary.

It is no secret that our prisons are overcrowded (the United Kingdom can now boast the highest rates of detention in Western Europe)[21] and that the past decade has seen a sharp rise in the numbers detained (a 50 per cent increase), without there being any discernible rise in the crime rate,[22] and it must be likely that breaches of ASBOs have directly contributed to that increase. According to Alvaro Gil-Robles (the former Commissioner for Human Rights of the Council of Europe), the chair of the Youth Justice Board conceded that the rise in the young offender population in custody in 2004 resulted mainly from breaches of ASBOs.[23] It is interesting to note that the *Magistrates' Court Sentencing Guidelines* list only aggravating factors – not a single mitigating factor is identified.[24]

The crisis in our prisons has been sporadically addressed in guideline judgments over the years, often by the Lord Chief Justice, in relation to a number of offences. An obvious example in recent times being *R v Kefford*[25] in relation to economic offences where the Court

18 5th Report from the Home Affairs Committee Session 2004–2005, *Anti-social Behaviour*, HC 80–I.

19 See www.crimereduction.gov.uk/asbos2.htm.

20 David Brogan, 'Anti-social Behaviour Orders: An assessment of current management information systems and the scale of Anti-social Behaviour Order breaches resulting in custody', Youth Justice Board, 2005, p25. Available at www.youth-justice-board.gov.uk.

21 Gil-Robles, note 9 above, para 123.

22 See Gil-Robles, note 9 above, paras 122–124. See also 5th Report from the Home Affairs Committee Session 2004–2005, *Anti-social Behaviour*, HC 80–I.

23 See Gil-Robles, note 9 above, para 118.

24 *Magistrates' Court Sentencing Guidelines*, p17. Guidelines reproduced in full on the JSB website: www.jsboard.co.uk/magistrates/adult_court/index.htm.

25 [2002] EWCA Crim 519; [2002] 2 Cr App R 495.

of Appeal held that custody was not inevitable even where there was a breach of trust and even more recently the guidelines on robbery sentencing issued by the Sentencing Guidelines Council.[26] There are no official sentencing guidelines in relation to ASBOs yet, although the recent case of *R v Christopher Lamb*[27] has suggested that breaches with little social impact (eg entering an excluded zone but not causing any harassment, alarm or distress) should be distinguished from those breaches that involve harassment, alarm or distress to the public (see chapter 9 on breaches). This is the first sign from the Court of Appeal that the consequence of every breach of an ASBO is not necessarily custody.

Rubber-stamping by the courts?

The other real issue about ASBOs is the disparity and quality of judicial supervision at the time of imposition. In the first six years of the ASBO regime (between 1 April 1999 and 31 March 2005), 5,557 ASBOs were applied for in England and Wales, and only 58 refused by the courts (in Wales, all of the 211 applied for were granted).[28] This translates as virtually a 99 per cent success rate. There is an absence of data about whether the orders are granted in the terms applied for. Certainly the High Court in *Wareham v Purbeck District Council*[29] would not be drawn into the argument that the statistics show that there is no real scrutiny by the magistrates' court when an ASBO application is made. Jack J said:

> If magistrates were granting orders without a proper consideration of their merits, that would be a serious breach of their duty. For my part I am not prepared to accept that has happened. It is equally an explanation for the figures that there is a considerable need for these orders to curb the activities of persons such as the appellant but local authorities and police forces are only applying for them in strong cases ...[30]

The absence of any data in relation to how many ASBOs are appealed, and to which court, makes it difficult to tell whether 99 per cent is a skewed statistic. However, the high levels of breaches to date may very well indicate that either ASBOs are not appealed very often or that

26 www.sentencing-guidelines.gov.uk.

27 [2005] EWCA Crim 2487; [2006] 2 Cr App R (S) 11.

28 www.crimereduction.gov.uk.

29 [2005] EWHC 358 (Admin).

30 Ibid, para 10.

they are not successfully appealed. Even if they are appealed, it may be too late given that a large number of ASBOs, particularly against youths, are breached in the very early stages.[31] The dramatic increase in the body of case law on ASBOs in 2005 and 2006 (analysed in later chapters), in particular the Court of Appeal decision of *R v Boness, Bebbington and Others*,[32] may well mean that there is a changing climate, both in terms of a greater willingness by lawyers to challenge ASBOs, as well as a recognition by the higher courts that the arbitrary application for and granting of ASBOs has had a serious impact upon our prison population over the past seven years.

Wide definition of anti-social behaviour

The other fundamental problem with ASBOs is the wide definition of anti-social behaviour. The current definition, for the purposes of obtaining an ASBO, is boundless and, it would seem, deliberately so (namely, behaviour which causes or is likely to cause harassment, alarm or distress to one or more persons who are not in the same household as the perpetrator).[33] In short, the test is whether others have been or are likely to be upset by it (see para 5.40). The consequences of such a definition are that the state may end up regulating behaviour which does not necessarily amount to a crime or indeed even a civil wrongdoing.

There are endless examples of behaviour which could cause harassment, alarm or distress. Some of them are arguably part and parcel of urban living. Some of them may materially affect the quality of life of a group of individuals in a particular locality. As Gil-Robles has noted, the inevitable result of the fact that ASBOs, unlike civil injunctions, are intended to protect not just specific individuals, but entire communities, is that 'the determination of what constitutes anti-social behaviour becomes conditional on the subjective views of any given collective'.[34] This in turn makes it extremely difficult to define the terms of orders in such a way that 'does not invite inevitable breach'.[35] But the task and challenge facing those defending such orders is to ask the important questions: are these acts anti-social

31 5th Report from the Home Affairs Committee Session 2004–2005, *Anti-social Behaviour*, HC 80–I, see also note 19 above.

32 [2005] EWCA Crim 2395. See chapters 5, 6 and 7.

33 Crime and Disorder Act (CDA) 1998 s1.

34 See Gil-Robles, note 9 above, para 110.

35 Ibid, para 110J.

within the meaning of the CDA 1998; if they are, is an ASBO really necessary or is there some other way of dealing with the behaviour? If an ASBO is necessary, are the terms proportionate?

CHAPTER 1

ASBOs compared with other civil remedies

What is an ASBO?

1.1 There are three different types of order commonly referred to as anti-social behaviour orders (ASBOs). They are civil orders[1] prohibiting behaviour considered to be anti-social, the breach of which results in a penal sanction of up to 5 years' imprisonment. The first type of ASBO to be introduced on 1 April 1999 was the 'stand-alone ASBO', described as an 'anti-social behaviour order' in section 1 of the Crime and Disorder Act (CDA) 1998.[2] In 2002, 'post-conviction ASBOs' (described as 'orders on conviction to prevent further anti-social acts' in CDA 1998 s1C) were introduced.[3] These two types of ASBOs are only available in the criminal courts and the criminal standard of proof applies.[4] In the same year, 'county court ASBOs' (described as 'orders in county court proceedings' in CDA 1998 s1B) came into being.[5]

1.2 While there are similarities between each of these ASBOs, there are vast differences in procedure. There have also been extensive amendments to each of the sections since their introduction at different times. Because of the complexity of each of these orders, a separate chapter is devoted to each kind of ASBO. As the law on the terms and duration of all ASBOs is the same, those aspects of an ASBO are dealt with in chapter 7 and readers will need to cross-refer. Similarly, as the ramifications of breaching an ASBO are the same, readers are referred to chapter 9, which is devoted to the law and procedure upon breach. The statutory test for obtaining an ASBO is a two-stage process and is exactly the same for stand-alone and county court ASBOs. This test is discussed in detail in chapter 5 and once more readers will need to cross-refer. In post-conviction ASBOs, the test is largely the same, with a slight difference, and therefore readers will need to refer to both chapters 5 and 6.

The range of civil remedies available

1.3 There is now a wide range of civil orders and injunctions available to counteract anti-social behaviour. Like many other countries, we have

1 See para 3.2 on why ASBOs are 'civil' and not 'criminal'. See chapter 4 on the use of hearsay evidence in ASBO proceedings in the criminal courts.

2 See chapter 5.

3 Police Reform Act (PRA) 2002 s64. See chapter 6.

4 See para 5.43.

5 PRA 2002 s63. See chapter 8.

long had injunctions and other orders to protect victims of domestic violence[6] as well as tenants in social housing exposed to excessive noise, harassment, abuse, etc.[7] Local authorities have had a statutory power since 1972 to 'promote or protect the rights of inhabitants in their area' by way of injunctive relief (commonly used to tackle begging, prostitution and kerb-crawling),[8] thus invoking the assistance of the civil court in aid of the criminal law.[9] Exclusion orders to counteract football hooliganism have been available in one form or the other since 1986.[10]

1.4 These powers have widened and grown enormously over the past few years, in particular with the introduction of the Crime and Disorder Act (CDA) 1998, the Police Reform Act (PRA) 2002 and the Anti-Social Behaviour Act (ASBA) 2003. CDA 1998 introduced not only ASBOs (limited to the criminal courts at that stage) but also parenting orders, sex offender orders, child curfew orders and child safety orders. PRA 2002 introduced ASBOs in the county court and increased their availability generally. ASBA 2003 further widened existing powers and brought in a raft of new measures including 'crack house' closure orders, dispersal orders[11] and new powers to tackle flyposting, graffiti, waste dumping and litter.[12] The Serious Organised Crime and Police Act (SOCPA) 2005 gave the Secretary of State the power to extend the list of authorities that can apply for ASBOs.[13] The Criminal Justice Act (CJA) 2003 introduced individual support orders[14] and, finally, the Drugs Act 2005 introduced

6 Non-molestation orders, occupation orders and common law injunctions. See also anti-harassment injunctions under the Protection from Harassment Act 1997.

7 Housing Act 1996 s153 (as amended).

8 Local Government Act 1972 s222. See in particular *Nottingham City Council v Matthew Zain (a minor)* [2001] EWCA Civ 1248 in which the Court ruled that s222 could be used to seek an injunction to prevent a public nuisance such as drug dealing which is discussed in detail at para 8.130.

9 Described as a comparatively modern power by the House of Lords in *Stoke-on-Trent City Council v B & Q (Retail) Limited* [1984] AC 754 at 776.

10 Football (Spectators) Act 1989 as amended by the Football (Disorder) Act 2000.

11 Interpreted as a permissive and not coercive power by the High Court in the first challenge in relation to this power: see *R (W) v Commissioner of Police for the Metropolis & The London Borough of Richmond-upon-Thames* [2005] EWHC 1586 (Admin).

12 See also Clean Neighbourhoods and Environment Act 2005 which amends and extends ASBA 2003 powers to deal with flyposting, graffiti, waste dumping and litter and introduces new powers such as 'dog control orders'.

13 SOCPA 2005 s139(3) amending CDA 1998 s1A.

14 CDA 1998 ss1AA and 1AB, inserted by CJA 2003 s322.

intervention orders,[15] although these orders can only be made in addition to an ASBO.

Who can apply for an ASBO?

What is the 'relevant authority'?

1.5 Only a 'relevant authority' within the meaning of CDA 1998 s1(1A)[16] can apply for an ASBO on a stand-alone basis.[17] The list has increased since 1999: now local authorities ('the council for a local government area'),[18] county councils (England only), police forces, British Transport Police (BTP), registered social landlords (RSLs) and housing action trusts (HATs) are included (see section 1(1A)(d) and (e) for full definitions of RSLs and HATs).[19] The Government announced on 20 December 2005 that it wanted to add the Environment Agency to the list and on 4 April 2006 it made the same announcement in relation to Transport for London. It was not until 3 August 2006 that a statutory instrument, making both those bodies relevant authorities, was laid before Parliament.[20]

1.6 In post-conviction cases, under CDA 1998 s1(C) the court makes the order, either of its own motion or if it is asked to do so by the prosecutor (namely the Crown Prosecution Service (CPS) or the advocate instructed on its behalf). Although the application is made by the CPS, the impetus will more often than not come from the police or the local authority (see chapter 6 on post-conviction ASBOs).

1.7 The 2006 Home Office Guidance[21] points out that there is no duty on the BTP or RSLs or HATs to apply for an ASBO should the anti-

15 CDA 1998 ss1G and 1H, inserted by the Drugs Act 2005 s20 which will come into force on 1 October 2006 (see the Drugs Act (Commencement No 4) Order 2006 SI No 2136). See para 5.148.

16 As amended by PRA 2002 s61 and ASBA 2003 s85. Reproduced at appendix A.

17 See also chapter 5 (stand-alone ASBOs), chapter 6 (post-conviction ASBOs) and chapter 8 (county court ASBOs) for more detail.

18 A 'local government area' in England is defined in CDA 1998 s1(12) as a district or London borough, the City of London, the Isle of Wight and the Isle of Scilly. In Wales it is a county or a county borough.

19 See chapter 8 on county court ASBOs for a definition of 'relevant authority'.

20 Crime and Disorder Act 1998 (Relevant Authorities and Relevant Persons) Order 2006 SI No 2137, to come into force 1 Sepetmber 2006. See para 5.2 and appendix A.

21 *A Guide to Anti-social Behaviour Orders* (Home Office, 2006), p11. Available at www.together.gov.uk.

social behaviour occur within their jurisdiction: the police or local authority can still apply on their behalf in accordance with their obligations and duties under CDA 1998 ss5, 6 and 17 (discussed below). Indeed, in the magistrates' court that is usually what happens: the applicant body is nearly always either the police or the local authority. Stand-alone ASBOs are not available in the county court. There, ASBOs can only be made in respect of a person who is already a party to proceedings underway in that court,[22] although there is a power to join others who are not party to the principal proceedings, as long as their alleged anti-social behaviour is material to the principal proceedings.[23]

1.8 As mentioned above,[24] under SOCPA 2005, the Secretary of State now has the power to add any 'person' or 'body' to the list of relevant authorities. Given the focus on 'community justice' in the recent launch of the Government's 'Respect' campaign,[25] it may be a matter of time before community groups such as tenants associations will be given the statutory power to apply for ASBOs.

Why an ASBO over other orders?

1.9 Despite the availability of so many alternative powers to combat anti-social behaviour, there has been a drive to promote ASBOs. There are numerous aspects which make ASBOs attractive to local authorities and other government bodies:

- they are easy to obtain: there is no real age bar (for example, housing injunctions are obtainable only against those aged 18 and over, while ASBOs are available against those as young as 10);[26]
- they apply to a very wide group of people who need only commit their alleged anti-social acts in the area under the geographical control of the relevant government body (by contrast, for a social landlord to obtain an anti-social behaviour injunction, the conduct complained of has to relate to or affect the housing management functions of a local landlord);[27]

22 CDA 1998 ss1B(2) and 1B(3) (as amended). See chapter 8.

23 CDA 1998 ss1B (3A)–1B(3C). See chapter 8.

24 Para 1.4, note 13.

25 See the 'Respect' Action Plan at www.respect.gov.uk, launched on 10 January 2006.

26 In Scotland the age limit is 12, see para 10.6 below. See also para 8.134.

27 Housing Act 1996 s153A (as amended). See para 8.126 on housing for more detail.

- they are individually tailored so a person can be prevented from doing almost anything (even something as innocuous as opening their front door in their underwear);[28]
- they provide an enhanced penalty (a criminal conviction plus up to five years' imprisonment, whereas the breach of a traditional injunction can attract up to two years' imprisonment and does not result in a conviction);
- there is no ban on publicising the identities of those subject to them,[29] even if they are children;[30]
- and most importantly, they are a very powerful political tool, purporting to 'put the law-abiding citizen first'.[31]

Costs to the Government

1.10 In addition to the advantages cited above, obtaining an ASBO is now much cheaper than it used to be, removing any resource based decision making by the applicant body from the picture. A recent 'Together' report on costs[32] shows that the average cost of obtaining an ASBO (excluding breach and appeal costs) was estimated at £4,800 in 2002. Research carried out in 2004 showed that this figure had dropped to £2,500 (ie, by approximately 50 per cent). The reasons cited for this decrease are the introduction of post-conviction orders in 2002[33] and possibly more efficient administrative and legal procedures, as practitioners have become more familiar with using ASBOs. The research also shows that ASBOs on conviction are generally cheaper to administer than other types of ASBO, costing on average £900 compared with £3,200 for stand-alones. Of course, stand-alones are a great deal more expensive if the evidence is contested and witnesses have to be called (the most expensive stand-alone in the survey conducted was £8,400). Home Office statistics show that in 2005 in Greater London

28 See Duncan Walker, 'Asbowatch V: War on a G-string', http://news.bbc.co.uk/1/hi/magazine/4319653.stm, 15 March 2005 (27-year-old mother of two subject to an interim ASBO banned from opening her front door or doing her gardening in her underwear).

29 See paras 5.140 and 10.48.

30 *R (Stanley) v MPC* [2004] EWHC 2229 (Admin).

31 See *Home Office Strategic Plan 2004–2008*, TSO 2004. 'We understand criminal behaviour often has complex and tragic antecedents. But out first duty is to the law-abiding citizen. They are our boss. It's time to put them at the centre of the CJS. That is the new consensus on law and order for our time.'

32 'Cost of Anti-Social Behaviour Orders – a summary report' available at www.together.gov.uk.

33 Introduced by PRA 2002 s64, which came into force 2 December 2002.

over 75 per cent of ASBOs issued were post-conviction ASBOs. In Greater Manchester post-conviction ASBOs accounted for 63 per cent of ASBOs imposed. In the West Midlands there seemed to be a decline in the use of post-conviction ASBOs as the figure in 2005 was 67 per cent (compared with 84 per cent in 2004).[34]

34 A breakdown of ASBOs according to whether they are stand-alone or post-conviction is available from the Home Office Anti-Social Behaviour Unit upon request.

CHAPTER 2

Pre-ASBO considerations

Introduction

2.1 It is important for defence practitioners to understand the ASBO process as a whole so that they are able to advise on whether alternatives to an ASBO could have been offered by the applicant body. Additionally, before a stand-alone or county court ASBO can be applied for, there is a statutory duty to consult. In order to ensure that that duty has been complied with and in order to identify what disclosure they may need to seek, practitioners need to have an insight into that process. Furthermore, consultation inevitably involves information sharing and defendants are often concerned about their personal data being wrongly or unlawfully disclosed to third parties. This chapter therefore focuses on the following issues:

- how the ASBO process begins;
- information sharing and data protection;
- alternatives to ASBOs;
- the statutory duty to consult;
- disclosure of the consultation process;
- and finally, the effect of non-consultation on an ASBO application.

How does the ASBO process begin?

Crime and disorder reduction partnerships and anti-social behaviour

2.2 The Crime and Disorder Act 1998[1] imposed a duty on 'responsible authorities' for a local government area to work together and with local agencies to formulate and implement a strategy for the reduction of crime and disorder in the area. The Police Reform Act (PRA) 2002 expanded the list of responsible authorities to include the local authority, the police, the fire authority, the Primary Health Care Trust (England) or the health authority (Wales).[2] These statutory partnerships have come to be known as Crime and Disorder Reduction Partnerships (CDRPs) (in England) or Community Safety Partnerships (CSPs) (in Wales). Local authorities and police authorities also have

1 CDA 1998 ss5 and 6, as amended by PRA 2002 s97 and the Clean Neighbourhoods and Environment Act 2005 s1.

2 There are Government plans to include a power to extend this list by way of secondary legislation instead of primary legislation: *Review of the partnership provisions of the Crime & Disorder Act 1998* (Home Office Review) available at www.crimereduction.gov.uk.

a general duty under CDA 1998 s17 to consider crime and disorder strategies.[3]

2.3 These CDRPs are required to carry out:

> ... a review of the levels and patterns of crime and disorder in the area (including anti-social and other behaviour adversely affecting the local environment) and of the level and patterns of the misuse of drugs in the area,[4]

and thereafter formulate and implement a strategy to reduce and combat crime and the use of drugs. In doing so, they are required to work in co-operation with local education, health and probation authorities as well as invite the co-operation of a range of local community and other groups, from within both the private and public sector.[5] These reviews (or crime and disorder audits as they are commonly known) currently have to take place on a three-yearly basis and have to be published.[6]

2.4 The audits are usually extremely detailed, recording not only the incidence and type of crime in the borough but also including comparisons with other sufficiently similar boroughs, population figures, measures of poverty and affluence within the borough, 'hotspot' analysis (prevalence of offences in a particular area), the cost of crime, the fear of crime, youth crime, and various reduction strategies. Given that central government has made clear that tackling anti-social behaviour is a priority, each audit contains a section on anti-social behaviour.

2.5 According to the Home Office's *Guide to Anti-social Behaviour Orders* (2006 Home Office Guidance)[7], all CDRPs have been advised to appoint an anti-social behaviour co-ordinator and according to the 2003 Home Office Guidance 90 per cent of them have done so.[8] The

3 There is a current government proposal to widen this requirement to include 'anti-social behaviour, behaviour adversely affecting the environment and substance misuse': see Home Office Review cited at note 2 above.

4 CDA 1998 s6 as amended by PRA 2002 s97(9) and the Clean Neighbourhoods and Environment Act 2005 s1.

5 See the Crime and Disorder Strategies (Prescribed Descriptions) Order 1998 SI No 2513 and the Crime and Disorder Strategies (Prescribed Descriptions) (Amendment) Order 1998 SI No 2452 for full list. See also www.crimereduction.gov.uk.

6 There are government plans to repeal this requirement and to replace it with six-monthly strategic assessments and annual rolling three-year community safety plans. See Home Office Review cited at note 2 above.

7 Available at www.together.gov.uk.

8 *A Guide to Anti-social Behaviour Orders and Acceptable Behaviour Contracts*, Home Office, 2003, p5.

anti-social behaviour co-ordinator would seem to have a number of roles including 'communication with the courts',[9] establishing and managing protocols and processes with other agencies for implementing ASBOs, developing an area-wide action plan and the co-ordination of CPS training.[10]

2.6 Despite the government drive to form such partnerships, the Home Office's *Review of the Partnership Provisions of the Crime and Disorder Act 1998*[11] suggests that the introduction of Local Strategic Partnerships (the 'partnership of partnerships' within local government areas of which CDRPs are apparently a part)[12] and Local Criminal Justice Boards,[13] has meant that there is 'a crowded delivery landscape'.[14] What can be gleaned from this report is that there are far too many 'partnerships' with similar remits within each local area, which is probably a bureaucratic as well as expensive nightmare for central government. The answer, it would seem, is to encourage CDRP mergers, although it is not entirely clear who would merge with whom and when.[15]

Information sharing and data protection

2.7 This level of multi-agency working means that potential ASBO cases will inevitably be identified in the process and each local authority will work within its established protocol on what it does next. CDA 1998 s115[16] authorises the disclosure of information to the police, a registered social landlord, a local probation board and a health authority (including a strategic health authority and a primary care trust) or to a person acting on behalf of any of those authorities,[17] 'in any

9 For example, arranging seminars for lay magistrates and clerks. In the case of Coventry this apparently included showing them a video 'which graphically illustrated the behaviour to which communities have been subjected' (2003 Home Office Guidance, pp23–24).

10 See the section on expert CPS prosecutors on www.together.gov.uk.

11 Available at www.crimereduction.gov.uk. Cited as Home Office Review at footnote 2 above and elsewhere in this chapter.

12 Home Office Review, para 2.4.

13 Home Office Review, para 2.6.

14 Home Office Review, para 2.9.

15 Home Office Review, para 2.10.

16 As amended by PRA 2002, Criminal Justice and Courts Services Act 2000, Housing Act 2004 and various statutory instruments.

17 There are current Government plans to legislate to include a power to extend these relevant authorities by way of secondary rather than primary legislation: see Home Office Review, para 3.18.

case where the disclosure is necessary or expedient for the purposes of any provision of the Act' (the prevention of crime and disorder being the primary purpose of CDA 1998). Although CDA 1998 confers this broad power to share data, it does not override other statutory and common law constraints on disclosure. On the contrary, the disclosure must not breach an individual's rights under either European Convention on Human Rights (ECHR) Article 8 or the law of confidence[18] or the terms of the Data Protection Act (DPA) 1998.[19]

2.8 While DPA 1998 requires those who process personal data to act in compliance with eight fundamental data protection principles, it also contains a number of exemptions. The most relevant exemption is under section 29: if personal data is being processed for the 'prevention or detection of crime' or 'the apprehension or prosecution of offenders', and to comply with certain obligations (including disclosure of that information to the data subject) would prejudice that purpose, then various rights of data subjects are overridden.[20]

2.9 The careful control of personal data that DPA 1998 insists upon has meant that information sharing has been more complex than envisaged by CDA 1998. Government agencies are fearful of falling foul of DPA 1998 provisions partly because the legislation is so complex that few people understand its implications. In a bid to counteract this, there is a current Government proposal to strengthen CDA 1998 s115 powers by placing a duty on responsible authorities to share 'depersonalised' data (data which has been 'cleansed' to a point where individuals are no longer identifiable) which is relevant for community safety purposes and already held in a 'depersonalised' format.[21]

Complaints about potential breaches of the Data Protection Act 1998

2.10 An individual can complain to the Information Commissioner if he or she thinks there has been non-compliance with DPA 1998 or ask the Information Commissioner to carry out an assessment as to

18 See the celebrated case of *(1) Michael Douglas, (2) Catherine Zeta-Jones, (3) Northern & shell PLC v Hello! Ltd & Others* [2005] EWCA Civ 595 for a comprehensive journey through the law of confidence.

19 DPA 1998 came into force in March 2000, after CDA 1998.

20 For more information see the Information Commissioner's website at www.informationcommissioner.gov.uk.

21 See Home Office Review, cited at note 2 above, paras 3.13–3.17.

whether the processing in question is in compliance.[22] An individual can seek compensation from the data controller via the courts if he or she suffers damage or both distress and damage as a result of any contravention of DPA 1998.[23]

Pre-ASBO measures

2.11 Usually, once a stand-alone ASBO case has been identified, there will be a case conference hearing involving the agencies who know something about the individual concerned, which should result in an 'action plan'. A lead officer[24] is identified to oversee each case (whose job will include instructing solicitors if appropriate). The lead officer should record the action plan. It may be decided at that stage that an ASBO should be applied for or alternatively an Acceptable Behaviour Contract (ABC) (see below) or a period of assistance, support and monitoring.

2.12 What course is taken will depend, in the main, on the seriousness of the anti-social behaviour and the extent of its impact on the local community. Some local authorities follow a 'problem-solving' approach which initially involves working with the person concerned (and his or her family in the case of a young person), identifying the unacceptable behaviour and offering support to change it; if that fails, issuing a verbal warning, followed by a written warning, then a 'challenge' meeting and finally an ASBO application. However, 'problem-solving' takes place behind closed doors and is a long-term strategy. Some local authorities may wish to reassure the local community that action is being taken against anti-social behaviour and therefore will apply for an ASBO as soon as an offender is identified. This will be particularly so in adult ASBO cases and in cases where the anti-social behaviour is considered to be too serious to try an interventionist approach.

2.13 Where the identified person is a young person, case management meetings should include representatives from education, social services and the Youth Offending Team.[25] If the young person is in care specific issues arise about the role of social services in the ASBO application process, which are dealt with in chapter 10.

22 DPA 1998 s42.

23 DPA 1998 s13.

24 *A Guide to Anti-Social Behaviour Orders*, Home Office, 2006, p20.

25 See para 10.41.

Acceptable behaviour contracts

2.14 Acceptable Behaviour Contracts (ABCs) were pioneered by the London Borough of Islington[26] and have been welcomed by many local authorities as a simple and cheaper alternative to ASBOs. They are most commonly used for tackling lower level anti-social behaviour by young people (such as graffiti and under-age drinking and smoking on housing estates) but not exclusively so. They are essentially a written agreement not to carry out various specified acts. Unlike ASBOs, which can only contain prohibitory terms (see chapter 7 on terms of an ASBO), an ABC can include mandatory terms to do something.[27] The 2003 Home Office Guidance suggests that support to address the underlying causes of the anti-social behaviour should be offered in parallel to the contract.[28] Contracts are usually drawn up for a six-month period but can be longer.[29]

Are lawyers involved at this stage?

2.15 ABCs are not legally binding or enforceable and lawyers are not usually involved in the process simply because there is no public funding available at this stage.[30] Those lawyers who are prepared to act on a *pro bono* basis are not usually welcomed by the local authority – some have flatly refused to let lawyers be present. Despite the fact that ABCs are on the face of it a non-legal mechanism, they come with the threat that, if breached, the relevant agency will apply for an ASBO or, where relevant, a possession order. If a child or young person is the signatory, then the parent or guardian is encouraged to take part in the process. It is particularly important for young people to have some kind of adult guidance and representation if they are signing up to an ABC because the breach of such an undertaking will

26 See 2003 Home Office Guidance, above, note 24, appendices E, F, G.

27 See 2003 Home Office Guidance, above, note 24, p60, for examples of terms of an ABC.

28 See 2003 Home Office Guidance, above, note 24, p53. Guidance on ABCs has been removed from the body of the 2006 Home Office Guidance but is referred to at Annex A.

29 See para 10.19 for information on parenting contracts as a potential pre-ASBO measure.

30 Advocacy Assistance is available for stand-alone and interim ASBOs (using Form CDS 3). It may be arguable where an ASBO is threatened that an ABC meeting is part and parcel of ASBO proceedings. See chapter 12 for details of the public funding regime.

almost inevitably result in legal proceedings of some kind.[31] Similarly, if there is a refusal to sign such a contract, the next step may well be an ASBO application or possession proceedings. There is no reason why a lawyer cannot be present if the child and/or parent or guardian wants one there. If solicitors regularly represent prospective ASBO defendants at this stage, and can show that their involvement has ultimately benefited the young person, there may be some basis for persuading the Legal Services Commission that there should be public funding available. Indeed, if solicitor involvement meant that the terms of the contract were fairer and the child was more likely to sign up to it and abide by it, the benefit to the applicant body would be even greater than to the child.

Is there a duty to offer an ABC before applying for an ASBO?

2.16 There is no duty on a local authority or other relevant body to offer an ABC before applying for an ASBO. If an ABC is entered into and breached, this evidence will be put before the court by the applicant body in an ASBO application to justify the need for the order. Similarly, evidence of non-attendance at meetings to discuss a proposed ABC and subsequent failure to sign up to an ABC will also be put before the court. Defendants are often aggrieved if they have not been offered an ABC or some other pre-ASBO intervention before an ASBO is applied for. While a failure to offer or try an alternative may be something that a defence lawyer can make submissions about when addressing the court on whether an ASBO is 'necessary' (see chapter 5 on the two-limb test), it is entirely within the applicant body's discretion as to what course it chooses to take. If the discretion is exercised unreasonably (in the *Wednesbury* sense), then as with all such decisions of public bodies, the decision to apply for an ASBO may well be susceptible to judicial review.[32]

31 SOCPA 2005 s144 (inserting CDA 1998 s13A) introduced parental compensation orders in the magistrates' court when a child has caused damage to property by committing an act which would constitute an offence if the child was over 10 or if the child has acted in an anti-social manner. However, that section is not yet in force.

32 See para 11.30.

Is there a duty to consult before applying for an ASBO?

2.17 CDA 1998[33] imposes consultation requirements upon applicant bodies before a stand-alone or county court ASBO can be applied for.[34] If a local authority is making the application, it must consult 'the chief officer of police of the police force maintained for the police area within which that local government area lies'.[35] The Chief Constable's power to consult and be consulted with can be delegated to an officer for whom he or she is responsible.[36] If it is the police making the application the relevant local authority is 'the council for the local government area in which the person in relation to whom the application is to be made resides or appears to reside'.[37]

2.18 Any other applicant (ie RSLs, HATs, BTP, the Environment Agency, Transport for London and county councils) must consult both the local authority *and* the police force. The language of the sub-section is such that it does not apply to post-conviction ASBOs (only to 'applications' for an ASBO and ASBOs in county court proceedings).

2.19 SOCPA 2005[38] has introduced the possibility of local authorities[39] contracting out of their ASBO functions, including the duty to consult, if the Secretary of State so provides by order. Before making an order, the statute does require the Secretary of State to consult with the National Assembly of Wales if the order relates to a relevant authority in Wales, such representatives of local government as he thinks appropriate and such other persons as he thinks appropriate. It is unclear what agencies the Government has in mind and to date there has been no such order published.

33 CDA 1998 s1E, inserted by PRA 2002 s66.

34 This became a statutory requirement for stand-alone ASBOs from 2 December 2002 (PRA 2002 (Commencement No 3) Order 2002 SI No 2750) and for county court ASBOs on 1 April 2003 (PRA (Commencement No 4) Order 2003 SI No 808).

35 CDA 1998 s1E(2).

36 *The Chief Constable of West Midlands Police v Birmingham Justices* [2002] EWHC 1087 (Admin).

37 CDA 1998 s1E(3).

38 SOCPA 2005 s142, inserting CDA 1998 s1F.

39 A local authority is as defined by the Local Government Act 1972 s270 as well as the Common Council of the City of London and the Council of the Isles of Scilly : SOCPA 2005 s142(12)

Proof of consultation

2.20 Once consultation has taken place, and the decision to obtain an ASBO has been made, the applicant authority should ensure that the application for an ASBO includes evidence that consultation has taken place. CPR 65 requires that an application for an order under CDA 1998 s1B(4) must be accompanied by written evidence, which must include evidence that CDA 1998 s1E has been complied with.[40] There is no equivalent written rule for stand-alone ASBOs in the magistrates' court, but good practice dictates that the same should be done there or the applicant body will not be able to show compliance with section 1E. The 2006 Home Office Guidance suggests that 'a signed document of consultation is all that is required by the courts'.[41] While there is no official rule requiring proof of consultation in the magistrates' court, there is, however, a related rule in the Magistrates' Courts (Anti-Social Behaviour Orders) Rules 2002,[42] which reads as follows:

> Any summons, copy of an order or an application required to be sent to the defendant under these Rules shall also be sent by the designated officer for the court to the applicant authority, and to any relevant authority whom the applicant is required by section 1E to have consulted before making the application and, where appropriate, shall invite them to make observations and advise them of their right to be heard at the hearing.[43]

2.21 This is a somewhat curious and unused rule. It seems to put the obligation on the court to 'double check' on the statutory consultation requirements. Consultation is required to take place *before* an application for a stand-alone ASBO is made and the application ought to contain confirmation that consultation has taken place. If it does not, lawyers representing the defendant ought to raise the point and, if appropriate, seek proof of consultation (see below as to disclosure of the consultation process and the effect of non-consultation).

2.22 This rule seems to leave open the possibility that a body that has not been consulted can be invited to share its views on the application or indeed, a body that has been consulted can be invited to do the same. In principle, there is nothing wrong with extending this invita-

40 See para 8.42.

41 *A Guide to Anti-Social Behaviour Orders* (Home Office, 2006), p22.

42 SI No 2784, as amended by Magistrates' Courts (Miscellaneous Amendments) Rules 2003 SI No 1236 and Courts Act 2003 (Consequential Provisions (No 2)) Order 2005 SI No 617. Reproduced at appendix B.

43 Ibid, r7(2).

tion if there is a dispute between the applicant body and the defendant as to whether consultation occurred. Additionally, although far less likely, if a consulted body has expressed the view that it does not agree with the decision of the applicant body to apply for an ASBO, it is in the defendant's interests for that body to be asked to attend court. However CDA 1998 does not confer any procedural or other *rights* upon consulted bodies and therefore, in so far as the Rules purport to confer a *right* to be heard upon such bodies, the Rules are clearly *ultra vires*. It may be that rule 7(2) is routinely ignored because in practice all local authority ASBO applications inevitably include witness statements from a local police officer involved with crime and disorder reduction strategies, although when the applicant is the police, it is not inevitable that there will be a local authority witness.

The consultation process

2.23 The 2006 Home Office Guidance makes plain that the purpose of consultation is information sharing and does not mean that the agencies must agree to the application being made. Rather, once told of the intended application, the agencies will have an opportunity to comment. This process should ensure that actions taken by each agency regarding the same individual do not conflict. It also states that while no agency has veto over another agency's application 'any reservations or alternative proposals should be discussed carefully, against the background of the overriding need to bring the anti-social behaviour to a speedy end'. It states that a signed document of consultation is all that is required by the court but: 'This should *not* indicate whether the party consulted was or was not in agreement. This is not required by the legislation.'[44]

Purpose and disclosure of the consultation process

2.24 While the statute only requires the police to consult with the local authority (and vice versa), and HATs, RSLs and the BTP to consult with the police and the local authority, the consultation may well take place in the context of a CRDP.[45] Arguably, if there is a good reason for not applying for an ASBO (for example, if social services or another agency taking part in a CRDP case conference believes the person is

44 At page 22.

45 See para 2.2.

suffering from mental health problems and an ASBO would be detrimental or inappropriate), it should be disclosed in order to both ensure fairness[46] and comply with Article 6 (1) of the ECHR.[47] It would make a mockery of the whole *raison d'être* of CDA 1998 if the purpose of information sharing was simply for one agency to tell another agency what it was doing. If the process was working properly, then a local authority would have considered its obligations under the NHS and Community Care Act 1990 to assess any adult who might be in need of community care services,[48] and/or its duties under Children Act 1989 to assess children 'in need' or 'at risk' and make provision for them,[49] rather than simply apply for an ASBO. There is also an obligation to assess the needs of those leaving hospital to ensure aftercare support.[50] A failure by the local authority to carry out, or properly carry out, such assessments is susceptible to judicial review.[51]

Disclosure of personal data under the Data Protection Act 1998

2.25 Individuals have the right to access personal data about themselves under DPA 1998 s7, a regime preserved by the Freedom of Information Act 2000.[52] 'Data' and 'personal data' are defined in DPA 1998 s1 and mean computerised information as well as information held in manual files (as long as the manual filing system is of sufficient sophistication to provide the same or similar ready accessibility as a computerised filing system). To understand the scope of that provision, it is extremely helpful to refer to the decision of the Court of Appeal in *Durant v Financial Services Authority*[53] which defines personal data as 'information that affects [a person's] privacy, whether in

46 Certainly CPR 31 requires a party to disclose documents which adversely affects its own case and although they do not apply in criminal courts, there is no reason why the same principle should not apply in ASBO hearings: see *R (on the application of Cleary) v Highbury Corner Magistrates' Court* [2006] EWHC 1869 (Admin) at para 34. See para 8.86 for a full discussion on disclosure obligations under the CPR.

47 See chapter 3 on the application of ECHR Art 6.

48 Sections 46 and 47. See also the Department of Health's *Fair Access to Care Services Policy Guidance*, available at www.dh.gov.uk.

49 Sections 17–29. See *R (AB & SB) v Nottingham City Council* [2001] EWCA 235 (Admin): considered in more detail at para 10.28.

50 Mental Health Act 1983 s117. See also MIND website at www.mind.org.uk.

51 See note 49 above.

52 Freedom of Information Act 2000 s40.

53 [2003] EWCA Civ 1746.

his personal or family life, business or professional capacity'.[54] The Court of Appeal recommended that regard should be had to whether the information is 'biographical in a significant sense' and whether the information has the individual as 'its focus'.[55]

2.26 The ASBO consultation process will, by definition, involve discussions that involve a person's privacy and if the ASBO application process discloses little or nothing of the background discussions, then it may be advisable to make a DPA 1998 s7 application to the relevant 'data controller': the lead agency would be the best first port of call. Such an application has the advantage of there being no 'relevance' test as there would be if an application was being made to a court. The application has to be made in writing[56] and a fee will be payable.[57] Data subjects are entitled to disclosure of personal data of which they are the subject as well as disclosure of the purpose for which they are being or are to be processed and the recipients to whom they are or may be disclosed. Data controllers have 40 days to respond to a proper request. Of course, the data controller may rely upon an exemption such as 'crime control', but they can only do so if disclosure would have a substantial chance of prejudicing the prevention or detection of crime or the apprehension or prosecution of offenders.[58]

2.27 Not every ASBO application will be about the prevention of crime because not every anti-social act sought to be prevented is a crime, so there may be circumstances in which those who are being discussed at these meetings can properly access minutes of meetings and/or other information being circulated about them. Furthermore, if an individual is aware of the ASBO application, it would be difficult for the data controller to argue that one of the purposes outlined in DPA 1998 s29 would be prejudiced by disclosure of information to the individual.

2.28 There are other exemptions available to the data controller, which are intended to protect individual interests, in particular the welfare of children. These are known as the health, social work and education exemptions.[59] Certain health and education information is exempt from the subject access rights available under DPA 1998 s7 to the extent that the application of those rights 'would be likely to cause serious

54 [2003] EWCA Civ 1746, para 28.
55 Ibid.
56 DPA 1998 s7(2)(a).
57 Usually a flat fee of £10.
58 DPA 1998 s29. 'Prosecution of offenders' is limited to criminal proceedings and does not cover civil proceedings.
59 DPA 1998 s30.

harm to the physical or mental health or condition of the data subject or any other person'[60] (unless it has already been seen by the data subject or is already within his or her knowledge, in which case it cannot be withheld). Similarly, personal data processed in connection with the provision of personal social services or other social work functions are exempt from most of the section 7 subject access rights where to disclose the information would be likely to prejudice the carrying out of social work 'by reason of the fact that serious harm to the physical or mental health or condition of the data subject or any other person would be likely to be caused'.[61] 'Serious harm' is a high test and therefore it does not give local authorities *carte blanche* to refuse requests.

Enforcing disclosure rights under the Data Protection Act 1998

2.29 DPA 1998 gives individuals the right of access to the High Court or County Court if a data controller fails to comply with a request in contravention of the Act, as well as the power to award compensation in certain circumstances.[62] Before litigating, it may be sensible to first ask the Information Commissioner to carry out an assessment as to whether the processing in question has taken or is taking place in compliance with DPA 1998.[63] The Commissioner has the power to seek information from data controllers if asked to carry out an assessment, and the failure by a data controller to comply with the Commissioner's requests can result in a criminal prosecution. Despite its laudable aim of protecting an individual's fundamental rights, notably the right to privacy and accuracy of personal data held by others, DPA 1998 is a complex and at times impenetrable statute. Those wishing to exercise their rights in accordance with it are advised in the first instance to seek help from the Commissioner's Office.[64]

60 The Data Protection (Subject Access Modification) (Health) Order 2000 SI No 413.

61 The Data Protection (Subject Access Modification) (Social Work) Order 2000 SI No 415.

62 DPA 1998 s13.

63 DPA 1998 s42.

64 Full details on how to contact the Commissioner's Office, how to make a complaint or a request for information as well as a comprehensive guide to DPA 1998 are available at www.ico.gov.uk.

What happens if there has been a failure to consult or to properly consult?

2.30 The only litigation in the High Court to date on an applicant authority's failure to properly consult with other authorities before applying for an ASBO is the unreported decision of *McClarty and McClarty v Wigan Borough Council.*[65] The case was argued before Beatson J sitting in the Liverpool Crown Court, in the context of a county court ASBO pursuant to CDA 1998 s1B. An appeal was brought against the decision of a county court judge to grant ASBOs against two boys, aged 14 and 12 respectively. The ground of appeal upon which permission was granted was that the county court judge did not have jurisdiction to grant an ASBO because the Wigan Metropolitan Borough Council did not comply with the statutory consultation requirements before making the applications. The High Court judge granting permission, directed the local authority to prepare and serve statements as to the consultation process it claimed had taken place in the applications for the ASBOs.

2.31 The appellants' complaint really arose out of the fact that such consultation as there had been was carried out by a tenancy relations manager of a housing management company solely owned by the council,[66] who was not a 'relevant body' within the meaning of CDA 1998 s1. It was therefore not authorised to apply for an ASBO. By the time of the appeal hearing there was some evidence of inter-agency meetings which were attended by officers from the local authority and the Greater Manchester Police.

2.32 The issues that Beatson J had to decide were first, the effect of non-compliance with the statutory requirement to consult (bearing in mind that the statute uses the word 'shall') and second, what is required to achieve consultation pursuant to the statutory requirement. In dealing with the first point, his Lordship relied on *R v Secretary of State for the Home Department ex p Jeyeanthan,*[67] a judgment of Lord Woolf when he was Master of the Rolls. Although this was a case decided in an immigration context, it decided an issue of general importance which had implications for the failure to observe procedural requirements outside the field of immigration, as was recognised in the judgment. Lord Woolf was of the view that in the

65 Unreported. Heard on 22 October 2003, judgment handed down on 30 October 2003 by the High Court sitting at Liverpool Crown Court.

66 Also known as an arm's length management organisation.

67 [2000] 1 WLR 354.

majority of cases it provides limited, if any, assistance to inquire whether the requirement is mandatory or directory:

> Because of what can be the very undesirable consequences of a procedural requirement which is made so fundamental that any departure from the requirement makes everything that happens thereafter irreversibly a nullity it is to be hoped that provisions intended to have this effect will be few and far between. In the majority of cases, whether the requirement is categorised as directory or mandatory, the tribunal before whom the defect is properly raised has the task of determining what are to be the consequences of failing to comply with the requirements in the context of all the facts and circumstances of the case in which the issue arises. In such a situation that tribunal's task will be to seek to do what is just in all the circumstances: see *Brayhead (Ascot) Ltd v Berkshire County Council* [1964] 2 QB 303, applied by the House of Lords in London and Clydeside *Estates Ltd v Aberdeen District Council* [1980] 1 WLR 182.[68]

2.33 The approach suggested by Lord Woolf (and adopted by Beatson J) is as follows:

> ... I suggest that the right approach is to regard the question of whether a requirement is directory or mandatory as only at most a first step. In the majority of cases there are other questions which have to be asked which are more likely to be of greater assistance than the application of the mandatory/directory test. The questions which are likely to arise are as follows:
> (a) Is the statutory requirement fulfilled if there has been substantial compliance with the requirement and, if so, has there been substantial compliance in the case in issue even though there has not been strict compliance? (The substantial compliance question.)
> (b) Is the non-compliance capable of being waived, and if so, has it, or can it and should it be waived in this particular case? (The discretionary question.) I treat the grant of an extension of time for compliance as a waiver.
> (c) If it is not capable of being waived or is not waived then what are the consequences of non-compliance? (The consequences question.)[69]

2.34 In determining what is required to achieve consultation, Beatson J noted that the statutory duty to consult in ASBO cases is not a step in the making of a valid administrative or legislative instrument but

68 [2000] 1 WLR 354 at 359. This statement has since had the benefit of endorsement by Lord Steyn in the House of Lords in *Attorney General's Reference No 3 of 1999* [2001] 2 WLR 56 at 62C and was referred to in *R v Daljit Singh Sekhon* [2002] EWCA 2954.

69 [2000] 1 WLR 354 at 362.

a preliminary step before launching court proceedings. Moreover, the obligation to consult is not with those who would primarily be affected by the order (namely, the prospective defendant). However, the guidance given by Webster J in *R v Secretary of State for Social Services, ex p Association of Metropolitan Authorities*[70] was relevant:

> ... to achieve consultation sufficient information must be supplied by the consulting to the consulted party to enable it to tender helpful advice. Sufficient time must be given by the consulting to the consulted party to enable it to do that, and sufficient time must be available for such advice to be considered by the consulting party. Sufficient, in that context, does not mean ample, but at least enough to enable the relevant purpose to be fulfilled.[71]

2.35 His Lordship concluded that the requirement in CDA 1998 s1E to consult is fulfilled by substantial compliance even though there may not have been strict compliance. This is because he formed the view that the purpose of section 1E was to ensure a degree of co-operation and co-ordination between agencies which have authority to institute proceedings under CDA 1998 s1,[72] which could be achieved in a number of ways including partnership working arrangements. He found support for this interpretation in the 2003 Home Office Guidance.[73] On the particular facts of the case, he found that the participation of the police and local authority representatives at regular 'Positive Action Team' meetings which discussed, among other issues, the behaviour of the McClarty brothers as well as strategies for dealing with it, constituted 'substantial compliance'.

2.36 Thus the second two of Lord Woolf's questions (the 'discretionary' and the 'consequences' questions) did not arise, leaving open the question of whether complete non-compliance would render subsequent ASBO proceedings a nullity. Certainly, the door remains open on this question and was specifically left open by Sedley LJ in *R (Chief Constable of the West Midlands Police) v Birmingham Justices*.[74] In that case the question was whether the Chief Constable's powers to consult and be consulted were delegable.[75] If they were not, the argument was that the proceedings thereafter would have been null

70 [1986] 1 WLR 1.

71 [1986] 1 WLR 1 at 4.

72 *McClarty and McClarty v Wigan Borough Council*, unreported, 22 October 2003, High Court sitting at Liverpool Crown Court, transcript at paras 25, 26 and 30.

73 See above, para 2.5.

74 [2002] EWHC 1087 (Admin).

75 [2002] EWHC 1087 (Admin).

and void. The Court found that they were delegable, hence Sedley LJ's observations:

> The argument therefore remains open, notwithstanding the conclusions reached above, that if no consultation has taken place, or if it has been conducted by somebody who lacks due authority on behalf of the Chief Constable, the resultant process is ... void or ... challengeable on grounds of unfairness ...[76]

Is there a duty to consult the prospective defendant?

2.37 There is no statutory or other duty to consult with the prospective recipient of an ASBO. In *Wareham v Purbeck District Council,*[77] the issue raised by the appeal (which was taken by way of case stated) was whether a person in respect of whom an authority is considering making an application to the magistrates' court for an ASBO has a right to be consulted, or heard, as part of that consideration. The argument was put on human rights grounds in that it was submitted that ECHR Articles 6 and 8 required there to be such a right. On the facts of that case, it emerged that the Purbeck CRDP had concluded that action needed to be taken about Mr Wareham's anti-social behaviour and had written to him to that effect. Thereafter, at a meeting attended by representatives of various bodies (including the police, the local council and the CRDP), it was decided that it was appropriate to apply for an ASBO. An ABC was ruled out on the basis that Mr Wareham had been subject to two supervision orders and had received a detention and training order. He was informed of the decision to apply for an ASBO by letter and advised to seek legal advice. He challenged that decision, arguing that he had the right to be consulted.

2.38 Unsurprisingly, the court held that neither Article 6 nor 8 was relevant at the decision-making stage. Jack J concluded that:

> ... in some, perhaps many, cases it may be worthwhile to involve the proposed defendant before a decision is taken. In other cases his behaviour and history will show that it would not be productive but would be a waste of time. It is for the decision-making group to consider the practical sense of involving the proposed defendant. What in my judgment is clear is that it is not required by law, either as a matter of statute or to secure compliance with Article 8 or Article 6.[78]

76 [2002] EWHC 1087 (Admin) at para 21.
77 [2005] EWHC 358 (Admin).
78 [2005] EWHC 358 (Admin) at para 12.

CHAPTER 3

ASBOs and ECHR Article 6

Introduction

3.1 When ASBOs were first introduced there was concern about the fact that although they were described as civil orders, given the penal sanctions upon breach, they were actually criminal in nature. The concern was that hearsay is automatically admissible in civil proceedings and therefore ASBO defendants were deprived of the full protection of European Convention on Human Rights (ECHR) Article 6.[1] This question was resolved by the House of Lords in the now well known case of *R (on the application of McCann) v Crown Court at Manchester; Clingham v K & C Royal Borough Council*.[2] This chapter summarises the arguments deployed in that case and seeks to explain how the House of Lords dealt with the ECHR Article 6 points.

Civil or criminal proceedings?

3.2 ASBOs are available in the magistrates' courts on a stand-alone basis and in the youth, magistrates' and Crown courts on a post-conviction basis. However, an ASBO is a civil order and the criminal court will be sitting in its civil capacity when considering an ASBO application, be it a stand-alone or post-conviction ASBO.[3] Following the House of Lords' decision in *McCann*,[4] there is now no doubt that ASBOs are civil in their complexion, despite the ramifications of breaching them. Although there have been attempts to distinguish post-conviction ASBOs from stand-alone ASBOs post-*McCann*[5] (both appeals in *McCann* were against stand-alone ASBOs: post-conviction ASBOs were not in existence at that time), the Divisional Court in *R (W) v Acton Youth Court*[6] confirmed that post-conviction ASBOs under CDA 1998 s1C are civil orders.

3.3 The question certified by the Divisional Court in Clingham's case was, 'Whether hearsay evidence is admissible in proceedings to

1 See also chapter 4, for a detailed discussion of hearsay in civil proceedings.
2 [2002] UKHL 39; [2002] 3 WLR 1313; [2002] 4 All ER 593, HL.
3 The youth court has no civil capacity, hence stand-alone youth ASBOs are heard in the adult magistrates' court. That said, post-conviction youth ASBOs, despite their civil character, are heard in the youth court because CDA 1998 s1C confers the power to impose one upon criminal conviction.
4 [2002] UKHL 39; [2002] 3 WLR 1313; [2002] 4 All ER 593, HL.
5 See for example *R (C) v Sunderland Youth Court* [2004] 1 Cr App R (S) 76 and para 6.6.
6 [2005] EWHC 954 (Admin).

secure the making of an anti-social behaviour order under the Crime and Disorder Act 1998?' (McCann's case went up by way of appeal from the Court of Appeal (Civil Division).) This was the first occasion on which the House of Lords examined CDA 1998 s1 (in its original, unamended form) and in essence, the main questions that fell to be determined were:

- whether as a matter of domestic classification, proceedings leading to the making of an ASBO are criminal in nature;
- whether under ECHR Article 6 such proceedings involve 'a criminal charge';
- whether under CDA 1998 s1 hearsay evidence is admissible in proceedings seeking such an order;
- what the standard of proof is in such proceedings.

ECHR Article 6 and the decision in *McCann*

3.4 Article 6 of the ECHR states:

> (1) In the determination of his civil rights and obligations or of any criminal charge against him, everyone is entitled to a fair and public hearing within a reasonable time by an independent and impartial tribunal established by law. Judgment shall be pronounced publicly but the press and public may be excluded from all or part of the trial in the interest of morals, public order or national security in a democratic society, where the interests of juveniles or the protection of the private lives of the parties so require, or to the extent strictly necessary in the opinion of the court in special circumstances where publicity would prejudice the interests of justice.
>
> (2) Everyone charged with a criminal offence shall be presumed innocent until proved guilty according to law.
>
> (3) Everyone charged with a criminal offence has the following minimum rights:
>
> (a) to be informed promptly, in a language which he understands and in detail, of the nature and cause of the accusation against him;
>
> (b) to have adequate time and facilities for the preparation of his defence;
>
> (c) to defend himself in person or through legal assistance of his own choosing or, if he has not sufficient means to pay for legal assistance, to be given it free when the interests of justice so require;
>
> (d) to examine or have examined witnesses against him and to obtain the attendance and examination of witnesses on his behalf under the same conditions as witnesses against him;

(e) to have the free assistance of an interpreter if he cannot understand or speak the language used in court.

3.5 While both CDA 1998 and the Human Rights Act (HRA) 1998 were enacted in 1998, the former came into force before the latter.[7] Technically HRA 1998 was not applicable in either McCann's or Clingham's case as the decisions being appealed pre-dated the coming into force of HRA 1998.[8] However, all parties invited the House of Lords to deal with appeals as if HRA 1998 was applicable, which it did. The appellants argued that, seen as a whole, the scheme provided by CDA 1998 for the making of and enforcement of ASBOs is punitive, rather than preventative, and therefore truly criminal. An ASBO could, for example, banish a person from the area in which he or she lived, and provided in the event of breach for higher penalties than many criminal offences.

3.6 As the ECHR distinguishes between criminal and civil proceedings, affording minimum rights in accordance with Article 6(2) and 6(3) to those charged with criminal offences, classification is all-important. The Strasbourg Court, in order to prevent states from circumventing the safeguards provided by the criminal law by simply reclassifying proceedings, has long insisted that 'criminal charge' is an autonomous concept.[9] That is to say that the Court will decide for itself whether the proceedings in question involve the determination of a 'criminal charge' and will not be bound by domestic classifications. The approach taken in the Strasbourg jurisprudence is to determine that issue by reference to three criteria: (a) the classification of the proceedings in domestic law, (b) the nature of the offence or conduct in question, and (c) the severity of the potential penalty.[10] The first issue is not as important as the second and third and, as was acknowledged by the House of Lords in *McCann,* the third is the most important.[11]

3.7 However, in relation to the third question, their Lordships were not prepared to view ASBO breach proceedings as part and parcel of the ASBO procedure. The Court formed the view that these were separate and independent procedures and the imposition of an ASBO did not result in any penalty whatsoever. An ASBO was a preventative and not a punitive measure. The Court found support for this

7 CDA 1998 came into force on 1 April 1999; HRA 1998 came into force on 2 October 2000.

8 See *R v Kansal (No 2)* [2002] 2 AC 69.

9 The leading case is *Engels v Netherlands* (1979–80) 1 EHRR 706.

10 *Engels v Netherlands* (1979–80) 1 EHRR 706.

11 [2003] 1 AC 787 at para 30.

view from various Strasbourg judgments. In *Guzzardi v Italy*,[12] for example, the applicant was suspected by the authorities to belong to a band of Mafiosi and was made subject to special supervision for a period of three years with an obligation of compulsory residence on an island off the tip of Sardinia. He was required to look for work, to report to the supervisory authorities twice a day (at least), he was forbidden from associating with those with criminal records and those subject to preventative or security measures, he was subject to a curfew, he was forbidden from entering bars or night clubs or taking part in public meetings and he had to tell the authorities whom he was telephoning in advance and from whom he was receiving a telephone call. He was liable to punishment of detention of 1–6 months if he failed to comply with any of his obligations.

3.8 While the Strasbourg Court found that he had been deprived of his liberty contrary to ECHR Article 5(1), it was of the view that the proceedings did not involve the determination of a criminal charge within the meaning of Article 6. In *McCann*, their Lordships accepted that an ASBO may well restrict the freedom of the defendant to do as he wants and to go where he pleases, but that those restrictions are imposed for preventative reasons and not for punishment. The Article 5 point was not taken in *McCann* as it was not relevant to the particular arguments in that case. Depending on the extent of the restriction on liberty, it is conceivably an argument that could be run in an appropriate ASBO case (see chapter 7 on terms of ASBOs).

3.9 In *McCann*, their Lordships distinguished *Steel v UK*,[13] which is authority for the proposition that bind over proceedings *do* involve the determination of a criminal charge for the purposes of Article 6, on the basis that the magistrates may commit a person who refuses to be bound over not to breach the peace where there is evidence to the criminal standard that his or her conduct caused or was likely to cause a breach of the peace. This 'was an immediate and obvious penal consequence',[14] unlike the ASBO position.

3.10 Having been taken 'on a *tour d'horizon* of the leading decisions of the European Court', Lord Steyn observed that there was 'no case in which the European Court has held proceedings to be criminal even though an adverse outcome for the defendant cannot result in any penalty'.[15] The House of Lords having taken the interpretative course

12 (1980) 3 EHRR 333.

13 (1998) 28 EHRR 603.

14 *McCann* [2002] UKHL 39 at para 32.

15 *McCann* [2002] UKHL 39 at para 31.

that it did, namely that there was no punitive element in ASBO proceedings, it followed that the proceedings were determined to be civil in character and their Lordships had no doubt that they should attract the fair trial guarantees under Article 6(1) (a fair and public hearing within a reasonable time by an independent and impartial tribunal). Although on the face of it an ASBO has nothing to do with a person's civil rights and obligations, it does engage Article 8 and that is a civil right by virtue of HRA 1998.[16] However, there was nothing about the machinery of the Civil Evidence Act 1995 or the Magistrates' Courts (Hearsay Evidence in Civil Proceedings) Rules 1999 that was incompatible with Article 6(1) and hearsay was therefore admissible.[17]

Is the decision in McCann *here to stay?*

3.11 There has been academic discussion and disapproval of this decision,[18] in particular in relation to the English court's interpretation of the Strasbourg jurisprudence. In *Welch v UK*,[19] for example, a confiscation order was held to be a penalty and part of the reason for that decision was the fact that there was a possibility of imprisonment in default. Given that in ASBO cases the penalty for breaching a preventative order is greater than for many criminal offences, the House of Lords' distinction between punitive and preventative was arguably disingenuous. Perhaps it is an issue that the European Court of Human Rights will have to revisit in due course. The one concession made by the House of Lords was that despite the fact that proceedings were civil, due to the 'seriousness of matters involved',[20] the criminal standard of proof should apply and there was no illogicality between that requirement and hearsay evidence.

The standard of proof and Article 6

3.12 As mentioned above, despite the finding that ASBO applications are civil proceedings, the House of Lords determined in *McCann* that the standard of proof applicable for the determination of anti-social behaviour is the criminal one. While the House of Lords refused (on

16 See *Re S (Minors) (Care Order: Implementation of Care Plan)* [2002] 2 AC 291, 320 at para 71.
17 See chapter 4.
18 See for example Andrew Ashworth, 'Social control and 'anti-social behaviour': the subversion of human rights?' (2004) LQR 280.
19 (1995) 20 EHRR 247.
20 Per Lord Steyn in *McCann* [2002] UKHL 39 at para 37.

the one hand) to accept that the making of an ASBO was a penalty within the meaning on Strasbourg jurisprudence, it ruled (on the other) that the criminal standard of proof should apply due to 'the seriousness of matters involved'.[21] In short, the Court, following earlier Court of Appeal decisions in relation to sex offender orders[22] and football banning orders,[23] was accepting that there should be procedural safeguards in place when Convention rights are engaged (in ASBO cases, the right most commonly engaged is that enshrined in Article 8). Some commentators have seen the granting of quasi-criminal status to such orders as something of a compromise by the English courts as well as a contradiction: how can hearsay ever satisfy the criminal standard?[24] In *McCann*, Lord Steyn rejected that suggestion: he was of the view that 'hearsay evidence, depending on its logical probativeness, is quite capable of satisfying the requirements of section 1(1) [of CDA 1998]'.[25]

3.13 What practitioners should be alert to is that the criminal standard of proof only applies to the first limb of the test for an ASBO (namely whether the defendant has acted in an anti-social manner) and not the second limb (namely whether an ASBO is necessary).[26]

21 Per Lord Steyn in *McCann* [2002] UKHL 39 at para 37.

22 *B v Chief Constable of Avon & Somerset Constabulary* [2001] 1 WLR 340, HL.

23 *Gough v Chief Constable of the Derbyshire Constabulary* [2002] 3 WLR 289.

24 See Gil-Robles, *Report by Mr Alvaro Gil-Robles, Commissioner for Human Rights, on his visit to the UK 4–12 November 2004*, Comm DH(2005)6, Strasbourg: Council of Europe.

25 *McCann* [2002] UKHL 39 at para 37.

26 The standard of proof applicable to both limbs is discussed in detail at para 5.43.

CHAPTER 4

Hearsay evidence in ASBO proceedings

Introduction

4.1 Chapter 3 examined the relationship between ECHR Article 6 and ASBOs. It explained that the criminal safeguards in Article 6(3) did not apply. However, Article 6(1) does. Further, the admissibility of hearsay is governed by the Civil Evidence Act (CEA) 1995. This chapter examines the following:

- the interrelation between Articles 6(1) and (3) and hearsay evidence;
- the Civil Evidence Act 1995;
- the procedural rules relating to the reliance on hearsay evidence;
- challenges to hearsay and tactical tips;
- special measures for vulnerable witnesses.

The definition of hearsay

4.2 'Hearsay' is defined in section 1(2) of the Civil Evidence Act 1995 as 'a statement made otherwise than by a person while giving oral evidence in the proceedings which is tendered as evidence of the matters stated'. References to hearsay in CEA 1995 include 'hearsay of whatever degree'. Civil proceedings are defined by CEA 1995 s11 as 'civil proceedings, before any tribunal, in relation to which the strict rules of evidence apply, whether as a matter of law or by agreement of the parties'. Given that there has been no doubt since *McCann* that CEA 1995 applies in relation to stand-alone ASBOs, it must also apply to post-conviction ASBOs which have also been deemed to be civil proceedings.[1] The procedure in relation to the reliance on hearsay is discussed below at para 4.30.

ECHR Article 6(3) and hearsay evidence

4.3 While the decision in *McCann* deprives defendants of the 'criminal' safeguards in ECHR Article 6(3), it is worth noting that even if the minimum rights guaranteed by Article 6(3) did apply to ASBO proceedings, as they do to criminal proceedings, they would not impose an absolute prohibition on hearsay evidence. The provision under Article 6(3)(d)[2] that a person charged has the right to examine witnesses giving evidence against him is one specific aspect of a fair trial,

1 See para 3.2.
2 Article 6 is reproduced at para 3.4.

but, if the opportunity was not provided, the question for the Strasbourg Court would be whether the proceedings as a whole were fair.[3] Applying the Strasbourg jurisprudence, the English courts in a series of cases have not interpreted Article 6(3)(d) as imposing an absolute prohibition on the admission of hearsay. This has arisen especially in the context of prosecution witnesses being too fearful to come to court because of improper threats or pressure from a defendant.[4]

4.4 In the very recent case of *Daltel Europe Ltd (In Liquidation) v Hassan Ali Makki*,[5] the Court of Appeal appears to have ruled that committal proceedings for either civil or criminal contempt are civil proceedings for the purposes of domestic classification and therefore CEA 1995 applied, but the full protection of Article 6 is available. However the Court went on to rule that Article 6(1) and Article 6(3)(d) (the right to examine witnesses), taken together, were not incompatible with hearsay evidence.

4.5 Further, the introduction of the Criminal Justice Act 2003 has brought about the reversal of common law rules against the admission of hearsay in criminal proceedings[6] and the use of hearsay is now becoming routine in criminal trials. The Lord Chief Justice, Lord Phillips, presiding in the Court of Appeal in the first case considering the new hearsay provisions, found those governing admissibility to be compatible with Article 6(3)(d), particularly because the statute gives the court the power to exclude that evidence if unfair.[7]

Article 6(1) and hearsay

4.6 Against that background, the question of admissibility of hearsay evidence needs always to be looked at in the context of the proceedings as a whole. In civil proceedings the protection afforded by Article 6(1)

3 *Trivedi v UK* 89 DR 136; *Unterpertinger v Austria* (1991) 13 EHRR 175; *Windisch v Austria* (1991) 13 EHRR 281; *Lüdi v Switzerland* (1993) 15 EHRR 173; *Barbera Messegue and Jabardo v Spain* (1989) 11 EHRR 360; *Bricmont v Belgium* (1990) 12 EHRR 217; *Delta v France* (1993) 16 EHRR 574; *Saidi v France* (1994) 17 EHRR 251; *Doorson v Netherlands* (1996) 22 EHRR 330; *P.S. v Germany* (2003) 36 EHRR 61; and *Sadak v Turkey* (2003) 36 EHRR 26.

4 See in particular *R v Imad Al-Khawaja* [2005] EWCA Crim 2697; *R v Sellick (Santino)* [2005] EWCA Crim 651; [2005] 1 WLR 3257 and *Steven Grant v The State* [2006] UKPC 2.

5 [2006] EWCA Civ 94 (applying *Al-Khawaja* and *Sellick*).

6 The new hearsay provisions came into force on 4 April 2005 (CJA 2003 ss114–117).

7 *R v Xhabri* [2005] EWCA Crim 3135.

of ECHR is still an important safeguard which can be used to ensure that hearsay evidence is dealt with fairly.[8]

4.7 The general requirement of fairness enshrined in Article 6(1) is to be construed broadly and not restrictively. The more detailed provisions of Articles 6(2) and 6(3) have been treated by Strasbourg as aspects of the requirement of fairness in Article 6(1), not as distinct, extra rights. In *Niderost-Huber v Switzerland*[9] the Court stated that, when it came to the question of adversarial proceedings, it was of little consequence that the proceedings in question concerned civil litigation: the right to adversarial proceedings was a fundamental principle guaranteed by Article 6(1) which was intended above all to secure the interests of the parties and those of the proper administration of justice.

4.8 Further, the fair trial guarantee in Article 6(1) includes the principle of equality of arms:

> The principle of equality of arms – one of the elements of the broader concept of fair trial – requires each party to be given a reasonable opportunity to present his case under conditions that do not place him at a substantial disadvantage vis-à-vis his opponent ...[10]

However it should be noted that the fact that ASBO proceedings must be procedurally fair has been recognised by the Divisional Court on more than one occasion without reference to Article 6.[11] What is fair will depend on the circumstances of each case. If, for example, the sole evidence against the defendant is from a single witness, it would be arguably unfair to admit that evidence as hearsay.

Admissibility of hearsay evidence in the criminal courts: which rules apply?

4.9 As explained at para 4.2 above the admissibility of hearsay in civil proceedings is governed by CEA 1995. In the High Court and county court the Civil Procedure Rules (CPR) 33.1–33.5 also apply.[12] As the

8 Although see *Solon South West Housing Association Ltd v James* [2004] EWCA Civ 1847 at para 29.

9 (1998) 25 EHRR 709.

10 (1998) 25 EHRR 709 at para 23. See also *Dombo Beheer BV v The Netherlands* (1993) 18 EHRR 213.

11 *R (C) v Sunderland Youth Court* [2004] 1 Cr App R (S) 76; *R (W) v Acton Youth Court* [2005] EWHC 954 (Admin).

12 Relevant sections reproduced in appendix H.

Civil Procedure Rules do not apply to the criminal courts (see CPR 2.1(1)), the Magistrates' Courts (Hearsay Evidence in Civil Proceedings) Rules (MC(H)R) 1999[13] apply in the magistrates' courts and other criminal courts instead.

4.10 When appealing a stand-alone ASBO from the magistrates' court to the Crown Court (as a defendant is entitled to do as of right), MC(H)R 1999 should logically apply in the Crown Court.[14] In the absence of any other applicable rules, MC(H)R 1999 should also apply in the Crown Court and youth court in relation to post-conviction ASBOs. Concerns about the complete lack of procedural guidance in relation to post-conviction ASBOs (particularly in the Crown Court) were raised by the Court of Appeal in the recent case of *Luke Paul Wadmore and Liam Philip Foreman v R.*[15] The Court doubted whether MC(H)R 1999 applied in the Crown Court but proceeded as if the principles set out in those rules applied by analogy. Unfortunately neither counsel was able to assist the Court on this issue so the fact that MC(H)R 1999 are routinely applied in the Crown Court on appeals against stand-alone ASBOs was not considered by the Court when it doubted that MC(H)R 1999 applied 'in relation to adducing hearsay evidence in support of an ASBO in the Crown Court'.[16] The Court sent out a plea:

> So it seems that although it is common for applications for ASBOs to be made in the Crown Court under CDA 1998 s1C, the procedure for serving and adducing evidence, in particular hearsay evidence, in support of those applications is not expressly governed by any one set of court rules. If this is indeed the case then it is most unfortunate. It means that the CPS, defendants and their advisers and judges in the Crown Court have no clear rules to follow. We hope that this question will be considered by the appropriate Rules Committee(s) as a matter of urgency.[17]

4.11 It is likely that some time in the foreseeable future the Government will extend the jurisdiction of the CPR to civil matters heard in the criminal courts in order to achieve some consistency. In the meantime, the principles in MC(H)R 1999 should be applied by analogy in *all* ASBO cases in the criminal courts. Like all primary and subordinate legislation, CEA 1995 and MC(H)R 1999 must be interpreted in

13 SI No 681. Reproduced in full in appendix D.

14 See para 11.9.

15 [2006] EWCA Crim 686.

16 [2006] EWCA Crim 686 at para 32.

17 [2006] EWCA Crim 686 at para 34.

accordance with Convention rights.[18] In this context, that means in accordance with Article 6(1).

The Civil Evidence Act 1995: admissibility and weight of hearsay evidence

4.12 CEA 1995 s1(1) states: 'In civil proceedings evidence shall not be excluded on the ground that it is hearsay'. As stated at the beginning of this chapter, hearsay is defined in section 1(2) as a 'statement made otherwise than by a person while giving oral evidence in the proceedings which is tendered as evidence of the matters stated'. Additionally, references to hearsay include hearsay of 'whatever degree'.

4.13 CEA 1995 s4 states:

(1) In estimating the weight (if any) to be given to hearsay evidence in civil proceedings the court shall have regard to any circumstances from which any inference can reasonably be drawn as to the reliability or otherwise of the evidence.
(2) Regard may be had, in particular, to the following –
  (a) whether it would have been reasonable and practicable for the party by whom the evidence was adduced to have produced the maker of the original statement as a witness;
  (b) whether the original statement was made contemporaneously with the occurrence or existence of the matters stated;
  (c) whether the evidence involves multiple hearsay;
  (d) whether any person involved had any motive to conceal or misrepresent matters;
  (e) whether the original statement was an edited account, or was made in collaboration with another or for a particular purpose;
  (f) whether the circumstances in which the evidence is adduced as hearsay are such as to suggest an attempt to prevent proper evaluation of its weight.

4.14 This is not an exhaustive list and it is a matter for the court to decide what factors to weigh in the balance. It should be noted that the use of the words 'if any' in section 4(1) gives a judge the power to discount the hearsay entirely and therefore there may be little difference between that and the power to exclude the evidence because while the judge may admit the evidence, he or she could then determine that it is not worthy of any particular weight.[19] That said, experience in

18 HRA 1998 s3.
19 See *Solon South West Housing Association Ltd v James* [2004] EWCA Civ 1847 at para 19.

the civil courts to date would suggest that a case in which a judge has accorded no weight to a piece of evidence is rare.

4.15 In *Moat Housing Group-South Limited v Harris & Hartless,*[20] a case involving possession proceedings, anti-social behaviour injunctions and ASBOs in the county court, a great deal of hearsay evidence was relied upon, some of it anonymous because of non-specific expressions of fear of reprisals. The Court of Appeal recognised the real dangers of hearsay evidence in these kinds of cases:

> The willingness of a civil court to admit hearsay evidence carries with it inherent dangers in a case such as this ... rumours abound in a small housing estate, and it is much more difficult for a judge to assess the truth of what he is being told if the original maker of the statement does not attend court to be cross-examined on his/her evidence.[21]

4.16 The importance of a proper evidential basis for not producing witnesses live (see CEA 1995 s4(2)(a)) was highlighted:

> While nobody would wish to return to the days before the Civil Evidence Act 1995 came into force, when efforts to admit hearsay were beset by complicated procedural rules, the experience of this case should provide a salutary warning for the future that more attention should be paid by claimants in this type of case to the need to state by convincing direct evidence why it was not reasonable and practicable to produce the original maker of the statement as a witness. If the statement involves multiple hearsay, the route by which the original statement came to the attention of the person attesting to it should be identified as far as practicable. It would also be desirable for judges to remind themselves in their judgments that they are taking into account the section 4(2) criteria ... so far as they are relevant.[22]

4.17 The Court of Appeal also made useful observations about the contemporaneity and section 4(2)(b) in the context of possession proceedings:

> The emphasis placed by section 4(2)(b) of the 1995 Act on contemporaneity merely goes to highlight the importance of a landlord giving a tenant contemporary notice of any complaints that are made against his/her behaviour, so that the tenant is not faced in court with serious complaints made by anonymous or absent witnesses about matters that took place, if at all, many months previously.[23]

20 [2005] EWCA Civ 287; [2005] 3 WLR 691.

21 [2005] EWCA Civ 287 at para 135.

22 [2005] EWCA Civ 287 at para 140.

23 [2005] EWCA Civ 287 at para 135.

4.18 In a non landlord-tenant relationship, 'contemporary notice' of complaints will only take place in the context of an arrest if the complaint made involves conduct that may amount to a crime or perhaps at an ABC or other strategy meeting. It is rare in stand-alone ASBO applications for a defendant to be on notice of the range and detail of complaints of alleged anti-social incidents. It is usually when an ASBO application is served along with volumes of crime reports, police 'intelligence' and witness statements from officers about accounts they have taken from anonymous witnesses (usually after the decision to apply for an ASBO) that a defendant becomes aware of how closely he or she is being monitored by the police and/or the local authority. Given that a defendant may be faced with old allegations, in order for a hearing to be fair, it is important that statements, albeit anonymous ones, are taken at the time of the complaint being made. If there is no contemporaneity, then any defence submissions as to weight or exclusion will be well-founded.

Business records

4.19 CEA 1995 ss9(1) and (2)[24] state:

> (1) A document which is shown to form part of the records of a business or public authority may be received in evidence in civil proceedings without further proof.
> (2) A document shall be taken to form part of the records of a business or public authority if there is produced to the court a certificate to that effect signed by an officer of the business or authority to which the records belong. For this purpose –
> (a) a document purporting to be a certificate signed by an officer of a business or public authority shall be deemed to have been duly given by such an officer and signed by him; and
> (b) a certificate shall be treated as signed by a person if it purports to bear a facsimile of his signature.

4.20 Section 9(5) provides the court with an opt-out clause:

> The court may, having regard to the circumstances of the case, direct that all or any of the above provisions of this section do not apply in relation to a particular document or record, or description of documents or records.

4.21 In *Luke Paul Wadmore and Liam Philip Foreman v R*[25] the Court of Appeal considered that a schedule of complaints from residents on an

24 See appendix C for the full text.

25 [2006] EWCA Crim 686, discussed at para 4.10 above.

estate, compiled by a Neighbourhood Housing Manager, as well as a spreadsheet of criminal incidents on the same estate, compiled from crime reports by a police constable, may well be business records for the purposes of section 9. It underlined the limited application of section 9(5) in post-conviction ASBO hearings (there is no reason why the same should not apply to stand-alone ASBO hearings):[26]

> The spreadsheets or schedules that are exhibited to the statements of Miss Mason and Miss Kwasniewski probably constituted documents that are *'part of the records of ... a public authority'* within *section 9 of the Civil Evidence Act 1995*. As such they are admissible as evidence of the facts stated in them in civil proceedings. But if a party wishes to rely on such documents, then they should be accompanied by a certificate to the effect that they are part of the records of a public authority, which is signed by an officer of the authority: *section 9(2)*. That requirement can be dispensed with by a court if it thinks it appropriate *'in the circumstances of the case': section 9(5)*. However we doubt whether that requirement should be waived in a case where proof is required to the criminal standard, as it is when an application for an ASBO is made under *CDA 1998 s1C*.[27]

Vulnerable and intimidated witnesses: special measures

4.22 The social problem used as a justification for introducing ASBOs and relying upon hearsay has often been epitomised by an image of an elderly resident on a housing estate, too terrified to give evidence against the young ruffians who are terrorising her neighbourhood. The resident is usually prepared to make an anonymous complaint or, if he or she is identified, is unwilling to come to court out of fear. If the applicant body is relying on 'fear' as a reason for not calling the witness live, it is important to explore whether there is a proper foundation for that fear:

- Does the witness have a direct connection with your client?
- Has he or she witnessed any violence or ever been put in fear of violence by your client?

If not, you will have a good reason to object to the evidence being adduced as hearsay.

26 [2006] EWCA Crim 686 at para 38.

27 Emphasis as given in the judgment.

4.23 It is important to note that SOCPA 2005 inserts a new section 1I into CDA 1998,[28] which imports (with some exceptions) the 'special measures' regime[29] in relation to vulnerable and intimidated witnesses available in the criminal courts. The measures available are the special measures in the Youth Justice and Criminal Evidence (YJCEA) Act 1999 ss23 to 30:

- the use of screens;
- the giving of evidence by live link;
- the giving of evidence in private and the use of video recorded evidence-in-chief;
- the use of video recorded cross-examination or re-examination;
- the examination of a witness through an intermediary; and
- aids to communication.

4.24 YJCEA 1999 s16 (entitled 'Witnesses eligible for assistance on grounds of age or incapacity') states:

> (1) For the purposes of this Chapter a witness in criminal proceedings (other than the accused) is eligible for assistance by virtue of this section –
> (a) if under the age of 17 at the time of the hearing; or
> (b) if the court considers that the quality of evidence given by the witness is likely to be diminished by reason of any circumstances falling within subsection (2).
> (2) The circumstances falling within this subsection are –
> (a) that the witness –
> (i) suffers from mental disorder within the meaning of the Mental Health Act 1983, or
> (ii) otherwise has a significant impairment of intelligence and social functioning;
> (b) that the witness has a physical disability or is suffering from a physical disorder.
> (3) In subsection (1)(a) 'the time of the hearing', in relation to a witness, means the time when it falls to the court to make a determination for the purposes of section 19(2) in relation to the witness.
> (4) In determining whether a witness falls within subsection (1)(b) the court must consider any views expressed by the witness.
> (5) In this Chapter references to the quality of a witness's evidence are to its quality in terms of completeness, coherence and accuracy; and for this purpose 'coherence' refers to a witness's ability in giving evidence to give answers which address the questions put to the witness and can be understood both individually and collectively.

28 SOCPA 2005 s143; see *Archbold* 2006, para 5-886b.

29 YJCEA 1999 Pt 2 Chap 1; see *Archbold* 2006, para 8-52.

4.25 YJCEA 1999 s17 (entitled 'Witnesses eligible for assistance on grounds of fear or distress about testifying') states:

> (1) For the purposes of this Chapter a witness in criminal proceedings (other than the accused) is eligible for assistance by virtue of this subsection if the court is satisfied that the quality of evidence given by the witness is likely to be diminished by reason of fear or distress on the part of the witness in connection with testifying in the proceedings.
> (2) In determining whether a witness falls within subsection (1) the court must take into account, in particular –
> (a) the nature and alleged circumstances of the offence to which the proceedings relate;
> (b) the age of the witness;
> (c) such of the following matters as appear to the court to be relevant, namely –
> (i) the social and cultural background and ethnic origins of the witness,
> (ii) the domestic and employment circumstances of the witness, and
> (iii) any religious beliefs or political opinions of the witness;
> (d) any behaviour towards the witness on the part of –
> (i) the accused,
> (ii) members of the family or associates of the accused, or
> (iii) any other person who is likely to be an accused or a witness in the proceedings.
> (3) In determining that question the court must in addition consider any views expressed by the witness.
> [(4) Not applicable.][30]

Rules in relation to special measures

4.26 SOCPA 2005 adopts the criminal courts' rules (subject to such rules being issued in relation to ASBO proceedings with any modifications as may be so provided) in relation to special measures applications and objections.[31] CDA 1998 s1I does not apply to the county court (although CPR 32.3 makes provision for evidence by video link or other means)[32] or, curiously, the youth court (despite the fact that the special measures regime applies in criminal trials in the youth

30 SOCPA 2005 s143 specifically excludes ss17(4); 21(1)(b); 21(5)–(7); 22(1)(b); 21(5)–(7); 27(10); 32; in force 1 July 2005.

31 CDA 1998 s1I, inserted by SOCPA 2005 s143(4). The criminal courts' rules are laid out in the Criminal Procedure Rules 2005, Part 29 and in *Archbold* 2006, para 8-56. No rules relating to ASBO proceedings have yet been issued.

32 See *Roman Polanski v Condé Nast Publications Ltd* [2005] 1 All ER 945.

court). That said, the youth court has no jurisdiction to hear stand-alone ASBO applications, only post-conviction ones, and perhaps it was thought that evidence in those hearings was less likely to be contested. Special measures would therefore seem to be available in stand-alone applications in the magistrates' court, post-conviction ASBOs in the magistrates' and Crown Courts, as well as for interim orders in the magistrates' court.

Special measures: a good thing?

4.27 While in criminal proceedings defence practitioners have historically fought to minimise the use of special measures in trials, particularly before a jury, in ASBO proceedings they can be used to challenge the contention that is necessary to admit the evidence as hearsay. As can be seen from the way in which sections 16 and 17 above are drafted, the assumption in criminal trials is that a witness will appear live and face the full thrust of cross-examination unless they are very old, very young, incapacitated or in fear, and even then there may be some statutory hurdles to get over before they can benefit from special measures. In criminal trials heard before juries defence practitioners are understandably concerned about the prejudicial impact when these measure are used in relation to prosecution witnesses. Conversely, when an ASBO is being applied for, defendants will be concerned about the weight accorded by a professional tribunal to an extremely prejudicial and untested piece of hearsay evidence and therefore will want to highlight the existence of measures such as screens and video link, in order to counteract the 'fear' justification for hearsay evidence. If special measures have not been applied for by the applicant body seeking to rely upon hearsay evidence, defence practitioners should ask why not, either at an early stage or during cross-examination (see below on tactics).

Should hearsay evidence be objected to? Some tips on tactics

4.28 Civil practitioners do not feel the same discomfort about hearsay evidence as criminal practitioners do. Traditionally, and until the introduction of the Criminal Justice Act 2003, hearsay has been inadmissible in criminal courts unless one of the exceptions apply. In civil hearings, hearsay has long been admissible and therefore county court practitioners do not feel as dismayed as magistrates' court practitioners do when they are served with a file full of hearsay evidence by a local authority applying for an ASBO. County court practitioners are used to dealing tactically with this evidence and making submissions as to its weight. If, for example, the applicant body is relying upon second or third hand hearsay, an important tactical question is: is it worth objecting to it? If a police officer or housing officer is reporting something a third party told them orally or via a complaint that was recorded on a telephone attendance note, it may be tactically better to cross-examine the professional witness as to the extent of the enquiries made of this witness, whether they were ever asked to make a statement or attend court or whether they were offered special measures, rather than serving a response to a hearsay notice which may result in the applicant body acquiring direct evidence against your client. Of course an application to cross-examine the witness must be made (see para 4.32 below).

4.29 In first hand hearsay situations, if your client does not accept the evidence, then an application to cross-examine must be made (the procedure is laid out below at para 4.32). However, if the application fails, depending on the nature and extent of the dispute, it may be better to have the evidence read than to hear it live, particularly if the defendant is going to contradict this evidence by giving live evidence. If there are only some aspects of the statement that are not agreed, the other side may be amenable to some editing, if it means saving the expense and inconvenience of bringing a witness to court.

Relying on hearsay: the Magistrates' Courts (Hearsay Evidence in Civil Proceedings) Rules 1999

4.30 CEA 1995 s2(1) requires a party to give notice of an intention to adduce hearsay. Section 2(2) of the Act makes provision for rules of court to be made as to the manner in which notices should be served and section 3 provides for rules to be made when a party wishes to cross-examine, with the leave of the court, a hearsay witness live. The Magistrates' Courts (Hearsay Evidence in Civil Proceedings) Rules (MC(H)R) 1999[33] have been enacted pursuant to CEA 1995 to give guidance as to the use of hearsay evidence in ASBO proceedings[34] (see discussion at paragraph 4.10 as to which criminal courts they apply to).

33 Reproduced in full in appendix D.

34 CEA 1995 ss2(2), 3 and 12 envisage rules of court regulating the practice or procedure of the court in relation to the provisions of CEA 1995.

Time limits

4.31 MC(H)R 1999 rr3-6 are the equivalent of CPR Part 33[35] and regulate time limits and the procedure for informing other parties and the court in the following circumstances:

- if a party wishes to rely upon hearsay evidence (rule 3); or
- if a party wishes to make an application to call evidence that has been served as hearsay (rule 4); or
- if a party wishes to attack the credibility of the maker of a hearsay statement or allege that the person has made a previous inconsistent statement (rule 5); and
- when service is to be effected, rule 6 defines the method.

Hearsay notices

4.32 Any party relying upon hearsay must serve a hearsay notice on every other party, and the court, 21 days before the date fixed for the hearing. Importantly, the notice must state why the witness will not be called.[36] In *Luke Paul Wadmore and Liam Philip Foreman v R*, the Court of Appeal underlined the importance of complying with this requirement:[37]

> ... we note the following: (i) we were not told when the CPS Applications were served on the defendants. The Magistrates' Hearsay Rules provides that at least 21 days' notice of hearsay evidence must be given. (ii) The Application Notices do not identify the hearsay evidence relied on, nor the person who made the statement which is to be given in evidence. This failure might have been cured in relation to the statements if, (which is not clear), they were attached to the Application Notice that was sent to the defendants and their advisers ... (iii) The Application Notice does not state *why* the person who is supposed to be identified will not be called to give oral evidence. (See: Magistrates' Hearsay Rules paragraph 3). (iv) Service of an application to adduce hearsay evidence must be served on either the defendant, or if he is represented by a solicitor, on his solicitor. It is not clear what was done in this case ...[38]

4.33 If another party wishes the witness(es) to attend, they must make an application within seven days of receiving the notice to the clerk to the justices (unless the court otherwise directs), stating why cross-

35 See appendix H. Note tighter time limits in the magistrates' court.

36 MC(H)R 1999 r3(f).

37 [2006] EWCA Crim 686 at para 38.

38 Emphasis as per judgment.

examination on the contents of the witness statement is necessary (MC(H)R 1999 r4(2)(b)). Neither CEA 1995 nor MC(H)R 1999 gives any guidance as to how the Court should exercise its discretion to allow a witness to be called live.[39]

4.34 Unlike CPR Part 33, the rules allow for the application to call a witness live to be made *ex parte* to the court 'if it is in the interests of justice to do so' (MC(H)R 1999 r4(6)), although it is difficult to conceive of a circumstance which would justify such a course and be compliant with the right to a public hearing enshrined in Article 6(1).[40] The confirmation of service of the application on all parties must be filed with the court.[41]

Attacking credibility

4.35 There is also a requirement pursuant to MC(H)R 1999 r5 to serve a notice if a party wishes to attack the credibility of a witness whose evidence has been served as hearsay or wishes to allege that the witness has made a previous inconsistent statement. This must be done no later than seven days after service of the hearsay notice (unless the justice's clerk otherwise directs). The notice must be served on the party tendering the hearsay evidence, as well as every other party and the court. If, as a result, the party decides to call the evidence live instead, then that party must notify the court and all other parties of this intention and must do so no later than seven days after receiving the notice from the party wishing to attack the credibility of the witness.

What constitutes service?

4.36 If a party is not represented or not known to be represented by a solicitor, then a notice will have to be delivered to the individual personally or delivered to the person's last known residence or sent to that address by first-class post. If the party is represented by a solicitor, then service is effected by delivering the document or sending it by first-class post to the solicitor's offices or by DX or by fax (see MC(H)R 1999 r6). If first-class post is used, unless the contrary is proved, a document will be deemed to have been served on the

39 See para 8.109 on hearsay applications under the Civil Procedure Rules.

40 Although ECHR Article 6(1) does not apply whenever civil rights and obligations are in issue, only when they are being 'determined', it is perfectly clear that such an application would have a direct impact on the determination of those rights and obligations.

41 Rule 4(7).

second business day after posting, If the DX is used, then service will be deemed to have been effected on the second day after it was left at the document exchange. Faxes have to be transmitted before 4 pm for a document to be deemed to have been served on that day, otherwise it will be deemed to have been served on the next business day.

What happens if a party fails to comply?

4.37 Importantly, a failure to comply with CEA 1995 s2(1) or with MC(H)R 1999 does not affect the admissibility of the evidence but must be taken into account by the court in considering the exercise of its powers with respect to the course of the proceedings and as a matter adversely affecting the weight to be given to the evidence in accordance with CEA 1995 s4[42] (see para 4.12 above). Practitioners will have to make tactical decisions as to whether it is worth taking a point about technical non-compliance with the rules, given that non-compliance does not affect admissibility. For example, if the statement of a professional witness is filled with second and third hand hearsay, and the applicant body is intending on calling this witness live, but has not served a notice relating to the hearsay elements of that statement, a practitioner will have to decide whether it is in the interests of the defendant to complain in advance that MC(H)R 1999 r3, and in particular MC(H)R 1999 r3(f), has not been complied with or to leave it to questions in cross-examination. As mentioned in para 4.28 above, advance notice of the complaint may result in a first hand hearsay statement being served.

42 CEA 1995 s2(4).

CHAPTER 5

Stand-alone ASBOs

continued

Introduction

5.1 The law relating to ASBO practice and procedure has developed considerably over the past six years. The most important area in the context of all ASBO applications is the statutory test for obtaining one. This chapter looks at the practice and procedure specific to stand-alone ASBOs and also looks in detail at that statutory test which is relevant to all three types of ASBO. The terms and duration of ASBOs are dealt with in chapter 7. The focus of this chapter is as follows:

- practice and procedure in the magistrates' court;
- interim ASBOs;
- whether you can consent to an ASBO;
- the two limbs of the statutory test;
- the reasonableness defence and the ECHR;
- when ASBO proceedings can amount to an abuse of process;
- variation and discharge;
- reporting restrictions and post-ASBO publicity;
- ancillary orders.

Practice and procedure in the magistrates' court

Who can apply for a stand-alone ASBO?

5.2 The applicant body could be any one of the empowered actors (a 'relevant authority')[1] who choose to take action: local authorities, county councils (England only), police forces, British Transport Police (BTP), registered social landlords (RSLs), Housing Action Trusts (HATs), The Environment Agency and Transport for London. As mentioned in chapter 2 and in the Home Office's *Guide to Anti-social Behaviour* 2006,[2] there is no duty on the BTP or RSLs or HATs to apply for an ASBO should the anti-social behaviour occur within their jurisdiction: the police or local authority can still apply on their behalf in accordance with their obligations and duties under CDA 1998 ss5, 6 and 17 (discussed in detail in chapter 2). Both the Environment Agency and Transport for London ('TfL') will become relevant authorities on 1 September 2006.[3] The Environment Agency was

1 CDA 1998 s1(1A) (as amended) and the Crime and Disorder Act 1998 (Relevant Authorities and Relevant Persons) Order 2006 SI No 2137.

2 (Home Office, 2006), page 11. Available at www.together.gov.uk.

3 Crime and Disorder Act 1998 (Relevant Authorities and Relevant Persons) Order 2006 SI No 2137. See appendix A.

established by the Environment Act 1995 and has various functions including waste regulation and pollution control.[4] It has responsibility for the land formerly controlled by the National Rivers Authority and the London Waste Regulation Authority.[5] Its principal aim in discharging its functions is to protect or enhance the environment and to work towards attaining the objective of achieving sustainable development.[6] It will be able to apply for stand-alone (and county court) ASBOs 'where a person has acted in an anti-social manner on, or in relation to, any land and the Environment Agency has a statutory function in relation to that land'.[7] Transport for London ('TfL') was established in 2000, as a functional body of the Greater London Authority.[8] It is responsible for London's buses, the Underground, the Docklands Light Railway (DLR) and the management of Croydon Tramlink and London River Services. TfL is also responsible for a 580km network of main roads.[9] It will be able to apply for stand-alone (and county court) ASBOs 'where a person has acted in an anti-social manner on, or in relation to, any land or vehicles used in connection with, or for the purposes of, the provision of a relevant transport service'.[10]

Against whom is a stand-alone ASBO available?

5.3 'Stand-alone' ASBOs are available against anybody, as long as they have reached the age of 10 and the statutory test described below is satisfied. The person against whom an ASBO is sought does not need to officially reside in the local government area of the applicant council or the police area of the applicant police force: it is the locality of the anti-social behaviour which determines who the applicant body is, geographically speaking. RSLs and HATs can apply for ASBOs against residents, as well as non-residents, as long as the persons they are seeking to protect have a connection with the housing they provide or manage (see para 5.114 below for the 'relevant persons' requirement).

4 See Environment Act (EA) 1995 s2.
5 EA 1995 s3.
6 EA 1995 s4.
7 SI 2006 No 2137, para 2(2). See appendix A.
8 Greater London Authority Act 1999 s154.
9 See www.tfl.gov.uk.
10 SI 2006 No 2137, para 3(2). See appendix A.

Where are stand-alone ASBOs heard?

5.4 They are brought by way of complaint to a magistrates' court.[11] Stand-alone ASBOs are not available in the county court. There, ASBOs can only be made in respect of a person who is already a party to proceedings underway in that court,[12] although there is a power to join others who are not party to the principal proceedings, as long as their alleged anti-social behaviour is material to the principal proceedings.[13]

5.5 The civil jurisdiction of the magistrates' court is conferred upon it by virtue of Part II of the Magistrates' Court Act 1980. Such a jurisdiction is not conferred on the youth court. Hence all stand-alone applications for ASBOs in relation to children and young persons will be heard in the adult magistrates' court.[14]

Which magistrates' court?

5.6 There is no longer any requirement that there be a connection between the commission area of the magistrates' court and where the alleged anti-social behaviour took place.[15]

The summons and the ASBO application

5.7 Once a complaint has been laid, a defendant will be issued with a summons to attend court on a particular date.[16] The court will usually adjourn the hearing and fix a date for the full hearing.[17]

5.8 The application for the ASBO will be attached to the summons. Since the amendment of the Magistrates' Courts (Anti-Social Behaviour Orders) Rules (MC(ASBO)R) 2002,[18] there is also no longer any requirement for an ASBO application to be in a particular form but it will be set out in a form similar to that in MC(ASBO)R 2002 Sch 1 (reproduced in appendix B). The application may also include a draft order, evidence in support of the application, hearsay notices and a certificate of consultation. In accordance with MC(ASBO)R 2002 r7,

11 CDA 1998 s1(3).

12 CDA 1998 s1B(2) and (3) (as amended).

13 CDA 1998 s1B (3A)–1B(3C). See Chapter 8.

14 See Chapter 10 for details.

15 CDA 1998 s1(3) was amended by Courts Act 2003 (Consequential Provisions) Order 2005 SI No 886. See appendix A for CDA 1998 s1.

16 MCA 1980 s51.

17 The power to adjourn is contained in MCA 1980 s50.

18 Magistrates' Courts (Anti-Social Behaviour Orders) Rules 2002 SI No 2784, as amended by Magistrates' Courts (Miscellaneous Amendments) Rules 2003 SI No 1236. Reproduced at appendix B.

service is effected by post to the last known address or if given to the defendant in person. Evidence in support of an ASBO will typically include:

- witness statements from neighbours, local shopkeepers or other people affected by the behaviour complained of;
- witness statements from police officers who attended at incidents;
- witness statements from an officer tasked specifically to deal with anti-social behaviour in the particular locality;
- crime reports (CRIS printouts);
- police intelligence (CRIMINT printouts);[19]
- witness statements from housing officers;
- CCTV evidence.

5.9 Some of this evidence will be hearsay and some of these witnesses may seek 'special measures' if required to come to court. These issues are discussed in full in chapters 3 and 4.

Contents of the ASBO application

Best practice

5.10 In *Luke Paul Wadmore and Liam Philip Foreman v R*,[20] a case decided in the context of post-conviction ASBOs, the Court of Appeal highlighted the importance of signing and dating applications for ASBOs and, perhaps more significantly, the imperative need for the prosecution (by analogy the applicant body) to identify the particular facts said to constitute anti-social behaviour. The Court made a distinction between facts and evidence: the facts relied upon have to be proved by evidence if the defendant does not accept them. If an ASBO application does not specify the occasions of anti-social behaviour relied upon (for example: 'On 1 January 2006, the defendant was observed intoxicated outside the Abbey National Bank on Camden High Street, asking users of the cashpoint for money. He was then seen to urinate against the wall outside the bank'), court time and public funds will be wasted.

5.11 Serving a large file of evidence including crime reports and CRIMINT printouts[21] spanning a long period of time along with a

19 If documents such as a schedule of complaints on a particular housing estate derived from housing records or a schedule of criminal incidents derived from crime reports are to be relied upon, then the requirements of CEA 1995 s9 must be complied with. As to the admissibility of such schedules see para 4.19.

20 [2006] EWCA Crim 686.

21 As to the admissibility of a schedule of criminal incidents produced by a police officer, see para 4.19.

general 'case summary' will not suffice. Neither the defendant nor the court will know what the applicant body is seeking to prove; the defendant will not be able to identify which witnesses he or she requires to attend for cross-examination; nor will he or she be in a position to save time by accepting the acts that he or she has carried out. If an applicant body fails to identify the specific anti-social acts relied upon, practitioners acting on defendants' behalf should write to the relevant body before the substantive hearing, asking for this to be done citing *Wadmore* if necessary. Such a request should be copied to the relevant court.

Interim ASBOs

5.12 In some circumstances the applicant body will want an interim order pending the determination of the application. They are usually in the form set out at MC(ASBO)R 2002 Sch 5, but do not have to be. The power to impose an interim order derives from CDA 1998 s1D, which was first brought into force by PRA 2002 and then later amended by SOCPA 2005. An interim order can only be applied for once an application for an ASBO has been made (interim ASBOs are also available when a post-conviction order is being considered and also in the county court when an ASBO application is made – see chapters 7 and 8). They can be made with notice or without notice (*ex parte*). The test for the court for imposing an interim ASBO (be it with notice or without notice) is whether it considers it is 'just' to make such an order (see para 5.18 below). An interim order should not be granted against a child in local authority care without there being a representative from social services present.[22]

5.13 The 2006 Home Office Guidance[23] hails the interim order as a quick stop to anti-social behaviour:

> The benefit of an interim order is that it enables the courts to order an immediate stop to anti-social behaviour and thereby to protect the public more quickly. It reduces the scope for witness intimidation by making it unlawful for the offender to continue behaviour while the ASBO application is being processed. It also removes any delay in the proceedings.

The quote above assumes the defendant to be the perpetrator. Furthermore, in many ASBO applications witness intimidation may not

22 See *R (M) v Sheffield Magistrates' Court & Sheffield City Council* [2004] EWHC 1830 (Admin) at para 57. See also para 10.34.

23 At p15. See note 2 above.

be an issue if the bulk of the evidence is served as hearsay or by way of anonymous witness statements.

The effect of an interim ASBO

5.14 Despite the fact that an interim order can be made *ex parte* (without notice) (see para 5.14 below), it will have the same effect on a defendant as full orders do (ie some prohibitions will engage rights enshrined in the ECHR and breach of an interim order carries the same punishment as breach of a full ASBO). Indeed the absence of a condition contained in an interim order from the final ASBO does *not* affect the gravity or otherwise of a breach of that condition.[24] Careful consideration should be given to the terms sought if the application is made *inter partes* (see chapter 7 on terms of orders). CDA 1998 s1D(4) requires that interim ASBOs must be for a fixed period.[25]

5.15 An interim ASBO will cease to have effect once the full ASBO application is determined. It should be noted that the fact that a defendant does not commit any anti-social behaviour in response to an interim ASBO is not a reason for not making a final order.[26]

Discharge and variation of an interim ASBO

5.16 Interim orders may be varied, renewed or discharged[27] and an appeal lies against the making of one in the same way as it does for full ASBOs.[28] If the order was obtained without notice, if a defendant applies to have the order discharged or varied, the court must not dismiss such an application without the defendant having an opportunity to make oral submissions (MC(ASBO)R 2002 r5(8)). If having received such an interim order, it contains terms that are disproportionate in the sense discussed in chapter 7, practitioners should apply to vary the order. A breach of an interim or full order is a breach even if the term is subsequently varied or set aside or indeed the whole ASBO is set aside.[29] If a term is so wide as to be unenforceable, then a defendant may have the defence of reasonable excuse available to him or her (see para 9.14).

24 *Parker v DPP* [2005] EWHC 1485 (Admin).

25 CDA 1998 s1D(4)(a).

26 See *S v Poole Borough Council* [2002] EWHC Admin 244 where the court described this as 'a hopeless argument'.

27 CDA 1998 s1D(4)(b).

28 CDA 1998 s1D(5): see chapter 11 on appeals.

29 *CPS v T (Michael)* [2006] EWHC 728 (Admin); [2006] 3 All ER 471.

Without notice (*ex parte*) interim ASBOs

Is an ex parte *hearing necessary?*

5.17 MC(ASBO)R 2002 r5 governs the procedure for the making of interim orders without notice. Such an application requires the leave of the justice's clerk. The test for whether it should be made without notice is if the justice's clerk is satisfied that it is 'necessary' to proceed without notice. Guidance for justice's clerks in making that decision was given in *R (Manchester Crown Court v Manchester Magistrates' Court)*.[30] The considerations for clerks include the likely response of the defendant if given notice, the vulnerability of complainants, urgency, the nature of the prohibitions sought, the rights of the defendant, and the limited period of order.[31] The court must then go on to decide if it is just to make such an order.

Does the court consider it to be 'just' to make such an order?

5.18 In *R (Luke Kenny) v Leeds Magistrates' Court*,[32] the Court held that the consideration of whether it is just to make an order without notice 'is necessarily a balancing exercise'. The court must balance the need to protect the public against the impact that the order sought will have upon the defendant. In addition, where a defendant is under 18 the court must have regard to the principle that his best interests are a primary consideration when addressing the question of whether it is just to make an order.[33] Importantly, Owen J added these words: 'it is implicit in the balancing exercise that the considerations weighing in favour of injunctive relief must be sufficiently serious to warrant what may amount to a serious interference with the civil rights of a defendant'.[34]

5.19 The 2006 Home Office Guidance[35] suggests that at the interim stage the applicant body may not have all the evidence it would rely upon to obtain a full ASBO but it should be able to put sufficient evidence of the urgent need to protect the community before the court.

30 [2005] EWHC 253 (Admin).

31 The 'necessity' test should not be confused with the whether it is 'just' test.

32 [2003] EWHC 2963 (Admin) at para 38.

33 See also *R (A) v Leeds Magistrates' Court and Leeds City Council* [2004] EWHC 554 (Admin) and para 10.3.

34 [2003] EWHC 2963 (Admin) at para 39.

35 At 15. See note 2 above.

5.20 The order does not take effect until it is served on the defendant.[36] MC(ASBO)R 2002 requires a without notice interim order (together with the ASBO application and summons to attend court on a particular date) to be served as soon as practicable.[37] If it is not served within seven days of being made, it will cease to have effect.[38] If the court refuses to make an interim order without notice being given to the defendant, it can direct that the application be made on notice.[39]

Without notice interim ASBOs and ECHR Article 6

5.21 In *R (M) v Secretary of State for Constitutional Affairs and others*[40] (which included one of the two cases heard by Owen J in *Kenny*), the Court held that, as long as the interim order followed its normal course, Article 6 would not be engaged. The reasoning was that the order could only be made for a limited period, when the court considered it just to make it and in circumstances where it could be reviewed or discharged on an early return date or on the hearing of the application for a full order. The Court of Appeal was of the view that it was impossible to say that the order 'determined' civil rights. The Court also said that the more intrusive an order, the more the court would require proof that it was necessary that it should be made, but it found that there was nothing intrinsically objectionable about the power to grant an interim ASBO without notice.[41]

5.22 The Court went on to say that if the ECHR applied it would be necessary to look at the process as a whole, bearing in mind that the application for an ASBO was a civil procedure to which an application for an interim order was ancillary, and on that basis there would be no contravention of Article 6. Furthermore, there was no justification for requiring the magistrates' court, when considering whether to make an interim ASBO, to decide whether the evidence in support of the full order disclosed an extremely strong prima facie case. The test remained the statutory test, whether it was 'just' to make the order in all the circumstances (including the fact that the application had been made without notice).[42]

36 MC(ASBO)R 2002 r5(4).
37 MC(ASBO)R 2002 r5(3).
38 MC(ASBO)R 2002 r5(5).
39 MC(ASBO)R 2002 r5(7).
40 [2004] EWCA Civ 312; [2004] 1 WLR 2298.
41 [2004] EWCA Gv 312 at para 39.
42 Ibid, para 39.

Challenges to interim ASBOs

5.23 In *R (A) v Leeds Magistrates' Court & Leeds City Council*,[43] the High Court identified the following routes of challenge:

> A defendant aggrieved by the making of an interim ASBO without notice to him has the following procedures available to him:
>
> (i) He may apply to the magistrates' court for the order to be discharged or varied.
> (ii) He may appear before the magistrates' court and oppose the making of a further interim order (as happened in this case on 11 December 2003) or oppose the making under section 1 of a full order.
> (iii) He may appeal to the Crown Court: section 4(1) of the 1998 Act as amended by section 65 of the 2002 Act.
> (iv) He may appeal to the High Court by way of case stated.
> (v) He may apply to the High Court for judicial review.
>
> Of these procedures, judicial review is the least suitable in a case such as the present, where it is not disputed that the evidence before the magistrates' court justified (although it did not necessarily require) the making of the order. In such a case, if the claimant establishes that the District Judge applied an incorrect test, the only relief this Court can grant is to quash the ASBO. In judicial review proceedings, the High Court cannot consider the evidence before the District Judge (or any evidence subsequently available) and itself decide whether, applying the correct legal test, the order should be upheld, save in cases in which no District Judge properly applying the law could have come to any conclusion other than that the order should be made. Nor can the High Court vary the terms of the ASBO so as to accommodate the contentions successfully made by the claimant. The High Court cannot substitute its discretion for that of the magistrates' court.[44]

Non-appearance of the defendant after a summons for an ASBO is issued

5.24 Failure to answer to a summons will result in a warrant being issued if the court is satisfied that the summons was served within a reasonable time of the hearing.[45] If a defendant fails to attend an adjourned hearing, the court will issue a warrant unless it is satisfied that the

43 [2004] EWHC 554 (Admin) at para 29.

44 Paras 29 and 30. See chapter 11 for fuller details of the appropriate routes of appeal.

45 MCA 1980 s55.

defendant did not have adequate notice of the time and place of the adjourned hearing.[46] If a defendant is arrested under a warrant, the court can remand him at a subsequent hearing, but not if he has already given evidence.[47] The court does have the power to hear a complaint in the absence of a defendant[48] but fair trial rights as protected by ECHR Article 6(1) (see para 4.7) may require his or her presence, particularly as the proceedings will involve a determination of the conduct of the defendant, as well as a potential restriction on other Convention rights (such as Article 8, the right to family life) if that conduct is proved.[49]

Legal representation

5.25 There may also be included with the summons a letter from the applicant body advising a defendant of a right to legal advice and telephone numbers of local CABs or law centres and/or the Law Society and a warning that if s/he do not seek such advice immediately, proceedings may go ahead without legal representation. This is apparently done to prevent delays when an ASBO defendant seeks an adjournment to get legal representation.[50] The idea that a defendant should be denied an adjournment because he or she has received such a letter is unsustainable. Any lawyer appearing on a first hearing or for the first time, either as duty solicitor or because recently instructed, will want to obtain public funding (see chapter 12), consider the evidence, respond to the hearsay notices and gather evidence on behalf of the defendant.

5.26 The mere fact that a defendant has been given telephone numbers of law centres or CABs (few and far between these days) or the Law Society should not be a bar to an adjournment. ASBO hearings are complex and have serious ramifications, as has been recognised time and time again by the higher courts.[51] The hearing also attracts the protection of ECHR Article 6(1) which includes the important principle of 'equality of arms' (see paras 3.10 and 4.8). Obviously, if a defendant has done absolutely nothing to obtain legal advice despite

46 MCA 1980 s55(4).

47 MCA 1980 s55(5) and (6).

48 MCA 1980 s51 (3).

49 But see *R v Jones* [2002] UKHL 5; [2001] 2 WLR 524, *R v O'Hare (Leigh James)* [2006] EWCA Crim 471.

50 Certainly that is the advice given by Pema and Heels in their book on ASBOs (Jordans Special Bulletin) (see chapter 5.3).

51 See, for example, *McCann* [2002] UKHL at para 37.

the court specifically adjourning for that purpose, the court will have to consider whether it is fair to proceed without a lawyer. However, given that public funding is available under the General Criminal Contract (see chapter 12), a defendant should have access to the duty solicitor at the very least. A court that is persuaded that a letter from an applicant body advising a defendant to seek legal advice is sufficient reason to refuse an adjournment will be acting unreasonably and unfairly and the decision would be susceptible to judicial review.

The hearing of the complaint

5.27 The procedure is described very simply in MCA 1980 s53(2): 'The court, after hearing the evidence and the parties, shall make the order for which the complaint is made or dismiss the complaint'.[52] Usually, the applicant body will outline the basis of the 'complaint', call evidence (evidence is given on oath[53]) or read evidence, the defendant does the same, and then both parties make submissions on the law and the facts. The defendant makes his/her submissions last.

5.28 Submissions as to the admissibility of hearsay or other evidence can be made at the outset or at the close of evidence depending on the nature of the objection (see para 5.85 below on 'out-of-time' incidents). The court may, upon agreement by both parties, be invited to retire and read sections of the bundles prepared by the applicant body as well as any evidence served by the defendant. It is likely that the tribunal will be unfamiliar with the civil jurisdiction of the criminal court and will need reminding of the fact that it is hearing a civil matter, of the applicability of the Civil Evidence Act 1995 and the relevant Magistrates' Court Rules (see chapter 4), as well as be reminded that, notwithstanding the civil nature of the hearing, the criminal standard of proof applies. It is sensible to draft a skeleton argument ready to hand out at the time of making submissions. It is also sensible to have the statutory material available (CDA 1998 s1; CEA 1995 ss1-4; MCRs 2002 and 1999) (see appendices A–D) as well as copies of any relevant authorities.

5.29 Vulnerable witnesses and special measures applications are discussed at para 4.22.

52 See also *Stone's Justices' Manual* 2005, para 1-582.

53 MCA 1980 s98.

Can you consent to an ASBO?

5.30 If consultation has taken place properly (see chapter 2 for a detailed discussion), the court must then move on to consider the statutory test (see para 5.40 below). The ASBO application will contain a draft order or there may already be an interim order in place (see para 5.12 on interim orders). An ASBO cannot be consented to: the court *must* be satisfied on both limbs of the test.

5.31 In *R (T) v Manchester Crown Court* [54] a stand-alone ASBO was sought by Manchester City Council against a 14-year-old whose mother purported to 'consent' to an ASBO on his behalf, the terms of which were widely drafted. T was legally represented at the time. The District Judge in the magistrates' court looked at the papers in the context of an unopposed application and made the order as applied for. The matter was subsequently appealed by the defendant to the Crown Court. Manchester City Council took a preliminary point: it argued that the appellant was barred from appealing the ASBO because he had effectively consented to an order. Civil orders are often consented to in the county court and different considerations apply when such an order is subsequently sought to be set aside: counsel was borrowing from the test laid down in the context of such orders. The argument found favour with the Crown Court judge and so the appellant appealed to the Administrative Court by way of judicial review. Manchester City Council, despite having taken the point in the lower court, did not oppose the challenge. Moses J found that an order cannot be made on the basis of consent alone and the Crown Court should have heard the appeal:

5.32 > ... it is clear to me that an order cannot be made merely on the basis of the consent of the claimant. The court considering the making of an order must itself be satisfied to the required standard of proof as to the matters under section 1(1)(a) and, further, must exercise its own judgment pursuant to section 1(1)(b) as to the necessity of making such an order.
>
> Of course, the cooperation and consent of the person who it is suggested should be made the subject of an order is welcome and relevant. If an applicant is prepared to consent, it would not only show a cooperative state of mind, but would afford considerable saving of time and money. In requiring the proof of those matters that the statute requires to be proved it is not intended in any way to discourage such cooperation or consent. But consent is only a factor, both in relation to the matters that are required to be proved, and as to

54 [2005] EWHC 1396 (Admin).

the value judgment that the court must exercise in deciding whether an order is 'necessary'.[55]

The ramifications of 'consent'

5.33 Although he found that consent did not bar the appeal, Moses J went on to say that if a defendant did consent in the lower court, 'that will be powerful evidence that there is absolutely nothing in the appeal'[56] and that he hoped that it would be rare that 'the time and effort of the Crown Court will be spent in considering an appeal where consent has been given to an ASBO before'.[57] Two issues arise from these comments which require closer scrutiny.

5.34 First, it is submitted that demonstrating a 'co-operative state of mind' and saving 'time and money' are not relevant or appropriate considerations for a court deciding an ASBO application. An ASBO defendant has little to gain from 'co-operating' or saving court time or money, unless co-operation is used as a negotiating tool for less onerous conditions with the applicant body before the hearing. By contrast, in a criminal prosecution, if a defendant admits guilt, he or she saves a great deal of time and expense, demonstrates remorse and saves witnesses from what could be gruelling cross-examination. The incentive, enshrined in statutory law, is that the court will effect a reduction in sentence.

5.35 An ASBO defendant does not get a shorter ASBO or less onerous conditions imposed by the court just because he or she consents to an order. Even when a defendant does not take issue with the anti-social acts alleged by the applicant authority, and thereby saves court time and money as well as saves the applicant body the expense of witnesses coming to court, the court still has to go on to consider whether an ASBO is necessary and, if it is, impose terms which are proportionate (see para 5.107 below). Necessity and proportionality are legal concepts that require an exercise of judgment, and are utterly unrelated to questions of co-operation and costs.

5.36 That said, local authorities are sometimes amenable to negotiation about the terms of an ASBO (for example, the extent of a geographical exclusion zone) if they can be saved the expense of a contested hearing. If there is agreement between the parties as to all the terms, the applicant body can then put an amended ASBO application before the

55 [2005] EWHC 1396 (Admin) at paras 14–17.
56 [2005] EWHC 1396 (Admin) at para 22.
57 [2005] EWHC 1396 (Admin).

court and at the same time tell the court that it is not objected to by the defendant. Of course the court must still satisfy itself that both limbs of the test are made out before imposing any such order but may gain comfort from the defendant's consent and not, for example, concern itself with human rights issues. Conversely, however, it is open to the court to reject the agreed terms and impose an ASBO in wider terms and for a length of time it considers appropriate. In *R v Pedder*,[58] a post-conviction case, the Court of Appeal strongly disapproved of the practice of putting agreed terms before the court.

5.37 Defendants should therefore not be advised to 'consent' to an ASBO unless:

- he or she agrees that he or she committed all the acts relied upon (a not uncommon situation); and
- the terms and the length of the ASBO are in the lawyer's view both necessary and proportionate within the meaning of the statute and existing case law.

5.38 Second, it is submitted that if an ASBO is 'consented' to, that in itself should not be interpreted as compelling evidence that there is nothing in the appeal (as suggested by Moses J).[59] If a defendant has been wrongly advised or ill-advised by a lawyer or a parent, a proper challenge to the ASBO may well have been overlooked. In T's case for example, not only was his mother at court, he was represented by counsel. One of the terms of the ASBO consented to was a term forbidding T from acting in 'any anti-social manner in the City of Manchester'.[60] This term is clearly too vague, too wide and consequently unenforceable and should never have been consented to. Indeed, the saga of T's ASBO and the appellate courts did not end there as, despite the fact that the matter was remitted back to the Crown Court to hear the appeal, it was never pursued and T was subsequently prosecuted for breaching the very wide term mentioned T appealed to the Court of Appeal who ruled that such a wide term should never again be included in an ASBO.[61]

5.39 In *R v Michael John Starling*,[62] the Court of Appeal varied an ASBO that had been agreed by counsel in the lower court:

58 [2005] EWCA Crim 3163 at para 21.

59 See note 48 above.

60 [2005] EWHC 1396 (Admin), at para 6.

61 *CPS v T (Michael)* [2006] EWHC 728 (Admin) at para 46; [2006] 3 ALL ER 471. See para 7.27.

62 [2005] EWCA Crim 227 at para 21.

It is not suggested in this Court that there had been any bar or estoppel standing in the way of an appeal against the ASBO in whole or in part, and indeed, counsel for the prosecution has, in our view rightly, not felt able to support the ASBO in all respects.

The statutory test

5.40 CDA 1998 s1 provides:

(1) An application for an order under this section may be made by a relevant authority[63] if it appears to the authority that the following conditions are fulfilled with respect to any person aged 10 or over, namely –
(a) that the person has acted, since the commencement date,[64] in an anti-social manner, that is to say, in a manner that caused or was likely to cause harassment, alarm or distress to one or more persons not of the same household as himself; and
(b) that such an order is necessary to protect relevant persons from further anti-social acts by him.

5.41 CDA 1998 s1(4) requires the conditions in section 1(1) to be 'proved' before a court can make an order, although the language of the statute suggests that the court does not have to make an order even if the subsection is proved:

(4) If, on such an application, it is proved that the conditions mentioned in subsection (1) above are fulfilled, the magistrates' court *may* make an order under this section (an 'anti-social behaviour order') which prohibits the defendant from doing anything described in the order.[65]

5.42 Although the circumstances will be rare in which a court despite being satisfied on both limbs of the test does not impose an ASBO, they are not inconceivable. For example, where the defendant is vulnerable because he or she suffers from acute depression or a compulsive disorder or a severe learning disability, then the terms of an ASBO may well not be understood and inevitably be breached. In those circumstances a court should be persuaded that it would be inappropriate to impose an ASBO. Vulnerable defendants are discussed in the context of 'necessity' at para 5.118 below (see also the discussion on 'ASBOs made to be breached' in the introduction to this book, page 3).

63 See para 5.2.
64 1 April 1999.
65 Emphasis added.

Standard of proof

5.43 Following *McCann*, it is clear from Lord Steyn's judgment in that case[66] that only the first limb of the test (section 1(1)(a)) involves a standard of proof: 'The inquiry under section 1(1)(b), namely that such an order is necessary to protect persons from further anti-social acts by him, does not involve a standard of proof: it is an exercise of judgment or evaluation.'[67] The first limb of the test must be proved to the criminal standard.

What does 'likely' mean?

5.44 If the applicant authority is relying upon somebody actually being caused harassment, alarm or distress, it must satisfy the court to the criminal standard.[68] However, when deciding the question of whether conduct was *likely* to cause the harassment, alarm or distress, following *Chief Constable of Lancashire v Potter*,[69] the court does *not* have to be satisfied so that it is sure that the acts complained of were likely to cause harassment, etc.[70] Auld LJ in *Potter* considered that section 1(a) may be broken up into three constituents:[71]

- first, that a person has acted in a certain manner; and
- second, that the manner is one that caused harassment, alarm or distress to one or more persons outside the defendant's household; or
- third, that the manner of acting was likely to cause such harassment, alarm or distress.

5.45 There was no dispute between the parties as to the requisite standard of proof in relation to the first two constituents. In light of *McCann*, it was accepted that the first two constituents must be proved to the criminal standard; the issue in *Potter* was the meaning of 'likely'. Auld LJ considered that for three or more centuries justices have managed to cope with breach of the peace, not only as to when conduct has caused such a breach but as to whether it was likely to do so.

66 [2002] UKHL 39 at para 37; [2002] 3 WLR 1313; [2002] 4 All ER 593. See chapter 3.

67 See para 5.107 for a full discussion on 'necessity'.

68 *R (on the application of McCann) v Crown Court at Manchester; Clingham v K & C Royal Borough Council* [2002] UKHL 39; [2002] 3 WLR 1313; [2002] 4 All ER 593, HL, per Lord Steyn at para 37.

69 [2003] EWHC 2272 (Admin).

70 See paragraph 5.40 above.

71 [2003] EWHC 2272 (Admin) at para 7.

He also referred to various instances of the use of the word 'likely' in the Public Order Act 1986.[72] His Lordship was of the view that the meaning of 'likely' in this context was a higher threshold than that of 'a real possibility':

> It is true that the making of an anti-social behaviour order is not a criminal sentence, and serves only to prohibit in specified ways further anti-social behaviour of the sort giving rise to it. However, breach of such an order is a serious matter and can lead to a substantial term of imprisonment or fine. I would give 'likely' the meaning in this context of 'more probable than not'. That meaning, it seems to me, is much more the same as that of the Divisional Court in *Parkin v Norman* [1983] QB 92, which concerned a charge of insulting behaviour 'likely' to occasion a breach of the peace ... As to the standard of proof required, probably the fairest and simplest solution is to say that a court, in conducting what is necessarily an evaluative exercise on this issue as well as under section 1(1)(b), must, on the evidence before it, be sure to the criminal standard that a defendant's conduct has caused the likelihood in the sense I have indicated. It seems to me that whether that is a matter of proof and/or of evaluation is no more a matter for philosophical analysis or agonising by courts than say, a magistrates [*sic*] or a jury having to decide to the criminal standard whether an accused's conduct was dishonest or intentional or reckless. As I have said, determining whether conduct had a likely effect is a frequent demand made on lay and professional decision-makers in our courts in all sorts of criminal offences.[73]

5.46 In short, 'likely' means 'more probable than not' and what the court has to be satisfied so that it is sure about is that the defendant's conduct caused the likelihood. In many cases there will be little necessity for 'philosophy' or 'agony' because the nature of the anti-social acts, once proved to the criminal standard to have been committed, will usually impact on the decision as to likelihood. For example, if it is found that a defendant verbally abused a member of the public, in the absence of evidence from the person who was abused, there would be no difficulty in finding that there was a likelihood that that behaviour caused harassment, alarm or distress. In other cases, such as *Potter* (where the conduct complained of was street prostitution) and *R (Mills) v Birmingham City Council*[74] (where the conduct relied upon was shoplifting), the likelihood issue will become an important one.[75]

72 [2003] EWHC 2272 (Admin) at para 29.

73 [2003] EWHC 2272 (Admin), at paras 32 and 33.

74 [2005] EWHC 2732 (Admin).

75 See paras 5.51–5.61 below.

The first limb of the test

5.47 ... has acted in an anti-social manner, that is to say, in a manner that caused or was likely to cause harassment, alarm or distress to one or more persons not of the same household as himself ...[76]

What is anti-social behaviour?

5.48 'Anti-social behaviour' is not described in CDA 1998 beyond the definition above. As mentioned in the introduction to this book, this is a boundless definition which incorporates non-criminal behaviour. During the passage of the Crime and Disorder Bill through Parliament, Lord Rodgers warned against introducing 'powers which can be used against anyone who does not conform to a standard pattern of respectable behaviour or a life-style which is acceptable'.[77]

5.49 Unlike section 5 of the Public Order Act 1986 (causing harassment, alarm or distress), there is no need for the anti-social behaviour to have actually caused any person harassment, alarm or distress; nor is there need for the conduct to have taken place within the sight and hearing of a person who might be caused harassment, alarm or distress;[78] nor is the intention of the person against whom the ASBO is sought relevant.[79] In other words, it matters not whether the defendant intended to cause harassment, alarm or distress or whether he or she was aware that his or her behaviour might cause harassment, alarm or distress. It is simply a question of whether it *did* cause harassment, alarm or distress or whether it was *likely* to do so (as discussed at para 5.44 above). That is necessarily an objective test.[80] Concerns raised at the Committee stage of the Bill's passage through Parliament in the House of Lords by Lord Goodhart about the lack of intent in the definition were overridden by Lord Falconer (the Solicitor-General at the time) who stated that, '[w]e believe that it is the heedless, careless anti-social actions that the order needs to target, not just those with deliberate intent'.[81] Lord Falconer said that he believed that there was

76 CDA 1998 s1(1)(a). The acts relied upon must have occurred since the commencement date of this section, namely 1 April 1999.

77 HL Debate vol 584, col 545, 17 March 1998.

78 See *Holloway v DPP* [2004] EWHC 2621 (Admin).

79 See by contrast the intention requirement for offences under the Public Order Act 1986 s6.

80 *R (Chief Constable of West Mercia Constabulary) v Boorman* [2005] EWHC 2559 (Admin).

81 HL Debate, vol 587, col 584, 17 March 1998.

sufficient protection in the Bill to prevent applications being made where the behaviour was trivial.[82]

5.50 The only qualification is that the anti-social conduct must affect a person 'not of the same household'. This clearly envisages public anti-social behaviour as opposed to 'domestic' which is regulated by the civil injunction regime.[83] Because a defendant's *mens rea* plays no part in the test, the anti-social acts can be proved by hearsay evidence from 'professional witnesses' (for example police officers, local beat officers, community safety officers, local councillors, housing officers, etc) (see chapters 3 and 4 and below on the question and use of hearsay evidence).

'Harassment, alarm or distress'

5.51 CDA 1998 does not define 'harassment', 'alarm' or 'distress' but these terms have been used in various public order offences and are (as is so often said in other contexts by our courts) ordinary English words. Conduct which may be irritating or distasteful to some (for example, street prostitution mentioned above), is not necessarily anti-social within the meaning of CDA 1998, that is, it may not be likely to cause harassment, alarm or distress.

Conduct that may not cause harassment, alarm or distress

Burglary of unoccupied premises

5.52 In *R v Suzanne Werner*[84] the Court of Appeal doubted whether breaking in to unoccupied hotel rooms to steal credit cards caused harassment or alarm although it accepted that such offences do, or are likely to, cause distress.

Driving while disqualified

5.53 In *R v Morrison*[85] the Court of Appeal doubted whether driving while disqualified on its own would come within the terms of the statute as it is not normally an offence which is likely to cause harassment, alarm or distress to a person not in the offender's household. If such driving was combined with driving with excess alcohol, for example, the situation might well be different (see also the discussion on prohibitions on driving in chapter 6 on terms of ASBOs).

82 HL Debate, vol 587, col 585, 17 March 1998.

83 Family Law Act 1996, Pt IV.

84 [2004] EWCA Crim 2931 at para 19.

85 [2005] EWCA Crim 2237.

Graffiti

5.54 Despite the fact that the 2006 Home Office Guidance[86] lists writing graffiti as an example of anti-social conduct, it is difficult to see how every case of writing graffiti is likely to cause harassment, alarm or distress. Home Office Minister Hazel Blears, introducing new powers for local authorities to tackle graffiti under the Clean Neighbourhoods and Environment Act 2005, described it as 'a depressing and unsightly menace in many communities'. She has also said: 'It affects people's quality of life, increases fear of crime and reduces pride in a community. It also costs us all millions of pounds a year to clean up – money which could be better spent on other valuable services.'[87] Graffiti may be guilty of all of the above, but is it likely to cause harassment, alarm or distress? In *R v Boness*,[88] the Court of Appeal suggested that a prohibition on being in possession of spray paint might tackle the problem of graffiti. However the Court was simply giving examples of preventative terms in ASBOs and did not consider whether graffiti writing would satisfy the first limb of the test. Whether the writing of graffiti is so capable will depend on when it was written, how it was written, how much of it was written and what it said. Given that most graffiti is incomprehensible to the majority of people (to some it is an art form) and that it is often carried out late at night when no one else is around, it will often be unlikely to cause harassment, alarm or distress by reason of its content or the manner in which it is written.

Swearing at a police officer

5.55 In *DPP v Orum*[89] the Divisional Court considered whether a police constable is capable of being a person who is caused harassment, alarm or distress by the use of threatening, abusive or insulting behaviour within the meaning of the Public Order Act (POA) 1986 s5. The defendant in that case was having an argument with his girlfriend late at night when approached by a police officer and told to quieten down. The defendant responded with the words 'You fuck off. This is a domestic and you can't do nothing' and 'You can't fucking arrest me. I know my rights. If you don't go away I'm going to hit

86 *A Guide to Anti-social Behaviour Orders* (Home Office, 2006), available at www.crimereduction.gov.uk and www.together.gov.uk.

87 'Fixed Penalties Tackle Graffiti', http://news.bbc.co.uk/1/hi/uk/4878686.stm, 6 April 2006.

88 [2005] EWCA Crim 2395 at para 36.

89 (1989) 88 Cr App R 261.

you'. The officer, obviously unable to resist the temptation, did then arrest him for causing a breach of the peace. He was charged under POA 1986 s5. Giving the judgment of the court, Glidewell LJ said:[90]

5.56 I find nothing in the context of the 1986 Act to persuade me that a police officer may not be a person who is caused harassment, alarm or distress by the various kinds of words and conduct to which section 5(1) applies. I would therefore answer the question in the affirmative, that a police officer can be a person who is likely to be caused harassment and so on. However, that is not to say that the opposite is necessarily the case, namely, it is not to say that every police officer in this situation is to be assumed to be a person who is caused harassment. *Very frequently, words and behaviour with which police officers will be wearily familiar will have little emotional impact on them save that of boredom. It may well be that in appropriate circumstances, justices will decide (indeed they might decide in the present case) as a question of fact that the words and behaviour were not likely in all the circumstances to cause harassment, alarm or distress to either of the police officers.* That is a question of fact for the justices to be decided in all the circumstances: the time, the place, the nature of the words used, who the police officers are and so on.[91]

This is a case worth bearing in mind if the application for an ASBO relies to a large extent on abusive and/or drunken behaviour directed solely at police officers when they seek to move a person on for being too loud or for drinking in a public place.[92]

Shoplifting

5.57 In *R (Mills) v Birmingham Magistrates' Court*,[93] Ms Mills was observed in a Next store in Birmingham City centre to take three pairs of gloves from a display and leave without paying. She was observed by a plain-clothes police officer who happened to be at the store. At no point was she obstructive or abusive to the police or to anyone else, and it was not suggested that she was other than fully cooperative to the police. When she was brought before the magistrates' court she pleaded guilty to theft. The court was told that she had numerous convictions of a similar kind.

90 (1989) 88 Cr App R 261 at 264.

91 Emphasis added.

92 See also *R v DPP*, 17 May 2006, unreported, DC (Richards LJ, Toulson J): calling a police officer a 'wanker' and making a masturbatory gesture was not distressing within the meaning of POA 1986 s4A.

93 [2005] EWHC 2732 (Admin).

5.58 The prosecution applied for a post-conviction ASBO and one was imposed prohibiting her from entering retail outlets within a demarcated zone. While she had numerous convictions for theft and related offences (68) committed largely in the Birmingham City area, it does not seem that details of how these offences were committed were ever before the magistrates' court. The court, it seems, made its decisions on the basis of the facts of the offence for which she was convicted. Ms Mills challenged the imposition of the ASBO by way of judicial review on the grounds that the statutory test had not been made out (in other words there was no evidence of anti-social behaviour within the meaning of CDA 1998) and the order was therefore *ultra vires* and/or perverse. Neither the magistrates' court nor the CPS attended the judicial review hearing and the challenge was therefore unopposed. Scott Baker LJ, giving the judgment of the court, did not rule out the possibility that shoplifting may cause harassment, alarm or distress but on the facts of this particular case had no difficulty in finding that the theft did not actually cause harassment, alarm or distress and nor could it have:[94]

5.59
> The question is whether the deputy district judge was justified that the claimant had acted in a manner that caused or was likely to cause harassment, alarm or distress. It is not suggested that what she did actually caused harassment, alarm or distress. Indeed no employee of Next was even aware of the theft until the police officer took the gloves back to the shop and told them. Further, I find it quite impossible to say that by stealing the gloves unbeknown to the store the claimant had done anything that was likely to cause either harassment, alarm or distress within the meaning of the section. It is apparent from the terms of the order that the deputy district judge essentially pinned the anti-social behaviour order to this particular theft and the circumstances of it. The court says in the acknowledgment of service that this particular theft was likely to cause harassment. Whilst I accept that the circumstances of some shopliftings or other thefts may very well fall within the relevant words of section 1C(2), it does not seem to me that harassment, alarm or distress inevitably follows or is likely to follow. Particularly is that so in the circumstances of the present case. There was, in short, nothing about the facts of this theft to trigger the section. Were the section to have been triggered in this case, it would be difficult to imagine any shoplifting that did not likewise trigger the section; and, in my judgment, that is plainly not the situation.

94 *R (Mills) v Birmingham Magistrates' Court* [2005] EWHC 2732 (Admin) at paras 11 and 12.

5.60 Like street prostitution (see the *Potter* case mentioned above at para 5.44), shoplifting may cause harassment, alarm or distress, but it depends entirely on the facts and circumstances. Practitioners should not simply accept that because a crime has been committed, the conduct is necessarily anti-social. In *R v H, Cyril John Stevens and David Lee Lovegrove*,[95] for example, the defendant Lovegrove had a long history of committing thefts and fell to be sentenced for two offences of theft by the Crown Court. They both involved stealing DVDs from two different supermarkets. An ASBO, with no limit of time, and it seems without any resistance from the defence, was imposed upon him in addition to an 18-month conditional discharge. He was also on licence for a drugs offence but the judge did not send him back to prison to serve any remaining period as he was then, it seems, entitled to do.[96] The terms of the ASBO included a geographical restriction as well as a prohibition on committing theft within England and Wales. On appeal to the Court of Appeal (Criminal Division), the ASBO was quashed. The Court found that on the evidence of those particular thefts, neither limb of the ASBO test was made out (ie, there was no evidence that members of the public were likely to be caused harassment, alarm or distress, nor was the order necessary). There was no discussion on the propriety of the particular conditions, as the ASBO itself should never have been made.

5.61 In *R v Israilov*[97] a shoplifter's post-conviction ASBO was overturned on appeal but only because it was too wide, too unclear and in addition to a term of imprisonment. The question as to whether the shoplifting he was accused of either caused or was likely to cause harassment, alarm or distress was never raised.

Does the anti-social behaviour have to be persistent and serious?

5.62 While CDA 1998, unlike offences under the Protection from Harassment Act 1997, does not spell out a requirement for a course of anti-social conduct to be established before an application is made, an applicant body would be likely to fail to persuade a court that an ASBO was necessary (second limb of the test, see para 5.107) if it relied upon

95 [2006] EWCA Crim 255.

96 Powers of Criminal Courts (Sentencing) Act (PCC(S)A) 2000 s116 of the has now been repealed by CJA 2003 for offences committed after 4 April 2005, although administrative recall remains firmly in place.

97 [2005] EWCA Crim 441.

a single incident or only a few incidents. In *McCann*, Lord Steyn said: 'Section 1 is not meant to be used in cases of minor unacceptable behaviour but in cases which satisfy the threshold of *persistent* and *serious* anti-social behaviour.'[98]

5.63 A plain reading of section 1(1)(a) does not suggest that the anti-social acts need to be 'serious' although the requirement of 'persistence' is common sense in light of the second limb. It would seem that Lord Steyn was echoing the language used by Jack Straw MP [99] in the Preface to the original Home Office Guidance, *Anti-social Behaviour Orders – Guidance*, written in 1999:

> The case studies attached at section 8 give some idea of the sort of behaviour which too many people have had to suffer for far too long. As a society we cannot allow this to continue. That is why we introduced the Anti-Social Behaviour Orders in the Crime and Disorder Act 1998. They are designed to tackle this kind of *persistent, serious*, anti-social behaviour in our communities and to make life better for many of our fellow citizens ... I hope these new orders will provide reassurance to the public and also make it clear to offenders that *persistent, serious* anti-social behaviour will not be tolerated ...[100]

These are also the words he used in the House of Commons during the Crime and Disorder Bill's passage through Parliament.[101]

5.64 The two case studies in section 8 of the 1999 Home Office Guidance are examples of very serious and persistent anti-social behaviour by one family on a particular housing estate and two brothers on another estate. Examples of cases where an ASBO might be appropriate are cited at paragraph 3.9. In this section the 1999 Home Office Guidance emphasises the need for recurring behaviour: it describes 'persistent unruly behaviour' and 'persistent abusive behaviour' in different contexts as well as 'serious and persistent bullying of children on an organised basis ...', 'persistent racial harassment or homophobic behaviour', 'persistent anti-social behaviour as a result of drugs or alcohol misuse'. The examples are prefaced with a warning that the definition of anti-social behaviour should not include 'run of the mill disputes between neighbours, petty intolerances, or minor or one-off disorderly acts' and that orders should not be used 'to penalise those who are merely different'.

98 *R (on the application of McCann) v Crown Court at Manchester; Clingham v K & C Royal Borough Council* [2002] UKHL 39; [2002] 3 WLR 1313; [2002] 4 All ER 593, HL at para 25. Emphasis added.

99 The then Home Secretary.

100 Emphasis added.

101 HC Debate, vol 310, col 373, 8 April 1998.

5.65 Crucially, at paragraph 3.10 the 1999 Home Office Guidance states:

> This is not a definitive list but is intended to illustrate the type of behaviour involved. The main test is that there is a *pattern* of behaviour which continues over a period of time but cannot be dealt with easily or adequately through the prosecution of those concerned for a single 'snapshot' or criminal event.[102]

5.66 In contrast, the 2003 Home Office Guidance[103] deploys completely different language: the words 'serious' or 'persistent' no longer appear when describing the kind of behaviour that would necessitate an ASBO. John Denham MP's[104] introduction to the 2003 Home Office Guidance describes anti-social behaviour as covering 'a whole complex of thoughtless, inconsiderate or malicious activity' and 'aggressive or loutish behaviour'.[105] Gone is the language of restraint and moderation and in its place is the 'ASBOs-for-all' rhetoric. There is a single reference to a 'pattern of behaviour' in the context of out-of-time incidents (discussed at para 5.85 below), but that comment is preceded by the suggestion that 'one incidence of serious anti-social behaviour may be sufficient for an order to be made'.[106] Although the ministerial introduction to the 2006 Home Office Guidance (*A Guide to Anti-social Behaviour Orders*) is much more measured and abandons the emotive language of the 2003 Guidance,[107] the words 'serious' and 'persistent' do not appear. Page 8 of the 2006 Guidance lists examples of anti-social behaviour that can be tackled by ASBOs and ABCs:

- harassment of residents or passers-by;
- verbal abuse;
- criminal damage;
- vandalism;
- noise nuisance;
- writing graffiti;
- engaging in threatening behaviour in large groups;
- racial abuse;
- smoking or drinking alcohol while under age;

102 Original emphasis.

103 Available at www.crimereduction.gov.uk. The 2006 Home Office Guidance, published 1 August 2006 is available at www.together.gov.uk.

104 The then Minister of State for Crime Reduction, Policing and Community Safety at the Home Office.

105 2003 Home Office Guidance, p3.

106 2003 Home Office Guidance, p28. Repeated at p24 of the 2006 Guidance.

107 2003 Home Office Guidance, p4.

- substance misuse;
- joyriding;
- begging;
- prostitution;
- kerb-crawling;
- throwing missiles;
- assault; and
- vehicle vandalism.

Some of these examples of anti-social behaviour could properly be classed as what Lord Steyn called 'minor, unacceptable behaviour' for which ASBOs should not be used. What is absent as a prefix to any of the above examples is the word 'persistent'. Persistent 'minor' behaviour could render it serious.

5.67 Practitioners should resist attempts by applicant bodies to rely upon the Home Office Guidance as a proper interpretation of CDA 1998. First, and importantly, the Home Office Guidance is non-statutory and has no legal force. This was the 'health warning' issued at the very beginning of the 1999 Guidance at paragraph 1.4: 'The guidance is non-statutory and should not be regarded as authoritative legal advice. If there is any doubt as to the application or interpretation of the legislation, advice should be sought from a legal adviser ...'

5.68 By 2003, the Government had dispensed with this disclaimer. What constitutes anti-social behaviour will depend on a proper interpretation of the statute. The case law in this area is an obvious aid to interpretation. The examples given above may be misleading because of the omission of the word 'persistent' and indeed any reference to the context. For example, as Auld LJ made plain in the *Potter* case, prostitution is not anti-social conduct as such: the circumstances are all-important.

5.69 Second, while the statute has been amended in various ways by Parliament since the 1999 Home Office Guidance was published, the statutory test has not been amended. The 1999 Guidance was a much more accurate reflection of the intention of Parliament when it introduced ASBOs. The 1999 Guidance is at pains to point that out at paragraph 1.4: 'An early draft of this document was made available to Members of Parliament during the passage of the Crime and Disorder Bill and it reflects discussion that took place in Parliament about how the provisions should operate in practice'.

5.70 Indeed a reading of the debates in Parliament during the passage of the Crime and Disorder Bill reveals that the Government stressed that an ASBO should only be sought when the conduct complained of is sufficiently serious.[108] Lord Falconer, speaking on behalf of the Government in the House of Lords, said:

> We see the order as a tool to deal with a serious and escalating problem of anti-social behaviour in our communities. It is not to be used lightly ... It is a last resort when other methods have failed. If it is not successful, as the structure of the order makes clear, the next step is the criminal law. We do not see it as a tool to deal with petty irritations, grievances or disputes between neighbours. The minimum two-year duration for an order is a mark of the seriousness with which we expect all those involved to view it.[109]

5.71 Third, the House of Lords in *McCann* has already read in the requirement of 'seriousness' and 'persistence', presumably not only because of a recognition that the making of an ASBO can have serious consequences as well as reflect seriously on the character of a person subject to one, but because it was reflecting the intention of Parliament (although there is no direct reference to the 1999 Guidance in the House of Lords' judgment, it was specifically mentioned by Lord Phillips in the Court of Appeal stage of *McCann*).[110]

Can a defendant's conduct be aggregated with that of others?

5.72 In the *Potter* case (discussed above at paragraph 5.44), one of the questions that arose for the High Court to resolve was whether it was permissible to look at the defendant's conduct together with that of other street prostitutes frequenting the same area at the same, or similar, time in deciding whether harassment, alarm or distress was caused or was likely to be caused. Auld LJ answered the question in this way:[111]

> ... Street prostitution in residential areas, whatever the extremes of behaviour by individual prostitutes, is clearly capable, when considered as a whole and depending on the circumstances, including the number, regularity and degree of concentration of activity, of causing or being likely to cause harassment, alarm or distress to others in the area. It is a question of fact whether any individual prostitute, by her contribution to that activity and its overall effect, has caused a 'problem' which is caught by section 1 (1) (a) ...

108 Lord Williams of Mostyn, HL Debate, vol 585, col 571–2, 17 March 1998.

109 HL Debate, vol 585, col 588, 17 March 1998.

110 *R (on the application of McCann) v Manchester Crown Court* [2001] EWCA Civ 281 at para 18.

111 [2003] EWHC 2272 (Admin) at para 41.

5.73 The Court agreed that not all street prostitution in a residential area would fall foul of the Act, especially when the conduct relied upon by the applicant body is that of a single prostitute or a small number of prostitutes or 'where, however few or many there are, there is no significant concentration of their activities in a particular area to mark it out as [sic] "red light district"'.112 Auld LJ's careful analysis may well assist in resisting cases where the police or local authority try to obtain an ASBO against a prostitute who tends to work regularly, but alone or with a small group, in a particular area and who has not been deterred by criminal prosecutions for non-imprisonable offences such as loitering and soliciting (see chapter 7 on terms of orders).

'Defence' of 'reasonableness'

5.74 If a defendant can show that any of the anti-social acts relied upon by the applicant body were 'reasonable in the circumstances', the court *shall* disregard those acts for the purpose of determining whether CDA 1998 s1(1)(a) is made out.[113] This is not a complete defence, of course, as there may be other acts relied upon which are not reasonable. There is a similar 'defence' in injunction cases under the Protection from Harassment Act 1997, s1(c): 'that in the particular circumstances the pursuit of the course of conduct was reasonable' as well as under the POA 1986 s5(3)(c) ('it is a defence for the accused to prove his conduct was reasonable'). This is an objective test.[114]

5.75 The wording of the statute suggests that the evidential and persuasive burden (ie, the legal burden) is on the defendant to show that his or her acts were reasonable, but the standard will be to the civil standard, as is usual in civil proceedings and in criminal law whenever there is a burden on the defendant.[115] That said, the circumstances in which a defendant can rely on 'reasonableness' are probably limited. The obvious circumstances will be when a defendant is acting in self-defence or in defence of another or when he or she is protecting property or generally preventing the commission of a crime or when he or she is in immediate peril of death or serious injury (otherwise known

112 [2003] EWHC 2272 (Admin) at para 46.

113 CDA 1998 s1(5).

114 *DPP v Clarke* (1992) 94 Cr App R 359.

115 See *Norwood v DPP* [2002] EWCH 1564 (Admin) at paras 19 and 20 for an analysis of where the burden lies when relying on the POA 1986 s5(3) defence.

as the defence of necessity).[116] The 1999 Home Office Guidance offers a single example of potentially 'reasonable' behaviour at paragraph 3.11: '... noise from public houses and village halls on a Saturday evening may cause distress, but could be argued to be reasonable in the circumstances'. There is no reported example of an ASBO being applied for or obtained against a pub or equivalent. Neither the 2003 Guidance nor the 2006 Home Office Guidance offers examples of what may be considered reasonable.

Reasonableness and Convention rights: ECHR Articles 9, 10 and 11

5.76 What is reasonable also has to be interpreted in the context of Convention rights. A body of case law has grown up in relation to 'protest' cases and the interaction between public order or breach of the peace prosecutions and the right to free thought, speech and peaceful public demonstrations enshrined in ECHR Articles 9, 10 and 11 (reproduced in appendix E), which may be a useful starting point.

5.77 Article 9 protects the right to freedom of thought, conscience and religion, Article 10 the right to freedom of expression, and Article 11 the right to freedom of peaceful assembly and association with others. None of the rights protected by Articles 8 to 11 of the Convention are absolute rights. They can be restricted if it is necessary to do so in the interests of public safety or for the prevention of disorder or crime or some other legitimate aim (see appendix E for the full text of the limitations in relation to each article). However, these limitations must be narrowly interpreted and the necessity for any restrictions must be convincingly established. 'Necessity' in the context of these Convention rights implies the existence of a 'pressing social need'.[117] Further, proportionality is also part of the necessity test: any interference must be proportionate to the legitimate aim pursued.[118]

116 As to whether an alleged international crime of aggression (eg, the war in Iraq) is a crime in domestic law, as well as the availability of the defence of necessity in the context of a prosecution for criminal damage, see *R v Jones (Margaret)* [2006] UKHL 16; [2006] 2 WLR 772; 2 All ER 741.

117 See for example *Sunday Times v UK (No 2)* [1992] 14 EHRR 123 at para 50.

118 The link between necessity and proportionality was first made in *Handyside v UK* (1979-80) 1 EHRR 737 (see para 5.79 below).

5.78 Although there has been no reported use of ASBOs to prevent peaceful non-obstructive protests or demonstrations to date,[119] it is not beyond the bounds of imagination that such an application may be made in the future. ASBOs for 'one-off' protests or demonstrations, even if they are not peaceful, will in any event fall foul of the statutory test in so far as the conduct will not have been shown to be persistent and therefore not necessary within the meaning of the second limb of the test (see para 5.62 below).

5.79 The human rights argument in relation to the 'reasonableness defence' is essentially this: a person's conduct will be reasonable if he or she is exercising Convention rights in circumstances in which an interference with that exercise would not be justified under Articles 9(2) or 10(2) or 11(2).[120] In the 1976 case of *Handyside v UK*,[121] which involved challenge to a prosecution under the Obscene Publications Act of 1959 and 1964 on article 10 grounds (see appendix E for full text of Article 10), the Strasbourg Court interpreted freedom of expression thus:

> Freedom of expression constitutes one of the essential foundations of such a society, one of the basic conditions for its progress and for the development of every man. Subject to paragraph 2 of Article 10 (Art. 10-2), it is applicable not only to 'information' or 'ideas' that are favourably received or regarded as inoffensive or as a matter of indifference, but also to those that offend, shock or disturb the State or any sector of the population. Such are the demands of that pluralism, tolerance and broadmindedness without which there is no 'democratic society'. This means, amongst other things, that every 'formality', 'condition', 'restriction' or 'penalty' imposed in this sphere must be proportionate to the legitimate aim pursued.[122]

5.80 *Redmond-Bate v DPP*[123] was a case involving a Christian fundamentalist who was prosecuted for obstructing a police officer in the execution of his duty as she refused to stop preaching on the steps of a cathedral when asked to, a crowd having gathered. It was decided before the coming into force of HRA 1998 but after its enactment.

119 In *R v Heather Shirley Nicholson* [2006] EWCA Crim 1518, an ASBO was imposed against an animal rights protestor who campaigned against Huntingdon Life Sciences and other companies. The case is decided in relation to breach and 'reasonable excuse' and so the facts that gave rise to the ASBO itself are unknown.

120 See *Hammond v DPP* [2004] EWHC 69 (Admin) at paras 21 and 22.

121 (1979–80) 1 EHRR 737.

122 (1979–80) 1 EHRR 737 at para 49.

123 (1999) 163 JP 789, DC.

Sedley LJ, echoing *Handyside* to an extent, described free speech as including:

> ... not only the inoffensive but the irritating, the contentious, the eccentric, the heretical, the unwelcome and the provocative provided it does not tend to provoke violence. Freedom only to speak inoffensively is not worth having ...

5.81 In *Hammond v DPP*,[124] Mr Hammond, an Evangelical Christian preacher, had on more than one occasion carried a large double-sided sign with the words 'Stop immorality! Stop homosexuality! Stop lesbianism!', while preaching in the centre of Bournemouth. This attracted a large crowd: some found the words on the placard insulting, others found them distressing, one person found them disgusting and annoying. The Divisional Court considered his actions in the context of article 10 and 11 and found that they were not reasonable within the meaning of POA 1986 s5(3)(c).

5.82 By contrast, in *Percy v DPP*,[125] an experienced protester who had for many years protested against the use of weapons of mass destruction and against US military policy (in particular 'Star Wars') defaced the American flag at a US air base. She wrote 'Stop Star Wars' across the stripes, stepped in front of a vehicle and placed the flag down in front of it and then stood on it. American service personnel and/or their families were distressed to varying degrees by her actions. In an appeal to the Divisional Court against her conviction under POA 1986 s5, she argued that her conduct was reasonable within the meaning of section 5(3)(c). She relied upon Article 10 of the ECHR. Her conviction was quashed on the basis that the District Judge gave insufficient weight to the question of proportionality when considering whether her conduct was reasonable. The Court highlighted the importance of striking the right balance when considering the right to protest against the rights of those affected:

5.83
> I have no difficulty in principle with the concept that there will be circumstances in which citizens of this country and visiting foreign nationals should be protected from intentionally and gratuitously insulting behaviour, causing alarm or distress. There may well be a pressing social need to protect people from such behaviour. It is, therefore, in my view a legitimate aim, provided of course that any restrictions on the rights of peaceful protesters are proportionate to the mischief at which they are aimed. Some people will be more robust than others. What one person finds insulting and distressing

124 [2004] EWHC 69 (Admin).
125 [2001] EWHC 1125 (Admin).

may be water off a duck's back to another. A civilised society must strike an appropriate balance between the competing rights of those who may be insulted by a particular course of conduct and those who wish to register their protest on an important matter of public interest. The problem comes in striking the balance, giving due weight to the presumption in the accused's favour of the right of freedom of expression.[126]

5.84 While different considerations apply to criminal prosecutions under POA 1986 than to ASBO applications (for example, invoking the criminal law is considered a greater interference with Convention rights than invoking the civil law, and therefore the question of proportionality may be considered differently), nonetheless the question of 'reasonableness' under CDA 1998 must be interpreted in the context of Convention rights. There is currently no reported authority on ASBOs and the mandatory requirement to disregard acts which are 'reasonable'.

Is there a time bar on incidents that can be relied upon by the applicant body?

5.85 A stand-alone ASBO is applied for by way of complaint to a magistrates' court (CDA 1998 s1(1)(3)).[127] MCA 1980 s127 (1) states:

> *Except as otherwise expressly provided by any enactment* ... a magistrates' court shall not try an information or hear a complaint unless the information was laid, or the complaint made, within 6 months from the time when the offence was committed or the matter of complaint arose.[128]

5.86 The general purpose of MCA 1980 s127 is to ensures the prompt prosecution of summary offences and the prompt bringing of complaints and to discourage delay (there is no such general rule in relation to indictable offences). Particular statutes may provide otherwise for their own purposes[129] and the language of MCA 1980 s127(1) makes clear that that is envisaged. There is nothing in CDA 1998 that displaces the general rule on the hearing of complaints. A written

126 [2001] EWHC 1125 (Admin) at para 28.

127 As amended by Courts Act 2003 (Consequential Provisions) Order 2005 SI No 886 and in force as of 1 April 2005. It is an application by way of *complaint* contrary to what is said in the commentary to *Boorman* in CLW/05/42/10.

128 Emphasis added.

129 See *Stone's Justices' Manual* 2005, Vol 1, 1-62 (note 3) for various examples of statutes with their own time limits.

complaint is made when it is received in the office of the clerk to the justices for the relevant area.

5.87 There is no dispute in any of the case law on the subject that at least one of the incidents relied upon has to be within the six-month time limit to satisfy MCA 1980 s127. The confusion usually arises where there are one or more 'in time' incidents and a number of other 'out of time' incidents. When the offence or complaint is a continuing one, then time starts running from each day the offence is committed. This rule is particularly relevant in prosecutions in harassment cases[130] and also in cases where there is a failure to comply with an enforcement notice or a failure to execute works when required to by a local housing authority.[131]

5.88 In the ASBO context, a court has to be satisfied to the criminal standard that the acts complained of were carried out by the defendant.[132] In what circumstances therefore can 'out of time' incidents properly and fairly assist in that task? The court also has to be satisfied, but not to any particular standard of proof, that the ASBO is necessary within the meaning of CDA 1998. Can 'out of time' incidents be admitted in relation to that task?

5.89 The 2006 Home Office Guidance states[133] that under MCA 1980 s127:

> ... a complaint must be made within six months from the time when the matter of the complaint (the behaviour) arose. One incidence of serious anti-social behaviour may be sufficient for an order to be made. *Earlier incidents may be used as background information to support a case and show a pattern of behaviour.* As long as the complaint is made within the six-month timeframe, a summons may be served outside this time period; although delay is not encouraged.[134]

5.90 It is not at all clear from the above when and in exactly what context such incidents should be considered by a court. The question of 'out of time' incidents was first considered in *R (Stevens) v South East*

130 See *DPP v Margaret Baker* [2004] EWHC 2782 where incidents covering a period of 2 years 8 months were admitted as either a continuing offence or were in any event admissible to establish the relevant background to the offence.

131 See for example, *Camden London Borough Council v Marshall* [1996] 1 WLR 1345.

132 For the first limb of the test to be satisfied, the anti-social acts have to be carried out since the commencement date, namely, since 1 April 1999 (see para 6.27).

133 At p24. See www.together.gov.uk.

134 Emphasis added.

Surrey Magistrates' Court.[135] Auld LJ acknowledged that stand-alone ASBOs are made by complaint and are subject to MCA 1980 s127. The facts of that case were that the Surrey Police sought to rely on hearsay evidence of 30 alleged incidents of anti-social behaviour, 8 of them within the six-month period and 22 before it, the oldest going back to some three years before the hearing. The hearsay was in the form of crime reports, other police incident reports and witness statements from victims who were unwilling to attend court for fear of reprisals.

5.91 Those acting on behalf of Surrey Police did not ask the magistrates' court to rely upon the 'out of time' incidents to support the 'in time' incidents as similar fact evidence, but rather to support the part of their case going to the second limb of the test, ie 'necessity'. The magistrates found the 'in time' incidents proved and imposed an ASBO. The single issue for the Divisional Court was whether section 127 prevents an authority in an application for an ASBO from adducing evidence of anti-social behaviour that occurred more than six months before the making of the complaint.

5.92 Auld LJ was troubled by the jurisdictional constraints of section 127 and considered, but doubted, whether a sound argument could be made on jurisdictional grounds to allow the acts to be relied upon. He came to the following conclusions:[136]

5.93
> But on the facts of this case – and I suspect many such applications based on a long course of alleged anti-social behaviour – the fairer and possibly more intellectually respectable approach is not one going to jurisdiction, but to the propriety and fairness of reliance on evidence of 'out-of-time' incidents in relation to 'in time' incidents alleged to constitute a course of anti-social behaviour. It is here where Lord Steyn's distinction between magistrates' function when determining the facts of such behaviour and what, if anything, it is necessary to do about it comes into play, the latter not dependent on proof so much as an evaluative judgment. In making that judgment it makes sense for them to look at what has happened in the past ... But of course all depends on the quality of such information, how relevant and reliable it is to the issue of the need for protection of others and, if so, the nature and range of prohibitions to secure that protection.[137]

5.94 Auld LJ seemed to be suggesting that the 'out of time' incidents may well fall foul of the jurisdictional bar, but the real question was

135 [2004] EWHC 1456 (Admin).

136 [2004] EWHC 1456 (Admin) at paras 18 and 19.

137 Emphasis added.

whether the acts were relevant to and admissible in deciding the question of 'necessity'. He went on to say:[138]

> An important factor going both to relevance and hence admissibility, and possibly to reliability, going to its weight, is the age of the earlier 'out-of-time' incidents to which magistrates are asked to have regard on this issue. (This also applies to evidence of such incidents where it is a candidate for admission as similar fact evidence in support of proof of harassment under section 1(1)(a).) *If they are very old and amount to only a single or very few incidents they may have little relevance or weight however reliable the evidence of them may be, looking at each incident on its own. On the other hand, if, as here, they indicate a solid and consistent line of anti-social behaviour beginning possibly well out-of-time and ending within-time they would usually be highly relevant to the decision whether an order is, in the circumstances, necessary and to what form it should take.*[139]

5.95 In the context of hearsay evidence, he added:[140]

> The only question is whether, in the individual circumstances of each case, it is fair to admit such evidence of 'out of time' conduct or what, if any, weight to give to it once admitted in order to persuade magistrates of the necessity for making an order if the 'within time' anti-social behaviour is proved to the criminal standard.

5.96 Auld LJ also made the point that MCA 1980 s127 does not apply to post-conviction or county court ASBOs and it would therefore 'be curious if that section were to have an additional role as an "evidential filter" for conduct outside the six months' limit denied to the county court and Crown Court'.[141]

5.97 The decision in *Stevens* was interpreted by courts and practitioners alike as meaning that 'out-of-time' incidents were admissible only in relation to the second limb of the test ('necessity'), unless the similar fact principle was being relied upon to prove the first limb. In *R (Boorman) v Chief Constable of West Mercia Constabulary*,[142] such an interpretation was said to be a false one. Unlike *Stevens*, which was a challenge by way of judicial review heard by a Divisional Court (ie, a two judge constitution), this was an appeal by way of case stated from the magistrates' court taken by the police in relation to an ASBO

138 [2004] EWHC 1456 (Admin) at para 19.

139 Emphasis added.

140 [2004] EWHC 1456 (Admin) at para 20.

141 [2004] EWHC 1456 (Admin) at para 21. Although Auld LJ does not mention the magistrates' courts and youth courts, MCA 1980 s127 does not apply there in the context of post-conviction ASBOs either.

142 [2005] EWHC 2559.

application that was dismissed. It was heard by an Administrative Court (a single judge constitution, in this case Calvert-Smith J). *Boorman*, as discussed below, does seem to go further than *Stevens*, and in so far as it does, it is submitted that *Stevens* is a proper statement of the law, not *Boorman*.

5.98 It is not at all clear from the *Boorman* judgment what the incidents relied upon were or how old the incidents were, but two of the questions for the High Court were whether the magistrates were correct in law to find that 'out of time' incidents should only go to the question of necessity and whether they were correct in law in refusing to admit 'out of time' incidents which might assist in proving the first limb of the test. Calvert-Smith J ruled that the magistrates were wrong in believing that they could not take account of 'out of time' incidents for the purpose of CDA 1998 s1(1)(a) (first limb of the test) and that *Stevens* should not be interpreted as laying down such a rule. He said that any such interpretation of Auld LJ's reasoning was a 'mistaken finding'.[143] He justified that by saying that, 'It is perfectly clear that, for instance, similar fact evidence may go to proof of harassment, ie under subsection (1)(a).'[144]

5.99 It is submitted that there may well be circumstances in which, in order to prove the identity of the defendant in relation to an 'in time' incident or incidents, the applicant body relies on similar fact evidence of an 'out of time' incident. In those circumstances, subject to the evidence being properly described as such, similar fact incidents are legally admissible in relation to the first limb.

5.100 The test for admissibility of similar fact evidence in civil proceedings is quite different from that in criminal proceedings because the same issues of prejudice and unfairness do not arise. The issue was recently debated in the House of Lords in the case of *O'Brien v Chief Constable of South Wales Police*.[145] The House of Lords ruled that to adopt the tests established in criminal law would make civil proceedings inappropriately inflexible. The simple test is that such evidence is admissible if it is potentially probative of an issue in the action.[146]

5.101 That is not to say that a judge does not have the power to exclude the evidence if he or she considers it unjust to admit it. The House of Lords, referring to the over-riding principles in the Civil Procedure

143 [2005] EWHC 2559 at paras 8 and 9.

144 [2005] EWHC 2559 at para 9.

145 [2005] 2 AC 534; [2005] 2 WLR 1038; [2005] 2 All ER 931.

146 [2005] 2 AC 534 at para 53.

Rules, said that the judge had a power to deal with a case in a manner which is proportionate to what is involved in the case and in a manner which is expeditious and fair, which includes a power to exclude evidence and to limit cross-examination.[147] Furthermore, where the admission of evidence runs the risk of prejudice to a party that is disproportionate to its relevance (particularly in the context of a civil jury trial), 'the judge will be astute to see that the probative cogency of the evidence justifies this risk of prejudice in the interests of a fair trial'. Of course, although neither the CPR nor jury trials are applicable to the ASBO context, the principles for exclusion enunciated by the Court and codified in the CPR are a reflection of the common law protections that have evolved over the years to ensure that civil proceedings are fair. Given the language and purpose of MCA 1980 s127, and the broad nature of the similar fact test, it is difficult to see in what *other* circumstances 'out of time' evidence could become admissible in relation to the first limb, as seems to be suggested by *Boorman*.

5.102 As Auld LJ pointed out, in relation to evidence which is relied upon by an applicant body for the purposes of convincing a court that an ASBO is necessary (the second limb), whether the court chooses to rely upon it will depend on its quality, its reliability and its relevance to the issue of 'necessity'. Furthermore, if the evidence is hearsay (whichever limb it is relied upon for), the court will give it weight (or no weight) in accordance with CEA 1995 s4 (see para 4.12 on hearsay evidence).

5.103 In practice, the proper course to follow in the generality of cases would be for the magistrates to hear all of the evidence and then, following submissions from the advocates, make decisions as to relevance and accordingly which limb of the test the particular evidence should go to, if at all. If the court is satisfied as to admissibility, then it will have to direct itself as to weight.[148] From a defendant's point of view it is important that an advocate directs the court as to what evidence it is entitled to rely upon in relation to each limb, particularly as there is an obvious danger that evidence which should technically only go to the second limb will be considered in relation to the first limb. Of course, if the first limb is not made out, that is the end of the matter.

5.104 There may be cases where the evidence is so obviously irrelevant or unreliable that submissions as to admissibility and weight can be

147 [2005] 2 AC 534 at para 55.

148 Certainly this is the procedure recommended in *Boorman* [2005] EWHC 2559.

made at the outset. For example, it is common practice for applicant bodies to serve bundles of CRIMINT data about a defendant which makes little sense to the untrained eye: often the only discernible data is the defendant's name or the fact he was stopped and searched on a particular date. It would seem perfectly reasonable for magistrates not to spend time reading pages and pages of data which is nothing but prejudicial (the mere repetition of a defendant's name in police intelligence files has prejudicial impact). As mentioned at para 5.10, applicant bodies should be put under pressure to identify the acts they seek to rely upon in relation to each limb prior to the full hearing in the interests of court time and expense. There is no logical reason why the overriding objective of dealing with cases justly, as described in CPR 1.1, should not apply to civil hearings in the criminal courts (see appendix H).

Can the applicant body rely upon incidents that have been the subject matter of criminal proceedings?

5.105 There is no statutory bar to relying upon incidents that have already been the subject matter of criminal prosecutions. In *S v Poole Borough Council*[149], the point was taken in relation to convictions for nuisance obtained under the Education Act 1996 s547(1), where an ASBO application relied upon incidents which included the same material which founded the convictions. Simon Brown LJ said:

> It seems to me perfectly proper to use the same material to found a criminal conviction and then in a civil process to support the making of an order akin to an injunction. Indeed it would seem positively eccentric to have omitted reference to part of the conduct which undoubtedly contributed to the public mischief when it came to seek to deter it in the future.[150]

5.106 Indeed, in the context of post-conviction ASBOs, CDA 1998 s1C(3B) specifically envisages that evidence that was admissible in the criminal proceedings which gives the court jurisdiction to make a post-conviction ASBO will be admissible in the related ASBO application.[151] Of course *Poole* was decided before either section 1C or section 1C(3B) came into force.[152]

149 [2002] EWHC 244 (Admin).

150 [2002] EWHC 244 (Admin) at para 16.

151 See para 6.26.

152 Section 1C was introduced by PRA 2002 and came into force on 2 December 2002; s1C(3B) was introduced by ASBA 2003 and came into force on 31 March 2004.

The second limb of the test (the 'necessity' test)

5.107 Once the court hearing an ASBO application is satisfied to the criminal standard of the test as described above, it must go on to consider the next limb: is an ASBO necessary to protect relevant persons from further anti-social acts by the defendant? It does not at this stage have to be satisfied to the criminal standard that an ASBO is necessary. In the oft quoted words of Lord Steyn in *McCann*, the second limb of the inquiry 'does not involve a standard of proof: it is an exercise of judgment or evaluation'.[153] When deciding whether an ASBO is 'necessary' in principle, the court will have to consider issues such as seriousness and persistency.[154]

5.108 This limb of the test is the key tool for effectively resisting the imposition of an ASBO altogether or limiting the terms of one.[155] One issue to bear in mind is that an ASBO is not an injunction to be used to regulate the relationship between two individuals. It is supposed to protect relevant person*s* (or person*s* in England and Wales) and not *a* person or relevant person. This is clear from the use of the word 'persons' in sections 1(1)(b), 1B and 1(6), as well as the requirement in section 1(1)(b) that the person caused harassment, alarm or distress must be 'not of the same household'. The various parliamentary debates during the passage of the Crime and Disorder Bill bear this out.[156]

5.109 Equally, in a non-domestic context (a neighbour dispute, for example) an order that prohibits direct or indirect contact with one particular individual will not be necessary to protect 'relevant persons' or 'persons in England and Wales'. It may well protect that individual but that was not the purpose of introducing the ASBO legislation. The fact that an individual cannot apply for an ASBO distinguishes it from the personal remedies already in existence, be they in the context of domestic violence or of harassment under the Protection from Harassment Act 1997.

5.110 Another important issue is that an ASBO is a preventative and not a punitive order and therefore each term of the order must be aimed

153 *R (on the application of McCann) v Crown Court at Manchester; Clingham v K & C Royal Borough Council* [2002] UKHL 39; [2002] 3 WLR 1313; [2002] 4 All ER 593, at para 37; see also para 5.43 above.

154 See para 5.62 on the question of persistency and seriousness, as well as para 5.85 on the question of 'Out-of-time' incidents and necessity.

155 See para 7.6 on necessity and proportionality.

156 See, for example, Lord Hardie in HL Debate, vol 585, col 1025–6, 10 February 1998.

at preventing the anti-social acts complained of in order to protect 'relevant persons' from further anti-social acts. Indeed CDA 1998 was designed to reduce crime by introducing preventative strategies. The preventative nature of an ASBO was highlighted in the case of *R v Boness; R v Bebbington*:[157] 'The purpose of an ASBO is not to punish an offender ... This principle follows from the requirement that the order must be necessary to protect persons from further anti-social acts by him. The use of an ASBO to punish an offender is thus unlawful ...'

5.111 As Pitchers J put it in *W v Acton Youth Court*:[158]

> Each condition imposed must be considered against this question: 'Does it appear to the court that this condition in these terms, taken together with the other conditions to be imposed, is necessary to protect persons in any place from further anti-social acts by the defendant?' I have included the words 'in these terms' to underline that it may be necessary to consider not simply whether a particular kind of prohibition is necessary but how broad it needs to be.

5.112 In *Boness*, the court further reinforced the point made in *W v Acton Youth Court*. It said that, once there had been a finding that the offender has acted in an anti-social manner, an order should only be made if *each* term of it was necessary to protect persons from further anti-social acts by the offender. It decried the use of standard ASBO terms being reproduced in every ASBO application: 'Any order should ... be tailor-made for the individual offender, not designed on a word processor for use in every case ...'[159]

5.113 Once a court decides that a term is necessary, it must go on to ensure that it is proportionate. The ambit of each term in the context of necessity and its inter-relation with the concept of 'proportionality' are discussed in chapter 7.

Necessity and 'relevant persons'

5.114 The original CDA 1998 s(1)(b) required that the order be found to be necessary to protect persons 'in the local government area in which the harassment, alarm or distress was caused or likely to be caused from further anti-social acts by him'. At that time ASBOs could only be applied for by the police or the local authority. As the

157 [2005] EWCA Crim 2395 at para 30.
158 [2005] EWHC 954 (Admin) at para 37.
159 [2005] EWHC 954 (Admin) at para 29.

powers were given to other local actors, section 1(1)(b) was amended by PRA 2002 to require that the order was necessary 'to protect relevant persons from further anti-social acts'.

5.115 CDA 1998 s1(1B) (as amended by PRA 2002) defines 'relevant persons' as persons within the local government area of the applicant council or within the county of an applicant county council or within the particular police area of the applying police force. For the purposes of BTP applications relevant persons are:

(i) 'persons who are within or likely to be within a place specified in section 31(a) to (f) of the Railways and Transport Safety Act 2003 in a local government area' or
(ii) 'persons who are within or likely to be within such a place'.[160]

What this somewhat convoluted drafting would seem to translate as is persons who are or are likely to be:

(a) on [a] track;
(b) on [a] network;
(c) in a station;
(d) in a light maintenance depot;
(e) on other land used for purposes of or in relation to a railway; and
(f) on other land in which a person who provides railway services has a freehold or leasehold interest.

For the definition of 'relevant persons' in relation to the Environment Agency and Transport for London, see appendix A.[161]

For the definition of 'relevant persons' in relation to RSLs and HATs, see para 8.27.

5.116 Although the rationale for allowing various local bodies to apply for stand-alone ASBOs is to protect that particular local community, there is now no bar on a prohibition within the ASBO that is much wider than that (for example a prohibition from begging in the whole of England and Wales).[162] The lawfulness of a condition as wide as that is discussed in full in chapter 7.

160 This definition came into force on 1 July 2004 – see British Transport Police (Transitional and Consequential Provisions) Order 2004 SI No 1573, which amends the definition in PRA 2002. It reads as quoted in the text above, which does not make any sense in that (ii) simply repeats (i). This may well be an error of the draftsman.

161 Crime and Disorder Act (Relevant Authorities and Relevant Persons) Order 2006 SI No 2137. See appendix A.

162 CDA 1998 s1(6).

Can an ASBO actually be *un*necessary?

5.117 In practice, once a series of anti-social acts has been properly established (particularly if there are many over a long period of time: ie, the 'persistency' requirement discussed at para 5.62 above is made out), it is difficult to persuade a court that an ASBO is in itself *un*necessary. Of course different considerations may apply in cases involving long custodial sentences (see chapter 6 on post-conviction ASBOs and incarceration) and in youth or 'looked-after children' cases if specific submissions can be made on why an ASBO in itself would conflict with the best interests of the young person.[163] Importantly, in cases where a local authority is applying for an ASBO against a child in its care, there must be a separation of functions so that the social worker concerned can properly represent the best interests of the child in question.[164]

'Necessity' and vulnerable defendants

5.118 In cases involving defendants with learning disabilities (for example autism or Asperger's Syndrome or Attention Deficit Hyperactivity Disorder), or specific mental health needs (depression, for example), or a psychological disorder (an obsessive-compulsive disorder, for example),[165] or even chronic alcoholism, there may be a compelling argument that alternative treatment and support ought to be made available or are available. In such cases, an ASBO 'made-to-be-breached' does not serve the purpose of preventing further anti-social acts (see the introduction to this book on ASBOs 'made-to-be-breached') and is therefore unnecessary. In *R v Suzanne Werner*,[166] for example, the Court of Appeal quashed a post-conviction ASBO imposed on a woman who had been diagnosed with a schizo-affective disorder for which she was receiving treatment, on the basis it was not necessary within the meaning of CDA 1998.

5.119 The first issue to consider is whether the local authority has a responsibility to the defendant in question and whether it has fulfilled

163 See *R (A) v Leeds Magistrates' Courts and Leeds CC* [2004] EWHC 554, discussed at 10.16.

164 See *R (M) v Sheffield Magistrates' Court* [2004] EWHC 1930 (Admin), discussed at 10.35.

165 See the excellent MIND website for information on different kinds of learning disabilities and mental health needs: www.mind.org.uk/Information/Booklets/Understanding/index.htm.

166 [2004] EWCA Crim 2931.

it. A local authority has various obligations to assess community care needs: under the NHS and Community Care Act 1990[167] it has a duty to assess any adult who may be in need of community care services; under sections 17–29 of the Children Act 1989 it has a duty to assess children 'in need' or 'at risk' and make provision for them,[168] rather than simply apply for an ASBO. There is also an obligation to assess the needs of those leaving hospital to ensure aftercare support.[169] A failure by the local authority to carry out, or properly carry out, such assessments is susceptible to judicial review.[170] These kinds of issues should have been flushed out at the consultation stage (see para 2.24, on pre-ASBO considerations, and the purpose and disclosure of consultation). If disclosure of that process shows that nothing or little has been done, then the onus should be put back on the local authority to consider its obligations rather than applying for or 'approving' an ASBO through the consultation process.

5.120 If the local authority has complied with its statutory obligations, and the applicant body still wishes to apply for an ASBO, then it is important to obtain relevant expert reports as to the nature of the disability or condition and the appropriate intervention.[171] If an ASBO application is served on someone who is not receiving learning or other support or has not had a diagnosis in relation to a particular disability, then the importance of obtaining relevant expert opinion may not be immediately obvious. The kind of behaviour complained about may be the best clue.

5.121 In cases where there is a documented history, the task of obtaining information and reports will be easier. Organisations such as MIND, the British Institute for Brain Injured Children, the National Autistic Society and the Dyslexia Association (see appendix J) have a great deal of awareness and expertise which can assist in identifying the disability as well as the kind of intervention that is usually appropriate.[172] The appropriate expert can also be asked to comment on the propriety of imposing an ASBO.

167 Sections 46–47. See also *Fair Access to Care Services (FACS) Policy Guidance* available at www.dh.gov.uk.

168 See *R (AB & SB) v Nottingham City Council* [2001] EWCA 235 (Admin): considered at para 10.28.

169 Mental Health Act 1983 s117 . See also MIND website: www.mind.org.uk.

170 See note 168.

171 Extensions from the LSC will have to be obtained for the purposes of instructing an expert: see chapter 12 on public funding.

172 See in particular www.mind.org.uk.

5.122 It should also be remembered that terms of ASBOs have to be understood by the recipient (particularly bearing in mind issues of age, educational attainment and intellectual ability)[173] and it may well be that applications against those with learning difficulties are unworkable in any event. In those circumstances, even if the court is satisfied of the necessity element, it does not have to go on to make an ASBO (see para 5.41 above).

Can ASBO proceedings be an abuse of process?

5.123 Unlike what happened in *Poole* (para 5.105 above), what would the position be if the defendant had been acquitted in criminal proceedings and the same or similar evidence was used to apply for an ASBO? In criminal proceedings, prior to the coming into force of CJA 2003,[174] the principle of double jeopardy prevented a defendant, in the absence of special circumstances, from being prosecuted a second time on the same or substantially the same facts as had given rise to an earlier prosecution that had resulted in his acquittal or conviction. An attempt to pursue a prosecution in breach of this principle of double jeopardy would justify a plea of *autrefois acquit* or *autrefois convict*, or an application to stay the proceedings as an abuse of process. CJA 2003 changes the position to an extent – it allows a retrial following an acquittal for certain serious offences, with permission from the DPP, if various requirements are satisfied, including that there is new and compelling evidence and it is in the public interest to re-prosecute.

5.124 ASBOs, however, are different creatures: they involve civil proceedings and a person is therefore not at risk of a second 'prosecution' during the order-making process, despite the fact that any breach of that order may result in a conviction. Additionally, although the first limb of the test has to be proved to the criminal standard, different considerations may apply in an ASBO hearing. For example, the *mens rea* of the defendant is never relevant in ASBO proceedings nor does an actual person have to have been caused harassment, alarm or distress (see para 5.49 above in relation to POA 1986 s5). Therefore, if a person is acquitted of an offence under POA 1986, for example, it does not necessarily follow that he has not committed an anti-social act

173 *B v Chief Constable of Avon & Somerset Constabulary* [2001] 1 WLR 340; [2001] 1 All ER 5; *R v P (Shane Tony)* [2004] EWCA Crim 287. See para 7.22.

174 The relevant section (Part 10) came in to force on 4 April 2005.

within the meaning of CDA 1998. Having said that, any application for an ASBO following an acquittal on the same facts may still be an abuse of process on the basis that it would bring the administration of justice into disrepute to permit the same issues to be re-litigated in ASBO proceedings. It is certainly arguable that ASBO proceedings in those circumstances would be a collateral attack on an earlier decision of a criminal court of competent jurisdiction. In *Hunter v Chief Constable of the West Midlands*[175] the House of Lords ruled that it is a general rule of public policy that such an attack is an abuse of process.

5.125 In the recent case of *Ali-Daar v Chief Constable of Merseyside Police*[176] abuse of process principles in civil litigation were considered. Ironically, this case was an application by the Chief Constable to strike out the respondent's claims for false imprisonment, assault and malicious prosecution as an abuse of process on the basis that the facts relied upon were the same facts that had founded a successful ASBO application made by the local authority. What the Court of Appeal had real difficulty in grappling with was that the Chief Constable took this argument despite the fact that the ASBO application relied upon four incidents that were the subject matter of earlier criminal proceedings at which the respondent was acquitted. For reasons unknown the abuse point in relation to the ASBO application was not taken in the lower court at the time of the ASBO hearing. While not deciding whether the ASBO proceedings were abusive, Laws LJ made some helpful *obiter* comments:

5.126 What is in my judgment of the first importance here is that the ASBO was obtained, as I have said, on proof to the District Judge of matters which expressly included allegations of which the respondent had been acquitted in the magistrates' court. I see no escape from the proposition, on these particular facts, that whatever other matters may have informed the ASBO application, it was a signal feature of that application that the applicant local authority invited the court to retry allegations on which the respondent had been acquitted. It is perhaps not fruitful to consider, and I certainly do not decide, whether the ASBO application might itself have been stayed as an abuse ...'[177]

5.127 The Court also went on to distinguish the case of *R v Z*,[178] relied on by the Chief Constable to apparently prove that ASBO proceedings could in any event have been shown not to be abusive on the basis that an

175 [1982] AC 529.

176 [2005] EWCA Civ 1774.

177 [2005] EWCA Civ 1774 at para 17.

178 [2000] 2 AC 483.

acquittal is not evidence of innocence and evidence rejected by a court can later be relied upon in subsequent criminal proceedings:

5.128 ... *Z* is really concerned with a specific issue as regards admissibility of evidence. It does not, as it seems to me, throw light on the very different question of whether some complaint might have been made about the bringing of the ASBO proceedings here, having regard to the fact of the previous acquittal. In the ASBO proceedings the local authority set out to prove the very facts of which the respondent had been acquitted as part of their substantive case for an ASBO. That it seems to me distinguishes the case from *Z* ...[179]

5.129 There may be a further or alternative argument available to a defendant in circumstances where s/he has been acquitted of a criminal offence the facts of which are later relied upon in an ASBO application. The defendant may be able to bring him/herself within CDA 1998 s1(5) 'disregard' by arguing that his/her acts were 'reasonable' in the circumstances (see para 5.74 on 'reasonableness' above). If, for example, a person was acquitted of assaulting a police officer in the execution of his duty because it was shown at trial that the officer was not acting in the execution of his duty and the defendant was therefore entitled to use reasonable force to defend him/herself, it would be perfectly open to the defendant to make submissions and/ or call evidence to show that s/he acted reasonably.

Is it permissible to have concurrent criminal and civil ASBO proceedings?

5.130 On the facts of *Poole* (para 5.105 above), Poole Borough Council laid informations against the appellant in relation to offences under the Education Act 1996 on the same date as it applied for an ASBO. As it happened, the criminal proceedings were completed before the hearing of the ASBO matter. There was no point taken about this in the Administrative Court nor could there be. Concurrent proceedings are not uncommon in our jurisdiction, particularly in family law matters, where there are often concurrent care and criminal proceedings (for neglect). It is also not uncommon for there to be concurrent proceedings in relation to injunctions under the Family Law Act 1996[180] in the county court and a criminal prosecution based on the same evidence

179 [2000] 2 AC 483 at para 21.

180 See Family Law Act 1996 Part IV: Family Homes and Domestic Violence.

under the Protection from Harassment Act 1997.[181] That said, it is also common for the criminal proceedings to take precedence over the civil ones (ie, to be heard first), usually because of the higher standard of proof and greater penalty involved. Any civil proceedings thereafter will be subject to the abuse of process doctrine discussed above. The likelihood of the *Poole* situation arising again must be low given that post-conviction ASBOs are now available. If a defendant is convicted of a criminal offence, an ASBO can be applied for based on that same evidence alone (although a single offence is highly unlikely to satisfy both limbs of the test) or combined with other evidence (see chapter 6 on post-conviction ASBOs), so there is no longer any need to launch a criminal prosecution at the same time as a civil complaint.

The duty to give reasons

5.131 ECHR Article 6 (1) requires that a court in civil proceedings should give reasons for its judgment.[182] The extent of the reasons that must be given will depend on the nature of the application. In *Boorman*[183] the court made the point that Article 6 places such a duty on the court and said that it was desirable for reasons to be given whichever way the decision went.

The form of the order

5.132 There is now no longer a requirement that the ASBO be on a standard form (MCR 2003 Sch 3, which contained a standard form, was revoked in June 2003).[184] Whatever form is used, it must contain the following:

- the anti-social acts that the court found proved;[185]
- the prohibitions imposed;
- the length of the order;
- any map and exclusion zone (as attachments);
- signature and date by the chair of the justices or their clerk.

181 See Protection from Harassment Act 1997 ss1–5.

182 See, for example *Van de Hurk v Netherlands* (1994) 18 EHRR 481 at para 61. See also *Stone's Justices' Manual* 2005, chap 1 at para 1-82.

183 *R (Chief Constable of West Mercia Constabulary) v Boorman* [2005] EWHC 2559 (Admin).

184 Magistrates' Courts (Miscellaneous Amendments) Rules 2003 SI No 1236.

185 See *R v P (Shane Tony)* [2004] EWCA Crim 287 at para 31.

Good practice dictates that there should be a record on the court file or on the order of when it was served on the defendant. The importance of the contents of the form being properly filled out was highlighted in *Luke Paul Wadmore and Liam Philip Foreman v R*.[186] Although that case is decided in relation to post-conviction ASBOs, the criticism directed at the Crown (for failing to sign and date the application for an ASBO and for failing to indicate when it was served on the appellants or their legal advisers or how service was effected) are equally applicable to stand-alone ASBOs, whether imposed or subsequently varied in the magistrates' court or varied on appeal to the Crown Court. In addition, the relevant parts of the *Wadmore* judgment read:

5.133 The form used in the present case ... does have a space in which the court must record the details of the behaviour that it has found constitutes anti-social behaviour by the offender. That part of the form was not completed in this case. It is important that this space is completed. Counsel should assist the court in doing so. In this case counsel for the Crown had inundated the judge with material without any attempt to elucidate it. As a result, perhaps not surprisingly, the judge had made no particular findings of fact in relation to either appellant concerning the details of their anti-social behaviour.[187]

5.134 Although in the earlier case of *R v English*[188] the Court of Appeal did not accept that a failure to fill in that part of the form invalidated an ASBO, the importance of doing so remains paramount.

5.135 In *R (Walkling) v DPP*,[189] the High Court held that the order is the one pronounced in open court and not the written order (where there is a discrepancy). That was a case where there was a discrepancy about the date of the order, when the order expired and whether the defendant was in fact in breach of it. The Court was not persuaded that the scheme of CDA 1998 s1 required a written order. The Court held that even if it was wrong and a written order was required, if the order was somehow defective (in this case it purported to be valid for less than two years, contrary to CDA 1998 s1(7)), that would not render it a nullity. In argument the Court's attention was not drawn to an earlier decision of the High Court (with Lord Bingham when he was LCJ presiding) in *B v Chief Constable of Avon & Somerset Constabulary*[190]

186 [2006] EWCA Crim 686. See also para 5.10 above.

187 [2006] EWCA Crim 686 at para 18.

188 [2005] EWCA Crim 2690.

189 [2003] EWHC 3139 (Admin) paras 34–43.

190 [2001] 1 WLR 340; [2001] 1 All ER 562.

which makes plain that the order made is the one announced in court. Although that decision was made in the context of CDA 1998 s2 (sex offender orders) the relevant wording of the section is identical.

A copy of the original ASBO, certified as such by the proper officer of the court which made it, is 'admissible as evidence of its having been made and of its contents to the same extent that oral evidence of those things is admissible in those proceeding'.[191] Advocates should therefore always check the written order before it is signed to see if it accords with what was said in court. It is particularly important to check that the terms and prohibitions are accurate at the stage the order is made. By the time it comes to breach proceedings, it will almost inevitably be too late to argue that the written order does not reflect what was said in open court. Although in civil proceedings, the justices have no power to amend or vary an order (as they would do in criminal proceedings under the 'slip rule'),[192] they are perfectly entitled to amend a written order so that it expresses the order made and announced in open court.[193]

Variation and discharge

5.136 An ASBO will have effect for a minimum period of two years (CDA 1998 s1(8)). It can only be discharged prior to the expiration of the two-year period by consent of both parties (section 1(9)). The two-year period starts running from the date the order is pronounced in open court despite the use of the words 'beginning with the date of service of the order' in section 1(9).[194]

5.137 Either 'side' can make an application to vary or discharge an ASBO (or interim ASBO). MC(ASBO)R 2002 r6 governs the procedure. The application must be made in writing to the magistrates' court that made the order and must specify the reasons why the applicant believes the court should vary or discharge. Except in the case of 'without notice' interims, the application can be determined without a hearing if the court thinks there are no grounds to conclude that the order should be varied or discharged. However, the circumstances in which a court refuses to hear oral submissions, particularly where

191 CDA 1998 s1(10C) as amended by SOCPA 2005 s139(2).

192 *Stone's Justices' Manual* 2005, chap 1, para 1-583. See also *R v English* [2005] EWCA Crim 2690 at para 12.

193 *B v Chief Constable of Avon & Somerset Constabulary* [2001] 1 WLR 340; [2001] 1 All ER 562.

194 *R (Walkling) v DPP* [2003] EWHC 3139 (Admin).

there is disputed evidence, must be rare. If the court believes that there are grounds upon which it might conclude that the order should be varied or discharged, it shall issue a summons, giving not less than 14 days' written notice of the date, time and place for a hearing (see appendix B for the full text of MC(ASBO)R 2002 r5). If the application is to vary or discharge an order which was made on appeal to the Crown Court from the magistrates' court, the order is treated as if it were an order of the magistrates' court from which the appeal was brought and *not* an order of the Crown Court.[195]

5.138 Variation and discharge applications will usually be made where there is a change of circumstances or the passage of time has had a positive effect on a defendant or has made the order redundant for some other reason.[196] Such applications should not be made when a defendant is aggrieved by the terms or a particular term of the ASBO either because it is too wide or if the ASBO is imposed for too long. The proper course in those circumstances would be to appeal to the Crown Court pursuant to CDA 1998 s4[197] (see chapter 11 on appeals).

5.139 The 2006 Home Office Guidance states that if an individual seeks variation or discharge, 'the agency that obtained the ASBO needs to ensure that a considered response is given to the court' and if the application is to be contested, the court should be given reasons 'supported as appropriate by evidence gathered in the course of monitoring the effectiveness of the order'.[198]

Reporting restrictions

5.140 There are no automatic reporting restrictions available in relation to ASBO applications, whatever the age of the defendant.[199] If the ASBO is being made against a child or young person, the court does have the power to impose restrictions on media reporting and/or the publication of photographs in the media pursuant to section 39 of the

195 CDA 1998 s4 (3).

196 See *R (Manchester City Council) v Manchester Crown Court* (2000) 13 October, QBD, unreported. See also para 6.44.

197 Ibid.

198 *A Guide to Anti-Social Behaviour Orders* (Home Office, 2006), p 50.

199 Furthermore, CDA 1998 s1C(9C)(a) specifically provides that CYPA 1933 s49 does not apply in respect of a child or young person against whom a post-conviction ASBO is made and s1(10D) even disapplies s49 in relation to breach proceedings against children and young people. See para 10.48.

Children and Young Persons Act (CYPA) 1933.[200] There will only be anonymity conferred under that particular provision if the court so directs, and it may so direct either generally or it may limit the nature of the publicity which can be given. The extent to which the established principles in the case law in this area should be modified, or their application affected, in a context where the child or young person in question is the subject of an anti-social behaviour order was considered at length in *R (T) v St Albans Crown Court*[201] and is discussed at para 10.50.

5.141 In *Keating v Knowsley Metropolitan Borough Council*,[202] the High Court endorsed Elias J's approach and said it applied equally to interim ASBOs. It did not agree with the proposition that there should be a presumption in favour of a CYPA 1933 s39 order, despite the unproven nature of the allegations at the stage that an interim order is imposed, although it accepted that it was a very important consideration.

Post-ASBO publicity

5.142 While the restrictions in CYPA 1933 s39 apply to the media alone, if such an order is in place, it must follow that the local authority and police are restricted in the same way. The basis for the order must be that publication will harm the interests of the child, having weighed up considerations of open justice and the public interest in disclosure. If a local authority were to publish information which a newspaper was not allowed to do, then it would circumvent the purpose of the section 39 order.

5.143 In the absence of a media reporting restriction, the question still arises as to the extent to which an ASBO and details of the person subject to it can be publicised by the local authority without breaching the ECHR Article 8 rights of the person subject to the ASBO. The March 2005 Home Office *Guidance on Publicising Anti-social Behaviour*[203] lists the following as guiding principles:

- Publicity is essential if local communities are to support agencies tackling anti-social behaviour. There is an implied power in CDA

200 CDA 1998 s1 (9C)(b). For the full text of CYPA 1933 s39 as amended see *Archbold* 2006, para 4-27.

201 [2002] EWHC 1129 (Admin).

202 [2004] EWHC 1933 (Admin).

203 Available at www.together.gov.uk. See also chapter 15 of *A Guide to Anti-social Behaviour Orders* (Home Office, 2006).

1998 and the Local Government Act 2000 to publicise an order so that the order can be effectively enforced.

- ASBOs protect local communities. Obtaining the order is only part of the process; its effectiveness will normally depend on people knowing about the order.
- Information about ASBOs obtained should be publicised to let the community know that action has been taken in their area.
- A case by case approach should be adopted and each individual case should be judged on its merits as to whether or not to publicise the details of an individual subject to an ASBO: publicity should be expected in most cases.
- It is necessary to balance the human rights of individuals subject to an ASBO against those of the community as a whole when considering publicising ASBOs.
- Publicising should be the norm not the exception. An individual who is subject to an ASBO should understand that the community is likely to learn about it.

5.144 This Guidance was published following the decision in *R (Stanley) v Metropolitan Police Commissioner.*[204] In that case the High Court accepted that a local authority did have power to publicise by necessary implication under the terms of CDA 1998 but that post-ASBO publicity might infringe rights under Article 8.1,[205] especially if use was made of photographs taken under the powers of the Police and Criminal Evidence Act 1984 (as was done on the facts of that case). It emphasised the need for those considering post-order publicity in future to have in mind the Convention rights of those against whom orders are made, and of the wider public (including past and potential victims of anti-social behaviour).

5.145 The facts of the *Stanley* case involved extremely serious anti-social behaviour by a group of youths on a housing estate in the London Borough of Brent that culminated in what the Court described as a mini-riot when the police sought to intervene. The Court ruled that the use of leaflets containing photographs and identities, as well as the use of newsletters and websites to publicise the ASBO proceedings, was not a disproportionate interference with the claimants' article 8 rights. Kennedy LJ said:

> It is clear to me that whether publicity is intended to inform, to reassure, to assist in enforcing the existing orders by policing, to

204 [2004] EWHC 2229 (Admin); [2005] UKHRR 115; [2005] HLR 8.

205 Article 8 is reproduced in appendix E.

inhibit the behaviour of those against whom the orders have been made, or to deter others, it is unlikely to be effective unless it includes photographs, names and at least partial addresses. Not only do the readers need to know against whom orders have been made, but those responsible for publicity must leave no room for mis-identification. As to the remainder of the content of any publicity, that must depend upon the facts of the case. If, as here, residents have been exposed to significant criminal behaviour for years, and orders have been obtained by reference to that behaviour and to bring it to an end, I see no reason why publicity material should not say so. It cannot, of course, assert that those against whom orders have been made have been convicted of any crime, but none of the material that we have had to consider made that assertion. The language used in some of the publicity was colourful, but having regard to the known facts already in the public arena it was entirely appropriate, and the colour was needed in order to attract the attention of the readership.[206]

.146 Few cases will be as extreme as the situation that arose in the *Stanley* case and if the publicity in a particular case goes beyond a legitimate purpose (ie, enforcement, reassurance of the local community or deterrence) or even if the purpose is legitimate, but the information revealed is not strictly necessary to meet that purpose, defence lawyers should consider a challenge by way of judicial review.[207]

Ancillary orders

.147 There are three ancillary orders which may be available in ASBO cases, a detailed consideration of which is beyond the scope of this book.[208] These orders are:

- intervention orders;
- individual support orders; and
- parenting orders.

The statutory powers in relation to intervention orders are summarised below. As the other two orders are only available in relation to a child or a young person,[209] they are dealt with at para 10.60. It is arguable that none of these orders is available in conjunction with post-conviction orders.[210]

206 [2004] EWCA Civ 2229 (Admin) at para 40.

207 But see also *Medway Council v BBC* [2002] 1 FLR 104, para 10.54 below.

208 See www.together.gov.uk.

209 See para 10.12 for a definition of 'child' and 'young person'.

210 See para 6.53.

Intervention orders

5.148 The Drugs Act 2005[211] introduced intervention orders into CDA 1998.[212] The purpose of the orders seems to be the targeting of drug use which is the underlying cause of anti-social behaviour. When the sections come into force, such orders will be available in relation to adults only, and then only when an ASBO (stand-alone) or an order under section 1B (county court ASBO) is made.[213] It envisages the defendant carrying out specified activities designed to address the 'trigger behaviour' which led to the ASBO being made in the first place for a maximum period of six months. Before such an order can be made, the relevant authority has to have obtained a report 'from an appropriately qualified person ... relating to the effect on the person's behaviour of the misuse of controlled drugs or of such other factors as the Secretary of State by order prescribes'[214] as well as consulted with prescribed persons[215] to ensure that any specified activities recommended are in fact available. The breach of such an order is a summary only offence punishable with a fine. This is an ambitious order which will be extremely costly to administer and monitor.

5.149 Terms and duration of ASBOs are dealt with in chapter 7. For appeals against ASBOs, see chapter 11. For costs and public funding, see chapter 12.

211 Section 20. In force 1 October 2006. See Drugs Act 2005 (Commencement No 4) Order 2006 SI No 2136.

212 Sections 1G and 1H.

213 CDA 1998 s1G(1)(a).

214 CDA 1998 s1G(1)(b). An 'appropriately qualified person' is a fully registered medical practitioner who is a specialist in the treatment of substance misuse or addiction: see Crime and Disorder Act 1998 (Intervention Orders) Order 2006 SI No 2138, para 4(b).

215 CDA 1998 s1G(1)(c). The persons to be consulted by the relevant authority are an NHS Trust, a Primary Care Trust and a local authority (where it is not the relevant authority) concerned with the provision of activities involving the provision of drug misuse treatment: see Crime and Disorder Act 1998 (Intervention Orders) Order 2006 SI No 2138, paras 2 and 4(a).

CHAPTER 6

Post-conviction ASBOs

continued

Introduction

6.1 The legislation refers to stand-alone orders arising under CDA 1998 s1 as 'anti-social behaviour orders' and orders arising under section 1C as 'orders on conviction to prevent further anti-social acts'. For convenience, orders on conviction are referred to as post-conviction ASBOs.

6.2 The popularity of post-conviction ASBOs has steadily increased since their introduction in 2002. The Home Office statistics show that by 2004, the number of post-conviction ASBOs imposed was greater than the number of stand-alones in most regions in England and Wales. By 2005, in Greater London, post-conviction ASBOs accounted for 75.4 per cent of the total number of ASBOs issued that year. In Greater Manchester, 63 per cent of the ASBOs imposed in 2005 were post-conviction ASBOs.[1]

6.3 This may reflect the fact that post-conviction ASBOs are generally cheaper (see para 1.10) and that there is no 'relevant persons' requirement in the second limb of the test (see para 6.24 below). Criminal practitioners are likely to be faced with ASBO applications on an extremely regular basis now. There are a number of overlapping issues between stand-alone and post conviction ASBOs and these are explored in chapter 5. In particular, the statutory test for imposing ASBOs is dealt with in that chapter. Terms and duration of an ASBO are dealt with in chapter 7.

6.4 This chapter's main areas of focus are as follows:

- the correct procedure to follow;
- rules relating to the use of hearsay evidence;
- imposing an ASBO in addition to a prison sentence;
- variation and discharge.

Which courts can impose post-conviction ASBOs?

6.5 Post-conviction ASBOs (sometimes referred to as CRASBOs) are available in the magistrates' court, the youth court and the Crown Court. CDA 1998 s1C was introduced by PRA 2002 and later amended by ASBA 2003[2] and SOCPA 2005.[3]

1 The Home Office Anti-Social Behaviour Unit provided these figures upon request.
2 ASBA 2003 s86, which came into force on 31 March 2004.
3 SOCPA 2005 s139, which came into force on 1 July 2005.

Civil or criminal?

6.6 A post-conviction ASBO application, even if heard immediately after a criminal hearing, is a civil matter. It is not part of the sentence hearing.[4] As mentioned in chapter 3, although there have been attempts to distinguish post-conviction ASBOs from stand-alone ASBOs since the House of Lords' decision in *McCann*[5] (see for example *R (C) v Sunderland Youth Court*),[6] the Divisional Court in *R (W) v Acton Youth Court*[7] had no doubt that post-conviction ASBOs under CDA 1998 s1C are civil orders. This is also the view taken by the Justices' Clerks' Society.[8]

6.7 As there is no difference in the substance and consequences of a stand-alone and a post-conviction ASBO it must be right that there should be no distinction between them as to their proper classification. As a result of their civil classification, the Civil Evidence Act 1995 applies and hearsay is admissible (see chapters 3 and 4).

6.8 Although the youth court has no civil jurisdiction conferred upon it by statute (ie, it cannot hear civil matters brought by way of information or complaint), CDA 1998 s1C gives it a specific power to impose an ASBO upon conviction. As post-conviction orders are not brought by way of complaint but are ancillary to criminal proceedings, it would seem that the youth court's lack of civil jurisdiction is no bar to hearing a post-conviction ASBO.

Who can apply for a post-conviction ASBO?

6.9 ASBOs under CDA 1998 s1C can be made when a person is convicted of a relevant offence (namely an offence committed after the coming into force of PRA 2002 s64).[9] The conviction need not be for any specific offence but the order can only be made in addition to a sentence or a conditional discharge.[10]

4 Although the appropriate venue of appeal from the Crown Court is the Court of Appeal (Criminal Division): *R v P (Shane Tony)* [2004] EWCA Crim 287. See para 11.2

5 *R (on the application of McCann) v Crown Court at Manchester; Clingham v K & C Royal Borough Council* [2002] UKHL 39; [2002] 3 WLR 1313; [2002] 4 All ER 593.

6 [2004] 1 Cr App R (S) 76.

7 [2005] EWHC 954 (Admin).

8 See *ASBO guidance for the judiciary* (May 2005), and the Justices' Clerks' Society's *Good Practice Guide* (April 2004) in relation to ASBO law and procedure in the magistrates' court.

9 2 December 2002.

10 CDA 1998 s1C(4).

6.10 The court may make an order which prohibits the offender from doing anything described in the order:

- if the prosecutor asks it to do so; or
- if the court thinks it is appropriate to do so.[11]

6.11 There is, on the face of it, no role for a local authority in the ASBO application. In some regions there is a great deal of co-ordination between the local authority, the police and the Crown Prosecution Service. Where there is such co-ordination, the likelihood is that the local authority or local police force will have compiled the ASBO application, usually because a stand-alone ASBO was being contemplated until the defendant was arrested and charged with a crime. It is common practice to hold back on a stand-alone ASBO if a criminal conviction is likely.

What is the correct procedure to follow?

6.12 The difference between stand-alone and post-conviction ASBOs is a procedural one. Stand-alone ASBOs are brought by way of complaint in the magistrates' court (see chapter 5) while post-conviction ASBOs are ancillary orders. Applications for ASBOs brought by complaint put defendants on notice well in advance of the final hearing as to what the evidence is and what the issues are. In post-conviction ASBOs the defendant is often taken by surprise upon conviction that the prosecution is applying for an ASBO.

6.13 The court is permitted to consider evidence led by the prosecution and the defence.[12] It is immaterial that evidence would have been admissible in the criminal proceedings in which the offender was convicted.[13] A new section inserted by SOCPA 2005 means that the court may now adjourn the ASBO proceedings, even after sentencing the offender.[14] This is an important new provision that defence lawyers should rely upon if they are taken by surprise or wish to contest the evidence or call evidence on behalf of a defendant. Indeed the hearsay rules (discussed at para 6.19 below) require that a defendant is given 21 days' notice of hearsay evidence. If a defendant fails to attend for any adjourned ASBO proceedings, the court has the power to further adjourn the proceedings or issue a warrant for his

11 CDA 1998 s1C(3).
12 CDA 1998 s1C(3A).
13 CDA 1998 s1C(3B).
14 CDA 1998 s1C(4A) (inserted by SOCPA 2005 s139).

or her arrest.[15] However, a warrant can only be issued if a court is satisfied that the defendant has had adequate notice of the adjourned proceedings.[16]

Procedural rules

6.14 The absence of specific procedural rules[17] in relation to the serving and adducing of evidence in post-conviction ASBO hearings has been commented upon by the Court of Appeal, as long ago as 2003 by Brooke LJ in *C v Sunderland Youth Court*[18] and, more recently, in *Luke Paul Wadmore and Liam Philip Foreman v R*.[19] As a result of a lack of rules, post-conviction ASBO applications are often haphazard. While there may not be written procedural rules in relation to the serving of evidence other than hearsay (for which see below), there are elementary rules of fairness that ought to be followed. The Court of Appeal has made this clear on more than one occasion.[20]

The procedure must be fair

6.15 In *R (W) v Acton Youth Court*,[21] Pitchers J observed that, 'The actual and potential consequences for the subject of an ASBO make it, in my judgment, particularly important that procedural fairness is scrupulously observed'.[22] The Court of Appeal in *Wadmore and Foreman* agreed with this point and sought to emphasise it. The Court gave further guidance:

> ... the defendant must have a proper opportunity to consider the evidence advanced by the prosecution in support of the ASBO, especially in a case such as this one, where the CPS wishes to rely upon material that goes far wider than the evidence concerning the particular offence of which the appellants were convicted. If the defendant wishes to challenge it, he must be given proper time to do so ...[23]

15 CDA 1998 s1C(4B).
16 CDA 1998 s1C(4C).
17 Other than the Magistrates' Courts (Hearsay Evidence in Civil Proceedings) Rules 1999 discussed at para 6.19 below.
18 [2003] EWHC 2385; [2004] 1 Cr App R (S) 76.
19 [2006] EWCA Crim 686.
20 *C v Sunderland Youth Court* [2003] EWHC 2385; [2004] 1 Cr App R(S) 76, *R (W) v Acton Youth Court* [2005] EWHC 954 (Admin).
21 [2005] EWHC 954 (Admin).
22 [2005] EWHC 954 (Admin) at para 30.
23 [2006] EWCA Crim 686 at para 37.

6.16 The Justices' Clerks' Society's *Good Practice Guide* (*JCS Guide*) in relation to ASBO law and procedure in the magistrates' court[24] recommends that the prosecution should give as much advance notice as possible of its intention to apply for a post-conviction order, to include the grounds for and terms of the order sought. It warns that 'any failure by the prosecution to give notice which results in a sustainable application for an adjournment could lead to the court refusing to hear the application'.[25] If the court is minded to make an order on conviction of its own motion, the *JCS Guide* recommends that the court informs the parties that it is so minded, outlines the prohibition proposed and gives the defence sufficient time to consider the issues involved (the JCS envisage a 'short stand down').[26] Of course, as stated above, there is a power to adjourn if necessary.

The facts relied upon must be particularised

6.17 As mentioned at para 5.10, the Court in *Luke Paul Wadmore and Liam Philip Foreman v R*[27] was emphatic in its message to the CPS that post-conviction ASBO procedure needed much more care and precision, in particular the need to give advance notice and to identify the facts relied upon:

> We are very concerned about the procedure adopted in this case in relation to the ASBO. First, as we have already noted, we do not know when or how the defendants were given notice of the ASBO application and the material in support of the application. Secondly, there is no indication that any procedure analogous to that set out in the Magistrates Hearsay Rules was used. Thirdly, the Case Summary attached to the Application for the ASBOs does not set out particular facts on which the CPS intended to rely, in addition to the facts constituting the robbery offence of which the appellants had been convicted. Instead it set out only a vague 'Overview of the Problem' and some 'Reasoning' in the terms we have reproduced above. Therefore there was no summary of facts that the judge could put to the offenders to see, quickly and easily, whether or not the facts were disputed by them. It is also unfortunate that the prosecution did not assist the judge or the defence in summarising the facts at the hearing when the ASBO was sought.
>
> ...

24 Justices' Clerks' Society's *Good Practice Guide* (April 2004).

25 *JCS Guide*, para 4.5(a)(i).

26 *JCS Guide*, para 4.5(b)(ii).

27 [2006] EWCA Crim 686.

> We suggest that in future cases in the Crown Court under *CDA 1998 section 1C*, it is imperative that the prosecution identifies the particular facts said to constitute anti-social behaviour. We emphasise the word *fact*, as opposed to evidence adduced to prove a fact to the criminal standard. If the offender accepts those facts, then they should be put in writing, in the same way that a 'Basis of Plea' should always be put in writing. If facts are not accepted, then they have to be proved to the criminal standard before they can be acted upon. The judge should state his findings of fact expressly and they should be recorded in writing on the Order made by the judge in the space provided on the form.[28]

6.18 As advised at para 5.11, if the CPS simply serves an incomprehensible bundle of documentation including crime reports and CRIMINT printouts[29] spanning a long period of time, with no attempt at particularising which acts they rely upon for the purposes of the ASBO application, the Crown should be required to do so in advance of any ASBO hearing. A failure to do so will make it impossible for the defence to obtain meaningful instructions, decide which witnesses they need or indicate the amount of court time that the hearing will require. This will lead to further delay of the hearing which will be a waste of public funds. If defence practitioners are in receipt of the evidence prior to a post-conviction ASBO hearing, and the facts relied upon have not been identified, they should write to the CPS to seek clarification, relying upon the authority of *Luke Paul Wadmore and Liam Philip Foreman v R*.[30]

Procedure to be followed in relation to hearsay evidence

6.19 In relation to the reliance on hearsay evidence, see chapter 4, para 4.9 for a discussion on why the Magistrates' Courts (Hearsay Evidence in Civil Proceedings) Rules (MC(H)R) 1999[31] should apply by analogy to the Crown Court.[32] In *Luke Paul Wadmore and Liam Philip Foreman v R* the court said that it presumed that the rules applied in the Crown Court by analogy. As already mentioned in chapter 4, the Civil

28 [2006] EWCA Crim 686 at paras 43–45.

29 As to the admissibility of schedules of criminal incidents produced by a police officer see para 4.21 below.

30 [2006] EWCA Crim 686.

31 SI No 681. Reproduced in full in appendix D.

32 Although as mentioned above, the youth court traditionally has no 'stand-alone' civil jurisdiction, it is empowered to hear post-conviction ASBO applications and the Magistrates' Courts (Hearsay Evidence in Civil Proceedings) Rules 1999 will of course apply there.

Procedure Rules do not apply and the Criminal Procedural Rules (which do not in any event apply to civil matters) are silent on the procedure to be followed. It is submitted therefore that until either of those rules are amended, the MC(H)R 1999 should apply to all post-conviction hearings regardless of which criminal court they take place in. Similarly, in applications to vary or discharge post-conviction ASBOs, the Magistrates' Court (Anti-Social Behaviour Orders) Rules (MC(ASBO)R) 2002 should apply by analogy to the Crown Court (and the youth court, which is of course a specialised section of the magistrates' court).[33]

6.20 The MC(H)R 1999 provide that defendant must be given 21 days' notice of hearsay evidence and the Civil Evidence Act (CEA) 1995 governs the weight to be attached to such evidence. Readers are referred to chapter 4 for the rules governing the service of hearsay evidence, its admissibility and the weight to be attached to it as well as discussion on the relevance of ECHR Article 6.[34]

If documents such as a schedule of complaints on a particular housing estate derived from housing records or a schedule of criminal incidents derived from crime reports are to be relied upon, then the requirements of CEA 1995 s9 must be complied with.[35]

Vulnerable witnesses and special measures applications

6.21 See para 4.22.

ASBOs as alternatives to prison

6.22 In *R v Boness and Bebbington*[36] (referred to in chapters 5 and 7), the Court of Appeal disapproved of the practice of defendants' advocates seeking an ASBO at the sentencing stage in order to avoid prison or some other penalty. It said: 'The court must not allow itself to be diverted in this way. Indeed it may be better to decide the appropriate sentence and then move on to consider whether an ASBO should be made or not after sentence has been passed, albeit at the same hearing.'[37]

33 See para 6.42 below.

34 Also see chapter 4 for the special measures regime available for vulnerable witnesses.

35 See para 4.21.

36 [2005] EWCA Crim 2395.

37 [2005] EWCA Crim 2395 at para 30.

It is established law that to use an ASBO to punish an offender is unlawful (an ASBO being a preventative not a punitive order)[38] and therefore ASBO considerations should be entirely separate from the sentencing exercise. An ASBO can only be imposed if the statutory test (see below) is satisfied. Its terms are designed to prevent particular behaviour reoccurring and not simply to restrict an individual's liberty.[39]

Can you consent to an ASBO?

6.23 See para 5.30 for a full discussion of this issue.

What is the statutory test that has to be satisfied?

6.24 As mentioned at para 6.19 above, an ASBO under CDA 1998 s1C can only be imposed if the offender has been convicted of a relevant offence[40] and in addition to a sentence or conditional discharge.[41] The statutory test for imposing an ASBO under CDA 1998 s1C(2) is as follows:

(a) that the offender has acted, at any time since the commencement date,[42] in an anti-social manner, that is to say in a manner that caused or was likely to cause harassment, alarm or distress to one or more persons not of the same household as himself, and
(b) that an order is necessary to protect persons in any place in England and Wales from further anti-social acts by him.

The first limb of the test is exactly the same as for stand-alone ASBOs but the second limb is slightly different. For a full analysis of the first limb of the test and its proper interpretation, see chapter 5. It should be noted that the 'reasonableness defence' in relation to anti-social acts in the first limb of the test is available only in stand-alone and county court ASBO applications and not post-conviction ones.[43]

6.25 The second limb of the test is less restrictive than for stand-alone ASBOs in that the 'necessity' test is not limited to 'relevant' persons.

38 [2005] EWCA Crim 2395 at para 30. See also chapters 3 and 7.
39 See chapter 7 for terms and duration of ASBOs.
40 CDA 1998 s1C(1): namely an offence committed after the coming into force of PRA 1998 s64, ie 2 December 2002.
41 CDA 1998 s1C(4).
42 1 April 1999.
43 See para 5.74.

See para 5.107 for a full discussion on what constitutes necessity for the purposes of the second limb and para 7.55 for a discussion on prohibitions that extend to the whole of England and Wales.

Evidence that can be relied upon

6.26 As mentioned at para 6.13 above, the court can consider evidence led by the prosecution or the defence and it is immaterial that that evidence would have been admissible in the criminal proceedings in which the offender was convicted. Reliance may therefore be placed on the facts giving rise to the conviction(s) that gave the court the power to impose the ASBO in the first place. However, if that is the sole evidence relied upon, it may not satisfy either limb of the statutory test (see chapter 5). It is usual for the CPS to rely upon the facts of the current conviction supplemented by a list of previous convictions. Not every criminal conviction involves harassment, alarm or distress,[44] so if convictions are relied upon the CPS should be pressed to provide details of the facts underlying those convictions. The dates of the commission of those offences should also be requested, as although all anti-social acts committed since 1 April 1999 are admissible, if they are as old as that, the second limb of the statutory test will not be necessarily made out.[45]

6.27 In *R v McGrath*[46] the Court of Appeal considered whether pre-1 April 1999 acts were admissible and ruled that provided the offender has acted in an anti-social manner after the commencement date, in determining whether an ASBO is necessary, the judge is entitled to take all the offender's conduct into account, both before and after the commencement date. The Court found that while the statute requires the offender to have acted anti-socially after the commencement date, it does not go on to preclude the judge from considering the totality of the offender's behaviour. It said that to read such a limitation into the statute would be artificial and wrong and would run contrary to the purpose of the legislation.

For guidance on the kind of evidence that a defendant can usefully rely upon to either resist the making of an ASBO or resist its ambit, see para 7.18.

44 See, for example, the discussion on shoplifting and burglary at para 5.52.

45 See para 5.85 for a discussion on 'out of time incidents' in relation to stand-alone ASBOs.

46 [2005] EWCA Crim 353.

Standard of proof

6.28 See para 5.43.

Interim ASBOs

6.29 Post-conviction interims were introduced on July 2005 by SOCPA 2005 s139. They must be for a fixed period but can be varied, renewed or discharged.[47] An interim will cease to have effect once the decision whether to make a final ASBO is made.[48]

6.30 As mentioned above, there is now a statutory power (also introduced by SOCPA 2005) to adjourn the ASBO part of the hearing, even after sentence has been imposed (and a power to issue a warrant for arrest for non-attendance).[49] The courts may find it an attractive proposition to impose an interim ASBO while a pre-sentence report is being prepared or if a non-custodial sentence is imposed and the ASBO part of the hearing is adjourned. The test for imposing one is whether it is 'just' to do so.[50] It is unlikely to be 'just' to make an interim ASBO if the defendant is sentenced to a term of imprisonment given that the urgent need for protection of the community/fear of reprisals issue will not arise (see below on the propriety of imposing ASBOs alongside custodial sentences). If a non-custodial penalty is imposed, any such order must be considered carefully to ensure that the terms do not in any way impinge upon the successful completion of a community penalty or interfere with any other support the offender is currently getting in the community.[51]

6.31 As stated in chapter 5, a breach of an interim or full order is a breach even if the term is subsequently varied or set aside or indeed the whole ASBO is set aside.[52] If a term is so wide as to be unenforceable, then a defendant may have the defence of reasonable excuse available to him or her (see chapter 9 on breaches).[53]

47 CDA 1998 s1D(4).

48 CDA 1998 s1D(4)(c).

49 CDA 1998 s1C(4A).

50 See *R (Luke Kenny) v Leeds Magistrates' Court* [2003] EWHC 2963 (Admin) and *R (M) v Secretary of State for Constitutional Affairs* [2004] EWCA Civ 312; [2004] 1 WLR 2298, discussed at paras 5.18–5.22.

51 See para 7.18.

52 In *Parker v DPP* (2005) *Times* 20 June, the absence of a condition contained in an interim order from the final ASBO did not affect the gravity or otherwise of a breach of that condition. See also *T (Michael) v CPS* [2006] EWHC 728 (Admin).

53 *T (Michael) v CPS* [2006] EWHC 728 (Admin).

32 Unlike stand-alone interim ASBOs, there is no procedure for without notice (*ex parte*) orders[54] and it is difficult to conceive of such a course ever being appropriate or necessary. The power only arises once the prosecutor makes the request for a post-conviction ASBO, or the court decides it is minded to make one, so the defendant will presumably be on notice.[55]

For challenges to interim orders see para 5.23.

Terms and duration of ASBOs

33 A post-conviction ASBO, like a stand-alone, will have effect for a period (not less than two years) specified in the order or until further order. See chapter 7 for a full discussion. Variation and discharge are discussed at para 6.42 below.

Incarceration plus an ASBO?

.34 CDA 1998 s1C(5) reads as follows:

> An order under this section takes effect on the day on which it is made, but the court may provide in any such order that such requirements of the order as it may specify shall, during any period when the offender is detained in legal custody, be suspended until his release from that custody.

.35 CDA 1998 therefore clearly envisages the combination of custody plus an ASBO, notwithstanding the requirement of 'necessity' in the second limb of the statutory test. There are now a number of authorities on this point. *R v P (Shane Tony)*[56] was the high point in that the Court of Appeal stated that, 'it is simply not possible for a court to determine that an order is necessary to protect members of the public at some future date, having regard to the real possibility that the custodial element of the sentence imposed will prove to be effective'. The Court observed that where custodial sentences in excess of a few months were passed and an offender was liable to be released on licence and therefore be subject to recall, the circumstances in which there would be a demonstrable necessity to make a suspended ASBO, to take effect upon release, would be limited, although there

54 See para 5.17.

55 CDA 1998 s1D(1)(c) and (d).

56 [2004] EWCA Crim 287.

would be some cases in which geographical restraints could properly supplement licence conditions.

6.36 In *R v Paul Rush*,[57] the lower court imposed a two-and-a-half-year custodial sentence plus a ten-year ASBO. While the Court of Appeal did not quash the ASBO (although it reduced both the length of the sentence and the length of the ASBO), it said that the making of an ASBO should not be a normal part of the sentencing process, especially if the case did not involve harassment or intimidation:

6.37 We turn to the Anti-Social Behaviour Order. The principal decision of this Court on the use of criminal Anti-Social Behaviour Orders is *R v P (Shane Tony)* [2004] 2 Cr App R(S) 63, page 343. The court held that the test for the use of this power is one of necessity to protect the public from further anti-social acts by the offender. There must be a demonstrable necessity for such an order. Furthermore, where a substantial custodial sentence is being imposed at the same time, on release from which the offender will be on licence and liable to recall, it should not generally be assumed that there is a necessity for this additional power of the court to be invoked. If we had been inclined to uphold the length of this sentence, in the light of that consideration we would have been likely to quash the Anti-Social Behaviour Order. The court held in *R v P (Shane Tony)* that it was wrong to impose such an order on a 15-year-old prolific robber of mobile phones and the like on whom a four-year custodial sentence was being imposed. However, the court did not rule out the use of such an order in appropriate cases and appropriate circumstances. It is clear, in our judgment, that the making of an Anti-social Behaviour Order should not be a normal part of the sentencing process, particularly in cases which do not themselves specifically involve intimidation and harassment. It is a course to be taken in particular circumstances ...[58]

6.38 In *R v McGrath*,[59] the Court of Appeal urged caution: '... ASBOs should be approached with a proper degree of caution and circumspection. They are not cure-alls. They are not lightly to be imposed. The sanction for breach, as we have already outlined, may well be a term of imprisonment – indeed imprisonment for up to five years.'[60]

However, since *P*, in a number of cases including *Rush*, the Court of Appeal has found 'exceptional' reasons for upholding an ASBO coupled with a long period of incarceration.[61]

57 [2005] EWCA Crim 1316.

58 [2005] EWCA Crim 1316 at paras 12 and 13.

59 [2005] EWCA Crim 353.

60 [2005] EWCA Crim 353 at para 12.

61 See for example: *R v Scott Parkinson* [2004] EWCA Crim 2757, *R v Vittles* [2004] EWCA Crim 1089, *R v Hinton* [2006] EWCA Crim 1115. Although see *R v Desmond James* [2006] EWCA Crim 1810 for a recent application of *P*.

.39 All of these authorities were reviewed in *Boness*,[62] and the Court of Appeal made the additional point that the court should not impose an order which prohibits an offender from committing a specified criminal offence if the sentence which could be passed following conviction for the offence should be a sufficient deterrent: '... if the offender is not going to be deterred from committing the offence by a sentence of imprisonment for that offence, the ASBO is not likely (it may be thought) further to deter and is therefore not necessary'.[63]

.40 The propriety of including a term not to commit a criminal offence is discussed in detail in chapter 7.

.41 In *Boness* the court did not rule out an ASBO plus incarceration for serious offences if the terms of the ASBO were, using the example in *P*, a prohibition from places (two parks and an airport) where the offender had committed the robberies he was being sentenced for. They formed the view that such an order would allow those responsible for the safety of the prescribed areas an opportunity to act before a robbery was committed by the offender.

Two ASBOs?

.41A An analysis of the most recent ASBO breach authorities reveals that there seems to be a movement towards applying for a second ASBO if a defendant is convicted of an offence after the imposition of the first ASBO (regardless of whether the first ASBO was stand-alone or post-conviction).[64] Although there has been no reported legal challenge to the imposition of a second ASBO, the propriety of such a course is questionable. If the CPS is relying on evidence that has already been litigated on by another court, this is likely to be an abuse of process.[65] Advisers should examine both applications carefully and consider whether the second application is a collateral attack on the decision of a court of competent jurisdiction. If so, the matter should be listed for an abuse of process hearing. If there is genuine concern from the applicant body that, for example, an exclusion zone is not wide enough and there is new evidence to support this, it is open to the applicant body to seek to vary the terms of the original ASBO

62 [2005] EWCA Crim 2395.

63 [2005] EWCA Crim 2395 at para 31.

64 See, for example, *R v Keith Blackwell* [2006] EWCA Crim 1671 and *R v Melvin Sidney Harris* [2006] EWCA Crim 1864.

65 See *Johnson v Gore Wood & Co* [2001] 2 WLR 72; [2001] 1 All ER 481. See also para 5.124.

(see para 6.44 below). If the CPS is applying for a second ASBO on the basis of the new conviction alone, it is difficult to see how a single incident would satisfy the necessity test (see para 5.107), not least because an ASBO is already in existence.

Variation and discharge

6.42 An offender subject to an ASBO can apply to the court which made it[66] for it to be varied or discharged.[67] As mentioned above, interim orders can also be varied or discharged by either the applicant or the defendant. Such applications are usually made when there has been a material change of circumstances.[68] An order cannot be discharged before the two-year minimum period unless the DPP consents.[69]

6.43 Additionally, the DPP can now apply to the court which made the order to vary or discharge a post-conviction ASBO.[70] Despite the fact other applicant bodies have no role to play in applying for a post-conviction order, a relevant authority may also apply to the court which made the post-conviction order for it to be varied or discharged under CDA 1998 s1C(4), but only if it appears that:

(a) in the case of variation, the protection of relevant persons from anti-social acts by the person subject to the order would be more appropriately effected by the variation of the order;
(b) in the case of discharge, that it is no longer necessary to protect relevant persons from anti-social acts by him by means of such an order.

As with applications for discharge made by the offender, any application to discharge made by the DPP or relevant authority before the end of the two-year period can only be made if the offender consents (of course the likelihood of an offender not consenting to such a course must be less than nil!).

6.44 The changes introduced by SOCPA 2005 include a requirement for the offender to send written notice of the application to vary or discharge to the DPP (and vice versa for the DPP and a relevant

66 By CDA 1998 s1CA(6), if the post-conviction order is made by a magistrates' court, the references to 'the court by which the order was made' in s1C include a reference to any magistrates' court acting in the same local justice area as that court.

67 CDA 1998 s1CA, as inserted by SOCPA 2005 s140.

68 See para 5.138.

69 CDA 1998 s1CA(7)(a).

70 CDA 1998 s1CA (3).

authority).[71] If variation applications by the DPP or a relevant authority attempt to extend the length of the ASBO or re-introduce terms that have already been litigated upon or introduce brand-new terms, they are arguably simply having a second bite at the cherry and are not seeking a 'variation' at all. If they are relying upon new evidence to justify any variation, then the procedural rules in relation to any hearsay evidence will have to be complied with.

.45 Other than the statutory requirement to make the application in writing to the relevant body, there is no other specific procedural rule in the Crown Court as to how the application should be dealt with: the Criminal Procedure Rules make no mention of variation or discharge of post-conviction ASBOs made in the Crown Court or magistrates' court. However, MC(ASBO)R 2002 r6 outlines the procedure for variation or discharge of stand-alone, post-conviction and interim ASBOs. That said, MC(ASBO)R 2002 pre-date the coming into force of the relevant sections of SOCPA 2005 and do not add much by way of procedural guidance.

.46 MC(ASBO)R 2002 r6(1) makes r6 applicable to all orders made under CDA 1998 ss1, 1C or 1D (although applications to discharge or vary without notice interim ASBOs are subject to the right to an oral hearing).[72] Rule 6 (2) reads as follows:

> An application to which this rule applies shall be made in writing to the magistrates' court which made the order, or in the case of an application under section 1C to any magistrates' court in the same local justice area, and shall specify the reason why the applicant for variation or discharge believes the court should vary or discharge the order, as the case may be.

There is no reason at all why the requirement to make an application in writing specifying the reasons for variation or discharge should not also apply to the Crown Court.

.47 Subject to the exception that applies to without notice interim orders, MC(ASBO)R r6(3) entitles the magistrates' court to determine the application without hearing representations from the applicant or any other person if it considers that there are no grounds for variation or discharge. The circumstances in which a court would simply refuse an application for variation without hearing representations (particularly if there is disputed evidence) must be rare. The 2006 Home Office Guidance states that if an individual seeks variation or discharge, 'the agency that obtained the ASBO needs to ensure that a

71 CDA 1998 s1CA (2) and (5).

72 See MC(ASBO)R 2002 r5(8).

considered response is given to the court' and if the application is to be contested, the court should be given reasons 'supported as appropriate by evidence gathered in the course of monitoring the effectiveness of the order'.[73]

6.48 If the court considers that there are grounds, then the designated officer of the magistrates' court must issue a summons giving not less than 14 days' notice in writing to all parties of the date, time and place of the hearing. In the Crown Court, the matter can be listed in the usual way with all parties being put on notice.

The form of the order

6.49 The only time the Criminal Procedure Rules make mention of ASBO procedure is in relation to the form to be used in post-conviction ASBO cases. Rule 50.4 reads as follows:

> *Anti-social behaviour orders made by the Crown Court on conviction*
> 50.4 An order made by the Crown Court under section 1C of the Crime and Disorder Act 1998 ... on conviction in criminal proceedings shall be in the form set out in the Practice Direction.

A copy of the form, which is identical to the form in Schedule 13 to the Crown Court (Amendment) Rules 2002,[74] is contained in appendix F.[75]

6.50 Post-conviction ASBOs in the magistrates' court need not be in a specified form but there is no reason why a form similar to that set out in the Criminal Procedure Rules should not be used. It is the content of the form rather than the form itself that is important. See para 5.32 above for details of what should be contained in the form and the ramifications of failing to complete it properly. The terms of the order are those pronounced in open court as opposed to those recorded on the order. See para 5.135 for a discussion of this issue.

The duty to give reasons for the decision

6.51 See para 5.132.

73 *A Guide to Anti-social Behaviour Orders* (Home Office, 2006), p50. Available at www.together.gov.uk.

74 SI No 2783 introduced on 2 December 2002 at the same time that CDA 1998 s1C came into force, amending the Crown Court Rules 1982.

75 Also available on the DCA website: www.dca.gov.uk.

Reporting restrictions and post-ASBO publicity

5.52 See paras 5.140–5.146 and para 10.48.

Ancillary orders

5.53 There are three ancillary orders which may be available when ASBOs are imposed, a detailed consideration of each of which is beyond the scope of this book.[76] These orders are:

- intervention orders;
- individual support orders;
- parenting orders.

The statutory powers in relation to intervention orders are summarised at para 5.148. As the other two orders are only available in relation to a child or a young person,[77] they are dealt with at para 10.60.

5.54 Furthermore, it is arguable that none of these orders is available in conjunction with post-conviction ASBOs. This is because CDA 1998 distinguishes between the three kinds of ASBO by referring to stand-alone ASBOs as 'anti-social behaviour orders' throughout the Act, to post-conviction ASBOs as 'an order under s1C' and county court ASBOs as 'an order under section 1B'. 'Orders under section 1C' are not mentioned in the context of any of the ancillary orders. In any event, post-conviction ASBOs are imposed in addition to a sentence and it is difficult to imagine any circumstances in which it would be appropriate to impose a second order.

5.55 For a discussion on appeals against ASBOs and interim ASBOs, see chapter 11. For a discussion on costs and public funding, see chapter 12.

76 Readers are referred to the 'Together' website for full details of each of these orders: www.together.gov.uk/.

77 See chapter 10 for a definition of 'child' and 'young person'.

Reporting restrictions and post-ASBO publicity

[illegible]

Ancillary orders

[illegible]

- [illegible]
- [illegible]
- parenting orders

[illegible]

CHAPTER 7

Terms and duration of ASBOs

Introduction

7.1 This chapter is devoted to the complex question of appropriate ASBO terms as well as the length of ASBOs. The case law in this area is extensive and at times contradictory, particularly on the controversial issue of whether the prohibition on committing a criminal offence can be properly included as an ASBO term. The chapter also examines the inter-relation between ECHR Article 8 and certain ASBO terms and explores the concept of proportionality.

The nature of the prohibitions

7.2 If the statutory test is made out, then the court *may* make an order that prohibits an offender from doing anything described in the order. This applies to all types of ASBO applications: stand-alones, post-conviction and county court (see CDA 1998 ss1(4), 1(C)(2) and 1B (4)). It is worth noting that the court does not have to make an order even when both limbs of the test are satisfied (see para 5.41 for a discussion of this issue).

7.3 As mentioned in chapter 5, the purpose of the prohibitions is to prevent the behaviour complained of from re-occurring. Prohibitions should not be aimed at punishing a defendant but should target the specific anti-social behaviour identified in the first limb of the test. Further, in order for a prohibition to be effective, it must be enforceable. In order to be lawful, it must be set out in negative terms. It should also be in clear language and it should be proportionate (these requirements are discussed in more detail below). In summary, a prohibition must be:

- proportionate;
- expressed in clear language;
- preventative not punitive;
- enforceable;
- in negative terms.

7.4 There is now a large body of case law and other guidance about the effective drafting of prohibitions. The case law has evolved since the inception of ASBOs in 1999 and most of the authorities are dealt with below. The most important authority to date on the nature and purpose of prohibitions is *R v Boness and Bebbington*[1] (already referred

1 [2005] EWCA Crim 2395.

to in chapters 5 and 6). While it is decided in the context of post-conviction ASBOs, it is of general importance. It is particularly useful because the Court of Appeal reviewed in detail the individual prohibitions in the ASBOs imposed upon each one of the eleven defendants in that case, giving practitioners a good insight into the kinds of terms which are deemed to be acceptable and those which are not. It is, in fact, compulsory reading.

7.5 When considering the propriety of a particular prohibition, practitioners may also wish to refer to the 2003 Home Office Guidance[2] and chapter 2 and Annex B of the *ASBO Guidance for the Judiciary*[3] compiled by a working party set up by Lord Justice Thomas. Both guides are cited in *Boness*[4] in the context of the helpful guidance they offer on the nature of prohibitions. However, neither guide has legal force and should not be treated as such. *ASBO Guidance for the Judiciary* suggests at paragraph 2.2 that the 2003 Home Office Guidance was 'approved and endorsed' by the Court of Appeal in *R v P (Shane Tony)*[5] but a reading of that judgment reveals no such approval or endorsement of the whole of the Guidance. The court in that case commented that it contained 'helpful instruction as to the drafting of such orders'.[6]

Prohibitions and ECHR rights: the concept of proportionality

7.6 Many ASBO prohibitions will engage a defendant's Article 8 rights (the right to private and family life); or Article 10 rights (freedom of expression); or Article 11 rights (freedom of association) (see appendix E where the articles are replicated in full).[7] If prohibitions are so extreme that a person's liberty is interfered with, then

2 *Guide to Anti-social Behaviour and Acceptable Behaviour Contracts* (2003) p34. A new version of the Guidance was published on 1 August 2006 and is available at www.together.gov.uk. See, in particular, pp29–32.

3 Published in May 2005. Available at www.youth-justice-board.gov.uk.

4 [2005] EWCA Crim 2395, paras 21–24.

5 [2004] EWCA Crim 287.

6 [2004] EWCA Crim 287 at para 29.

7 See also *Archbold* 2006, chapter 16, which details each of the rights guaranteed by the ECHR and summarises the relevant case law.

Article 5 (the right to liberty) may be engaged.[8] Article 8 is the right most commonly engaged in the context of ASBO applications (for example a prohibition on entering an area in which family members live or a prohibition on associating with a particular friend or friends may interfere with a person's personal development, see below).

ECHR Article 8

7.7 Article 8 is intended to protect people from arbitrary interference by the state with their private and family life, home and correspondence. It also imposes a positive obligation on the state to actively respect private and family life.[9]

7.8 'Private life' is a broad concept, the definition of which includes the moral, psychological and physical integrity of the person.[10] In *Botta v Italy*, the court explained that:

> Private life, in the court's view, includes a person's physical and psychological integrity; the guarantee afforded by article 8 is primarily intended to ensure the development, without outside interference, of the personality of each individual in his relations with other human beings.[11]

7.9 Relationships are essential to a person's personal development and thus his or her 'private life'. Relationships are not limited to an 'inner circle' but extend to those formed in the course of working lives.[12]

7.10 'Family life' is not confined to the nuclear family: it incorporates a number of other relationships including, for example, unmarried couples in a stable relationship (even if they are not living together),[13] siblings,[14] uncles and aunts and nieces and nephews,[15] grandparents

8 See, for example, *Guzzardi v Italy* (1980) 3 EHRR 333, discussed in detail in chapter 3. See also *Secretary of State for the Home Department v JJ and others* [2006] EWCA Civ 1141 in which the Court of Appeal found control orders imposed under the Prevention of Terrorism Act 2005 to be a deprivation of liberty and therefore in breach of Article 5.

9 *Marckx v Belgium* (1979) 2 EHRR 330 at para 31.

10 *Niemietz v Germany* (1993) 16 EHRR 97; *Stubbings v UK* (1997) 23 EHRR 213; *Botta v Italy* (1998) 26 EHRR 241; and *Von Hannover v Germany* (2005) 40 EHRR 1.

11 (1998) 26 EHRR 241 at para 32.

12 *Niemietz v Germany* (1993) 16 EHRR 97 at para 29.

13 *Kroon v Netherlands* (1995) 19 EHRR 263 (the couple in this case had four children although they did not live together).

14 *Moustaquim v Belgium* (1991) 13 EHRR 802.

15 *Boyle v UK* (1995) 19 EHRR 179.

and grandchildren.[16] In *Ghaidan v Godin-Mendoza,*[17] a case involving a human rights challenge to an aspect of housing law, the House of Lords said that 'a homosexual couple, as much as a heterosexual couple, share each other's life and make their home together'.

Qualifications on the rights protected

7.11 The scheme of ECHR Articles 8–11 is first to set out the positive right protected and then circumscribe the grounds upon which it can legitimately be restricted (for example, the prevention of crime and disorder or the protection of the rights and freedoms of others are legitimate aims: see appendix E where the articles are replicated in full). So while an ASBO term may infringe Article 8, it may be justified (for example, it may be necessary to impose the term to prevent crime and disorder).

7.12 However Strasbourg jurisprudence over the years has established the following ways of interpreting restrictions on such rights: restrictions on qualified rights must be narrowly construed,[18] be prescribed by law, have a legitimate aim and be necessary in a democratic society. 'Necessity' in the context of these Convention rights implies the existence of a 'pressing social need'.[19] Furthermore, proportionality is also part of the necessity test, ie any interference must be proportionate to the legitimate aim pursued.[20] The burden of establishing that the interference is proportionate lies on the state.[21]

What is proportionality?

7.13 In *De Freitas v Permanent Secretary of Ministry of Agriculture, Fisheries, Lands and Housing*[22] the Privy Council said that in determining whether a limitation (by an Act, rule or decision) is arbitrary or excessive (ie, not proportionate) a court should ask itself three questions:

> (1) whether the legislative objective is sufficiently important to justify limiting a fundamental right;

16 *Marckx v Belgium* (1979) 2 EHRR 330 at para. 45.

17 [2004] 3 WLR 113. See also *Fitzpatrick v Sterling Housing Association Ltd* [2001] 1 AC 27, HL.

18 *Sunday Times v UK (No 2)* (1992) 14 EHRR 123 at para 50.

19 *Sunday Times v UK (No 2)* (1992) 14 EHRR 123.

20 The link between necessity and proportionality was first made in *Handyside v UK* (1979–80) 1 EHRR 737.

21 See for example *Smith & Grady v UK* (1999) 29 EHRR 493 at para 73.

22 [1999] 1 AC 69, PC, Lord Clyde at p80.

(2) whether the measures designed to meet the legislative objective are rationally connected to it; and
(3) whether the means used to impair the right or freedom are no more than is necessary to accomplish that objective.

7.14 The leading post-HRA 1998 case on how to approach an interference with a qualified right (in that case Article 8) is the House of Lords decision in *R v Secretary of State for the Home Department ex p Daly*,[23] which approved the test in *De Freitas* and described it as defining 'the contours of the principle of proportionality'.[24] The use of the term 'necessary' in CDA 1998 is directed at the protection of relevant persons or persons in England and Wales from further anti-social acts by a defendant ('the legislative objective'). Even if a court decides that a particular prohibition is necessary to achieve that end, if such a prohibition infringes upon a fundamental human right such as Article 8, it must also consider whether the term is proportionate.

7.15 When considering proportionality, the questions to bear in mind are:

- Can the conduct that is sought to be prohibited be prevented in any other way?
- Do the prohibitions go no further than is strictly necessary to serve the end they are intended to serve?
- Or are they arbitrary and excessive?

7.16 This approach was confirmed in *Boness*:[25]

> Not only must the court before imposing an order prohibiting the offender from doing something consider that such an order is necessary to protect persons from further anti-social acts by him, the terms of the order must be commensurate with the risk to be guarded against. This is particularly important where an order may interfere with an ECHR right protected by the Human Rights Act 1998, eg Articles 8, 10 and 11.

Geographical exclusion zones and ECHR Article 8

7.17 If a defendant is receiving support or services from the local community, then a term prohibiting access to such services or support will engage Article 8 as the defendant's 'private life' is affected. 'Support or services' could include for example:

23 [2001] UKHL 26.
24 [2001] UKHL 26, Lord Steyn at para 27.
25 [2005] EWCA Crim 2395 at para 38.

- drug rehabilitation;
- a drop-in centre;
- a homeless project;
- a drug dependency unit;
- a particular chemist to get a methadone script;
- an Alcoholics Anonymous or Narcotics Anonymous group;
- free meals;
- a church group;
- probation services;
- Youth Offending Team (YOT);
- regular medical treatment;
- after-school clubs.

7.18 In order to argue effectively that such a prohibition is a disproportionate interference with that right, it is important to obtain details of the support being received and its exact geographical location. Witness statements (from probation officers, hostel workers, support workers, drugs workers) should be taken to demonstrate the importance of maintaining those particular relationships in that particular locality. It may be difficult to obtain statements from social workers or YOT workers if they are employed by the local authority which is applying for the ASBO. This is a particular problem with children in care (see para 10.35). Practitioners should give consideration to applying for a witness summons (or order in the county court) in such a situation, although the fact that this may alienate the witness cannot be discounted. However, the use of a witness summons or order may be required, even if the social worker or other professional is willing to give favourable evidence, in order that the witness is given protection against his or her employer.

7.19 It is equally important to obtain witness statements from family members or close friends who rely upon the defendant for any of their support needs. All the evidence should deal in specifics and explain how exclusion from a particular area would leave the defendant isolated and deprived of contact with her/his family and/or friends.

Exclusion zones and 'hot spots'

7.20 Some local authorities rely upon Crime and Disorder Audits (carried out pursuant to CDA 1998 and PRA 2002) to establish the existence of alleged drug and other crime 'hot spots'. Using this evidence, they then seek orders excluding defendants from those zones as well as neighbouring zones, to avoid what is called 'displacement' (for example, not to enter the London Boroughs of Camden and Islington and the City of

Westminster). However, if this argument is taken to its logical conclusion, a defendant would simply move to the next 'hot spot', and eventually there would be nowhere in England and Wales for a defendant to live. Additionally, it may simply serve to move the problem on without addressing the root causes.

7.21 Practitioners should ensure that the witness who can speak to such a report is required to attend the full hearing. Drug 'hot spotting' is not an exact science, especially as the spots move and change frequently, depending on a variety of external factors. Typically, a community police officer or anti-social behaviour co-ordinator will have compiled a report about these problem areas and then purport to give 'expert' opinion on the likelihood of a defendant moving to another 'hot spot' if excluded from his or her present location. One way of challenging such theories is to instruct a criminologist. There is a handful of such experts who are familiar with the 'science' of 'hot spotting' as well as the theory of 'displacement' in the context of ASBO applications. They can be very effective in showing that 'hot spotting' is an unreliable 'science'.

Clear and precise language

7.22 The terms should be clear, precise, unambiguous and expressed in simple language so that they can be understood by all (particularly bearing in mind issues of age, educational attainment and intellectual ability).[26] The findings of fact giving rise to the making of the order must be recorded, the exact terms of the order must be explained to the offender and pronounced in open court and the written order must accurately reflect the order as pronounced.[27] In *Boness* the Court of Appeal reinforced the point: 'Because an ASBO must obviously be precise and capable of being understood by the offender, a court should ask itself before making an order: "Are the terms of this order clear so that the offender will know precisely what he is prohibited from doing?"'[28] A term will not be clear if a breach cannot be readily identified or proved. Excluded areas must be clearly delineated. A map should be attached. Lines should not be drawn in the middle of roads as a defendant may not know if he or she is on the right side.

26 *B v Chief Constable of Avon & Somerset Constabulary* (2001) 1 WLR 340; (2001) 1 All ER 5; *R (C) v Sunderland Youth Court* [2003] EWHC 2385; *R v P (Shane Tony)* [2004] EWCA Crim 287.

27 *R v P (Shane Tony)* [2004] EWCA Crim 287.

28 [2005] EWCA Crim 2395 at para 20.

Unacceptably wide terms and their effect on breach proceedings

.23 There have been a number of cases in the Divisional Court and Court of Appeal (Criminal Division) considering the width or propriety of various prohibitions. Although some of those cases turn on their own facts, it is useful to look at the kinds of terms the higher courts have found to be unacceptably wide. The widest ever ASBO term imposed to date is the one in *R (W) v DPP*[29] which was an order not to commit 'any criminal offence'. The Divisional Court had no doubt that it was too widely drawn. W was only 14 years old at the relevant time and the Court formed the view that he might well not know what amounted to a criminal offence.

.24 What happens when a breach is alleged of a too widely drawn order? Despite conflicting decisions on the issue (discussed below), an order is valid until it is set aside, however badly drafted, wide or unenforceable it may be. In other words, a defendant *may* be liable for any breach of an ASBO committed before it is set aside.

.25 In *W*, the defendant stole sweets and a bottle of Lucozade after the ASBO described above was imposed. He was convicted of breaching the ASBO. The Divisional Court (Brooke LJ, Field J) held that the order not to commit a criminal offence was so wide it was plainly invalid and the conviction for the breach should effectively be set aside. The decision in this case was based on a concession by the respondent that a case called *Boddington v BTP*[30] was authority for the proposition that if an ASBO term is plainly invalid, then a court dealing with an alleged breach can refuse to act on it.

.26 This judgment has been criticised in the very careful judgment given in *CPS v T (Michael)*.[31] That Divisional Court (Richards LJ and Clarke J) formed the view that the concession on which the court acted in *W* was wrongly made and declined to follow it. It is submitted that the reasoning in *T* is correct since it reflects the normal rule in civil proceedings that an order of the court remains valid unless it is set aside. The Court in *T* did go on to say that a wide and uncertain order (in this case a prohibition on acting 'in an anti-social manner in the City of Manchester'), did not leave a magistrates' court

29 [2005] EWCA Civ 1333.

30 [1999] 2 AC 143.

31 [2006] EWHC 728 (Admin). This case is part 2 of the decision in *R (T) v Manchester Crown Court* [2005] EWHC 1396, referred to at para 5.31 on the issue of 'consent'.

in a position whereby it was compelled to convict the defendant for breaching the ASBO when he subsequently pleaded guilty to interfering with a motor vehicle:

> It does not follow that the District Judge lacked any means of giving effect to the concerns he had about width and uncertainty of the order. It was open to him to consider whether the relevant provision lacked sufficient clarity to warrant a finding that the respondent's conduct amounted to a breach of the order; and whether if a breach was established, it was appropriate in the circumstances to impose any penalty for the breach ...[32]

The death of the prohibition on anti-social conduct?

7.27 The decision in *T* is important for another reason. The Court found that T (who was aged 13 at the time the two-year ASBO was made) could not be taken to know the ambit of the words 'act in an anti-social manner' or indeed the geographical ambit of the City of Manchester. Such a prohibition was not just inappropriate for young people. The Court went on to say: 'In our judgment, such a wide provision as 'not to act in an anti-social manner', without further definition or limitation, should never again be included in an ASBO.'[33] If the definition of 'anti-social manner' included the explanatory words contained in the statutory definition, namely the words 'that is to say in a manner that caused or was likely to cause harassment, alarm or distress to one or more persons not of the same household as himself', it is unlikely that a court would interfere with it. That said, a prohibition worded so may not be appropriate for young defendants, such as T and W. In *Boness* such a prohibition was not disapproved of in relation to an adult but the court said that it would prefer some geographical limit in the absence of good reasons for having no such limit.[34]

Further examples of unacceptable terms

7.28 In *R v Mcgrath*[35] a prohibition from entering any car park in Hertfordshire, Bedfordshire and Buckinghamshire was considered unjustifiably draconian and too wide. The Court of Appeal also quashed a prohibition on 'trespassing on any land belonging to any person whether legal or natural' within the same three counties, as well as a

32 [2006] EWHC 728 (Admin) at para 37.
33 [2006] EWHC 728 (Admin) at para 46.
34 [2005] EWCA Crim 2395 at para 78.
35 [2005] EWCA Crim 353.

prohibition framed as follows: 'having in his possession in any public place any window hammer, screwdriver, torch or any tool or implement which could be used for the purposes of breaking into motor vehicles'. The court found them both to be unjustifiably wide. The use of the words 'tool or implement' was criticised on the basis that the meaning of those words was impossible to ascertain.

7.29 In *Boness* numerous provisions were struck out as being unnecessary or too wide or too vague or too difficult to understand. Each decision has to be read in the context of the facts that led to the making of the order, therefore each quashed term is not repeated here. However, there are some that will have general application and are worth repeating. The following prohibition (or a variation of it) is commonly suggested in ASBO applications to prevent the wearing of 'hoodies':

> In any public place, wearing, or having with you, anything which covers, or could be used to cover, the face or part of the face. This will include hooded clothing, balaclavas, masks or anything else which could be used to hide identity, except that a motorcycle helmet may be worn only when lawfully riding a motorcycle.[36]

7.30 It was presumed in *Boness* that this prohibition was based upon an assertion that the defendant was 'forensically aware' and would use items to prevent detection. The Court agreed with the submissions that, first, the terms were too wide, resulting in a lack of clarity and consequences which were not commensurate with the risk the prohibition sought to address and, second, the phrase 'having with you anything which covers ... the face' incorporates a huge number of items including a jumper, a scarf and a newspaper.

7.31 Another prohibition that was found to be both unclear and disproportionate was: 'Having any item with you in public which could be used in the commission of a burglary, or theft from vehicles except that you may carry one door key for your house and one motor vehicle or bicycle lock key ...'[37] The Court agreed with the submission that a credit card, a mobile phone or a pair of gloves could be used in the commission of a burglary and yet the term as drafted would prevent such items being carried.

7.32 In *R v H, Stevens and Lovegrove,*[38] a post-conviction ASBO term preventing a 16-year-old boy from returning to his home after release from custody was varied on the basis that it 'would be a troublesome

36 [2005] EWCA Crim 2395 at para 60.

37 [2005] EWCA Crim 2395 at para 63.

38 [2006] EWCA Crim 255.

start to his rehabilitation' and likely to reduce the prospects of successful rehabilitation. The Court varied this term of its own motion as the point was not taken by the appellant. Although the point did not arise, an exclusion of a youth from his parents' home for a period of ten years would undoubtedly be in breach of Article 8.

In *R v Keith Blackwell*,[39] the term 'consuming, being under the influence of, or in possession of any intoxicating liquor in a public place' was replaced with 'Not to be in a state of drunkennness in any public place in England and Wales'.

Prohibitions must be negative

7.33 Orders should contain terms which are prohibitions directed to the anti-social behaviour. Negative prohibitions, which are in truth mandatory orders to do something 'specific', are not permissible (for example: not to reside at any address other than XYZ). In *R (M) v Sheffield Magistrates' Court* (a case discussed in full in chapter 10 in the context of children in local authority care), Newman J made the following *obiter* comment:[40]

> Orders should contain prohibitions directed to the anti-social behaviour. Care should be taken not to include by negative prohibitions what in truth amount to mandatory orders to do something specific. In this instance, a condition of residence was imposed by prohibiting M from living other than at one address. It is unnecessary in this case to decide whether the order as granted was outside the Act.

7.34 In *R (Ashley Lonergan) v Lewes Crown Court*,[41] the prohibition challenged by way of judicial review was in these terms:

> Being in any place other than 30 Stephens Road, or 16 Brentwood Road or 41 Brentwood Road or 35 Hodshrove Road, Brighton (or any other address as directed by the Youth Offending Team), or moving between those addresses, between the hours of 11.30 pm and 06.00 am.

The High Court (Maurice Kay LJ giving the judgment of the Court) found this to be prohibitory and not mandatory:

> Whatever words are used, the essence of a curfew is a positive obligation to remain in a certain place for a specified time. The positive

39 [2006] EWCA Crim 1671.

40 [2004] EWHC 1830 (Admin) at para 57.

41 [2005] EWHC 457 (Admin).

> or mandatory substance cannot be circumvented by expressing it in a superficially negative prohibition ... Whilst I accept that the statute requires the order to be substantially and not just formally prohibitory, I am satisfied that the restraint upon leaving or travelling between specified premises between particular times meets that test.[42]

7.35 There is therefore nothing legally objectionable in the inclusion of a curfew provision in an anti-social behaviour order if it is necessary for the protection of others. The Court commented that there was nothing in Newman J's *obiter* remarks that were inconsistent with that conclusion. It was unimpressed with the further argument advanced by the claimant that a curfew is a penalty. The Court had no doubt that, although a curfew restricted freedom of movement, its purpose was preventative and not punitive when imposed as a term of an ASBO. Importantly, the Court also pointed out that, although an ASBO had to run for a minimum of two years, it did not follow that every prohibition within the order had to endure for the life of the order.[43]

> ... I do think that it behoves magistrates' courts to consider carefully the need for and duration of a curfew provision when making an ASBO. Just because the ASBO must run for a minimum of two years it does not follow that each and every prohibition within a particular order must endure for the life of the order. A curfew for two years in the life of a teenager is a very considerable restriction of freedom. It may be necessary but in many cases I consider it likely that either the period of the curfew could properly be set at less than the full life of the order, or that in the light of behavioural progress, an application to vary the curfew under section 1(8) might well succeed.

This aspect of Maurice Kay LJ's judgment, although doubted in *ASBO Guidance for the Judiciary*,[44] was specifically approved in *Boness*.[45]

Prohibition on committing a crime: a misuse of power?

7.36 There is some conflict between higher court authorities on this point. In *R v P (Shane Tony)*[46] the Court of Appeal, presided over by Lord

42 [2005] EWHC 457 (Admin) at para 7.

43 [2005] EWHC 457 (Admin) at para 13.

44 Published in May 2005. Available at www.youth-justice-board.gov.uk/PractitionersPortal/CourtsAndOrders/Disposals/ASBOs/.

45 [2005] EWCA Crim 2395 at para 27.

46 [2004] EWCA Crim 287.

Woolf CJ (as he then was), did not find that there was any objection in principle to including an order that prohibits the commission of a criminal offence:

> ... it is submitted that the prohibitions imposed by paragraphs 2 and 7 are redundant as they prohibit conduct which is already subject to a general prohibition by the Public Order Act 1986 and the Prevention of Crime Act 1953 respectively. In that regard we are by no means persuaded that the inclusion of such matters is to be actively discouraged. So far as minor matters are concerned, we take the view that there is no harm in reminding offenders that certain matters do constitute criminal conduct, although we would only encourage the inclusion of relatively minor criminal offences in the terms of such orders.[47]

7.37 However, the fact that an ASBO may be used to give a court a greater sentencing power following breach than would have been available if a defendant had been convicted of the substantive offence has caused the Court of Appeal some consternation. Initially, in *R v Hall*,[48] the Court of Appeal following *P*, saw no difficulty with a prohibition from driving without a licence, the breach of which would result in up to five years' imprisonment, while if he was convicted of the criminal offence, the offender could only receive a maximum of six months. The Court of Appeal was unconcerned despite the fact that the judge in that case had said the following to the defendant:

> If you drive a motor car in this country on a public road without getting through a test and getting a licence after your period of disqualification, you will be in breach of this order and you will not then be liable merely to six months' imprisonment for driving whilst disqualified, you will be liable to imprisonment of up to five years.

7.38 Subsequently, in the case of *R v Kirby*[49] decided in May 2005, after *Hall*, but with no reference to it, the Court of Appeal put the brakes on ASBOs which prohibited driving while disqualified. The Crown Court judge in *Kirby* imposed an ASBO prohibiting him from driving or attempting to drive until the expiration of his period of disqualification. The defendant was also prohibited from driving, attempting to drive or allowing himself to be carried in a vehicle taken without

47 It should be noted that in *Boness* the Court of Appeal pointed out that the test for making an ASBO was not whether an offender needed reminding that certain matters do constitute criminal conduct, but whether it was necessary: [2005] EWCA Crim 2395 at para 32.

48 [2004] EWCA Crim 26.

49 [2005] EWCA Crim 1228.

consent. The judge had told the defendant that 'it actually increases the penalty that the courts can impose on you for those offences, which are now maximum six months. It increases the penalty to five years.' Quashing the ASBO, the Court of Appeal said this:

7.39 > ... to make an anti-social behaviour order in a case such as the present case, where the underlying objective was to give the court higher sentencing powers in the event of future similar offending, is not a use of the power which should normally be exercised ...
>
> In our judgment the making of an order of this sort should not be a normal part of a sentencing process, particularly in cases which do not in themselves specifically involve intimidation, harassment and distress. It is an exceptional course to be taken in particular circumstances. There was, in our judgment, nothing in this case, despite the deplorable record of the appellant for offences of this sort, to justify the use of this power in the present case. Its effect was no more than to transform any such offence into a different offence, namely breach of an anti-social behaviour order, so as to increase the potential penalty. In our judgment that was unwarranted in this case in the absence of exceptional circumstances.[50]

7.40 In *R v Theo Yestin Williams*[51] the Court of Appeal heard full argument from both sides (*Kirby* and *Hall* were both appeals against sentence where only the appellant was represented) and preferred *Kirby* over *Hall*. It quashed an ASBO prohibiting the defendant from driving until the expiration of his disqualification period. In *R v Morrison*[52] and *R v Lawson*[53] (both driving cases) the Court of Appeal again followed and endorsed *Kirby*. In *Lawson* the term of the ASBO was '... not to own nor borrow any motor vehicle or occupy the driver's seat of a motor vehicle on a road or other public place until further order.' The Court quashed it on the basis of the reasoning in *Kirby*.

7.41 In *Morrison* the term of the ASBO prohibited the appellant, a disqualified driver, from being in the front or passenger seat of any motor vehicle in England and Wales. The Court (a two judge court comprising Hughes J and Goldring J) made the point that, while driving while disqualified on its own would not usually cause harassment, alarm or distress,[54] the order was appropriate since the appellant was also drink driving. Unlike the other cases mentioned, *Morrison* was an appeal against sentence for the breach of an ASBO as opposed to

50 [2005] EWCA Crim 1228 at paras 9 and 11.

51 [2005] EWCA Crim 1796.

52 [2005] EWCA Crim 2237.

53 [2005] EWCA Crim 1840.

54 See para 5.5.

an appeal against the ASBO itself. Indeed there had never been an appeal against the ASBO. Instead the Court asked this question:

> ... if an anti-social behaviour order is made which has the effect of prohibiting behaviour which would in any event be a criminal offence, then the question arises: what is the proper approach to sentencing if the offender subsequently commits such a criminal offence and in consequence is also in breach of the ASBO?[55]

7.42 It answered the question by considering the statutory maximum for driving while disqualified:

> The maximum has been fixed by Parliament; it is fixed at six months. It is not open to this Court to evade that maximum by imposing an Anti-Social Behaviour Order and then taking advantage of the maximum for breach of that order in the event that a further offence is committed. That, we are satisfied, follows from *R v Kirby* and *R v Williams*, and we are satisfied also that it follows from elementary principles.[56]

The Court quashed the sentence of 12 months imposed for the breach and reduced it to four months.

7.43 Following these cases the position seemed quite clear: the *Kirby* principle was one approved of by the Court of Appeal: it was wrong in principle in most cases to impose an ASBO where the underlying objective was to give the court a higher sentencing power in the event of future similar offending. If the ASBO was not appealed and was subsequently breached, then the *Morrison* approach would apply. This was a fair and principled way of dealing with the potential abuse of ASBOs by the lower courts. Parliament had after all determined the maximum penalty available for all criminal offences and the House of Lords in *McCann*[57] had decided that ASBOs are preventative, not punitive. How could it be permissible therefore to simply increase the statutory maximum for persistent offenders with whom the court had lost all patience by imposing an ASBO term which was equivalent or identical to a criminal offence, knowing it would be breached?

7.44 The question is a complex one. Terms of ASBOs can turn non-criminal behaviour into crimes when breached (ie a prohibition on entering a particular location may result in a prison term if disobeyed). The statute permits that. So why is it impermissible to give

55 [2005] EWCA Crim 2237 at para 13.

56 [2005] EWCA Crim 2237 at para 19.

57 *R (on the application of McCann) v Crown Court at Manchester; Clingham v Kensington and Chelsea Royal Borough Council* [2002] UKHL 39; [2003] 1 AC 787.

courts the power to increase the sentence for those who persist in committing them? The answer must lie in the purpose of the term. Is it *necessary* to protect people from further anti-social acts (see chapter 5) or is it simply a device to keep a persistent offender off the streets and in prison for longer periods?

7.45 In *Hall, Kirby, Williams, Morrison* and *Lawson* the ASBO term really did nothing other than increase the existing penalty for driving while disqualified. Numerous past disqualifications and present sentences did not act as a sufficient deterrent for any of these defendants. The ASBO in each case had no other purpose than to increase the penalty. It did not try to prevent behaviour which led, for example, to the anti-social driving. It is submitted that the Court of Appeal was right to put a stop to this practice for that reason and, despite conflicting authorities since *Morrison* (discussed below), it remains the proper approach in such cases.

7.46 In *Boness* the Court of Appeal conducted a comprehensive review of the significant post-conviction ASBO decisions of the Court of Appeal and Divisional Court. It did not consider *Morrison* and other breach authorities (some of which conflicted with *Morrison*). None of the 11 appellants it was considering was subject to a prohibition from driving but nonetheless the Court of Appeal examined the principle. It too preferred *Kirby* over *Hall*.[58] It explained the importance of preventative measures:

> There is another reason why a court should be reluctant to impose an order which prohibits an offender from, or merely from, committing a specified criminal offence. The aim of an ASBO is to prevent anti-social behaviour. To prevent it the police or other authorities need to be able to take action before the anti-social behaviour it is designed to prevent takes place. If, for example, a court is faced by an offender who causes criminal damage by spraying graffiti then the order should be aimed at facilitating action to be taken to prevent graffiti spraying by him and/or his associates before it takes place. An order in clear and simple terms preventing the offender from being in possession of a can of spray paint in a public place gives the police or others responsible for protecting the property an opportunity to take action in advance of the actual spraying and makes it clear to the offender that he has lost the right to carry such a can for the duration of the order.[59]

7.47 Of course there is a risk of a person being criminalised for being in possession of spray paint in a public place. But that is a different (and political) issue. Is there a legal bar to such a term or is it precisely what

58 See para 7.40 above.

59 [2005] EWCA Crim 2395 at para 36.

was intended by CDA 1998? The first question to consider is whether the persistent spraying of graffiti caused or was likely to cause harassment, alarm or distress (see para 5.54). Assuming that, on the facts, a particular bout or bouts of graffiti spraying did satisfy both limbs of the statutory test in CDA 1998 s1, a term preventing the possession of a can of spray paint in a public place is clear, concise, designed to prevent further graffiti writing, potentially proportionate and strictly preventative.

7.48 Addressing the issue of anti- social driving (speeding and racing), the Court suggested the following:

> If a court wishes to make an order prohibiting a group of youngsters from racing cars or motor bikes on an estate or driving at excessive speed (anti-social behaviour for those living on the estate), then the order should not (normally) prohibit driving whilst disqualified. It should prohibit, for example, the offender whilst on the estate from taking part in, or encouraging, racing or driving at excessive speed. It might also prevent the group from congregating with named others in a particular area of the estate. Such an order gives those responsible for enforcing order on the estate the opportunity to take action to prevent the anti-social conduct, it is to be hoped, before it takes place. Neighbours can alert the police who will not have to wait for the commission of a particular criminal offence. The ASBO will be breached not just by the offender driving but by his giving encouragement by being a passenger or a spectator. It matters not for the purposes of enforcing the ASBO whether he has or has not a driving licence entitling him to drive.[60]

7.49 In this passage the Court demonstrates the difference between using an ASBO to punish those who persistently commit a particular crime and the prevention of anti-social conduct that causes or is likely to cause harassment, alarm or distress. That said, the judgment in *Boness* is not quite the end of the story on whether the prohibition of a particular crime in an ASBO is permissible.

7.50 In *R v H, Stevens and Lovegrove*,[61] the term of the ASBO that was breached in Stevens' case was the prohibition on being drunk in a public place. He was sentenced to nine months' imprisonment. On appeal it was argued, relying on *Morrison*, that this was wrong in principle given that the statutory maximum sentence for being drunk in a public place was a fine. The Court of Appeal (presided over by Sir Igor Judge, president of the Queen's Bench Division) considered this proposition in light of three other breach cases, not considered in

60 [2005] EWCA Crim 2395 at para 37.

61 [2006] EWCA Crim 255.

Boness, namely *R v Braxton*,[62] *R v Tripp*[63] and *R v Lamb*.[64] All three of these cases were in conflict with *Morrison*.[65] In each of these differently constituted Courts of Appeal, the Court did not find that there was anything wrong in principle in ASBO breach cases to punish behaviour which was also equivalent to a criminal offence with a greater penalty than the statutory maximum for the offence. The court in *H, Stevens and Lovegrove* declined to follow *Morrison*:

51 ... It is obvious that when passing sentence for breach of an anti-social behaviour order, the court is sentencing for the offence of being in breach of that order. Plainly, any sentence, in any court, must be proportionate or, to use the word with which all sentencers are familiar, 'commensurate'. Therefore, if the conduct which constitutes the breach of the anti-social behaviour order is also a distinct criminal offence, and the maximum sentence for the offence is limited to, say, six months' imprisonment, that is a feature to be borne in mind by the sentencing court in the interests of proportionality. It cannot, however, be right that the court's power is thereupon limited to the six months maximum imprisonment for the distinct criminal offence. That would treat the breach as if it were a stand-alone offence, which at the time when it was committed did not amount to a breach of the court order. In reality, the breach is a distinct offence in its own right, created by statute, punishable by up to five years' imprisonment. We therefore reject the submission that it was wrong in principle for the judge to have imposed a custodial sentence, where, for the instant offence of drunkenness, the maximum sentence would have been a fine. To the extent that the submission of the appellant on this particular aspect of the appeal is supported by *Morrison*, we respectfully conclude that its authority has been wholly undermined.[66]

52 The Court did not, however, seek to over-rule the principle established in the *Kirby* line of cases, approved of in *Boness*. It made a distinction between cases where the inclusion of a distinct criminal offence was used as a device to circumvent statutory maximums and those where an ASBO term was appropriately imposed to prevent harassment, alarm or distress caused by anti-social behaviour:

For the avoidance of controversy, we must add that we are not suggesting, and should not be taken to suggest, that an ASBO should be imposed as a kind of device to circumvent maximum penalties

62 [2005] 1 Cr App R(S) 167.

63 [2005] EWCA Crim 2253.

64 [2005] EWCA Crim 2487.

65 These cases are also discussed in chapter 9.

66 [2006] EWCA Crim 255 at paras 26 and 27.

which are believed to be too modest. That is a distinct point which does not arise here. The principle is covered by two decisions of this Court, *R v Kerby* [*sic*] [2005] EWCA Crim 1228 and *R v Boness* [2005] EWCA Crim 2395. As we repeat, that is a distinct principle which relates to the circumstances in which it is proper to make an ASBO, not to the consequences which may follow its breach.[67]

7.53 Unless and until the House of Lords considers all of these authorities, the principles to be extrapolated are as follows:

- The purpose of an ASBO is to prevent the recurrence of particular anti-social behaviour. The court should begin by considering in each case whether the conduct complained of caused or was likely to cause harassment, alarm or distress. If it does not, an ASBO should not be made as the statutory test has not been satisfied.
- Any prohibition should be designed to prevent the particular behaviour complained of. This may mean that it is inappropriate to impose an ASBO that simply prohibits a distinct criminal offence. *Boness* makes plain that courts should be reluctant to take such a course.
- *Kirby* remains good law but its effect is to restrain courts from using ASBOs as a device to circumvent statutory maximums.
- In so far as the decision in *Morrison* prohibits a greater sentence for a breach than is available for the equivalent criminal offence, it is wrong and should not be followed. However, sentencing courts should only impose sentences for breaches that are commensurate with the seriousness of the offence in the ordinary way. Where the conduct amounting to a breach is also a distinct criminal offence, the court should bear in mind the statutory maximum when considering what sentence is commensurate.[68]

7.54 It is not always possible to know when a court is deliberately using an ASBO as a 'device' and when it is not. An inadvertent decision can have the same effect as a deliberate one. Practitioners will have to be vigilant in ensuring that the principle established in *Kirby* and approved of in *Boness* is not eroded as a result of the decision in *H, Stevens and Lovegrove.*

67 [2006] EWCA Crim 255 at para 28.

68 See *R v Angol*, unreported 20 July 2006, CA, and chapter 9.

The geographical ambit of a prohibition: the whole of England and Wales?

55 The original CDA 1998 s1(6) allowed prohibitions that went further than those made simply in order to protect persons in the local government area: it allowed for orders that protected persons in 'any adjoining local government area'. The rationale for that (presumably) was to prevent the problem of anti-social conduct simply being shifted to the neighbouring borough. CDA 1998 s1(6) was subsequently amended by PRA 2002 to read as follows:

> The prohibitions that may be imposed by an anti-social behaviour order are those necessary for the purpose of protecting persons (whether relevant persons or persons elsewhere in England & Wales) from further anti-social acts by the defendant.[69]

.56 The rationale for this amendment to CDA 1998 was 'to enable anti-social behaviour orders to travel with the people on whom they have been served',[70] the assumption being that when a person travels they take their anti-social behaviour with them.

.57 At the same time that this section was introduced, so was CDA 1998 s1C (post-conviction ASBOs). The second limb of the test for imposition of post-conviction ASBOs is 'that an order under this section is necessary to protect persons in any place in England and Wales from further anti-social acts by him' (see chapter 6 on post-conviction orders). In essence the very introduction by PRA 2002 of post-conviction ASBOs altered the original character of ASBOs as it became permissible to impose ASBOs in order to prevent anti-social conduct outside a local area. Of course the difference with a post-conviction ASBO is that it is applied for by the CPS or imposed by a court of its own motion and not upon the request of a local actor, and therefore the second limb of the test could not sensibly have had a 'relevant persons' requirement.

.58 It would seem that the proper approach to stand-alone ASBOs is to first consider whether 'relevant persons' need protecting and then consider whether the prohibition, if any, to be imposed requires a wider geographical condition.

.59 The question as to whether a prohibition as wide as the whole of England and Wales is necessary will depend on the evidence and how itinerant a lifestyle the applicant body suggests the defendant

69 This section came into force on 2 December 2002.

70 HL Debates vol 631, col 506, 2 February 2002.

has or could have. It does not necessarily follow (despite the popularity of nationwide ASBOs)[71] that if local people need protection, so does the whole population of England and Wales. The 2006 Home Office Guidance explains the purpose of CDA 1998 s1(6) as follows:[72] 'The power to make an order over a wide area is for use where there is reason to believe that the person concerned may move or has already moved. It goes some way to addressing the problem of offenders moving to other areas and continuing the behaviour'.

7.60 The Guidance then gives examples of ticket touting at different train stations, anti-social behaviour on trains[73] as well as 'the minority of the travelling community who persistently engage in anti-social behaviour around the country'.[74]

7.61 The fact that the Home Office has chosen to highlight one group ('the travelling community') is worth considering further. It seems to stem from a contribution made by John Denham[75] to a House of Commons Standing Committee debate on the Police Reform Bill that was made without any evidential foundation:

> One group that we had in mind in developing the clause was the minority in the traveller community who engages in persistent nuisance more or less wherever they go. That may involve moving from one end of the country to another, and a stay in a particular area may be brief. The disruption caused may be significant but with no possibility of collecting the evidence necessary for the local authority to get an ASBO.[76]

7.62 It is difficult to understand this reasoning. If a local authority or other applicant body cannot collate evidence of anti-social behaviour there can be no ASBO application. If alternatively the suggestion is that the second limb cannot be made out because there is insufficient evidence of necessity to protect relevant persons because the person has moved on, then the ASBO application would fail to satisfy the second limb of the test.

71 In Greater Manchester, for example, 31 per cent of ASBOs issued between September 1999 and September 2005 included a prohibition that extended to all of England and Wales. See www.crimereduction.gov.uk.

72 *Guide to Anti-social Behaviour Orders* (2006) p14. Available at www.together.gov.uk.

73 It should be noted that ticket touting may not satisfy the first limb of the test. See para 5.48 and 2006 Home Office Guidance at pp14–15.

74 See *R v Hinton* [2006] EWCA Crim 115 for an example of an ASBO that prevents anti-social behaviour on a train.

75 Then Minister for Policing, Crime Reduction and Community Safety.

76 SC Deb (A) 25 June 2002, col 375.

7.63 If on the other hand what is being suggested is that there is sufficient evidence of anti-social behaviour in a particular area in relation to a defendant who is also a member of a travelling community, that in itself does not mean it is necessary to impose prohibitions which will be valid across the country. Any such suggestion by an applicant body would be quite wrong. A person may commit a particular anti-social act in a particular area for particular socio-economic or other reasons, while movement to another area may have a positive impact on their behaviour. Equally, somebody may have a nomadic habit of life but has temporarily or permanently ceased to travel.[77] Each application must be looked at on an individual basis. An ASBO imposed as a result of assumptions being made because a defendant belongs to a particular group would be discriminatory under the Race Relations Act 1976[78] and potentially in breach of ECHR Article 14 (the prohibition on discrimination).[79]

7.64 Recent Home Office statistics reveal that prohibitions that are valid nationwide (ie in England and Wales) are commonly imposed.[80] Practitioners should be alive to the fact that Parliament's intention in widening CDA 1998 s1(6) was to ensnare those who move around either deliberately so that they can continue their anti-social behaviour elsewhere or those whose anti-social behaviour is carried with them as they move (along a train line for example). The applicant body must have some evidential basis for suggesting that anti-social acts are likely to be committed outside a particular locality. Furthermore, in order to be enforceable, a geographical limit (as opposed to 'England and Wales') is inevitably necessary.

Negotiating terms of ASBOs

7.65 The local authority or relevant authority is often open to 'negotiation' about the terms of an ASBO (for example, the extent of a geographical exclusion zone), particularly if they can save the costs of a full contested hearing with the expense of professional and other witnesses having to attend. That said, it is of course ultimately a matter for the

77 See *South Buckinghamshire District Council v (1) Andrew Smith (2) James Smith* [2006] EWHC 281 (QB).

78 On the basis that the applicant body is a public body under the Race Relations Act 1976 and travellers are a racial group within the meaning of that Act.

79 ECHR Article 14 is not a free-standing right: the facts must fall within the ambit of another Convention right (Article 8 for example).

80 See note 71 above.

court, which has to be satisfied of both limbs of the statutory test since it is not possible to 'consent' to an ASBO.[81]

Duration of ASBOs

7.67 ASBOs must be imposed for a minimum of two years (although as mentioned above, it was said in *Lonergan* and *Boness* that not every prohibition need be as long as the term of the ASBO imposed). The order comes into effect on the day it is made[82] but as explained above at para 6.34, it can be suspended until release from any period of custody. There is also the power to vary or discharge an order before the end of the two-year period (see chapters 5 and 6).

7.68 There is no maximum duration: the court has the power to impose an order 'until further order'. However, such a course has not to date been approved of by the Court of Appeal (see para 7.69 below). The court imposing the ASBO must consider the twin concepts of necessity and proportionality when deciding on the length of an order. The age of the defendant is an important consideration in deciding the length of an ASBO.[83] The 2006 Home Office Guidance is at pains to point out that orders issued to children and young people should be reviewed annually and that 'careful consideration must be given to the case for applying for such orders to last beyond two years'.[84] If an ASBO is imposed as well as custody, clearly the effect of the sentence itself should play a part in deciding the length of any ASBO (see chapter 6 on post-conviction ASBOs).

7.69 In *Hall*,[85] when considering whether a lifetime ASBO prohibiting driving without a valid licence was appropriate, the Court of Appeal said the following: 'The matter which has concerned us ... is the indefinite nature of this order. Just as it is not advisable to make long periods of disqualification, because it only makes it much more difficult for somebody to comply, in our view the specific terms of the anti-social behaviour order should have been set out, rather than an indefinite order.' The length of the order was reduced to two years.

81 *R (T) v Manchester Crown Court* [2005] EWHC 1396. Discussed in detail at para 5.30.
82 *W v DPP* [2003] EWHC 3139 (Admin).
83 See, for example, *R v H, Stevens and Lovegrove* [2006] EWCA Crim 255.
84 Page 32. See also p45, where it is suggested tht annual reviews of youth ASBOs is likely to become a statutory requirement in the near future – see para 10.4.
85 [2004] EWCA Crim 26. This aspect of *Hall* remains good law.

7.70 In *R v Paul Rush*,[86] a ten-year ASBO, preventing harassment of the offender's parents by the offender, was reduced to five years. The Court of Appeal emphasised the importance of ensuring that the necessity test applied to the duration of the order, as well as the need to give reasons not just for imposing an ASBO but for its length:

> ... we consider that the duration of the order was excessive. It implies that the need for that protection will last until the appellant is in his mid-thirties. Having regard to the potential sentence for breach of an anti-social behaviour order, which can include activity which would not otherwise amount to a criminal offence, we consider that the court needs to give careful consideration to the length of the order. We question whether the judge did so because he gave no particular reasons for his decision to make it ten years in length.[87]

86 [2005] EWCA Crim 1316. This case is discussed further at para 6.36.

87 [2005] EWCA Crim 1316 at para 15.

CHAPTER 8

ASBOs in the county court

by Rajeev Thacker

continued

Introduction

8.1 The power to apply for an ASBO in the county court was introduced by the Police Reform Act (PRA) 2002, with the majority of the relevant statutory framework coming into force on 1 April 2003.[1] Further changes were created by the Anti-Social Behaviour Act (ASBA) 2003, extending the range of parties which could obtain and be subject to ASBOs with effect from 31 March 2004.[2]

8.2 The most distinctive feature of the county court ASBO is that it can only be obtained where other proceedings, termed the 'principal proceedings', are in train. There is accordingly no scope for an application for a stand-alone ASBO in the county court. Furthermore, while many of the legal principles which apply in the county court are similar to those discussed in earlier chapters, there are numerous different procedural and tactical considerations.

8.3 The first part of this chapter sets out the legislative basis which governs applications for ASBOs in the county court, and considers both law and procedure. Since some of the statutory language is similar to that considered in earlier parts of this book, there will be an element of cross-referencing, although the most important points are repeated for convenience.

8.4 The second part of this chapter deals with the issues which may arise at each stage of the ASBO process in the county court, and considers the strategy and tactics which advisers might employ when seeking to defend applications for ASBOs.

The statutory framework

8.5 CDA 1998 s1B, entitled 'Orders in county court proceedings', provides the statutory underpinning for the making of an ASBO:

> (1) This section applies to any proceedings in a county court ('the principal proceedings').
> (2) If a relevant authority –
> (a) is a party to the principal proceedings, and
> (b) considers that a party to those proceedings is a person in relation to whom it would be reasonable for it to make an application under section 1,

1 See Police Reform Act 2002 (Commencement No 4) Order 2003, SI No 808, art 2(f).

2 See Anti-social Behaviour Act 2003 (Commencement No 2) Order 2004, SI No 690, art 2(b).

it may make an application in those proceedings for an order under subsection (4).

(3) If a relevant authority –

(a) is not a party to the principal proceedings, and

(b) considers that a party to those proceedings is a person in relation to whom it would be reasonable for it to make an application under section 1,

it may make an application to be joined to those proceedings to enable it to apply for an order under subsection (4) and, if it is so joined, may apply for such an order.

(3A) Subsection (3B) applies if a relevant authority is a party to the principal proceedings and considers –

(a) that a person who is not a party to the proceedings has acted in an anti-social manner, and

(b) that the person's anti-social acts are material in relation to the principal proceedings.

(3B) The relevant authority may –

(a) make an application for the person mentioned in subsection (3A)(a) to be joined to the principal proceedings to enable an order under subsection (4) to be made in relation to that person;

(b) if that person is so joined, apply for an order under subsection (4).

(3C) But a person must not be joined to proceedings in pursuance of subsection (3B) unless his anti-social acts are material in relation to the principal proceedings.

(4) If, on an application for an order under this subsection, it is proved that the conditions mentioned in section 1(1) are fulfilled as respects that other party, the court may make an order which prohibits him from doing anything described in the order.

(5) Subject to subsection (6), the person against whom an order under this section has been made and the relevant authority on whose application that order was made may apply to the county court which made an order under this section for it to be varied or discharged by a further order.

(6) Except with the consent of the relevant authority and the person subject to the order, no order under this section shall be discharged before the end of the period of two years beginning with the date of service of the order.

(7) Subsections (5) to (7) and (10) to (12) of section 1 apply for the purposes of the making and effect of orders made under this section as they apply for the purposes of the making and effect of anti-social behaviour orders.

8.6 While it is convenient to refer to a county court order prohibiting anti-social behaviour under CDA 1998 s1B(4) as an ASBO, it is important to note that, strictly speaking, an 'anti-social behaviour order' is an order made under CDA 1998 s1(4).[3] This technical difference is important in certain circumstances which will be made clear where appropriate. However, unless it is necessary to make this distinction, reference to a county court ASBO in this chapter is to an order made under s1B(4).

8.7 Practitioners should also be aware of the difference between a county court ASBO and other orders which the court may make in order to prohibit alleged anti-social behaviour. Such orders, in so far as civil proceedings are concerned, will invariably be in the form of an injunction. They are discussed in more detail below.

8.8 With these points in mind, the key aspects of a county court ASBO can be summarised as follows:

- The county court proceedings within which the application for an ASBO is made are called the 'principal proceedings'.
- Such 'principal proceedings' can be any proceedings, although they will in practice be concerned with alleged anti-social behaviour, most commonly in the housing field.
- The only body that can make an application for an ASBO is a 'relevant authority'. The 'relevant authority' is uniformly defined through the legislation[4] and in the county court it is most likely to be a local authority or a registered social landlord.
- The relevant authority may or may not be a party at the outset of the principal proceedings.
- If the relevant authority is not a party to the principal proceedings, then it may apply to be joined to those proceedings.
- If the person against whom an ASBO is sought is not a party to the principal proceedings, then the relevant authority can apply for that person to be joined, but only if the anti-social acts are 'material' to the principal proceedings.
- It is not possible for a non-party relevant authority to be joined in order to seek an ASBO against a non-party. This is because s1B(3) states that the application to join may be made to 'enable it' to apply for an ASBO against a person who is a party to the principal proceedings.
- The criteria for granting an ASBO are as in s1(1).[5]

3 See CDA 1998 s18(1).

4 See also para 5.2.

5 See chapter 5.

- A county court ASBO remains in force for a minimum of two years from the date of service of the order, unless the parties consent to it being discharged at an earlier date.[6]

The 'relevant authority' in the county court

8.9 CDA 1998 s1(1A) lists those relevant authorities which are entitled to apply for ASBOs.[7] They include local authorities, registered social landlords (RSLs) and housing action trusts (HATs). The body most likely to bring the application for a county court ASBO is a landlord where the alleged anti-social behaviour has arisen in relation to its housing functions and it is seeking to obtain possession of a tenant's home on the basis of that anti-social behaviour.

8.10 However, it is important to bear in mind that local authorities, RSLs and HATs have wide powers to apply for orders without simultaneously seeking the possession of a person's home – such as anti-social behaviour injunctions.[8] There is no reason why these proceedings cannot constitute the 'principal proceedings' within which the application for an ASBO is made.

Local authorities

8.11 As well as their other responsibilities, local authorities remain providers of social housing. There should be no difficulty in establishing the fact that a local authority is a landlord since its name should appear on the tenancy agreement. This will be an essential document if the 'principal proceedings' consist of a claim for possession of residential property or an application for an anti-social behaviour injunction.

Registered social landlords (RSLs)

8.12 An RSL is, broadly speaking, a non-profit-making body which makes housing available for letting. Many are housing associations[9] which are registered as a charity, but they may also be a society registered under the Industrial and Provident Societies Act 1965 or a company

6 Section 1B(6).

7 But see also the Crime and Disorder Act 1998 (Relevant Authorities and Relevant Persons) Order 2006 SI No 2137, which makes the Environment Agency and Transport for London relevant authorities for the purpose of county court ASBOs as of 1 September 2006. See appendix A.

8 See Housing Act 1996 ss153A–158 and below at paras 8.126–8.128.

9 Defined in section 1 of the Housing Associations Act 1985.

under the Companies Act 1985. The full definition of an RSL is contained in s2 of the Housing Act 1996. This makes it clear that the RSL is permitted to have additional objects or purposes, such as constructing houses to be acquired on shared ownership schemes and managing properties.

Housing action trusts (HATs)

8.13 HATs were established under s62 of the Housing Act 1985. They were designed to achieve specific aims in relation to urban regeneration and were time-limited. Six were created for the areas of Castle Vale (Birmingham), Liverpool, North Hull, Stonebridge, Tower Hamlets and Waltham Forest (the latter three in London). With the exception of Stonebridge HAT, the others have all ceased operating. The Stonebridge HAT has indicated that it expects to cease its operations in 2007.

8.14 Those HATs that are no longer in operation have been dissolved and their rights and liabilities transferred to English Partnerships, which is a governmental development agency. This would seem to suggest that English Partnerships also has the right to bring proceedings for anti-social behaviour, since that was a right available to HATs. However, it seems highly unlikely that this would ever occur in practice, since the housing stock for which each housing trust was previously responsible will have been transferred to housing associations or local authorities, which would then be in a position to bring the proceedings.

Other bodies managing housing stock

8.15 Section 27 of the Housing Act 1985 permits a local authority, with the approval of the Secretary of State (or, in Wales, the National Assembly for Wales), to contract out its housing management functions to certain other bodies. There are three categories of such bodies:

- arm's length management organisations;
- tenant management organisations;
- private companies.

8.16 It is important to note that none of these is, at present, a 'relevant authority' for the purposes of CDA 1998 s1(1A). However, the Office of the Deputy Prime Minister[10] recently consulted on this issue[11] and

10 Now the Department for Communities and Local Government.

11 *Enabling local authorities to contract their Anti-Social Behaviour Order functions to organisations managing their housing stock*, ODPM Publications (November 2005).

proposed that local authorities could ask those managing its properties under s27 to carry out all or some of its ASBO functions on their behalf. If this proposal were to be implemented, it would be by way of an order under s1F of the CDA 1998. At the time of writing, no such draft order has been made.

Are RSLs or HATs public authorities?

8.17 This question may be relevant for two reasons. First, if an attempt is made to challenge the decision of an RSL or HAT to bring proceedings for an ASBO, either by way of a public law defence in the county court or by way of judicial review in the High Court, it will be necessary to establish that it is a public authority. Second, by virtue of the Human Rights Act (HRA) 1998 s6(1),[12] if it is alleged that a body has violated a person's Convention rights, it will again be necessary to show that the body is a public authority.

8.18 The position of RSLs has been considered by the Court of Appeal in *Poplar Housing and Regeneration Community Association Ltd v Donoghue.*[13] Here, the issue was whether the tenant in a possession action brought by the claimant housing association was entitled to rely upon a defence based on HRA 1998. She could only do so if the housing association came within the definition of public authority under HRA 1998. In turn, to show that the housing association came within this definition, the tenant had to establish that it was performing functions of a public nature under s6(3)(b) of the 1998 Act.

8.19 The Court of Appeal rejected the submission that a housing association should always be regarded as a public authority for the purposes of HRA 1998. The mere fact that the housing association was performing functions which would otherwise have been performed by a local housing authority did not convert its activities from private to public. It went on, however, to find that the defendant was, on the facts of the case, a public authority. The relevant principles can be summarised as follows:

- There is a close similarity between the test for deciding what is a public authority for the purposes of HRA 1998 and the approach of the courts to the issue of whether a body is public for the purposes of judicial review proceedings.
- The act of providing accommodation to rent is not, without more, a public function for the purposes of HRA 1998 s6.

12 But see the decision of the House of Lords in *Kay v Lambeth LBC* [2006] UKHL 10; [2006] 2 WLR 520 discussed at para 8.156.

13 [2001] EWCA Civ 595; [2002] QB 48.

- The mere fact that a body is a charity or conducts itself on a not for profit basis does not necessarily point to it being a public authority, even though it is likely to be motivated by the public interest.
- It is necessary to consider those features or a combination of features which impose a public character or stamp on the relevant act of the public authority. The fact that an act is done under statutory authority will help to mark the act as being public, and the more that acts that could be of a private nature are enmeshed in the activities of a public body, the more likely they are to be public.
- There is often no clear demarcation line which can be drawn between public and private bodies and functions. In some borderline cases, the decision will be one of fact and degree.
- While a body may be public for the purposes of some of its activities, this does not mean that it will be so in relation to everything it does. In particular, the act of a housing association in raising finance may be private.
- In the case itself, it was relevant that the housing association was created by a local authority which had transferred its stock to it. In addition, the housing association was subject to the guidance of the local authority in so far as its relationship to the tenant was concerned. Furthermore, the intention of the parties was that the housing association would step into the shoes of the previous local authority landlord.

8.20 It is important to bear in mind, however, that the jurisprudence in relation to proper definition of 'public authority' is in a constant state of development and that *Poplar*[14] is by no means the last word on the subject. Indeed, the Court of Appeal emphasised the importance of considering the facts of each case carefully. In particular, if a housing association or other social landlord is exercising functions which would otherwise be performed by a public authority, such as dealing with alleged anti-social behaviour, it is more likely to be amenable to a public law challenge.

8.21 In this connection, the decision of the Court of Appeal in *R (Beer (trading as Hammer Trout Farm)) v Hampshire Farmers' Markets Ltd*[15] is of interest. Here, a county council had established farmers' markets under statutory powers. The claimant was a stallholder, having applied to the council to run a stall. The defendant subsequently took over the running of the markets. It was a limited company and

14 See note 12 above.

15 [2003] EWCA Civ 1056; [2004] 1 WLR 233.

was initially registered at the council's offices. The defendant then rejected an application by the claimant to become a stallholder. The claimant sought judicial review of this decision and an issue arose as to whether the defendant was susceptible to such a challenge.

8.22 The Court of Appeal pointed out that in cases where the source of a decision-maker's power was not statutory, it was necessary to carefully consider the nature of that power and the function of the body to decide whether it was sufficiently public. In this case, the company had been created by the council. It had stepped into its shoes and performed the functions that had been previously carried out by the council. Further, the company had been established on a non-profit-making basis to carry out functions which were in the public interest. In those circumstances, it was amenable to judicial review and was acting as a public authority within the meaning of HRA 1998.

8.23 On this basis, a HAT is likely to fall within the category of public authority. It is described by the Department for Communities and Local Government as a 'non-departmental public body' which has aims created by statute. Furthermore, a HAT is managed and run by a board which is appointed by the Secretary of State. Both HATs and English Partnerships fall within the definition of public authority.

What needs to be established to obtain a county court ASBO?

8.24 The conditions that need to be satisfied before an ASBO is granted in the county court are the same as those set out in CDA 1998 s1(1). These are:

- that the person against whom the order is sought has acted, since the commencement date,[16] in an anti-social manner, that is to say, in a manner that caused or was likely to cause harassment, alarm or distress to one or more persons not of the same household as himself; and
- that such an order is necessary to protect relevant persons from further anti-social acts by him.

8.25 As with stand-alone ASBOs, the court must disregard any act that the defendant shows was 'reasonable' in the circumstances.[17] In addition,

16 As to which, see the discussion at para 8.33 below.

17 See CDA 1998 s1B(7) which applies s1(5) to the making of county court ASBOs.

the order can only prohibit the defendant from doing certain things. These prohibitions must be set out in the order.[18]

8.26 Reference should be made to chapter 5 for a detailed analysis of the two-stage test identified above, how it has been interpreted and its scope. Reference should also be made to chapter 7 for permissible terms of ASBOs and their interaction with ECHR rights. The specific considerations that apply in the county court context are considered later in this chapter but there are two particular points which can be conveniently addressed at this stage.

The identity of 'relevant persons'

8.27 The second limb of the test requires the court to consider whether the order is necessary to protect 'relevant persons' from further anti-social actions by the party subject to the ASBO (CDA 1998 s1(1)(b)). In county court proceedings, when the party applying for the ASBO is the local authority, the relevant persons will be those within the local government area or the county, as the case may be (sections 1(1B)(a) and (aa)).

8.28 However, where the body applying for an ASBO is an RSL or a HAT, section 1(1B)(d) provides that the relevant persons are:

(i) persons who are residing in or who are otherwise on or likely to be on premises provided or managed by that authority; or
(ii) persons who are in the vicinity of or likely to be in the vicinity of such premises.

8.29 There is of course no difficulty with the use of the word 'residing', since it will be a question of fact as to whether the people whom it is sought to protect actually live in the properties provided or managed by the RSL or HAT. Similarly, the question of whether somebody is actually 'otherwise on' premises will be a question of fact. There are, however, three aspects of section 1(1B)(d) which deserve more detailed analysis.

8.30 First, although the word 'premises' is used, rather than specific reference to housing accommodation, the intention of the provision is clearly to protect those persons who live in or visit such accommodation. This is made clear by the use of the phrase 'residing in or who are otherwise on'.

8.31 Second, in so far as reliance is placed by the applicant authority on the fact that persons are 'likely' to be on premises or in the vicinity of

18 See CDA 1998 ss1(5) and 1(6) which are applied to county court ASBOs by virtue of CDA 1998 s1B(7).

premises, it will be necessary for it to provide evidence of this likelihood. If an ASBO is sought on this basis, it will probably be in relation to employees or contractors of the authority, particularly housing officers.

8.32 Third, the reference to protecting those who are or are likely to be in the 'vicinity' of the premises provided or managed by the RSL or HAT extends coverage beyond those who are not neighbouring occupiers. However, the use of the word 'vicinity' also envisages a geographical limitation and, since RSLs and HATs have been given the power to apply for ASBOs in the interests of managing their housing stock, a generalised assertion that members of the public need protection is unlikely to satisfy the second limb.

The 'commencement date' for the purposes of section 1B

8.33 Section 1B does not itself set out the criteria that have to be satisfied in order for an ASBO to be made. Rather, it refers back to s1 and the issue of whether a relevant authority in county court proceedings would otherwise consider it appropriate to make an application under that section. However, it will be recalled that s1 allows an application to be made where it is alleged that a person has acted, since the 'commencement date', in an anti-social manner. The question which arises, bearing in mind that s1B did not come into force until 1 April 2003,[19] is whether the 'commencement date' is in fact that date rather than 1 April 1999, which is the specified commencement date for s1.

8.34 In *Moat Housing Group-South Ltd v Harris*[20] the Court of Appeal mistakenly thought that the commencement date for s1B was 2 December 2002,[21] this actually being the date when CDA 1998 ss1C and 1D came into force for the purposes of post-conviction and interim ASBOs. However, leaving this aside, it clearly formed the view that the 'commencement date' would not be 1 April 1999 if the claim was made in the county court. It does not seem, however, that it heard any argument on the impact of s1B(7). This provides, among other things, that s1(12) is to apply for the purposes of the making and effect of county court orders as it applies for the purposes of the making and effect of orders under s1. It is s1(12) which stipulates 1 April

19 See Police Reform Act 2002 (Commencement No 4) Order 2003 SI No 808 art 2(f).

20 *Moat Housing Group-South Ltd v Harris* [2005] EWCA Civ 287; [2005] 3 WLR 691.

21 [2005] EWCA Civ 287 at para 165.

1999 as being the commencement date of s1. There may therefore be an argument that s1B(7) has the effect of transposing across 1 April 1999 as the 'commencement date' for the purposes of county court ASBOs.

8.35 This is unlikely to make any difference in practice since any ASBO application now made in the county court will almost certainly be based on allegations after 1 April 2003. However, if an authority does seek to rely upon the earlier date, both the views of the Court of Appeal in *Moat Housing*[22] and the general principle that Parliament does not intend to legislate with retrospective effect, can be invoked in order to argue the contrary position.

Ancillary orders

8.36 As indicated at para 5.147, a criminal court can make various additional orders upon imposing an ASBO, such as individual support orders and parenting orders. However, subject to one exception,[23] it is not open to a county court to proceed in this way. This is because the ability to make such an order is dependent upon an 'anti-social behaviour order', as defined by CDA 1998 s1(1), being made. Since this provision defines an 'anti-social behaviour order' as having the meaning set out in CDA 1998 s1(4), it is not apt to cover an order made under s1B(4), that is, a county court ASBO. This is accordingly one of the situations where the difference between a true ASBO under CDA 1998 s1(4) and a county court ASBO is of relevance.

Interim orders

8.37 CDA 1998 s1D(1)(b) enables an applying authority to obtain an interim county court ASBO where it has made an application for a final ASBO under s1B. As discussed previously,[24] the question for the court on such an interim application is whether it is 'just' to make the order. The interim order has to be for a fixed period, can be varied, renewed or discharged and automatically comes to an end when the court makes a decision on the substantive application for the ASBO.[25]

22 [2005] EWCA Civ 287; [2005] 3 WLR 691.

23 This being an intervention order under CDA 1998 s1G, which provision was inserted by the Drugs Act 2005, and which can be made by a county court by virtue of CDA 1998 s1G(1)(a) (in force as of 1 October 2006). See chapter 5 for more details.

24 See para 5.12.

25 CDA 1998 s1D(4).

The procedure which applies in respect of interim orders in the county court is dealt with below.

Applying for a county court ASBO

Procedure

8.38 Section IV of CPR 65[26] and the corresponding Practice Direction govern the procedure to be followed when applying for an ASBO.[27] There are different considerations depending upon whether the authority is involved in the principal proceedings and whether the person against whom the ASBO is sought is a party in those proceedings. The key points in each scenario are as laid out below.

Relevant authority a party in the principal proceedings (CPR 65.22)

8.39
- Where the relevant authority is the claimant in the principal proceedings, then an application for the order must be made in the claim form.
- Where the relevant authority is the defendant, for example, in a claim by a tenant for damages for disrepair, then the application for an ASBO is to be made by a Part 23 application notice.[28] This should be filed with the defence.
- If, however, the application for an ASBO is not made when it should have been, because the relevant authority only subsequently becomes aware of circumstances which make such an application necessary, it should apply as soon as possible by way of a Part 23 application notice.

Relevant authority not a party in the principal proceedings (CPR 65.24)

8.40
- The relevant authority will first need to be made a party to the proceedings. This is to be done in accordance with CPR 19, which governs the addition and substitution of parties to civil proceedings. Again, this involves using an application notice.
- The application for the ASBO must be made in the same application notice.
- The applications should normally be made on notice.

26 See appendix H for relevant sections of CPR.

27 The most up to date version of the Civil Procedure Rules, and the relevant forms, can be found at www.dca.gov.uk.

28 This is the standard terminology used in respect of all applications made in the civil courts. The standard form is N244.

- The applications must be made as soon as possible after the authority becomes aware of the principal proceedings.

Proposed subject of ASBO not a party (CPR 65.23)

8.41
- Again, the application to add a party must be made in accordance with CPR 19.
- The application to add the party should be contained in the same application notice as the application for the substantive order.
- It should be made 'as soon as possible' after the relevant authority considers that the subject of the proposed order has acted in an anti-social manner and that his or her acts are material to the principal proceedings.
- The application notice has to contain the relevant authority's reasons for claiming that the person's anti-social acts are material in relation to the principal proceedings and details of the alleged anti-social acts.
- The application should normally be made on notice.

8.42 In all cases, CPR 65.25 provides that the application for the ASBO must be accompanied by written evidence. This will normally be in the form of a witness statement, although it is open to a claiming authority to include it within the body of the application notice. CPR 65.25 specifically provides that the supporting evidence must include information indicating that there has been compliance with the consultation requirements of CDA 1998 s1E.[29]

Procedure on interim orders

8.43 The CPR has its own specific provisions which set out the procedure to be followed when applying for any interim order in the county court. They are found in CPR 25 and, by virtue of CPR 65.26, the rules contained within that Part are to apply where there is any application for an interim ASBO. CPR 65.26 additionally provides that the application should normally be made in the claim form or application notice seeking the interim order and should, again, be on notice.

8.44 These aspects of CPR 25 are relevant for present purposes:

- an interim remedy may be granted at any stage of proceedings;
- an application for an interim remedy may be made without notice if there are good reasons for not doing so;

29 As to the statutory requirement to consult, see *McClarty & McClarty v Wigan Borough Council*, unreported, 22 October 2003, and the discussion of that case at para 2.30.

- where a without notice application is made, the evidence in support of the interim order should contain an explanation as to why this course has been taken;
- the order, if made without notice, should be served by the claiming party on the respondent as soon as possible;
- the order, if made without notice, should provide for a return date at which time the court can give further consideration to the order.

8.45 CPR 25 does permit an application for an interim remedy to be made, and for the remedy to be granted, prior to a claim being started. However, CDA 1998 s1D(1)(b), which introduced interim orders, is expressly stated only to apply where an application for an ASBO under CDA 1998 s1B is made. Accordingly, it is impossible for an interim ASBO to be made prior to the issue of a claim or application, no matter how urgent the situation is said to be. This was confirmed by the Court of Appeal in *Manchester City Council v Muir.*[30] The Court also made the point in this case that there is an obligation, at the interim stage, to consider whether there has been compliance with the consultation requirement imposed by CDA 1998 s1E:

8.46 > ... So, a necessary pre-condition to an application under section 1B for an interim order was, in this case, an application under 1B. By section 1E(2), before such an application might be made the necessary consultation has to have taken place. Accordingly, a judge hearing an application for an interim order under section 1D not only has jurisdiction to decide whether there has been sufficient consultation, but is obliged to do so if the issue is raised, as it was before HHJ Holman. The fact, as Mr Stark submits, that when it comes to considering whether to make an interim order under section 1D, the test is whether it is just to do so does not alter the fact that a necessary pre-condition of considering that matter is that there should be a valid application under section 1B in existence. As Kennedy LJ said in *B v Secretary of State for Constitutional Affairs and the Lord Chancellor* [2003] 1 All ER 531 at paragraph 39, the court on an application for an interim order must consider whether the application for a final order has been properly made.[31]

8.47 *Muir* is also authority for the proposition that it is not possible for a court, when considering the application for a final ASBO, to re-open the finding of the court, at the interim stage, that the consultation requirement has been satisfied. Accordingly, if any challenge is to be

30 [2006] EWCA Civ 423.

31 [2006] EWCA Civ 423 at para 21.

made to a court's decision on an interim ASBO, in so far as it relates to the consultation requirement, this must be the subject of a separate appeal immediately after the making of the interim ASBO.

Without notice applications for interim ASBOs

8.48 There may be circumstances in which an applying authority seeks to obtain an interim ASBO without giving notice to the proposed subject. However, there is no specific procedure set out in CPR 65 for obtaining such an order without notice. It is accordingly necessary to consider CPR 23, which sets out the general rules for making applications without notice. The following points are of importance:

- an application must be made by using a standard application notice, unless the court orders otherwise;
- the court has power to order that an application be made without notice. This order will normally be sought within the body of the application notice seeking the without notice order;
- if the court has permitted an application to be made without notice, a copy of the application notice must be served along with the order;
- the order must contain a statement of the respondent's right to apply to have the order set aside or varied.

8.49 In *R (on the application of M) v Secretary of State for Constitutional Affairs*[32] the Court of Appeal considered, among other things, the circumstances in which it would be appropriate to make without notice interim ASBOs. Although the case was concerned with applications in the magistrates' court, it is likely that applying authorities will seek to suggest that the following guidance given by the Court in *M* should apply in the county court:[33]

- it is unusual for an order to be made without notice;
- however, such an order can be made when it is 'necessary to do so' and is made subject to safeguards which give the person affected the opportunity to apply at an early stage to have the order reviewed or discharged;
- the more intrusive the order the more the court will require by way of proof that it is necessary that it should be made;
- but 'there is nothing intrinsically objectionable about the power to grant an interim ASBO without notice';

32 [2004] EWCA Civ 312; [2004] 1 WLR. 2298. This case is further discussed at para 5.21.

33 [2004] EWCA Civ 312, para 39.

- the court has to consider whether the application for the final order has been properly made, but there is no need for the applying authority to establish that there is 'an extremely strong prima facie case'.

8.50 It is important to stress the fact that the making of a without notice application is very much an exceptional course to take. This was reaffirmed by the Court of Appeal in *Moat Housing Group-South Ltd v Harris*:

> It needs to be clearly understood, however, that to grant an injunction without notice is to grant an exceptional remedy. There is a useful discussion of the topic in Zuckerman's *Civil Procedure* (2003), paras 9.133–9.136, although the author for understandable reasons does not concern himself with the kind of issues relating to personal safety which are of most concern in a family law or ASBI context. He says, correctly, at para 9.133, that: 'Notice of an application for an interim injunction must be given to the respondent as a matter of elementary justice.' He goes on to cite a passage in the judgment of the High Court of Australia in *Thomas A Edison Ltd v Bock* (1912) 15 CLR 679, 681 (a case which is also cited in the section on *ex parte* injunctions in Spry, *The Principles of Equitable Remedies* (5th ed, 1997) at p 511): 'There is a primary precept governing the administration of justice, that no man is to be condemned unheard; and therefore, as a general rule, no order should be made to the prejudice of a party unless he has the opportunity of being heard on defence.' It would in our judgment be best if judges in the county courts, when deciding whether to exercise their discretion to make an ASBI without notice, followed the guidance given in section 45(2)(a) of the Family Law Act 1996. They should bear in mind:
> (1) that to make an order without notice is to depart from the normal rules as to due process and warrants the existence of exceptional circumstances;
> (2) that one such exceptional circumstance is that there is a risk of significant harm to some person or persons attributable to conduct of the defendant if the order is not made immediately;
> (3) that the order must not be wider than is necessary and proportionate as a means of avoiding the apprehended harm.[34]

8.51 Of course, these comments were made in the context of an application for an injunction rather than an ASBO. Further, the approach of the Court of Appeal in *M*,[35] discussed above, seems to be more relaxed in so far as seeking a without notice interim ASBO is concerned. Indeed,

34 [2005] EWCA Civ 287; [2005] 3 WLR 691 at paras 71–72.

35 *R (on the application of M) v Secretary of State for Constitutional Affairs* [2004] EWCA Civ 312; [2004] 1 WLR. 2298.

since the statutory language for the grant of an interim ASBO, under s1D of the CDA 1998, is whether it is 'just' to make such an order, it may be argued that the courts should be more willing to grant without notice interim ASBOs.

8.52 It is suggested, however, that it would be wrong to countenance any relaxation of the general principles applicable to the making of without notice orders, as restated in *Moat Housing*.[36] The stricter approach retains its force because the issue under consideration is one of making any order without notice, rather than the criteria to be applied when deciding whether to grant a particular type of order. In particular, a county court, when faced with an application for a without notice interim ASBO, will need to be particularly alive to the obligation of full and frank disclosure. For example, in *Moat Housing*[37] itself, the district judge who made the exclusion order was unaware that it would be executed outside office hours and had not considered the question of where the family was to live.

Discharging without notice applications

8.53 As noted above, an order obtained on a without notice basis must contain a provision enabling a person affected by it to make an application for it to be discharged. In many cases, it will not be worthwhile making an application to discharge as there is likely to be sufficient evidence to justify obtaining an interim order. Furthermore, there may be good tactical reasons as to why such an application should not be made.

8.54 First, while the evidence in support of the interim order will be sufficient to justify the interim order, it is frequently not enough to enable a final order to be made. This is especially the case where the same evidence is relied upon in support of a possession claim in housing cases, which is the most common type of 'principal proceedings' in which the ASBO will be made. If an application is made to discharge the interim order, this may galvanise the applicant authority into obtaining further, stronger evidence.

8.55 Second, minor procedural flaws are unlikely to lead a court to discharge an ASBO and may well be counterproductive, unless it is possible to show real prejudice as a result of the failure to comply with the relevant rules. If an application is to be made in such circumstances, then it is essential that the witness statement in support of the application identifies the prejudice which has been caused.

36 [2005] EWCA Civ 287; [2005] 3 WLR 691.

37 [2005] EWCA Civ 287; [2005] 3 WLR 691.

8.56 However, there are cases where a prompt application to discharge should be made. The two situations that are most likely to arise are where there has been a material non-disclosure or a failure to establish expediency. In some cases, it may be possible to establish some bad faith or serious incompetence. If this is the case, the application to discharge could be coupled with an application to strike out the substantive claim for the ASBO, although care should be taken before embarking upon this course since the evidence in support will have to be strong.

After the ASBO

Service

8.57 The order, whether final or interim, must be served personally on the person who is the subject of the ASBO.[38] The date of service is significant because this is when the two-year minimum duration period of an ASBO begins.[39]

Applications to discharge or vary

8.58 An application for variation and/or discharge of the ASBO can be made at any time by the applying authority or the person against whom the order was made.[40] However, it can only be discharged before the two-year minimum period if both parties consent.[41]

An application to vary or discharge should be made by way of a Part 23 application notice supported by evidence. Such an application might be made, for example, where the specific persons who made a complaint about the defendant's behaviour have moved away and there is no evidence of anti-social conduct towards any other individuals.

8.59 There is no formal requirement as to what needs to be in the notice. However, it will need to be relatively detailed, setting out the basis upon which the ASBO was made, what has occurred since the making of the order, and explaining why this justifies a discharge or variation of the order. It is important that any supporting evidence, including that from any support or educational organisations, is included, as well as any relevant medical evidence.

38 CPR PD 65 para 13.1.

39 CDA 1998 s1B(6).

40 CDA 1998 s1B(5).

41 CDA 1998 s1B(6).

8.60 The hearing of such an application will not normally involve oral evidence, but rather be by way of submissions on the basis of the evidence filed. However, if the facts are contested, then a trial of the issues may be necessary.

Breach

8.61 If an ASBO made in the county court is breached without reasonable excuse it is a criminal offence.[42] Either the CPS or a local authority may bring the prosecution. Breaches of ASBOs are dealt with separately in chapter 9.

8.62 Dyson LJ has indicated, in his role as the Deputy Head of Civil Justice, that judges should not actually be seeking to commit for the breach of an ASBO on the basis that it can be dealt with as a criminal offence.[43] It is not clear, however, whatever the merits of a committal application, whether this view is legally correct, since a county court ASBO is an order of a civil court and a failure to comply with such an order is normally punishable by way of committal.

8.63 The procedure for a committal application is set out in Part 29 of the County Court Rules 1984.[44] However, this is unlikely to be a particularly attractive option for the applicant authority because of the costs involved and the fact that it is relatively unusual for a sentence of imprisonment to follow.

8.64 It is important to note that, if the alleged breach of a county court ASBO is pursued by way of prosecution under CDA 1998 s1(10), that provision contains a defence of reasonable excuse. However, if it is sought to punish the breach of an ASBO by way of committal proceedings in the county court, the only issue is whether it has been shown beyond reasonable doubt that the term of the ASBO has been breached, although the county court will be bound to take into account the degree of wrongdoing when considering penalty.

Appeals

8.65 The practice and procedure relating to appeals are dealt with in chapter 11.

42 CDA 1998 s1B(7), which reads across the relevant provisions of s1 into county court orders.

43 See Nic Madge, 'Anti-social behaviour orders: case-law reviewed', December 2004 *Legal Action* 22.

44 This remains in force and can be found in CPR Sch 2.

Issues

8.66 In considering the various issues set out below, it is important to bear in mind that the rules which govern proceedings in the county court have to be read in light of the overriding objective contained in CPR 1. There is an obligation on the parties to assist the court in promoting the overriding objective. The cards on the table approach which exists in civil litigation means that it is essential to adopt a co-operative approach to litigation where possible, as well as bearing in mind the emphasis placed by the courts on proportionality. Accordingly, procedural points should not be made just for the sake of taking them, and concessions should be made where appropriate.

8.67 It is also important to bear in mind CPR 3.10 which provides as follows:

> Where there has been an error of procedure such as a failure to comply with a rule or practice direction –
> (a) the error does not invalidate any step taken in the proceedings unless the court so orders;
> (b) the court may make an order to remedy the error.

8.68 Accordingly, while the discussion of directory and mandatory steps in relation to the consultation requirement in chapter 2[45] remains valid in relation to requirements set out in primary and other secondary legislation, the distinction does not apply in the context of a failure to comply with a procedural requirement set out in the Civil Procedure Rules, since CPR 3.10 makes express provision for errors of procedure. However, it is unlikely that the court will be willing to correct substantial procedural errors which cause prejudice to a party. Rather, since Rule 3.10 appears in the context of the court's case management powers, it should be seen as one of the rules available to enable justice to be done between the parties, rather than giving one party licence to ignore procedural safeguards.

The drafting of the application for an ASBO

8.69 As discussed in chapter 5, it is not unusual for authorities seeking an ASBO to be rather lax in the drafting of the matters which are the subject of complaint. It is likely that a county court judge will insist on a greater degree of precision. The information which needs to be provided will depend upon the way in which the ASBO application has reached the court.

45 See para 2.30.

8.70 If the applicant is the claimant in the principal proceedings, then the application will usually be made in the claim form. CPR 16 sets out what needs to be included. CPR 16.2(1) provides that the claim form itself should contain a concise statement of the nature of the claim and specify the remedy which the claimant seeks. The Particulars of Claim should, by virtue of 16.4(1), include a concise statement of the facts relied upon by the claimant.

8.71 If, on the other hand, the ASBO application is made independently of the claim form, it will be contained in an application notice. CPR 23.6 indicates that an application notice must state the order sought and brief details of why it is sought. There is no specific requirement to serve evidence but, as pointed out in paragraph 9.1 of the Practice Direction to CPR 23, the court will, in general, need to be satisfied by evidence of the matters set out in the application notice. Paragraph 9.3 of the Practice Direction states that the evidence should be served with the application notice.

8.72 Having said this, it is likely that the facts supporting the claim or application for an ASBO will be similar to those in the principal proceedings, such as possession proceedings. If this is the case, those principal proceedings may well be sufficiently particularised and there is no objection to the applicant authority in relying upon those allegations.

8.73 There is nothing to prevent the respondent to an ASBO application from seeking more particularity about the basis of the claim. This should be done under CPR 18, which deals with requests for further information. No particular form is prescribed for making such a request and it can be done by way of letter. The easiest way of setting out the request is by isolating those parts of the particulars of claim or application notice in respect of which further information is sought and asking a question. So, for example, there may be a paragraph in the particulars of claim which baldly states 'On 2 January 2006 the defendant shouted in the street'. A Part 18 request for further information would quote this and then ask for various clarifications such as 'Please state the time when this is alleged to have occurred', 'Please name the street where this is alleged to have occurred', 'Please set out the words the defendant is alleged to have shouted' and so on.

The timing of the ASBO application

8.74 As noted above, an application for an ASBO where the applying body is a claimant or defendant in the principal proceedings can be made at various stages. If the ASBO is not sought in the claim form, or in an application notice filed with the defence, it can only be made at a later stage where relevant facts have subsequently come to the attention of an applicant body, and even then it must be made as soon as possible.[46] This would preclude a subsequent application for an ASBO if those facts were in the possession of the relevant authority when the principal proceedings were instituted or in train.

8.75 If the relevant authority seeks to make a late application for an ASBO, it will be necessary to act quickly in order to dispose of it. On the basis that the applicant authority did not come into possession of the relevant information late in the day, the following steps should be taken:

(1) Write to the applicant pointing out that it has made a late application without any basis and ask it to withdraw the application.
(2) If it refuses to withdraw the application for an ASBO, put it on notice that an application to strike out will be made.
(3) Consider making the application to strike out at a case management or directions hearing in order to save costs.

Joining parties

8.76 As indicated above, applications by authorities to become a party or to make another person a party require them to apply under CPR 19. It is by no means automatic that a party will be joined to proceedings. The specific considerations which apply to the two scenarios are set out below, but it is important to bear in mind that joinder under CPR 19 is a matter of discretion for the court and is subject to the overriding objective.

8.77 The hearing of an application under CPR 19 follows the same form as any other application. It is necessary for the applying party to file and serve an application notice under Part 23 with evidence in support. Although it is very unusual to hear live evidence at such an application, there is no reason why this cannot be considered in an appropriate case.

Additional considerations where an authority seeks to be joined

8.78 In this scenario, CDA 1998 s1B(3)(b) indicates that it is necessary for the authority to come to the conclusion that it would be reasonable for it to make an application for an ASBO. Accordingly, a witness statement in support of the application for joinder should set out the

46 See CPR 65.22(2).

basis for reaching such a view. It is important to bear in mind that the purpose of the statutory provision is to enable a multiplicity of proceedings to be avoided. Accordingly, if there appears to be some collateral or improper purpose behind the application for joinder, it may be legitimately resisted.

Additional considerations where an authority seeks to join a party

79 There are three particular issues which arise here. The first concerns the requirement that the application to join is made 'as soon as possible' after the occurrence of the acts which are both alleged to constitute the anti-social behaviour and said to be material to the principal proceedings. The wording of CPR 65.23(1)(c) indicates that the relevant authority has to make a subjective judgment as to whether the criteria relating to occurrence and materiality are satisfied. In practice, if there is sufficient evidence of anti-social behaviour, a court is likely to find that the relevant authority has acted 'as soon as possible' even if there is scope for arguments about true expedition. Nevertheless, the process of disclosure should lead to the documents which recorded the decision-making process being revealed, thereby enabling an adviser to judge whether the relevant authority did indeed act sufficiently quickly.

.80 Of more interest is the requirement in CDA 1998 s1B(3C) that a person can only be joined to the 'principal proceedings' where the acts of that person are 'material' to those proceedings. This is not merely a matter for the judgment of the relevant authority, although it will have to establish a subjective belief that the acts are indeed material.

.81 The word 'material' is found in legislation dealing with many different areas. As Lord Millett pointed out in *Malekshad v Howard De Walden Estates Ltd*,[47] it can mean both 'substantial' and 'relevant', depending upon the context. In the context of s1B(3C), it must have the latter meaning. In other words, there must be some connection between the anti-social acts alleged against the party whom it is sought to join and the 'principal proceedings'. Furthermore, those alleged anti-social acts must be 'material in relation to the principal proceedings'. This suggests that it is insufficient for the anti-social acts to form part of the history or background to the principal proceedings. Rather, they must be in issue in those proceedings.

82 Some assistance as to the meaning of the word 'material' comes from *Post Office v Jones*,[48] a case in the field of disability discrimination.

47 [2002] UKHL 49 at para 66; [2003] 1 AC 1013.

48 [2001] EWCA Civ 558; [2001] ICR 805; [2001] IRLR 384.

One of the issues under consideration here was the proper construction of a statute where an employer's reason for treatment of a disabled employee had to be 'material' to the particular circumstances of the case. Arden LJ made the following point:

> [Counsel for the employer] submits that 'material' means 'relevant'. As to this, it is often said that there are degrees of relevance. In this context, I would add to [this] submission the rider that it is not sufficient that the connection is an extenuated one. The use of the word 'material' rather than 'relevant' or 'applicable' indicates to me that there must be a reasonably strong connection between the employer's reason and the circumstances of the individual case. The strength of this connection involves largely a factual enquiry.[49]

8.83 Therefore, in so far as ASBOs are concerned, the materiality requirement will not be satisfied, for example, where a tenant facing possession proceedings has a son or daughter who is committing anti-social behaviour which is not mentioned or relied upon in the proceedings by the landlord. Indeed, even if the child's anti-social behaviour forms part of the background to the possession proceedings, it may still not be 'material'.

8.84 Finally, as the Court of Appeal pointed out in *Manchester City Council v Muir*[50] there is nothing in the language of CDA 1998 s1B which prevents a claim for an ASBO being pursued against a joined party even when the principal proceedings have come to an end.[51] However, it made some further comments as to proper use of the procedure to join a non-party:

> That is not to say that it would be a proper use of this statutory procedure to start county court proceedings against a principal defendant for the sham purpose only of joining another person, to enable an order under s1B(4) to be made in relation to that person. Stand-alone applications for anti-social behaviour orders have to be made in a magistrates' court ...[52]

Disclosure of documents

8.85 Part 31 of the Civil Procedure Rules[53] governs the disclosure and inspection of documents. It is important to remember that, technically speaking, disclosure does not mean the physical provision of a

49 [2001] EWCA Civ 558 at para 37.
50 [2006] EWCA Civ 423.
51 [2006] EWCA Civ 423 at para 26.
52 [2006] EWCA Civ 423 at para 27.
53 See appendix H for CPR 31.

document. Rather, under CPR 31.2, a party discloses a document by stating that it exists or that it has existed. There is then a right, under CPR 31.3, to inspect that document, save in certain specified circumstances.

86 It should be borne in mind that, as with all other aspects of the CPR, a court will apply the overriding objective when deciding whether it is appropriate to make an order. Since the process of disclosure inevitably requires time and expense, advisers should always carefully consider whether a document sought is really required, having regard to the issues in dispute between the parties.

The scope of disclosure

87 Under CPR 31.5, when a court makes an order for disclosure, the obligation is to provide 'standard disclosure'. Under CPR 31.6, this means that the following must be disclosed:

- the documents on which a party relies;
- the documents which adversely affect the disclosing party's case;
- the documents which adversely affect another party's case;
- the documents which support another party's case;
- any other documents which a relevant practice direction require the party to disclose.

.88 However, in so far as standard disclosure is concerned, a party is only required to make a reasonable search for these documents (CPR 31.7). In deciding upon the reasonableness of a search, the following factors are relevant:

- the number of documents involved;
- the nature and complexity of the proceedings;
- the ease and expense of retrieval of any particular document;
- the significance of any document which is likely to be located during the search.

.89 If a party has not searched for a category or class of document on the grounds that to do so would be unreasonable, he must state this in his disclosure statement and identify the category or class of document.

.90 In addition, a party may disclose a document but assert that it would be disproportionate to the issues in the case to permit inspection of documents within a particular category or class of document disclosed. This might be the case, for example, where there are a large number of pages comprising a document relating to telephone records, but they extend over many years and the applicant is only relying upon the fact of a few calls which are recorded in the document.

In those circumstances, it may well be disproportionate to copy and provide all the pages in the document.

The process of disclosure

8.91 CPR 31.10 sets out the procedure to be followed in respect of disclosure. It involves drafting a list of documents on the standard court form, identifying in particular:

- those documents in respect of which the party claims a right or duty to withhold inspection;
- those documents which are no longer in the party's control, along with an explanation of what has happened to those documents.

8.92 The list will also include a disclosure statement, which is in a standard wording on the court form. This statement will:

- set out the extent of the search that has been made to locate disclosable documents;
- certify that the person making the statement understands the duty to disclose documents;
- certify that the person has, to the best of his or her knowledge, carried out that duty.

Where a party wishes to withhold inspection of a document on the basis of disproportionality, this must also be stated in the disclosure statement (CPR 31.3(2)(b)).

Withholding disclosure or inspection

8.93 CPR 31.10(4) permits a party to indicate that there are documents in respect of which it claims a right or duty to withhold inspection. If this right or duty is upheld or not challenged, then CPR 31.3(1)(b) means that there is no right to inspect the document. In such a case, the details of the document will appear in the disclosure list but will not actually be physically provided.

8.94 In addition, a party may seek, under CPR 31.19, to withhold disclosure of a document, that is, not even to mention its existence in a disclosure statement. Such an order can be made without notice and any order will not normally be served on anybody else. However, the court may permit any party to make representations on the application.

8.95 These rules are in place because of issues concerning legal professional privilege, litigation privilege and public interest immunity (PII). In the case of the former two categories, a party will almost certainly refer to the fact that there is a class of privileged documents, and there is a specific part of the standard court form which deals with it. In so far as the latter is concerned, a party may not even mention the fact that these documents exist but instead apply to the court, without notice, in order to prevent the other party from even learning of their possible existence. The most common example of PII is in the context of police informers (known as Covert Human Intelligence Sources, or CHISs). However, where ASBOs are concerned, it may be that the police pass a document to an applying authority which then has the duty of deciding whether to make any claim to PII.

8.96 Claims to legal professional privilege, which encompass communications between legal advisers and their clients, both acting in their professional capacities, will not normally require any challenge. However, this is sometimes confused with litigation privilege, which can apply when the communication is between a solicitor and a third party. This will most commonly arise where the solicitor obtains witness statements in contemplation of pending litigation, in which case privilege will attach and there is no obligation to permit inspection. However, it is important to remember that communications are not privileged simply because they are confidential. Accordingly, where a housing officer, for example, asks a person to keep diary sheets which are then used to draft a witness statement, the diary sheets are not privileged from production, although a draft copy of the witness statement might be.

8.97 In this connection, it is worth making the point that the wishes of any witnesses who prefer to retain their anonymity do not determine whether evidence should be disclosed. The 2006 Home Office Guidance suggests that 'evidence should not be disclosed without the express permission of the witness'.[54] This is legally incorrect, unless a claim can be made in respect of litigation privilege for the relevant evidence. Furthermore, this Guidance ignores the fact that the evidence of the witness may not assist the authority's case but might assist the defendant's case, in which case it has to be disclosed.

Specific disclosure and inspection

8.98 It is also open to a party to seek specific disclosure or inspection. The procedure is governed by CPR 31.12 and works in two ways. First, in so far as disclosure is concerned, it may be claimed that a relevant document has not been disclosed or that the class of documents

54 *A Guide to Anti-social Behaviour Orders* (Home Office, 2006) p33. Available at www.together.gov.uk.

which should be disclosed goes beyond standard disclosure by reason of a particular feature of the case. If such an application is to be made, then cogent reasons for it will need to be provided with particular reference as to why justice cannot be done unless the additional documents are disclosed.

Disclosure against non-parties

8.99 An application can also be made to obtain disclosure from somebody who is not a party to the proceedings. However, since this will involve the expenditure of time and resources by a body which has no direct interest in the outcome of the case, there are additional hurdles to be overcome. They are contained in CPR 31.17 and enable the court to make an order only where:

- the documents sought are likely to support the case of the applicant or adversely affect the case of one of the other parties to the proceedings;
- disclosure is necessary in order to dispose fairly of the claim or to save costs.

8.100 Accordingly, where such an application is made, it is essential that the evidence in support clearly addresses the relevant criteria. Of course, the first step before making the application is to seek voluntary disclosure from the third party. It is good practice to address the above criteria in any informal request so that the proposed respondent has an opportunity to explain why it will not be providing the documents. If these reasons are weak, it will strengthen any subsequent application to the court.

8.101 The most likely candidates for non-party disclosure are bodies which have been involved with defendants in other capacities. This will include local authorities, the police, schools and hospitals. In many cases, it will be possible to obtain the required information under data protection or freedom of information legislation, especially where the information concerns the client or the client's family.[55] The position is more complicated when information about other individuals is involved, for example, where it is thought that a witness on behalf of a claimant may have criminal convictions or medical problems which might render their evidence unreliable. In such circumstances, the best way of dealing with the position is by way of a CPR Part 18 request for further information from the applying authority or a notice, under CPR 32.18, to admit certain facts.

55 The impact of the Data Protection Act 1998 is discussed in full in chapter 2.

Witness evidence

8.102 It is frequently the case that authorities applying for ASBOs rely upon hearsay evidence from employees and officers in order to make good their contention that a respondent has been involved in anti-social behaviour. This evidence is often hearsay on the basis that the victims of the alleged anti-social behaviour are fearful of coming to court. Additionally, this evidence is sometimes anonymised. Depending on the seriousness of the allegation, it can be very difficult to persuade a court to treat such evidence with the appropriate degree of circumspection.

8.103 There is nothing wrong in principle in relying upon hearsay evidence. As illustrated in chapter 4, CEA 1995 expressly allows for the adducing of hearsay evidence. The failure to follow the relevant rules of procedure are matters which go to weight, although it is of course open to a judge to rule that no weight should be attached to a particular piece of evidence.

8.104 In *Solon South West Housing Association Ltd v James*[56] the appellants sought to argue, despite the decision of the House of Lords in *R (on the application of McCann) v Crown Court at Manchester; Clingham v K & C Royal Borough Council*,[57] that the trial judge had erred in admitting hearsay evidence. It was asserted that the admission of such evidence, on the facts, breached the appellants' right to a fair trial under ECHR Article 6. The Court of Appeal disagreed, making the following points:

> The issue becomes, rather, the case-specific issue: whether the way in which [the trial judge] addressed the hearsay evidence and the weight which he attached to it was in all the circumstances appropriate and fair, or whether he acted in some way unfairly in its treatment, or attached disproportionate weight to it in such a way as to make the proceedings unfair. It seems to me that in this respect the Convention adds little to what would anyway be involved in the proper application of the discretion provided under section 4 of the 1995 Act.[58]

8.105 However, although it is now commonplace for judges to admit hearsay evidence with very little by way of argument, it is important to bear in mind that the admission of such evidence cannot be treated as automatic. In *Moat Housing Group-South Ltd v Harris*,[59] while holding

56 [2004] EWCA Civ 1847.

57 [2002] UKHL 39; [2003] 1 AC 787. This case is discussed in full in chapter 3.

58 *Solon South-West Housing Association Ltd v James* [2004] EWCA Civ 1847 at para 29.

59 [2005] EWCA Civ 287; [2005] 3 WLR 691.

that the trial judge had been entitled to rely upon hearsay evidence in the way that he had, the Court of Appeal said this:

> While nobody would wish to return to the days before the Civil Evidence Act 1995 came into force, when efforts to admit hearsay evidence were beset by complicated procedural rules, the experience of this case should provide a salutary warning for the future that more attention should be paid by claimants in this type of case to the need to state by convincing direct evidence why it was not reasonable and practicable to produce the original maker of the statement as a witness. If the statement involves multiple hearsay, the route by which the original statement came to the attention of the person attesting to it should be identified as far as practicable. It would also be desirable for judges to remind themselves in their judgments that they are taking into account the [CEA 1995] section 4(2) criteria so far as they are relevant.[60]

8.106 It is worthwhile reminding judges of this, as well as the specific problems that can occur when there is over-reliance on hearsay evidence. The extent to which hearsay evidence can become contaminated is often overlooked and it is important for advisers to carefully probe the way in which the evidence from witnesses was collected. This can be done at an early stage of the proceedings by making CPR 18 requests for further information. The advantage of this approach is that it does not involve any specific procedure or form and can simply be done by letter. Providing that the correspondence clearly indicates that the request is being done under Part 18 and gives a reasonable amount of time to answer the questions posed, which should be expressed simply and not be disproportionate in terms of information sought, it can be a valuable weapon.

8.107 Other problems which may be caused by hearsay evidence were also highlighted in *Moat Housing*,[61] and are again worth raising in an appropriate case:

> The willingness of a civil court to admit hearsay evidence carries with it inherent dangers in a case like this. As Mr Macdonald said, rumours abound in a small housing estate, and it is much more difficult for a judge to assess the truth of what he is being told if the original maker of the statement does not attend court to be cross-examined on his/her evidence. The emphasis placed by section 4(2)(b) of the 1995 Act on contemporaneity merely goes to highlight the importance of a landlord giving a tenant contemporary notice of any complaints that are made

60 [2005] EWCA Civ 287 at para 140.

61 [2005] EWCA Civ 287 at para 135.

against his/her behaviour, so that the tenant is not faced in court with serious complaints made by anonymous or absent witnesses about matters that took place, if at all, many months previously.

8.108 The form of the hearsay evidence upon which reliance is placed also needs to be carefully considered. If there is a formal witness statement, then the party which seeks to adduce the evidence needs to explain, at the time of serving the witness statement, why the witness cannot attend court to give evidence.[62] Where the hearsay evidence is not in a witness statement, then there needs to be a notice identifying the hearsay evidence, stating that reliance will be placed upon it and explaining why the witness will not be called.[63] A failure to comply with these requirements does not mean that the evidence becomes inadmissible but can be taken into account by the court when deciding what weight to put on the hearsay evidence.[64] From a practical point of view, the failure by a party to explain why a party cannot come to court to give evidence is likely to be the issue which most concerns a judge.

8.109 It is open to a party to make an application to cross-examine the maker of a hearsay statement under CPR 33.4.[65] This application must be made not later than 14 days after the service of a notice indicating an intention to rely upon hearsay evidence. It should be noted that, where the hearsay evidence is a witness statement, the service of the statements also constitutes the relevant notice.[66]

8.110 Whether or not an application to cross-examine should be made will of course depend upon the circumstances of the particular case. A court is unlikely to grant the application where there is cogent evidence of fear or other inability to attend. On the other hand, the interests of justice may mandate attendance for cross-examination where the only evidence against a defendant comes from one source. It should also be borne in mind that the late service of witness statements may prejudice the right of a party to apply for cross-examination, and so this is a point which should be taken into account by a court when deciding whether to allow an applicant authority to adduce hearsay evidence at the last minute.

62 CPR 33.2(2).

63 CPR 33.2(3).

64 CEA 1995 s2(4).

65 See appendix H for CPR 33.

66 CPR 33.2(1).

The hearing

8.111 Since the application for the ASBO in the county court will be an adjunct to the main proceedings, some consideration will need to be given to how the evidence can be dealt with most conveniently. However, it is difficult to envisage cases where the evidence in support of the ASBO will not form an integral part of the main proceedings. Accordingly, in the vast majority of cases, the format will be that of an ordinary civil trial, with witness statements standing as the evidence in chief, and the usual procedural rules applying in relation to the giving of evidence, submissions and judgment.

8.112 Where the evidence in support of an ASBO is distinct from that which is relevant to the principal proceedings, it may appear that, in theory, some issues arise. For example, where a claim is made for possession based on non-payment of rent and the alleged anti-social behaviour is raised after the issue of proceedings, it might be argued that the evidence relating to the ASBO should be considered after a judgment on the possession claim is made, especially since a court may be less favourably inclined to a tenant who had committed acts of anti-social behaviour. However, given that all the evidence will be in the same hearing bundle, and the judge will have probably read the witness statement of the applying authority beforehand, or at least the application notice seeking the ASBO, there may not be a great difference in practice.

8.113 Nevertheless, it is worth paying attention to the different burdens of proof which may be involved. In relation to possession proceedings, the allegations will need to be proved on the balance of probabilities. However, where the same acts are relied upon in support of an application for an ASBO, the court will need to consider whether the allegations are made out to the criminal standard, albeit only for the purposes of the ASBO.

Drafting of the order

8.114 There is a standard form of the order which, at the time of writing, is not available on the website of the Department of Constitutional Affairs. However, it is available from the Government's 'Together' website[67] and a copy is reproduced in appendix G.

8.115 Although the court form is said to apply to applications under s1B(4), there is no reason why it cannot be used when an application

67 Form N113: see www.together.gov.uk.

is made for an interim ASBO under s1D, especially since it contains a swhich enables a return date to be added.

8.116 In *Moat Housing Group-South v Harris*,[68] the Court of Appeal adopted the principles set out in the criminal case of *R v P (Shane Tony)*[69] about the content of a county court ASBO:

- the terms of the order must be precise and capable of being understood by the respondent;
- the findings of fact giving rise to the making of the order should be recorded;
- the order must be explained to the respondent;
- the exact terms of the order must be pronounced in open court;
- the written order must accurately reflect the order as pronounced.

8.117 The court emphasised the importance of ensuring that, in the event of a breach, a court should be able to understand the facts on which the original order was made without having to incur the expense of commissioning a transcript of the county court judgment.

It is common for county court orders to be drafted by advocates at court and for the order to be comprehensive of all the issues between the parties.

Consent orders

8.118 It has already been pointed out[70] that, in the context of magistrates' courts, it is not open to a party to consent to an ASBO. This is because the court needs to be satisfied that both limbs of the statutory test have been made out.

8.119 The same principle applies in the county court. A judge will have to make his or her own judgment as to whether the necessary conditions are satisfied and a defendant cannot agree to an ASBO being made. In this respect, the position is similar to residential possession proceedings where the court has to be satisfied that it is reasonable to make an order.[71]

8.120 However, there is nothing to prevent a person facing an application for an ASBO from expressing a willingness to submit to such an order. First, s/he can admit the factual basis of the claim. This will

68 [2005] EWCA Civ 287 at para 34; [2005] 3 WLR 691. See also para 5.132 on form of the order; and chapter 7 on terms and duration of orders for more on this issue.

69 [2004] EWCA Crim 287. See chapter 7 on terms of orders.

70 See *R (on the application of T) v Manchester Crown Court* [2005] EWHC 1396 and the discussion of this case at para 5.33.

71 See, for example, *Knowsley Housing Trust v McMullen* [2006] EWCA Civ 539 at para 6.

obviate the need for the judge to make the relevant findings of fact. Second, it is open to him or her to advance no argument as to the second limb of the statutory formula. Although the circumstances in which such a course should be taken are likely to be rare, because of the criminal sanctions which could follow if the ASBO was breached, it should not be ruled out as an option in all cases. For example, if the choice is between submitting to an ASBO and risking the loss of a home in possession proceedings, the view may be taken that the ASBO is the lesser of the two evils.

Children and young persons

Making an order

8.121 Although there is nothing in CDA 1998 which prevents a relevant authority from making an application against any person aged 10 or over, it is important to bear in mind the principle that an order in the civil courts will not generally be made against those who are under the age of 18. This is because of the problems that are faced in seeking to enforce the breach of an injunction order. An example of this is supplied by the case of *Harrow London Borough Council v G*[72] where the High Court held that it had been wrong to have made an injunction order against a 13-year-old boy since he could not be imprisoned nor was there any evidence that any other financial sanction could be imposed upon him for breach.

8.122 Stand-alone ASBOs can be made against any person aged 10 or over. The position is slightly different in the county court. There is no general power to make a county court ASBO against a person under 18. However, there is a pilot scheme in certain county courts, which has operated since October 2004 and is due to end on 1 October 2006, which enables ASBOs to be made against those under 18.[73] The extent to which this interrelates with the general principle relating to orders against those under 18 is yet to be seen. Reference should also be made to chapter 10 and the discussion of the considerations which apply when making ASBOs against young people, in particular, the importance of taking into account the interests of the child.

72 [2004] EWHC 17 (QB).

73 See reg 4(1) of the Anti-Social Behaviour Act 2003 (Commencement No 4) Order 2004, SI No 2168 (as amended by the Anti-Social Behaviour Act 2003 (Commencement No 4) (Amendment) Order 2006, SI No 835). Reg 4(2) lists the following pilot county courts: Bristol, Central London, Clerkenwell, Dewsbury, Huddersfield, Leicester, Manchester, Oxford, Tameside, Wigan, Wrexham.

Reporting restrictions

8.123 Section 39 of the Children and Young Persons Act 1933 permits the court to give a direction which prevents the identification of a child concerned in ASBO proceedings. The principles which govern the making of such a direction, and how the interests of the child are to be balanced against the general rule that proceedings are to be held in public,[74] were discussed in *R (on the application of T) v St Albans Crown Court*.[75] Here, Elias J pointed out that there was a public interest in disclosure when an ASBO had been made since this might assist in enforcement of the order. Having said this, the fact that the prospects of rehabilitation would be enhanced if anonymity was preserved would also be a relevant consideration.

Representation

8.124 CPR 21.2(2) provides that a child must have a litigation friend to conduct proceedings unless the court orders otherwise. A person may not take any step against a child without the child having a litigation friend, save for issuing and serving proceedings and applying to the court for the appointment of a litigation friend.[76] Any other step which is taken while the child has no litigation friend shall be of no effect unless the court orders otherwise.[77]

8.125 CPR 21 also sets out the procedure to be followed when a litigation friend is to be appointed and who can be a litigation friend. Reference should be made to the detailed provisions of Part 21 if required.

Alternatives to ASBOs

8.126 As highlighted in earlier chapters, there have long been many options available to those seeking to prevent what is frequently referred to as anti-social behaviour. In the civil field, the most obvious remedy is the injunction. The scope of such injunctions in the housing field has grown rapidly in recent years, with social landlords now having the power to obtain anti-social behaviour injunctions (ASBIs) to restrain a wide range of activity which affects their housing management

74 See CPR 39.2(4).

75 [2002] EWHC 1129 (Admin). Judgment was given at the same time in the linked case of *Chief Constable of Surrey Police v JHG (1) and DHG (2)*. See also para 10.48.

76 CPR 21.3(2)(b).

77 CPR 21.3(4).

functions. Under the Housing Act (HA) 1996 the court can make the following orders on the application of the relevant landlord:

8.127 (1) An injunction under section 153A to prohibit conduct which is capable of causing nuisance or annoyance to any person and which directly or indirectly relates to or affects the housing management functions of the relevant landlord providing that:
   (a) the person against whom the injunction is sought is engaging, has engaged or threatens to engage in such conduct and
   (b) the conduct is capable of causing nuisance or annoyance to any of the following:
      (i) a person with a right to reside in or occupy housing accommodation owned or managed by the relevant landlord;
      (ii) a person with a right to reside in or occupy other housing accommodation in the neighbourhood of housing accommodation referred to in (i) above;
      (iii) a person engaged in lawful activity in or in the neighbourhood of housing accommodation referred to in (i) above; or
      (iv) a person employed, whether or not by the relevant landlord, in connection with the exercise of the relevant landlord's housing management functions.

(2) An injunction under section 153B to restrain conduct that consists of or involves the use or threat to use housing accommodation owned or managed by a relevant landlord for an unlawful purpose.

(3) Under section 153C, an exclusion order and/or power of arrest if an injunction is granted under section 153A or 153B and the court considers that:
   (a) the conduct complained of consists of or includes the use or threatened use of violence; or
   (b) there is a significant risk of harm to a person mentioned in section 153A whom the anti-social behaviour is capable of affecting.

(4) An order under section 153D excluding a person from entering or being in any specified premises or area and/or granting a power of arrest when an application is made for an injunction to prevent the breach or anticipated breach of a tenancy agreement where the tenant is:
   (a) engaging or threatening to engage in conduct that is capable of causing nuisance or annoyance to any person, or
   (b) is allowing, inciting or encouraging any other person to engage or threaten to engage in such conduct

and the conduct complained of:

(i) includes the use or threatened use of violence, or

(ii) means that there is a significant risk of harm to any person.

8.128 A relevant landlord is defined as a local authority, an RSL or a HAT.[78] In addition, a charitable housing trust which is not registered as a social landlord can apply for the last type of order mentioned above.[79] The applications can be made without notice and, where a power of arrest is sought, this can also be granted without notice.[80]

8.129 In addition to these specific types of order, available to both the county court and the High Court, the civil courts have wide powers to grant injunctions to prohibit other civil wrongs, ranging from assaults to trespass on land. It is also worth considering the power available to a local authority under s222(1)(a) of the Local Government Act (LGA) 1972, which is in the following terms:

> Where a local authority consider it expedient for the promotion or protection of the interests of the inhabitants of their area ... they may prosecute or defend or appear in any legal proceedings and, in the case of civil proceedings, may institute them in their own name ...

8.130 In *Nottingham City Council v Zain*[81] the local authority brought proceedings in order to prevent a suspected drug dealer from entering a housing estate in its area. It argued that what was being done by the defendant, and what he would continue to do, amounted to a public nuisance and so it was entitled to bring proceedings in its name in order to prevent that nuisance from occurring. The Court of Appeal agreed. It held that a nuisance was public if 'it materially affects the reasonable comfort and convenience of life of a class of Her Majesty's subjects' and the question of whether it did so affect individuals was a matter of fact. Schiemann LJ explained his reasoning as follows:

> [I]n my judgement it is within the proper sphere of a local authority's activities to try and put an end to all public nuisances in its area provided always that it considers that it is expedient for the promotion or protection of the interests of the inhabitants of its area to do so in a particular case. Certainly my experience over the last 40 years tells me that authorities regularly do this and so far as I know this has never attracted adverse judicial comment. I consider that an authority would not be acting beyond its powers if it spent time and money in trying

78 HA 1996 s153E(7).

79 HA 1996 s153E(8).

80 HA 1996 s154.

81 [2001] EWCA Civ 1248.

> to persuade those who were creating a public nuisance to desist ... It follows that, provided that an authority considers it expedient for the promotion and protection of the interests of the inhabitants of its area, it can institute proceedings in its own name with a view to putting a stop to a public nuisance.[82]

8.131 Schiemann LJ also made the following point about the relationship between the local authority's rights LGA 1972 s222 and the criminal law:

> On the assumption that I am right that an authority has the right to sue in its own name for a public nuisance, at any event if the nuisance covers a sphere in relation to which the authority has express duties, I see no reason to deprive it of that right simply because carrying out the activity which it is seeking to inhibit also involves the commission of a crime. Indeed if the fact that the acts alleged amount to a crime had the effect of depriving the authority of the right to sue in public nuisance it would do so whenever public nuisance is alleged since the commission of a public nuisance is itself a crime.[83]

8.132 In the light of these apparently wide powers available to local authorities and other social landlords, there may well be arguments available to a defendant as to the failure to consider alternatives to an ASBO. When rights under the European Convention on Human Rights (ECHR) are engaged, which they frequently will be, especially in the housing context, there may well be arguments that the use of an ASBO constitutes a disproportionate measure, bearing in mind the other available options.

8.133 Given that ASBOs made in the county court are likely, in many cases, to engage Article 8 of the ECHR, it will be necessary for an applicant to show, and a court to be satisfied, that the order is strictly necessary, or proportionate, to deal with the conduct which it is sought to suppress.[84] Most obviously, this means that an order must not be drawn too widely. However, it also requires consideration of alternatives to an ASBO since the doctrine of proportionality means that the means used to deal with the alleged anti-social behaviour must not be excessive, having regard to the aim which is sought to be achieved. In some circumstances, this may mean not making any order at all, particularly since breach can result in a criminal sanction.

82 [2001] EWCA Civ 1248 at para 13.

83 [2001] EWCA Civ 1248 at para 15.

84 See chapter 7 for a full discussion.

8.134 There are various arguments, however, which may be deployed by an applying authority to explain why an ASBO should be sought instead of an injunction:

(1) It may be said that an ASBO can prohibit any conduct whereas an injunction is more limited. However, within the context of the principal proceedings, it would be an unusual case where an injunction would not cover the subject area of the conduct which it is sought to prevent. Similarly, since a housing injunction can prevent anti-social conduct by a former tenant in the neighbourhood of his or her previous accommodation, it can apply even after a tenant has been evicted.

(2) It is commonly said that an injunction cannot be made against a person under 18, whereas an ASBO can. It is true that the courts are reluctant to make injunction orders against those under 18, since the penalty of imprisonment for contempt is not available,[85] and financial penalties would be in effective. However, in *Harrow London Borough Council v G*,[86] the High Court, in allowing an appeal against an interim injunction made in the county court, did not rule out the possibility that an injunction might be appropriate if there was evidence of the defendant possessing assets. Furthermore, where the principal proceedings rely upon a parent's breach of a tenancy agreement, in the sense that s/he is allowing a child to act in an anti-social manner, there is no reason why, in an appropriate case, an injunction against the parent should not be sought as opposed to an ASBO.

(3) It is true to say that the minimum two-year length of an ASBO is greater than most injunctions which might be granted and that, further, both the sanction for breach and the range of penalties are greater than in the case of a breach of an injunction. However, given that the purpose of both injunctions and ASBOs is to provide protection, rather than punish, it is arguable that the focus should be on the ability of the order to prevent the anti-social behaviour from reoccurring. Since a party subject to an ASBO or an injunction will be made equally aware that one of the possible consequences of breach is imprisonment, the differences

85 See Power of Criminal Courts (Sentencing) Act 2000 s89, which in fact does not permit any person under the age of 21 to be committed to prison for contempt. The section has been amended by Criminal Justice and Court Services Act 2000 (see s74 and Sch 7 Pt II paras 160 and 180) so as to reduce the age to 18 but the amendment has not yet been brought into force.

86 [2004] EWHC 17 (QB).

between the two are perhaps more apparent than real in so far as deterrence is concerned.

ASBOs and possession proceedings

8.135 Within the context of possession proceedings, it is important to remember that, in so far as statutorily protected tenants are concerned, the court will need to be satisfied that it is reasonable to make an order for possession. Furthermore, even where the court is so satisfied, it may be possible to argue that an order should be suspended, or made conditional, on terms. In cases of alleged anti-social behaviour, it is typical that a possession order is made but its execution is suspended on the basis that the defendant complies with the terms of the tenancy agreement which prohibit the commission of acts of nuisance. It could be argued that this will be sufficient to prevent future anti-social behaviour and therefore give adequate protection to other individuals. It can further be argued that this would constitute a proportionate response.

8.136 Conversely, it might be said that, given the protection which might be given through the grant of an ASBO, whether stand-alone or within county court proceedings, it would be inappropriate to make an order for possession. Both these sets of arguments have been considered in various cases.

8.137 In *London & Quadrant Housing Trust v Root*[87] there had been numerous breaches of the defendant's tenancy agreement, which included intimidation and threats, by her former partner. He was joined to the proceedings and an ASBO made against him. This prohibited him from coming to within a mile of the neighbourhood, but he regularly came to the edge of the proscribed zone in order to see his son. The Court of Appeal, while not specifically addressing the defendant's arguments that the trial judge should have considered more carefully whether the ASBO provided sufficient protection, dismissed her appeal on the basis that the judge had been entitled to make an outright order for possession.

8.138 In *Manchester City Council v Higgins*[88] the local authority appealed against the fact that the trial judge had suspended a possession order which had been made largely on the basis of the defendant's 12-year-old son's behaviour. The judge had found that the defendant had displayed an indifference to her son's behaviour but also commented

87 [2005] EWCA Civ 43; [2005] HLR 28.

88 [2005] EWCA Civ 1423.

on her inadequate parenting skills. One of the issues on appeal was the extent to which the existence of an ASBO, which had been made against the son in the case, was relevant to the making of a possession order.

8.139 The Court of Appeal held that the judge had been wrong to suspend the possession order. Ward LJ made the following observations about the ASBO:

> The mere fact that the ASBO remained in force until James attained the age of 16 and that the police had powers to deal with future breaches would give the neighbours no sufficient protection for the reasons I have explained. He cocked a snook at it within days of its imposition: indeed he demonstrated his contempt for the order by his rampage of destruction on the two motor cars on 14 December. The making of an ASBO could in some cases be the harbinger of better times but the mere fact of its having been made and remaining in place serves in this case more to emphasise the seriousness of the misbehaviour and therefore the need for immediate protection from it than the hope without more that it will cause the offending to cease.[89]

8.140 Gage LJ made it plain that it was not possible to give any guidance as to the factors to be taken into account when deciding whether or not to suspend a possession order, save in the most general terms as follows:

> In other words, when deciding whether or not to suspend the order the court will amongst other things be concerned to devise the best method of protecting the needs of neighbours against the re-occurrence of the anti-social behaviour which gave rise to the order for possession being made. In some cases, of which in my opinion this is one, an ASBO will provide no real protection for neighbours. In other cases it may well provide adequate protection. Each case must be determined on its own facts.[90]

8.141 The Court of Appeal again considered the relationship between possession proceedings and ASBOs in *Knowsley Housing Trust v McMullen*.[91] Here, the trial judge had made a suspended possession order on the basis of the behaviour of the tenant's son. The terms of the suspension were dependent upon the son not committing any further acts of anti-social behaviour. In the Court of Appeal the tenant argued, among other things, that it was wrong to make the order, or suspend it on the terms relating to the son's behaviour, because there was an ASBO

89 [2005] EWCA Civ 1423 at para 42.
90 [2005] EWCA Civ 1423 at para 55.
91 [2006] EWCA Civ 539.

against the son which provided sufficient protection. This submission was rejected, with Neuberger LJ explaining his reasoning as follows:

8.142 I can see no intrinsic reason why the existence of an ASBO against the person responsible for the nuisance should prevent the making of an order for possession, whether outright or suspended, based on ground 14 [ie, the statutory ground entitling a landlord to claim possession on the basis of nuisance]. Indeed, it seems to me wrong that there should be some sort of rule or practice that a landlord, who has the benefit of a covenant against nuisance and of a statutory right to possession (if it is established to be reasonable) under ground 14, should be forced to rely on enforcing an ASBO, rather than pursuing its own rights. The two orders are conceptually quite different; further, the order for possession would survive the revocation of the ASBO, and the ASBO would survive notwithstanding the execution, or the reversal, of the order for possession.

I would therefore reject, on the basis of principle, practice and authority, the notion that, in a case where the landlord relies on ground 14, the court should not make an order for possession, whether suspended or otherwise, simply because it can be said that the person responsible for the acts of nuisance is subject to an ASBO which is, in effect, directed to preventing the same sort of acts. However, I accept that, as a matter of principle, and, in the light of Ward LJ's observations, on the basis of authority, the existence of an ASBO can be a relevant matter when the court is deciding whether it is reasonable to make an order for possession, and whether to suspend it.

The existence of an ASBO may be of particular assistance to the tenant (especially in resisting an outright order for possession) where, as here, the person responsible for the nuisance is not the tenant, and the tenant cannot control the behaviour of that person.[92]

On the facts of the particular case, the Court of Appeal found that the judge had been entitled to make the order which he had.

8.143 The following principles can be drawn from this series of cases:

- The existence of an ASBO will not prevent a court from making an order for possession, whether outright or suspended on terms.
- Conversely, the fact that a possession order may be suspended on terms, thereby making it clear to the tenant that any further breaches of the order will lead to dispossession of the home, does not mean that an ASBO should not be made.
- However, the existence of an ASBO, along with any other behavioural restraints, is a relevant consideration when deciding whether or not a possession order should be made and if any order which is made should be suspended.

92 [2006] EWCA Civ 539 at paras 37, 43 and 44.

- It will also be relevant to consider whether the ASBO has been breached since, if it has not, this will be evidence from which the court can conclude that the objectionable behaviour is being adequately controlled.

Offers to settle

8.144 Although, as indicated above, it is not possible to consent to an ASBO, there is nothing to prevent a party from making offers which fall short of giving such consent. In broad terms, there are two options available. First, a defendant can make an open offer to settle the claim, for example, by agreeing to give undertakings to the court instead of an ASBO. Alternatively, the defendant can formalise any settlement proposal by way of a Part 36 offer, which cannot be disclosed to the court, and has certain costs consequences.

8.145 CPR 36 sets out the process for making offers which will not be brought to the attention of the court until the issue of costs comes to be decided.[93] Of course, the ASBO aspect of any claim will not involve money, but if the principal proceedings do, for example in a claim for rent arrears and/or disrepair, then slightly different rules apply. What follows sets out the basics of Part 36 and full reference should be made to the relevant part of the CPR if required.

Offers to settle non-money claims

8.146 This is governed by CPR 36.5. An offer to settle must be in writing and relate to the entire claim or any issue which arises in it. It must state whether it relates to the whole claim or just an issue in the claim, as well as whether it takes into account any counterclaim. It should usually be made more than 21 days before the start of the trial and

(a) be expressed to remain open for acceptance for 21 days from the date it is made;
(b) provide that after 21 days the offeree may only accept it if:
  (i) the parties agree the liability for costs; or
  (ii) the court gives permission.

Where the Part 36 offer is made less than 21 days before the start of the trial it must state that the offeree may only accept it if:

(a) the parties agree the liability for costs; or
(b) the court gives permission.

93 See CPR 36.19.

Offers to settle money and non-money claims

8.147 The process to settle money and non-money claims is similar to that outlined above, save that, where there is a defendant to the money claim, s/he must follow up the offer with a payment into court.

Advantages of a Part 36 offer

8.148 The rationale behind Part 36 is that parties should attempt to settle their differences with minimum expense and by avoiding litigation where possible. Accordingly, there are incentives and penalties where parties do better or worse than Part 36 offers. Where a claimant accepts a defendant's Part 36 offer s/he will be entitled to the costs of the claim up to the date of acceptance; where a defendant accepts a claimant's Part 36 offer, then the claimant will again be entitled to the costs of the claim up to the date of acceptance

8.149 However, where a claimant at trial fails to obtain a judgment which is more advantageous than a defendant's Part 36 offer, then, unless it is unjust to do so, the court will order the claimant to pay any costs incurred by the defendant after the latest date on which the payment or offer could have been accepted without needing the permission of the court.[94]

8.150 Where a judgment against a defendant is more advantageous to the claimant than the proposals contained in a claimant's Part 36 offer the court can order penalty interest and/or costs on the indemnity basis unless it is unjust to do so.[95] While this will not make a great difference in many cases as far as those facing ASBO applications are concerned, there are two circumstances where it might be relevant:

- where the applying authority also has a rent arrears claim, in which case it could obtain penalty interest on any arrears found to be owing;
- where the defendant is not publicly funded, in which case the amount of personal liability will be greater.

8.151 Finally, it is also important to bear in mind that any offer, even if not made in accordance with Part 36, may still have adverse consequences if the offering party does better than his or her offer at trial.[96]

94 CPR 36.20.

95 CPR 36.21.

96 See *Stokes Pension Fund v Western Power Distribution (South West) Plc* [2005] EWCA Civ 854.

Mediation and other forms of alternative dispute resolution

8.152 In *Halsey v Milton Keynes Hospital General Trust*[97] the Court of Appeal made it clear that a party cannot be compelled to enter into mediation or another form of ADR in order to resolve a legal dispute. However, there is no doubt that an unreasonable failure to consider mediation can have adverse costs consequences. In *Burchell v Bullard*,[98] the Court of Appeal found that there had been such a failure but declined to mark its disapproval by a costs sanction on the sole basis that the law had not fully developed on the issue when the offer to mediate had been refused. However, Ward LJ had this to say about the current position:

8.153 The profession must, however, take no comfort from this conclusion. *Halsey* has made plain not only the high rate of a successful outcome being achieved by mediation but also its established importance as a track to a just result running parallel with that of the court system. Both have a proper part to play in the administration of justice. The court has given its stamp of approval to mediation and it is now the legal profession which must become fully aware of and acknowledge its value. The profession can no longer with impunity shrug aside reasonable requests to mediate. The parties cannot ignore a proper request to mediate simply because it was made before the claim was issued. With court fees escalating it may be folly to do so. I draw attention, moreover, to paragraph 5.4 of the pre-action protocol for Construction and Engineering Disputes – which I doubt was at the forefront of the parties' minds – which expressly requires the parties to consider at a pre-action meeting whether some form of alternative dispute resolution procedure would be more suitable than litigation. These defendants have escaped the imposition of a costs sanction in this case but defendants in a like position in the future can expect little sympathy if they blithely battle on regardless of the alternatives.[99]

8.154 Furthermore, public funding is available to enable a party to pursue alternative forms of dispute resolution and so the barriers which might have previously prevented a publicly funded party from making an offer of mediation no longer apply.

97 [2004] EWCA Civ 576; [2004] 1 WLR 3002.

98 [2005] EWCA Civ 358.

99 [2005] EWCA Civ 358 at para 43.

Judicial review

8.155 There are numerous powers exercised by relevant authorities under CDA 1998 s1B which involve the exercise of a judgment. So, for example, the power to seek an ASBO is couched in permissive terms; a relevant authority 'may' apply for an ASBO if it considers that certain conditions are satisfied. It is therefore open to the person who is the subject of an application to seek to claim judicial review of any decisions made in the exercise of such powers, assuming of course that the relevant authority is a public authority.[100] However, in order to succeed in such an application, it will be necessary to show that the decision reached by the public body is one to which no reasonable local authority could have come.[101] This is a high hurdle to surmount. Furthermore, if the decision to seek an ASBO reaches this level of unreasonableness, it is likely to be because there is insufficient evidence. In such a case, an application to strike out the claim, in so far as it relates to an application for an ASBO under CPR 3 or CPR 24, will be quicker and more cost-effective.

8.156 Other cases where a public law challenge may be considered is where the relevant authority has acted unlawfully in some other respect, perhaps by not complying with its own policy or by declining to enter into an acceptable behaviour contract[102] but then seeking to commence proceedings in breach of an agreement reached. However, even then, serious consideration should be given to the possibility of raising this public law challenge in the county court proceedings. Although there has been much debate over the extent to which it is open to a party to raise a public law issue in private law proceedings, all the members of the House of Lords, in *Kay v London Borough of Lambeth*,[103] seemed to be of the view that these could nearly always be raised in the private law proceedings.[104]

100 While local authorities etc will be public authorities, the question of whether a registered social landlord comes within this category is very much a fact-sensitive issue. See the discussion earlier in this chapter at paras 8.18–8.24.

101 See also paras 11.30–11.31 on appeals.

102 See para 2.16.

103 [2006] UKHL 10; [2006] 2 WLR 570.

104 [2006] UKHL 10, see Lord Bingham at para 30, Lord Nicholls at paras 58–60, Lord Hope at para 110, Lord Scott at para 174, Lady Hale at para 188 and Lord Brown at para 208.

Policies of applying authorities

8.157 Under HA 1996 s218A, every social landlord, which includes local authorities, RSLs and HATs, is required to have a policy relating to anti-social behaviour and procedures in place for dealing with occurrences of such behaviour. Anti-social behaviour is defined by reference to HA 1996 ss153A and 153B, which means that it is limited to conduct:

- which is capable of causing nuisance or annoyance to any person and which directly or indirectly relates to or affects the housing management functions of the relevant landlord; or
- which consists of or involves using or threatening to use housing accommodation owned or managed by a relevant landlord for an unlawful purpose.

8.158 In devising these policies and procedures, the landlord is required to take into account any guidance issued by the Secretary of State, in the case of an English local authority or HAT, or the Housing Corporation in the case of an English RSL. If the local authority or RSL is Welsh, then the relevant guidance is issued by the National Assembly for Wales.[105]

8.159 The various pieces of guidance issued by the Secretary of State, the National Assembly for Wales and the Housing Corporation are all entitled *Anti-Social Behaviour: Policy and Procedure.*[106] The three documents are all in similar terms and contain various aspects when advising a party faced with proceedings for an anti-social behaviour order. It is also important to bear in mind that local authorities will have other guidance which may well be relevant. For example, there may be guidance in relation to their obligations to prevent homelessness and keeping families together.

8.160 These documents, which should be available on the individual authority's website, can be used in numerous ways. First, if the authority has failed to comply with its own policies, such as taking less intrusive steps to prevent alleged anti-social behaviour, the shortcoming can be raised in correspondence and the body invited to comply with its own policies. In an appropriate case, the matter can be

105 Because although the relevant authority in both these cases is the Secretary of State, the effect of Regulation 2 and Schedule 2 of the National Assembly for Wales (Transfer of Functions) Order 1999 SI No 672 is that these functions are to be exercised by the Welsh National Assembly.

106 See www.housingcorp.gov.uk for the Housing Corporation's version of the guidance.

taken up with local politicians or a Member of Parliament. In the case of RSLs, the failure can be brought to the attention of the Housing Corporation, which is the statutory body that regulates the activities of RSLs. Another option is to raise the matter with the Local Government Ombudsman.

8.161 Second, a failure to follow a policy can be the basis for a claim for judicial review, providing that the body which it is sought to challenge comes within the definition of public authority (see paras 8.18–8.24 above). It can also be raised as a public law challenge in the county court, as discussed above.

8.162 Third, the failure by an applying authority to properly consider its own policies may be evidentially significant. A housing officer, for example, can sometimes be usefully questioned as to why s/he pursued the application for an ASBO without further considering other alternatives.

8.163 Fourth, the alternative methods set out in the policy for dealing with the anti-social behaviour, if not attempted, or not properly attempted, can be used as concrete examples of proportionate steps which could have been taken to deal with the issue. The fact that the guidance sets out less intrusive options can form the foundation of a submission that an ASBO is not required on the facts of any particular case.

Disability discrimination

8.164 The Disability Discrimination Act (DDA) 1995 gives some protection to disabled persons who are subject to less favourable treatment on the basis of their disability. A full analysis of the provisions is beyond the scope of this book.[107] What follows, therefore, is an analysis of those parts of the 1995 Act which are relevant to the making of ASBOs.

The definition of disability

8.165 Under DDA 1995 s1(1) a person has a disability for the purposes of the legislation, if he has a physical or mental impairment which has a substantial and long-term adverse effect on his ability to carry out normal day-to-day activities. However, it is important to note that this definition does not exist in a vacuum. Rather, it is necessary to analyse Schedule 1 in order to decide whether the conditions set out in s1(1) are indeed satisfied:

107 See C Palmer et all, *Discrimination Law Handbook* (2nd edn, forthcoming, 2006), Legal Action Group.

8.166 First, the effect of an impairment is a long-term effect if:

- it has lasted at least 12 months;
- the period for which it lasts is likely to be at least 12 months; or
- it is likely to last for the rest of the life of the person affected.

8.167 Second, an impairment is to be taken to affect the ability of the person concerned to carry out normal day-to-day activities only if it affects one of the following:

- mobility;
- manual dexterity;
- physical co-ordination;
- continence;
- ability to lift, carry or otherwise move everyday objects;
- speech, hearing or eyesight;
- memory or ability to concentrate, learn or understand;
- perception of the risk of physical danger.

8.168 Third, there are various deeming provisions which may need to be considered, such as:

- where an impairment ceases to have a substantial adverse effect on a person's ability to carry out normal day-to-day activities, it is to be treated as continuing to have that effect if that effect is likely to recur;
- an impairment which would be likely to have a substantial adverse effect on the ability of the person concerned to carry out normal day-to-day activities, but for the fact that measures are being taken to treat or correct it, is to be treated as having that effect (except in relation to an impairment concerning a person's sight, to the extent to which it is correctable by spectacles or contact lenses);
- a person who has cancer, HIV infection or multiple sclerosis is deemed to have a disability, and hence to be a disabled person.

Disability discrimination in relation to premises

8.169 Section 22(3) makes it unlawful for a person managing any premises[108] to discriminate against a disabled person, as defined in s1, who is occupying those premises, as follows:

(a) in the way he permits the disabled person to make use of any benefits or facilities;

108 But note also the exception from this duty in respect of small dwellings under DDA 1995 s23.

(b) by refusing or deliberately omitting to permit the disabled person to make use of any benefits or facilities; or
(c) by evicting the disabled person, or subjecting him to any other detriment.

8.170 It is subsection (c) which deserves further attention in this context. While an application for an ASBO will not be an attempt to evict an occupier, it will certainly constitute a detriment. In *Shamoon v Royal Ulster Constabulary*[109] the House of Lords made it clear, in an employment context, that the concept of detriment was not restricted to an economic or physical consequence of discrimination but rather referred to any impact which the victim of discrimination could reasonably regard as being to his or her disadvantage.

8.171 It is necessary to consider, next, the definition of discrimination in so far as premises are concerned. This is set out in s24, which provides that discrimination occurs, for the purposes of s22(3), when:

(a) for a reason which relates to the disabled person's disability, another person treats him less favourably than he treats or would treat others to whom that reason does not or would not apply; and
(b) he cannot show that the treatment in question is justified.

8.172 It is important to bear in mind that the issue is not whether the less favourable treatment is precisely linked to the disabled person's disability.[110] Rather, all that is needed is a connection to a reason related to that disability. So, for example, a person who has possession proceedings brought against him/her because of rent arrears, which have been caused by an inability to complete housing benefit forms because of depression, will be treated less favourably for a reason related to his/her disability.

8.173 Furthermore, treatment can only be justified, for present purposes, in the following circumstances. First, in the alleged discriminator's opinion, either or both of the following conditions are satisfied:

(a) treatment is necessary in order not to endanger the health or safety of any person (which may include that of the disabled person);
(b) the disabled person is incapable of entering into an enforceable agreement, or of giving an informed consent, and for that reason the treatment is reasonable in that case.

8.174 Second, even if one of these conditions is satisfied, it has to be reasonable, in all the circumstances of the case, for the alleged discriminator to hold that opinion.

109 [2003] UKHL 11; [2003] ICR 337.
110 *Clark v Novacold* [1999] IRLR 318.

It is clear that the test for justification is partly subjective and partly objective. Furthermore, the opinion of the alleged discriminator has to be tested by reference to the material before him/her at the time of the act of alleged discrimination.[111]

Disability discrimination in relation to let premises

8.175 From 4 December 2006, it will be unlawful for a person (called the controller) who lets premises to a disabled person to discriminate against that person, or a disabled person who is a lawful occupier under that letting, by failing, without justification, to comply with certain duties.[112] These duties are set out in DDA 1995 ss24C and 24D. In broad terms, they do two things. First, the controller is required to take such steps as are reasonable to enable the disabled person to use any auxiliary aid or service provided by the controller. Second, and perhaps more relevantly in relation to ASBOs, the controller has to take such steps as are reasonable in the circumstances to stop any policy, practice or procedure which makes it impossible or unreasonably difficult for the disabled person to enjoy the premises.

8.176 DDA 1995 s24K enables a person to justify a failure to comply with a duty on the same basis as set out above, namely, the subjective belief that a particular condition applied and the reasonableness of that belief. The two conditions which are capable of forming the basis of the justification defence are also the same.

Justification

8.177 The most likely basis for justification will be that the person with a disability is committing acts of anti-social behaviour and it is necessary to treat him or her less favourably in order to protect the health or safety of others. In *Manchester City Council v Romano*[113] the Court of Appeal gave a wide reading to the phrase 'health and safety'. It adopted the World Health Organisation's definition of health as being 'a state of complete physical, mental and social well-being and not merely the absence of disease and infirmity'.

8.178 This approach was followed by the Court of Appeal in *Knowsley Housing Trust v McMullen.*[114] However, neither of these cases throws

111 *Post Office v Jones* [2001] EWCA Civ 558; [2001] ICR 805. See Pill LJ at paras 25–27, Kay LJ at para 32 and Arden LJ at para 41.

112 DDA 1995 s24A.

113 [2004] HLR 47.

114 [2006] EWCA Civ 539, discussed in more detail at paras 8.141–8.142 above.

doubt upon the principles to be applied where the landlord is seeking an ASBO on the basis of behaviour which does not constitute a threat to the health or safety of others. In *North Devon Homes Limited v Brazier*[115] the High Court rejected the landlord's contention that the eviction of the tenant was justified on health or safety grounds, not least because there was no evidence before the trial judge that such an opinion had ever been formed at the time of the alleged discrimination.

The application of disability discrimination law in the ASBO context

8.179 The cases cited above are all concerned with possession proceedings. However, providing that the body bringing the claim for an ASBO is the landlord, or somebody else managing the accommodation in which the defendant resides, the principles will be the same. It can be seen, therefore, that the bringing of ASBO proceedings against a disabled person has the potential to constitute unlawful discrimination. It will be necessary to show the following in order to succeed in such a claim:

- that the proposed subject of the ASBO is disabled;
- that the reason why the ASBO is sought is related to that person's disability;
- that the seeking of the ASBO cannot be justified within the meaning of s24.

8.180 A person who claims that another has acted in a way which constitutes discrimination under s22 may bring a civil claim in the county court.[116] The court has power to grant any remedy which it might grant in any other claim. Accordingly, consideration should be given to bringing a counterclaim in an appropriate case. Furthermore, there is no reason why a defendant cannot claim an injunction preventing an application for an ASBO being made if the making of the ASBO injunction would constitute an unlawful act.

8.181 The interesting issue is what impact, if any, the finding of unlawful discrimination would have on an application for an ASBO. A number of views are possible. The first is that if the conditions which are capable of justifying the making of an ASBO are satisfied, then the order can be made in any event. Another, at the opposite end of the spectrum, is that no ASBO should be made since the court should

115 [2003] EWHC 574 (QB); [2003] HLR 59.

116 DDA s25.

not be a party to an unlawful act. The compromise position is that a court may take the fact of discrimination into account when deciding whether to exercise its discretion to make an ASBO.

8.182 It is suggested that the proper result is that no ASBO should be made where the bringing of the proceedings amounts to unlawful discrimination. This is not only because of the general principle that a court should not be used as a vehicle for unlawful conduct but also for two further reasons particular to the discrimination legislation. First, as the courts have constantly recognised, there is a public interest in ensuring that discrimination is eliminated. Second, there is a specific provision in DDA 1995, as there is in all discrimination legislation, which treats a person who knowingly aids another person to do an unlawful act as himself doing the same kind of unlawful act.[117] Although a court is not a 'person' for the purposes of this provision, it would be incongruent if DDA 1995, in the context of ASBOs, did not prevent the court from doing the very act which would be unlawful if done by another person.

117 See DDA s57(1).

CHAPTER 9

Breach of an ASBO

Introduction

9.1 Breach of an ASBO (or interim ASBO) without reasonable excuse is a criminal offence.[1] This applies to stand-alone, post-conviction and county court ASBOs:[2] there is no distinction between them when it comes to criminal sanctions.[3] This chapter discusses the following:

- which court a breach will be heard in;
- potential abuse of process arguments;
- the defence of 'reasonable excuse';
- relying upon a too widely drawn term of an ASBO as a defence;
- sentencing principles and a summary of the case law.

Which court?

Breach of an ASBO is an 'either way' offence

9.2 Breach of an ASBO or interim ASBO is an either way offence and can be tried summarily or on indictment. If tried summarily the maximum penalty is six months' imprisonment or a maximum £5,000 fine or both.[4] If tried on indictment the maximum penalty is five years' imprisonment or a fine or both.[5] The nature and seriousness of the alleged breach will determine which court an adult is tried[6] and sentenced[7] in (sentencing is discussed below). Even if the magistrates' court accepts jurisdiction at the mode of trial stage, it can commit the defendant to the Crown Court for sentence upon conviction if new information is revealed (for example, a string of previous convictions for prior breaches of the ASBO). If a defendant is contesting the breach, it may be that s/he will in any event elect trial by jury.

1 CDA 1998 s1(10).
2 See CDA 1998 ss1B (7) (county court ASBOs) and 1C(9) (post-conviction ASBOs) which make s1(10) applicable.
3 Although see para 8.63 for a discussion on committal proceedings for breach.
4 CDA 1998 s1(10)(a).
5 CDA 1998 s1(10)(b).
6 The mode of trial is determined in accordance with Magistrates' Court Act 1980 s16. See 'Mode of trial guidelines' reproduced in the *Adult Bench Book* at www.jsboard.co.uk.
7 See 'Magistrates' Court Sentencing Guidelines' reproduced in the *Adult Bench Book* at www.jsboard.co.uk. Aggravating features include a previous breach and the use of violence.

Under-18s will be tried in the youth court

9.3 Breaches by children and young persons (that is, all those under 18 years of age)[8] will be dealt with in the youth court. The maximum penalty there is a two-year detention and training order,[9] although under-15-year-olds have to be persistent offenders before they can receive a detention and training order and those under 12 cannot currently be sentenced to a term of detention.[10] In determining whether an offender under the age of 15 could be considered a 'persistent offender', the court can take account of offences in respect of which a person has been cautioned (and by analogy, reprimanded or warned).[11] It is not necessary for the offender to have committed a series of offences of a similar character, or that he should have failed to respond to a previous order of the court for him to be considered a 'persistent offender'.[12] Further, an offender with no previous conviction who is convicted on the same occasion of a number of offences committed within a short space of time may be deemed a persistent offender.[13]

9.4 For reporting restrictions in the youth court, see para 10.55.

Who can bring breach proceedings?

9.5 Both the CPS and now the local authority may bring proceedings for breach of an ASBO. Section 1(10A) was introduced by ASBA 2003[14] giving both 'a council which is a relevant authority' and 'the council for the local government area in which a person in respect of whom an anti-social behaviour order has been made resides or appears to reside' the power to prosecute. Section 1(10) applies by virtue of s1(7) to county court ASBOs and therefore an appropriate local authority would have the right to prosecute the breach of such an ASBO.

9.6 The position in relation to post-conviction ASBOs is slightly unclear due to unnecessarily complex drafting, in that section 1C(9)

8 For a statutory definition of 'children' and 'young people' see para 10.12.

9 Powers of Criminal Courts (Sentencing) Act 2000 s100.

10 See Powers of Criminal Courts (Sentencing) Act 2000 s100 (2)(b)(ii) and *Archbold* 2006, para 5-348.

11 *R v D* [2001] 1 Cr App R(S) 59, CA.

12 *R v B* [2001] 1 Cr App R(S) 113, CA.

13 *R v S(A)* [2001] 1 Cr App R(S) 18, CA.

14 CDA 1998 s1(10A) was inserted by ASBA 2003 s85 which came into force on 31 March 2004.

(as amended by SOCPA 2005) does not apply s1(10A) to post-conviction orders. However, s1C(9A) gives 'the council for the local government area in which a person in respect of whom an anti-social behaviour order has been made resides, or appears to reside' the power to bring breach proceedings.

9.7 In short, it would seem that this power to prosecute is vested in the relevant local authority in relation to breaches of all types of ASBOs (ie, stand-alone, county court and post-conviction).[15]

9.8 These enhanced powers were probably introduced due to the lack of familiarity displayed by CPS representatives in relation to ASBO breach prosecutions and the concomitant frustration felt by local authorities, particularly if they had been the body that applied for the ASBO in the first place. Local authority representatives have had a much longer involvement with the mechanics of ASBOs than the CPS, given that post-conviction orders were not introduced until December 2002.

Abuse of process

9.9 The doctrine of abuse of process was discussed in chapter 5 in relation to the reliance on the same act or acts to obtain an ASBO that were insufficient to found a criminal conviction. In breach proceedings, there is the spectre of concurrent proceedings in the criminal courts for the breach of an ASBO (by the commission of an act which is both a criminal offence and a breach of the term or terms of an ASBO) as well as a prosecution of the substantive offence itself. If these matters were tried separately, there would be a risk of offending the principle of double jeopardy, as the defendant would be in peril of being twice prosecuted on the same or similar facts. An attempt to pursue a prosecution in breach of this principle would justify a plea of *autrefois acquit* or *autrefois convict*, or an application to stay the proceedings as an abuse of process. The sensible course is for the substantive offence and the breach to be tried together. If a defendant is convicted of both offences, he or she must not be punished twice for the same act and this should be reflected in the sentence imposed.[16]

15 CDA 1998 s1B(7) makes s1(10) applicable to county court ASBOs (which must include s1(10A)); s1C(9A) specifically repeats s1(10A) at s1C(9A).

16 See by analogy *Lomas v Parle* [2003] EWCA Civ 1804; see also *CPS v Michael T* [2006] EWHC 728 (Admin) at para 48.

Proving the ASBO

9.10 A copy of the original ASBO, certified as such by the proper officer of the court that made it, is 'admissible as evidence of its having been made and of its contents to the same extent that oral evidence of those things is admissible in those proceedings'.[17] Any defects in the written order do not nullify the ASBO itself.[18]

What happens if there is a breach alleged of an order that is too wide?

9.11 Despite conflicting decisions on the issue, however badly drafted, wide or unenforceable an order is, it is valid until it is set aside.[19] That is, a person *may* be liable for any breach committed of it before it is set aside. In *R (W) v DPP*[20] Brooke LJ had suggested that a 'plainly invalid' order could be challenged in breach proceedings but *CPS v T (Michael)*[21] has thrown doubt on that decision. A breach court does not have the power to strike down a term that is too wide or otherwise unworkable.

9.12 However, as pointed out in chapter 7, that did not mean that a court was compelled to convict when faced with a situation as the District Judge in *T* was faced with. In T's case he faced a prohibition on acting 'in an anti-social manner in the City of Manchester' and was subsequently convicted of interfering with a motor vehicle. The Divisional Court held that it was open to the district judge to consider whether the relevant provision lacked sufficient clarity to warrant a finding that the respondent's conduct amounted to a breach of the order; whether the lack of clarity provided a reasonable excuse for non-compliance with the order; and whether, if a breach was established, it was appropriate

17 CDA 1998 s1(10C), inserted by SOCPA 2005 s139(2), is applicable in the case of stand-alone and post-conviction ASBOs.

18 See *R (Walkling) v DPP* [2003] EWHC 3139 (Admin); *B v Chief Constable of Avon & Somerset Constabulary* [2001] 1 WLR 340; [2001] 1 All ER 562; *R v English* [2005] EWCA Crim 2690 discussed at para 5.135.

19 See para 7.23.

20 [2005] EWCA Civ 1333.

21 [2006] EWHC 728 (Admin). This case is part 2 of the decision in *R (T) v Manchester Crown Court* [2005] EWHC 1396 referred to in chapter 5 on the issue of 'consent'.

in the circumstances to impose any penalty for the breach.[22] On the facts of that case, the court concluded the case in the following way:

9.13 What then is to be done in the present case? The district judge having not been entitled to strike down the offending paragraph of the ASBO, it remained in force until it expired in October 2005. It was in force when the respondent committed the offence of vehicle interference, and indeed it was still in force when the breach proceedings were heard. Thus, however inappropriate he considered it to be, he should have gone on to determine whether there was a breach of the order and, if so, to consider the question of penalty.

It may very well be that the district judge would have been entitled to hold that there was no breach of the order. We think it unnecessary, however, to dwell on that issue. It is sufficient for present purposes to consider the question of penalty if a breach had been established. It should be remembered that the respondent was duly sentenced for the substantive offence which he committed. The penalty for breach of an ASBO is of course distinct from the sentence for any underlying offence and can in an appropriate case exceed the maximum sentence for that underlying offence (see *R v Stevens* [2006] EWCA Crim 255; *Times*, 24 February 2006). In the particular circumstances of the present case, however, we take the view that it would have been wrong in principle to impose any penalty additional to that imposed in respect of the underlying offence.[23]

The defence of 'reasonable excuse'

9.14 As with other criminal offences which include a statutory defence of 'reasonable excuse', the standard of proof (on the defendant) is the balance of probabilities.[24] As contended by the High Court in the case of *Michael T* discussed above, if an order is drawn too widely, it is open to a defendant to rely on lack of clarity as a reasonable excuse as a defence at trial. Whether the defence is made out will depend on the facts of each case. In a jury trial, whether a defence amounts to a reasonable excuse is for the jury to decide and judges should be slow to withdraw any such defence from them. In *R v Heather Shirley Nicholson*[25] the judge ruled as a preliminary issue that 'without reasonable excuse' should be narrowly construed so as to exclude ignorance, forgetfulness and, by implication, misunderstanding.

22 [2006] EWHC 728 (Admin) at para 37.
23 [2006] EWHC 728 (Admin) at paras 47–48.
24 See for example *R v Brown* (1971) 55 Cr App R 478.
25 [2006] EWCA Crim 1518; (2006) *Times* 13 June.

The defendant pleaded guilty as a consequence. The facts of that case were that the defendant was an animal rights campaigner who was subject to an ASBO prohibiting her from going within 500 metres of numerous premises including a laboratory called Halifax House. She had subsequently attended a demonstration within 500 metres of Halifax House. She contended that she had no recollection of having heard that name as the name of the laboratory she was excluded from. The Court of Appeal quashed her conviction. The Court referred to the words of Dyson LJ in *R v Dorothy Evans*:[26]

9.15 It is of some significance that a defendant who is alleged to have acted in breach of a restraining order contrary to section 5(5) of the 1997 Act has the protection that the prosecution must prove that he or she has acted 'without reasonable excuse'. Thus, for example, there may be cases where there is room for legitimate differences of view as to the meaning of a restraining order. If in such a case the defendant raises the issue that he or she believed that the conduct of which complaint is made was permitted by the order, the prosecution will have to prove that he or she did not have reasonable excuse for the prohibited conduct. Acting under a reasonable misapprehension as to the scope and meaning of the order is capable of being a reasonable excuse for acting in a manner which is prohibited by the order.

9.16 The Court of Appeal held that there was no material distinction between the Protection from Harassment Act 1997 and CDA 1998 and that such matters as had been raised as a defence by the defendant were issues of fact and value judgment for the jury, not the judge, to consider.

9.17 In ASBO cases, there will be situations where a defendant quite innocently crosses into a prohibited area or misunderstands the scope of a particular term. Whether or not the misapprehension is reasonable will depend on factors such as how long he or she has been subject to the ASBO and whether there has been a breach of the same term in the past.

Sentencing principles

The nature and seriousness of the breach

9.18 CDA 1998 s1(11) prevents a court from imposing a conditional discharge for breach of an ASBO. Therefore, the sentence imposed will depend on the nature and seriousness of the breach and the

26 [2005] 1 Cr App R 549 at para 21.

defendant's past record in particular previous breaches of an ASBO. Indeed, a perusal of the breach authorities to date makes it quite apparent that immediate custody is the most likely disposal once an ASBO has been breached by the offender acting in an anti-social manner, particularly where there have been repeated breaches of the order.[27]

9.19 A recent breach authority, *R v Christopher Lamb*,[28] draws a distinction between ASBOs which are breached by the offender simply going into a geographical exclusion zone and those breaches which involve harassment, alarm or distress.[29] The Court was troubled by this distinction for the purposes of sentencing:

> We are confronted with the problem of an offender who, without committing a crime, or in fact harassing or causing distress to any member of the public, repeatedly breaches the order of the court. As Judge Whitburn observed, flouting such an order is itself a serious matter. How should it be tackled?[30]

9.20 It reviewed the existing breach authorities and came to the following conclusion, worth quoting in full:

> The vital distinction between [*Curtis Braxton* [2004] EWCA Crim 1374, [2005] 1 Cr App R (S) 36] and the circumstances with which we are concerned is that albeit the deliberate and multiple flouting of the order is the same (indeed, there are more breaches of the ASBO in this case), the social impact of this appellant's offending is very much less and, indeed, did not impact on the public in any way. Save for one occasion when the appellant was drunk (without there being any suggestion that he was causing a nuisance), none of these breaches have resulted from anti-social behaviour as such. The ever longer sentences have been driven only by the determination of the court to ensure that its orders limiting the appellant's movements are not flouted.
>
> We recognise that this is an important objective in itself. An order of the court must be obeyed. We do not accept, however, that being found in a place within the proscribed area without any evidence of associated anti-social behaviour deserves to be visited with a sentence as long as 22 months' imprisonment. Where breaches do not involve

27 See in particular *R v Curtis Braxton* [2003] EWCA Crim 1037 and *R v Curtis Braxton* [2004] EWCA Crim 1374; [2005] 1 Cr App R (S) 36, *R v John Anthony Thomas* [2004] EWCA Crim 1173; [2005] 1 Cr App R (S) 9 and most recently *R v Neil Russell Swain* [2006] EWCA Crim 1621.

28 [2005] EWCA Crim 2487.

29 But see also *R v Kearns* [2005] EWCA Crim 2038.

30 [2005] EWCA Crim 2487 at para 14.

> harassment, alarm or distress, community penalties should be considered in order to help the offender learn to live within the terms of the ASBO to which he or she is subject. In those cases when there is no available community penalty (into which category we include this case given the appellant's refusal to engage with agencies prepared to help him and the frequency of his breaches), custodial sentences which are necessary to maintain the authority of the court can be kept as short as possible. This approach is consistent with that adopted by the Court in the albeit unrelated area of shoplifting: see *Page* [2004] EWCA Crim 3358 in which the Vice-President spoke of the need for proportionality between the sentence and the particular offence.[31]

Breach of an interim ASBO

9.21 In *Parker v DPP*[32] the absence of a condition contained in an interim order from the final ASBO did not affect the gravity or otherwise of a breach of that condition. Rose LJ gave the following guidance:

> In my judgment, however, it by no means follows that the absence from the final ASBO of a condition inserted at the interim stage itself affects the gravity or otherwise of the breach of that condition. The gravity of the breach of the interim condition depends on all the circumstances of the case by reference, for example without purporting to be exhaustive, to the nature of the conduct giving rise to the breach and the flagrancy of the breach, having regard, for example, to the relevant time scale – that is to say, a breach which occurs very soon after an order has been made may very well be a good deal more serious than a breach occurring some time later. Equally, the repetition of the same breach may well result in the sentencing court taking a graver view of the quality of the breach for which sentence is to be passed.[33]

These comments apply equally to the gravity or otherwise of a breach of a full ASBO.

Breach of a term which prohibits a criminal offence

9.22 The propriety of prohibiting actions that constitute a criminal offence as an ASBO term, whether a court can impose a greater sentence for breach than is available for the criminal offence prohibited and the apparent conflict in the authorities (in particular between *R v Kirby*,[34]

31 [2005] EWCA Crim 2487 at paras 18–19.

32 [2005] EWHC 1485 (Admin).

33 [2005] EWHC 1485 (Admin) at para 10.

34 [2005] EWCA Crim 1228.

R v Morrison[35] and the latest case of *R v H, Stevens and Lovegrove*)[36] are discussed at length at para 7.36. In short, while an ASBO should not be used as a device for increasing the available penalty, the *Stevens* case confirms that a breach is a distinct offence and therefore it is open to the court to impose a greater sentence than the maximum that would be available for the criminal offence. The court was prepared to concede, however, that the maximum sentence was a factor to be taken into consideration:

> Plainly, any sentence, in any court, must be proportionate or, to use the word with which all sentencers are familiar, 'commensurate'. Therefore, if the conduct which constitutes the breach of the anti-social behaviour order is also a distinct criminal offence, and the maximum sentence for the offence is limited to, say, six months' imprisonment, that is a feature to be borne in mind by the sentencing court in the interests of proportionality ...[37]

9.23 On the facts of *Stevens*, the Court of Appeal upheld a nine-month sentence for the breach of the prohibition on being drunk in a public place. A similar decision was made in the earlier case of *R v Dickinson*[38] in which 18 months for a breach of an ASBO by an alcoholic prohibited from being drunk in a public place was reduced to eight months. Sadly, the breach authorities reveal that ASBOs are regularly made against those suffering from chronic alcoholism[39] and that the questions of 'necessity' and vulnerable defendants discussed at para 5.118 do not seem to have been considered at the stage at which the ASBOs were made.

9.24 For public funding of breach proceedings, see chapter 12.

35 [2005] EWCA Crim 2237. See also chapter 5 on whether driving while disqualified can satisfy the first limb of the ASBO test.

36 [2006] EWCA Crim 255.

37 [2006] EWCA Crim 255 at para 26.

38 [2005] 2 Cr App R (S) 489(78).

39 See *R v John Anthony Thomas* [2004] EWCA Crim 1173; [2005] 1 Cr App R (S) 9; *R v Caiger* [2005] EWCA Crim 3114; *R v Karen Bulmer* [2005] EWCA Crim 3516; *R v Tripp* [2005] EWCA Crim 2253: all cases of alcoholics sentenced to imprisonment for breaches of ASBOs for drunken anti-social behaviour.

CHAPTER 10

Children and young persons

Introduction

10.1 The use of ASBOs against young people has been at the forefront of media reporting over the past few years.[1] Since their introduction in 1999, a total of 7,356 ASBOs have been issued across England and Wales, 2,995 of which have been imposed on 10- to 17-year-olds.[2] A closer look at the statistics shows that in 2003 almost half of all ASBOs applied for were against 10- to 17-year-olds and in 2004 and 2005, this figure fell to about 40 per cent.[3]

Young people and breaches of ASBOs

10.2 As mentioned in the introduction to this book, the most worrying Government ASBO statistics in 2003 were that 42 per cent of ASBOs are breached, 55 per cent of breaches are punished with a custodial term and 46 per cent of young people receive immediate custody for breach of an ASBO.[4]

On 7 February 2006, Home Office Minister Hazel Blears was asked the following parliamentary question, amongst others, about ASBOs: 'How many anti-social behaviour orders had been issued up to the latest date for which figures are available, in respect of people aged (a) 10–17 years, (b) 17–20 years, and (c) 21 years and over; and how many of those orders have so far been breached?' Her response:

10.3 The information held centrally, on the Court Proceedings Database, as held by the Office for Criminal Justice Reform, only covers breach proceedings where there has been a conviction. Anti-social behaviour order (ASBO) breach data are currently available from 1 June 2000 to 31 December 2003 for ASBOs issued since 1 June 2000. During this period 392 persons aged 10–17, 137 persons aged 18–20, and 264 persons aged 21 and over breached their ASBO on one or more occasions.

Given that the Home Office has still not published any up-to-date breach statistics it is difficult to assess whether the breach rate has escalated or remained static or whether young people are disproportionately affected.

1 See, for example, Goodchild, 'The ASBO kids: a lost generation', *Independent on Sunday*, 23 April 2006 and 'Making our kids criminals', *Channel 4*, broadcast Friday 24 February 2006.

2 www.crimereduction.gov.uk.

3 www.crimereduction.gov.uk.

4 The 5th Report from the Home Affairs Committee Session 2004–2005, *Anti-social behaviour*, HC 80–I, HMSO. See also www.asboconcern.org.uk.

10.4 That said, past research has revealed that young people are most likely to breach ASBO terms which involve geographical restrictions and restrictions on association with others (the terms most commonly imposed on youths) and most will breach in the first quarter of their ASBO term.[5] Despite the trends revealed by surveys and statistics, the use of ASBOs against children and young people has not abated. In Greater London, for example, there were 77 ASBOs imposed on 10- to 17-year-olds in 2004 and in 2005 the figure had increased to 116.[6] On 21 December 2005, Hazel Blears announced that all youth ASBOs would be reviewed after a period of one year (despite the statutory 'minimum term' of two years) but at the time of writing no such statutory scheme had been introduced.

That said, the 2006 Home Office Guidance (*A Guide to Anti-social Behaviour Orders*) advises that all orders issued to young people should be reviewed every year.[7] In particular it says:

> Agencies need to be alert to the prospect that this should become a statutory requirement in the near future. Adopting this as best pracrtice now will enable them to achieve compliance more readily.[8]

Stigmatising children: turning the pesky into the pariah?

10.5 In his report following his visit to the United Kingdom in November 2004, Alvaro Gil-Robles, the then Commissioner for Human Rights, raised a number of concerns about ASBOs.[9] His concerns about the use of ASBOs against children were expressed as follows:

10.6 Particular concerns arise in respect of the application of ASBOs to children. ASBOs can be served on children as young as 10 in England and Wales and 12 in Scotland. It is one thing to intervene in respect of seriously and repetitively troublesome youths, in respect of whom ASBOs may, on occasion, be appropriate. It is another to slap them on youths that are generally up to no good. There is a world of difference between hassle and harassment. It is not because a child is causing inconvenience that he should be brought to the portal of the criminal

5 David Brogan, 'Anti-social behaviour orders: An assessment of current management information systems and the scale of anti-social behaviour order breaches resulting in custody', Youth Justice Board, 2005, available at: www.youth-justice-board.gov.uk.

6 www.crimereduction.gov.uk.

7 2006 Guidance, p45.

8 2006 Guidance, p45.

9 Gil-Robles, *Report by Mr Alvaro Gil-Robles, Commissioner for Human Rights, on his visit to the UK 4–12 November 2004*, CommDH(2005)6, Strasbourg: Council of Europe, paras 117–119. See also introduction to this book.

> justice system. Here again, however, I heard numerous complaints of excessive, victimising ASBOs being awarded. The concern is that the excessive use of ASBOs is more likely to exacerbate anti-social behaviour and crime amongst youths than effectively prevent it and this is for two reasons. Firstly, ASBO breaches have resulted in large numbers of children being detained – 46 per cent of young people received immediate custody upon conviction for breach, though only 17 per cent were sentenced to custody for breach where no other offence was considered. The chair of the Youth Justice Board has conceded that the rise in the young offender population in custody in 2004 resulted mainly from breaches of anti-social behaviour orders. Given the high reconviction rates for detained juvenile offenders, one wonders whether the detention of juveniles for non-criminal behaviour will not lead to more serious offending on release. It is to be recalled, in any case, that the detention of children should be a last resort – detaining children for activity that is not itself criminal can scarcely be consistent with this principle. I was pleased to note that children under 16 cannot be detained for breaching ASBOs in Scotland and would strongly encourage the extension of this rule to the rest of the United Kingdom. Secondly, ASBOs risk alienating and stigmatising children, thereby entrenching them in their errant behaviour. Whilst the first of these consequences is perhaps involuntary, if inevitable, the second effect seems rather to be expressly encouraged ...

10.7 He recommended that the age at which children in breach of terms of ASBOs may be sentenced to custody be raised to 16 in England and Wales. Given that CDA 1998 itself originally introduced detention and training orders for 12- to 17-year-olds, it was inevitable that such a recommendation would be ignored.

Specific issues relating to children and young people

10.8 This chapter aims to highlight specific issues that arise in relation to children and young persons in the ASBO context which have not been dealt with elsewhere in this book. It is not a 'stand-alone' guide to ASBOs and young people. Consequently, readers must refer to previous chapters. This chapter focuses on the following issues:

- the best interests of the child;
- 'children in need';
- 'looked after children';
- youth offending teams;
- alternatives to ASBOs;
- reporting restrictions;
- ancillary orders.

Which courts deal with youth ASBOs?

10.9 As previously mentioned, given the youth court's lack of civil jurisdiction (it cannot hear civil matters brought by way of information or complaint), all stand-alone ASBO applications are heard in the adult magistrates' court, although in relation to young people there is a Practice Direction on the preferable constitution of that court (see below).

10.10 Post-conviction ASBOs in relation to young people will be applied for in the court that convicted them (either the youth court or the Crown Court). As explained in chapter 6, although the youth court has no civil jurisdiction conferred upon it by statute, CDA 1998 s1C gives it a specific power to impose an ASBO upon conviction. As post-conviction orders are not brought by way of complaint but are ancillary to criminal proceedings, it would seem that the youth court's lack of civil jurisdiction is no bar to hearing a post-conviction ASBO.

10.11 Breaches of ASBOs are 'either way' criminal offences and children and young people will be tried in the youth court (see chapter 9 for details of breach proceedings and sentencing principles). Reporting restrictions are dealt with below at para 10.55.

Definition of 'child' and 'young person'

10.12 The references to 'child' and 'young person' in CDA 1998 have the same meaning as in the Children and Young Persons Act (CYPA) 1933. 'Child' means a person under 14 years old and 'young person' means a person who has attained the age of 14 and is under the age of 18 years.[10]

The best interests of the child

10.13 Article 24(1) of the European Union Charter of Fundamental Rights provides that:

> (1) Children shall have the right to such protection and care as is necessary for their well-being.
> (2) In all actions relating to children, whether taken by public authorities or private institutions, the child's best interests must be a primary consideration.

10 CYPA 1933 s70 (as amended).

10.14 Article 1 of the UN Convention on the Right of the Child is in very similar terms:

> In all actions concerning children, whether undertaken by public or private social welfare institutions, courts of law, administrative authorities or legislative bodies, the best interests of the child shall be a primary consideration.

10.15 CYPA 1933 s44 reflects those principles in the following way:

> Every court dealing with a child or young person who is brought before it, either as an offender or otherwise, shall have regard to the welfare of the child or young person.

10.16 In *R (Luke Kenny) v Leeds Magistrates' Court,*[11] the Court of Appeal held, in the context of interim ASBOs,[12] that the best interests of the child should be a primary consideration when deciding whether it was 'just' to make an interim order. In *R (A) v Leeds Magistrates' Court and Leeds City Council,*[13] Stanley Burnton J held that the lower court was undoubtedly right in treating the interests of A as a primary consideration, but not as the primary consideration. He added that the interests of the public are themselves a primary consideration. It is clear from the judgment that a general assertion that an ASBO or a particular term is not in the best interests of a child will not suffice to persuade a court not to impose an order:

10.17

> If it is contended that the special interests of a child require either that there be no order, or an order in terms different from those proposed by the local authority, it is incumbent on a defendant to provide an explanation of his case and some relevant evidence. There will be cases where it is inappropriate to make any ASBO in respect of a child by reason of his age. That is not the present case: as I have stated, it is not contended that the evidence before the district judge did not justify the making of an order against the claimant, who was aged 16 and was allegedly participating in seriously anti-social behaviour. The phrase 'the best interests of the child as a prime consideration' is not a magic talisman which, if not pronounced in a case concerning a child, will necessarily invalidate the order made.[14]

11 [2003] EWHC 2963 (Admin).

12 See para 5.12.

13 [2004] EWHC 554 (Admin).

14 [2004] EWHC 554 (Admin) at para 51.

Alternatives to ASBOs

10.18 Pre-ASBO measures which apply to both adults and youths are discussed in chapter 2. The measures discussed include acceptable behaviour contracts (ABCs), which although not youth-specific, are most commonly used for young people. Readers are referred to para 2.14 for details on how they work.

Parenting contracts

10.19 Parenting contracts were introduced by ASBA 2003.[15] Like an ABC, such a contract is a voluntary agreement which is not legally enforceable and does not attract a criminal penalty on breach. This legislation, combined with parenting orders under CDA 1998 (see para 10.65 below), reflects the fact that the prevailing Government view is that it is not enough to simply require the attendance of parents or guardians at court when a young person is brought before it[16] but to put the responsibility on them to increase their supervision of children as well as improve their parenting skills. The joint Home Office, Department for Constitutional Affairs and Youth Justice Board circular, *Parenting Contracts and Orders Guidance* (the Guidance)[17] explains the reason for this approach:

10.20 > Inadequate parental supervision is strongly associated with offending. For example, a Home Office study[18] showed that 42 per cent of juveniles who had low or medium levels of parental supervision had offended, whereas for those juveniles who had experienced high levels of parental supervision the figure was only 20 per cent. The same research showed that the quality of relationship between the parent and child is crucial. Research[19] also shows that the children of parents whose behaviour towards their children is harsh and erratic are twice as likely to offend. In the United States, a study as long ago as 1973 showed that by training parents in negotiation skills, in sticking to clear rules and rewarding good behaviour, offending rates

15 ASBA 2003 ss19 and 25.

16 CYPA 1933 s34A.

17 February 2004, paras 2.1–2.3. Available at www.crimereduction.gov.uk.

18 Graham and Bowling, *Young people and crime* (1995), Home Office Research Study No 145.

19 Farrington, 'Family backgrounds in aggressive youths', in Hersov (ed.), *Aggressive and anti-social behaviour in childhood and adolescence*, Pergamon Press, 1978.

were halved.[20] Parenting can also be an important protective factor that moderates a child's exposure to risk.[21] Parenting programmes are designed to develop parents' skills to reduce parenting as a risk factor and enhance parenting as a protective factor. The Government believes that for many parents whose children get into trouble, help from trained professionals and contact with other parents in the same situation may prove invaluable.

10.21 Given the above justification for such orders, if the pre-conditions for entering into one are satisfied, and a parent or guardian of a youth who is being considered for an ASBO is willing to enter into one, there is no reason why a parenting contract should not be tried as an alternative to an ASBO.

10.22 The relevant section of ASBA 2003 in the context of anti-social behaviour is section 25. It provides that where a child or young person has been referred to a youth offending team (YOT) that team may enter into a parenting contract with a parent or guardian of that child or young person, if a member of that team has reason to believe that the child or young person has engaged, or is likely to engage, in criminal conduct or anti-social behaviour.[22]

10.23 The Guidance contemplates the use of parenting contracts by youth offending teams in the following circumstances:

- when a child or young person has been reprimanded or warned for an offence;
- when a child or young person has been convicted of an offence;
- where a child under 10 years is believed by the youth offending team to have committed an act which would have constituted a crime if the child had been older;
- where a child is identified (by local initiatives such as youth inclusion projects or anti-social behaviour teams) as being at risk of offending.

10.24 A s25 parenting contract is a document which contains:

- a statement by the parent or guardian that he or she agrees to comply for a specified period with requirements specified in the contract;

20 Alexander and Parsons, 'Short term behavioural intervention with delinquent families: impact on family process and recidivism', *Journal of Abnormal Psychology*, 81(3) 1973.

21 See various Youth Justice Board research including *Risk and protective factors associated with youth crime and effective interventions to prevent it* (2001) and *The evaluation of the validity and reliability of the Youth Justice Board's assessment for young offenders.*

22 ASBA 2003 s25(1) and (2).

- a statement by the youth offending team agreeing to provide support to the parent or guardian for the purposes of complying with the contract.[23]

The contract may include a requirement for a parent or guardian to attend a counselling or guidance programme.[24] A parenting contract must be signed by the parent and signed on behalf of the youth offending team.[25] The contract does not create any enforceable obligations.[26] However, failure to agree on the terms to be included in a contract or to comply with the terms of the contract may result in the YOT applying for a parenting order.[27] ASBA 2003 does not specify a time limit for contracts. According to the Guidance, duration is a question of what is reasonable and effective.[28]

10.25 The contract requirements imposed on a parent or guardian should have the purpose of preventing the child or young person from engaging in criminal conduct or anti-social behaviour. Examples given in the Guidance[29] include the following:

- to ensure their child stays away unless supervised from a part of town where he or she has misbehaved;
- to ensure their child is effectively supervised at certain times;
- to ensure their child avoids contact with certain disruptive individuals;
- to ensure their child avoids contact with someone he or she has been harassing.

10.26 The Guidance also recommends, 'that where there is separate work being carried out with the child it may be helpful for the contract to support this or bring together work involving parents and child. For instance the requirements of a parenting contract could mirror requirements agreed in an ABC'.[30] If there is such a combination in place, given that the aim of both these contracts is to prevent a child or young person from engaging in criminal conduct or anti-social behaviour, there can be no necessity for an ASBO. Obviously, as discussed at para 2.15 in the context of ABCs, non-compliance with the contracts may mean that there will be an application for an ASBO.

23 ASBA 2003 s25(3).
24 ASBA 2003 s25(4).
25 ASBA 2003 s25(6).
26 ASBA 2003 s25(7).
27 ASBA 2003 s27(1)(a).
28 Guidance para 3.20.
29 Guidance, para 3.13.
30 Guidance, para 3.14.

Statutory consultation

10.27 The statutory requirement to consult before applying for a stand-alone or county court ASBO under CDA 1998 s1E, as well as the ramifications of a failure to consult, is discussed in detail at para 2.17.

'Children in need'

10.28 As mentioned in chapter 2, if the consultation process was working properly, then a local authority would have considered its duties under sections 17–29 of the Children Act 1989 to assess children 'in need' or 'at risk' and make provision for them (as supplemented by Children Act 1994 s10),[31] rather than simply apply for an ASBO. A failure by the local authority to carry out, or properly carry out, such assessments is susceptible to judicial review.[32]

10.29 In *R (AB and SB) v Nottingham City Council*,[33] a challenge by judicial review was taken against the local authority by a 14-year-old child (SB) and his mother (AB) for failing to assess and provide for their needs. SB had a learning disability and suffered from Attention-deficit hyperactivity disorder (ADHD) and other behavioural and emotional difficulties. He had been out of education for two years. His mother had been subject to domestic violence and had developed a drug habit as a result. SB was the subject of an ASBO application and part of the claimants' challenge was that such an order should not be made in circumstances where the local authority had failed properly to assess SB's needs and to consider other ways of dealing with him short of applying for an ASBO.

10.30 SB was accepted to be a 'child in need' within the meaning of s17 of the Children Act 1989. A 'child in need' is entitled to certain support from the local authority:

> 17(1) It shall be the general duty of every local authority (in addition to the other duties imposed on them by this Part) –
> (a) to safeguard and promote the welfare of children within their area who are in need; and
> (b) so far as is consistent with that duty, to promote the upbringing of such children by their families,
>
> by providing a range and level of services appropriate to those children's needs.

31 See *R (LH and MH) v Lambeth LBC* [2006] EWHC 1190 (Admin) at para 19.

32 See *R (AB and SB) v Nottingham City Council* [2001] EWCA 235 (Admin) and *R (LH and MH) v Lambeth LBC*[2006] EWHC 1190 (Admin).

33 [2001] EWCA 235 (Admin).

10.31 Section 17 (10) defines a 'child in need':

> 17(10) For the purposes of this Part a child shall be taken to be in need if –
> (a) he is unlikely to achieve or maintain, or to have the opportunity of achieving or maintaining, a reasonable standard of health or development without the provision for him of services by a local authority under this Part;
> (b) his health or development is likely to be significantly impaired, or further impaired, without the provision for him of such services; or
> (c) he is disabled,
> and 'family', in relation to such a child, includes any person who has parental responsibility for the child and any other person with whom he has been living.

10.32 The claimants argued that the defendant council had failed to properly assess SB's needs and, in particular, had failed to follow relevant guidance issued by the Secretary of State in exercising their social services functions. Adopting the interpretation of the way in which the Guidance should be applied to s17 laid down in *R v Lambeth LBC ex p K*,[34] the High Court ruled that there should be a systematic assessment of needs which takes into account a child's developmental needs, parenting capacity and family and environmental factors. After an identification of needs, a care plan should be produced and the identified services provided. In SB's case those requirements were not met. In conclusion, Richards J said this:

10.33

> Finally on the general issue of assessment of need, I have to say that I am left with the impression that the defendant has concentrated unduly on the anti-social behaviour proceedings and insufficiently on the discharge of its duty, in particular under section 17 of the Children Act, to assess SB's needs and make provision for them. No doubt the focus has been the result of SB's very serious behavioural problems, but these problems cannot excuse a failure to comply with the section 17 duty.[35]

Practitioners should always consider whether a child or young person against whom an ASBO is sought is a 'child in need' within the meaning of s17 and, if so, whether a proper needs assessment has been carried out.

34 (2003) 6 CCLR 141 at 144H.

35 *R (AB and SB) v Nottingham City Council* [2001] EWCA 235 (Admin) at para 48.

'Looked after children' and ASBO applications

10.34 A 'looked after child' is a child in local authority care or a child accommodated by the local authority.[36] In 2003–2004, some 61,000 children were in local authority care.[37] A local authority's duty to a 'looked after child' is defined in s22 of the Children Act 1989, the material parts of which are as follows:

> (1) In this Act, any reference to a child who is looked after by a local authority is a reference to a child who is –
> (a) in their care; or
> (b) provided with accommodation by the authority in the exercise of any functions ...
>
> (3) It shall be the duty of a local authority looking after any child –
> (a) to safeguard and promote his welfare; and
> (b) to make such use of services available for children cared for by their own parents as appears to the authority reasonable in his case.
>
> (4) Before making any decision with respect to a child whom they are looking after, or proposing to look after, a local authority shall, so far as is reasonably practicable, ascertain the wishes and feelings of –
> (a) the child;
> (b) his parents;
> (c) any person who is not a parent of his but who has parental responsibility for him; and
> (d) any other person whose wishes and feelings the authority consider to be relevant,
>
> regarding the matter to be decided.
>
> (5) In making any such decision a local authority shall give due consideration –
> (a) having regard to his age and understanding, to such wishes and feelings of the child as they have been able to ascertain;
> (b) to such wishes and feelings of any person mentioned in subsections (4)(b) to (d) as they have been able to ascertain; and
> (c) to the child's religious persuasion, racial origin and cultural and linguistic background.
>
> If it appears to a local authority that it is necessary, for the purpose of protecting members of the public from serious injury, to exercise their powers with respect to a child whom they are looking after in a manner which may not be consistent with their duties under this section, they may do so.

36 See Children Act 1989 s22(1).

37 *Children looked after in England (including adoptions and care leavers): 2003–2004*, report from National Statistics Office, available at www.dfes.gov.uk.

10.35 If a local authority in relation to a child in its care makes an ASBO application, there is likely to be a conflict of interest as that local authority also has parental responsibility for that child.[38] This issue was considered in *R (M) v Sheffield Magistrates' Court and Sheffield City Council*.[39] M had been in care since the age of six. He was aged 15 at the time of the ASBO application. Under s22(3) of the Children Act 1989 (see above), a local authority has a duty to safeguard and promote the welfare of a child in its care. Newman J approached the issue on the basis that the welfare of a child may or may not be furthered by the making of an ASBO but the interests of the child in the decision-making process and in the court process must be protected. In M's case the decision to consider an ASBO application was made at a meeting which included police officers and representatives from Sheffield City Council housing department as well as M's social worker (the social worker discharging parental responsibility on behalf of Sheffield City Council). At a subsequent meeting of an ASBO panel, it was decided that a report from social services would be appropriate before proceeding with an ASBO application. There was reference to the fact that a social worker had raised a concern that M's grandmother believed he may have ADHD. A brief report in the form of an ASBO panel pro-forma report was prepared for the next ASBO panel meeting by the social worker. The social worker expressed reservations about an ASBO, given the progress that M was making since the involvement of various professionals. Notwithstanding that, the panel decided to proceed with the ASBO application.

10.36 During the ASBO proceedings lawyers acting for M had real difficulty accessing YOT staff and M's social worker, who in their view was a potential witness. The Director for Legal Services at Sheffield City Council warned M's lawyers that YOT workers were local authority employees and should not be approached directly in relation to the ASBO matter. Further, the Director informed M's lawyers that the social worker concerned would only meet them in the presence of a line manager and a legal representative. Such a meeting was arranged, but to add to the complete failure by social services to consider M's welfare in the context of ASBO proceedings, it transpired that the legal representative who attended on behalf of the social worker was also the legal representative conducting the ASBO application on behalf of the local authority.

10.37 Newman J sought to provide guidance on how the interests of a

38 Children Act 1989 s33.

39 [2004] EWHC 1830 (Admin).

child in care can be protected when the authority responsible for the child's care makes an application for an ASBO against the child. He pointed out that an ASBO places a person subject to it at risk of penal sanction and that sanction will regularly involve loss of liberty. He added: 'Any parent, whether natural or statutory, and no matter how determined to bring discipline to bear on a child, would hesitate to place their child at risk of detention in custody.'[40]

10.38 He had no doubt that a conflict of interest arose for local authorities in the circumstances under consideration in M's case. Further on the facts of M's case, he was satisfied that the conflict gave rise to prejudice to M. His guidance can be summarised as follows (although practitioners are advised to read the judgment in full if advising on this issue):

- Under s22(4) of the Children Act 1989, a decision to apply for an ASBO requires the local authority to ascertain the 'wishes and feelings' of the child and any other person who is not a parent but has parental responsibility for him, and any other person whose wishes and feelings the local authority consider to be relevant.
- The material should be prepared and presented not as though it is a report for the ASBO panel, but as a report for the authority on behalf of the child.
- The ASBO panel should consider the material before it proceeds to make an ASBO application as the considerations to which s22(4) will give rise are likely to be relevant to the 'necessity' test.[41]
- If an application to make an ASBO is to be made, then the lead agency must communicate that decision to all parties.
- The relevant social worker must not participate in the decision to apply for an ASBO.
- The social worker/workers for the local authority should be available to assist and be witnesses at court, if so requested by the child in question.
- No court should make an order against a child in care without someone from the social services who can speak to the issue being present except in exceptional circumstances.
- The solicitor responsible for the relevant authority's ASBO application should not attend meetings with the child's solicitors and social services representatives (the need for the attendance of a solicitor for the social worker should be rare).

40 *R (M) v Sheffield Magistrates' Court and Sheffield City Council* [2004] EWHC 1830 (Admin) at para 44.

41 See para 5.107.

- Once a decision has been taken to apply for an ASBO there should be no contact on the issue between the ASBO team and the social services without the child's solicitor being present.

10.39 Practitioners may well be faced with difficulty when seeking to secure the co-operation or attendance at court of a social worker (or a YOT worker), notwithstanding this judgment. The court should be alerted to the issue and if necessary, a witness summons obtained. After all, according to Newman J, it is the court's duty to hear from social services before making a decision on the ASBO question. It is also open to defence lawyers to give evidence of any conversations they have had with social workers on the propriety or otherwise of an ASBO (or to serve a statement in accordance with the hearsay rules).[42]

10.40 Although the M case related to a stand-alone ASBO, if the impetus for a post-conviction ASBO, although applied for by the CPS, in reality came from the local authority, the principles laid down in *M* may well be equally applicable. Furthermore, although M was in care, this judgment must apply equally to all 'looked after children' within the meaning of s22(1) of the Children Act 1989.

See para 2.24 for guidance on obtaining disclosure of the consultation process.

Role of the Youth Offending Team (YOT)

10.41 YOTs were established under CDA 1998 s39, whose principal aim is to prevent youth offending.[43] Each local authority has such a team and each team should comprise a social worker, probationer officer, police officer, a representative each from the health authority and the education authority.[44] YOTs should be involved in the decision to apply for an ASBO against a young person.[45] YOT involvement is particularly important in ensuring that any proposed prohibitions do not adversely affect work already being undertaken with the young person by other agencies.[46]

42 See chapter 4.

43 CDA 1998 s37.

44 CDA 1998 s37(5). See also s37(6).

45 Readers are referred to the joint Youth Justice Board, ACPO & Home Office publication, *A guide to the role of Youth Offending Teams in dealing with anti-social behaviour* available at www.youth-justice-board.gov.uk and www.together.gov.uk.

46 See also para 7.18.

10.42 In relation to the YOT's view on the propriety of an ASBO application, *A guide to the role of Youth Offending Teams in dealing with anti-social behaviour*[47] says this: 'There will be occasions when ASBO applications are pursued when the YOT is not in full agreement. In these circumstances, the YOT maintains a responsibility, alongside other interested partner agencies, to support the implementation of the order and ensure that it leads to positive outcomes for the young person and the community.'

10.43 This advice is contradictory and potentially undermines the purpose of statutory consultation. If, for example, it is the YOT's view that an ASBO is not necessary within the meaning of CDA 1998 (for which see para 5.107) or that it will not prevent offending, the YOT will not be in a position to 'ensure' that an ASBO leads to 'positive outcomes'. Bearing in mind the guidance issued in the case of M discussed above, the relevant YOT representative should be available at court to assist in the determination of this issue, if the young person so requests.

Court procedure

Composition of benches for under-18s

10.44 When an ASBO defendant is under 18 and the ASBO application is for a stand-alone or variation or discharge of a stand-alone, the following *Practice Direction on the Composition of Benches* issued by the President of the Queen's Division on 24 February 2006 applies (emphasis added):

> (1) Where there is an application to a magistrates' court for an anti-social behaviour order under section 1 of the Crime and Disorder Act 1998 (the Act), or an application to a magistrates' court for an anti-social behaviour order to be varied or discharged under section 1(8) of the Act, and the person against whom the order is sought is under 18, *the justices constituting the court should normally be qualified to sit in the youth court.*
>
> (2) Applications for interim orders under section 1D of the Act, including those made without notice, may be listed before justices who are not so qualified.
>
> (3) If it is not practicable to constitute a bench in accordance with paragraph 1, in particular where to do so would result in a delayed hearing, this direction does not apply.[48]

47 Available at www.youth-justice-board.gov.uk and www.together.gov.uk.

48 [2006] 1 WLR 636; [2006] 1 All ER 886.

10.45 It remains to be seen whether young people will in fact have the benefit of a specialist bench given the wide terms in which paragraph 3 is drafted. As an appeal to the Crown Court of a stand-alone ASBO is by way of a complete rehearing, presumably the Practice Direction will apply there. If a young person was denied a specialist bench at the first hearing, it may be a good reason for insisting upon one upon appeal.

10.46 If there is concern about the effective participation of a young defendant in ASBO proceedings, practitioners should consider asking the court to make adaptations in line with the relevant parts of the Practice Direction[49] introduced in the Crown Court following the Strasbourg decisions of *T v UK; V v UK*.[50]

10.47 If an ASBO is being applied for against an under-16-year-old, CYPA 1933 s34A requires the attendance of a parent or a legal guardian or in the case of a 'looked after child', a representative from the local authority. If a child is under 14 and is giving evidence, then it will be unsworn. If over 14, then it will be given on oath.[51]

Reporting restrictions

Adult courts

10.48 As explained in chapter 5, no automatic reporting restrictions apply in the adult courts. Further, CYPA 1933 s49, which is the section that imposes automatic reporting restrictions on proceedings in the youth court, does not apply to post-conviction ASBOs in the youth court, although CYPA 1933 s39 does.[52]

10.49 However, CYPA 1933 s39 confers a discretion on all courts to impose one. It reads as follows:

> **Power to prohibit publication of certain matter in newspapers**
>
> 39(1) In relation to any proceedings in any court ... the court may direct that –
>
> (a) no newspaper report of the proceedings shall reveal the name, address, or school, or include any particulars calculated to lead to the identification, of any child or young person concerned in the proceedings, either as being the person [by or against]

49 Practice Direction (CA (Crim Div): Criminal Proceedings: Consolidation) [2002] 1 WLR 2870 at para IV.39; *Archbold* 2006, para 4-96a.

50 30 EHRR 121.

51 MCA 1980 s98.

52 CDA 1998 s1C(9C) as introduced by SOCPA 2005 s139.

or in respect of whom the proceedings are taken, or as being a witness therein;

(b) no picture shall be published in any newspaper as being or including a picture of any child or young person so concerned in the proceedings as aforesaid;

except in so far (if at all) as may be permitted by the direction of the court.

(2) Any person who publishes any matter in contravention of any such direction shall on summary conviction be liable in respect of each offence to a fine not exceeding [level 5 on the standard scale].

10.50 The extent to which the established principles in the case law in this area should be modified, or their application affected, in a context where the child or young person in question is the subject of an ASBO was considered at length in *R (T) v St Albans Crown Court*.[53] Elias J first identified the following as principles established by the existing case law:

(i) In deciding whether to impose or thereafter to lift reporting restrictions, the court will consider whether there are good reasons for naming the defendant.

(ii) In reaching that decision, the court will give considerable weight to the age of the offender and the potential damage to any young person of public identification as a criminal before the offender has the benefit or burden of adulthood.

(iii) By virtue of section 44 of the 1933 Act, the Court must 'have regard to the welfare of the child or young person'.

(iv) The prospect of being named in court with the accompanying disgrace is a powerful deterrent and the naming of a defendant in the context of his punishment serves as a deterrent to others. These deterrents are proper objectives for the court to seek.

(v) There is strong public interest in open justice and in the public knowing as much as possible about what has happened in court, including the identity of those who have committed crime.

(vi) The weight to be attributed to the different factors may shift at different stages of the proceedings, and, in particular, after the defendant has been found, or pleads, guilty and is sentenced. It may then be appropriate to place greater weight on the interest of the public in knowing the identity of those who have committed crimes, particularly serious and detestable crimes.

(vii) The fact that an appeal has been made may be a material consideration.

10.51 He then went on to consider the ASBO context. He was not persuaded that ASBO hearings were less serious than proceedings in the crim-

53 [2002] EWHC 1129 (Admin). Judgment was given at the same time in the linked case of *Chief Constable of Surrey Police v JHG (1) and DHG (2)*.

inal courts because of their civil nature and hence the public interest in disclosing identities was not as great. His ruling on whether ASBO applications required modification of the factors referred to above is necessary to repeat in full:

10.52 ... In my judgment, where an anti-social behaviour order has been imposed, that is a factor which reinforces, and in some cases may strongly reinforce, the general public interest in the public disclosure of court proceedings. There are two reasons for this. First, disclosure of the identity of the individuals may well assist in making an order efficacious. If persons in the community are aware that the order has been made against specified individuals, then it must improve the prospect of that order being effectively enforced. Any subsequent breach is more likely to be reported back to the authorities. Second, the very purpose of these orders is to protect the public from individuals who have committed conduct or behaviour which is wholly unacceptable and of an anti-social nature. The public has a particular interest in knowing who in its midst has been responsible for such outrageous behaviour. In my judgment, this latter factor does not constitute simply 'naming and shaming' which Lord Bingham in *McKerry*[54] thought it would be difficult to justify. This is not simply publicity to satisfy a prurient public: the local community has a proper interest in knowing who has been seriously and persistently damaging its fabric. Moreover, in so far as shaming may, and often will, have a legitimate deterrent effect, it is a relevant factor to weigh against its potential adverse effects, as the judgment of Simon Brown LJ indicates. However, I do not accept that the consequence of this is that in every case it raises a presumption in favour of refusing to make a section 39 direction. It is a weighty factor to be taken into consideration against upholding any claim for anonymity, but, in my judgment, it is not helpful in a case of this kind to talk about presumptions one way or another. In each case there will be a wide variety of factors which will have to be considered, and in each case the balance has to be struck between the desirability of public disclosure on the one hand and the need to protect the welfare of the individual at trial on the other after a full appreciation of the relevant considerations.[55]

10.53 Elias J also considered whether the effect on a family was a relevant consideration or a good reason for granting a direction under section 39.[56] He decided it was not, other than in the most exceptional of cases. In *Keating v Knowsley Metropolitan Borough Council*,[57] the High Court

54 *McKerry v Teesdale and Wear Valley Justices* (2000) 164 JP 355, DC.

55 [2002] EWHC 1129 (Admin) at para 22.

56 Ibid, paras 47–53.

57 [2004] EWHC 1933 (Admin).

endorsed Elias J's approach to the application of CYPA 1933 s39 to ASBO hearings and said it applied equally to interim ASBOs. The court accepted that the unproven nature of the allegations was a very important consideration in deciding where the balance lies.

Youth courts

10.54 Although the youth court usually has automatic reporting restrictions by virtue of CYPA 1933 s49, SOCPA 2005 specifically disapplies s49 in relation to ASBO breach proceedings against a child or young person[58] and, as mentioned above, in relation to post-conviction ASBO hearings.

10.55 In its place, CDA 1998 purports to offer protection to young people facing a criminal prosecution in the form of s45 of the Youth Justice and Criminal Evidence Act (YJCEA) 1999.[59] However, to complicate matters, YJCEA 1999 s45 is still not in force and until it is, references to s45 in CDA 1998 s1(10D)(b) and (10E) are to be read as references to CYPA 1933 s39.[60] When (or if) s45 does come into force, it will replace s39 (which by CYPA 1933 s39(3) will no longer have any application in criminal proceedings).[61]

The usual application of CYPA 1933 s49 in youth court proceedings

10.56 CYPA 1933 s49(1) provides in effect that there should be no disclosure of information which would reveal the identity of the child or young person concerned, but an exception is then provided in subsection (4A) as follows:

> If a court is satisfied that it is in the public interest to do so, it may, in relation to a child or young person who has been convicted of an offence, by order dispense to any specified extent the requirements of this section in relation to any proceedings before it to which this section applies ...

10.57 In *McKerry v Teesdale and Wear Valley JJ*[62] Lord Bingham said that the jurisdiction to dispense with reporting restrictions should be exercised with great care, caution and circumspection and that it would be only very rarely that the statutory criteria are met:

58 CDA 1998 s1(10D) inserted by SOCPA 2005 s141 2005. in force from 1 July 2005.

59 CDA 1998 s1 (10D) (b) and (10E).

60 SOCPA 2005 s141(4).

61 See *Archbold* 2006, para 4-27.

62 164 JP 355, DC.

> ... the privacy of a child or young person involved in legal proceedings must be carefully protected, and very great weight must be given to the welfare of such child or young person. It is in my judgment plain that power to dispense with anonymity, as permitted in certain circumstances by section 49(4A), must be exercised with very great care, caution and circumspection. It would be wholly wrong for any court to dispense with a juvenile's prima facie right to anonymity as an additional punishment. It is also very difficult to see any place for 'naming and shaming' ...[63]

10.58 Despite the historical respect for a child's privacy, reflected both in CYPA 1933 s49 and its interpretation, Parliament has chosen to remove that right in relation to ASBO breaches. It is difficult to see how there could be any justification for treating ASBO breaches differently from other criminal prosecutions. Defence lawyers must be prepared to argue that CYPA 1933 s39 orders can and should apply.

Post-ASBO publicity

10.59 Even when reporting restrictions are not imposed, defence lawyers need to be alert to the fact that any post-ASBO publicity disseminated by a public body will engage Article 8 and should therefore be reasonable and proportionate. For a discussion of this issue and the case of *R (Stanley) v Metropolitan Police Commissioner*,[64] see para 5.142.

Ancillary orders

10.60 There are two ancillary orders which may be available when ASBOs are imposed on children and young people, a detailed consideration of each of which is beyond the scope of this book.[65] These orders are individual support orders and parenting orders.

10.61 It is arguable that neither of these orders is available in conjunction with post-conviction ASBOs. This is because the language of CDA 1998 distinguishes between the three kinds of ASBOs by referring to

63 164 JP 355, DC, para 25.

64 [2004] EWHC 2229 (Admin). See also *Medway Council v BBC* [2002] 1 FLR 104 in which a local authority failed to obtain an injunction to restrain the BBC from broadcasting an interview with a 13-year-old child in its care who was subject to an ASBO.

65 Readers are referred to the 'Together' website for full details of each of these orders: www.together.gov.uk.

stand-alone ASBOs as 'anti-social behaviour orders' throughout the Act, to post-conviction ASBOs as 'an order under s1C' and county court ASBOs as 'an order under s1B'. 'Orders under section 1C' are not mentioned in the context of any of the ancillary orders. Certainly it is the view of the Youth Justice Board, for the reasons set out above, that the individual support order provisions do not apply to orders made post-conviction.[66] Further, given that any sentence of the court ought to address issues such as the prevention of further anti-social behaviour, it is difficult to see how subjecting a youth to a sentence plus two preventative orders could ever be necessary or appropriate.

Individual support orders (ISOs)

10.62 These were introduced into CDA 1998 (s1AA) by the Criminal Justice Act 2003 on 1 May 2004. The court is required to consider the making of such an order when an ASBO is made against a child or young person. Before making an individual support order the court shall obtain from a social worker of the local authority social services department or a member of the youth offending team any information which it considers necessary to determine whether the individual support conditions are fulfilled or what requirements should be imposed by any individual support order.[67] Various pre-conditions have to be met before an ISO can be made. They are as follows:

- an ISO would be desirable in the interests of preventing any repetition of the kind of behaviour which led to the making of the ASBO;
- the defendant is not already subject to an ISO;
- the court has been notified by the Secretary of State that arrangements for implementing ISOs are available in the area in which the young person resides or will reside.[68]

10.63 The order requires a child or young person to comply with specified activities for a period of six months. If the court is not satisfied that the conditions for the making of an individual support order are fulfilled it should state this in open court and give reasons.[69]

10.64 A failure to comply with the terms of an ISO without reasonable excuse is a summary offence punishable with a fine of up to £1,000

66 See www.youth-justice-board.gov.uk. Click on the Practitioners' Portal and go to FAQs.

67 CDA 1998 s1AA(9).

68 CDA 1998 s1AA(3).

69 CDA 1998 s1AA(4).

for those aged 14 or over at the time of conviction and £250 for those under 14 at that time. For appeals against ISOs see para 11.2.

Parenting orders

10.65 These orders were introduced by CDA 1998 s8 and have been available since 30 September 1998.[70] Various statutes since have amended the section.[71] They are available in a number of circumstances including when an ASBO is made in respect of a child or young person. The court must make such an order if the defendant is under the age of 16 and it is satisfied that such an order is desirable to prevent the repetition of the kind of behaviour which led to the making of the ASBO.[72] Where a defendant is 16 or over, the court has a discretion.

10.66 Where a defendant is under 16, the court must obtain and consider information about the person's family circumstances and the likely effect of the order on those circumstances before it can make an order. The order places specific requirements on parents or carers to comply with, specified for a period of up to 12 months. It also requires parents or carers to attend a parenting or counselling programme for up to three months. A failure to comply with the order without reasonable excuse is a summary offence punishable with a fine of up to level 3.

10.67 For an analysis and discussion of appeals against ASBOs, costs and public funding, see chapters 11 and 12.

70 Crime and Disorder Act 1998 (Commencement No 2 and Transitional Provisions) Order 1998 SI No 2327.

71 See appendix A.

72 CDA 1998 s9(1B).

CHAPTER 11

Appeals against ASBOs

with Rajeev Thacker

Introduction

11.1 Once an ASBO has been made, it is essential to be aware of the various rights of appeal which may be available. Because of the unusual nature of such orders, in that they are civil orders which are most often made in the criminal courts, the correct route of appeal is not always obvious. In addition, the time limits applicable to appeals are short.

Appeals to the Crown Court

Stand-alone ASBOs

11.2 CDA 1998 s4 provides for a right of appeal to the Crown Court against the making by the magistrates' court of an ASBO, an interim ASBO and an individual support order.[1] There is accordingly no need to obtain permission to appeal. Since the right of appeal is given against the 'making' of such an order, the applicant body has no power to appeal against the decision of a court not to make such an order. The appeal is by way of a full rehearing[2] and remains civil in character.

11.3 Under CDA 1998, the Crown Court may make such order as may be necessary to give effect to its determination on the appeal.[3] In addition, it may make any incidental or consequential order as it considers just.[4]

11.4 An order that is made by the Crown Court on appeal from the magistrates' court is treated, for the purposes of any application to vary or discharge,[5] as an order of the magistrates' court.[6] Therefore applications to vary or discharge such an order will be upon application to the magistrates' court.[7]

11.5 The general powers of the Crown Court on appeal are set out in s48 of the Supreme Court Act (SCA) 1981. SCA 1981 s48(1) indicates that the Crown Court may, in the course of hearing an appeal, 'correct any error or mistake in the order or judgment incorporating the decision which is the subject of the appeal.'

1 See para 10.62 for ISOs. See appendix A for CDA 1998 s4.
2 See Supreme Court Act 1981 s79(3).
3 CDA 1998 s4(2)(a).
4 CDA 1998 s4(2)(b).
5 Under CDA 1998 ss1(8) and s1AB(6).
6 CDA 1998 s4(3).
7 See chapters 5 and 6 for variation and discharge of ASBOs and interim ASBOs.

11.6 Under SCA 1981 s48(2), upon the 'termination of the hearing of an appeal' the Crown Court has the following powers:

- to confirm, reverse or vary any part of the decision appealed against;
- to remit the matter with its opinion thereon to the authority whose decision is appealed against;
- to make such other order in the matter as the court thinks just, and by such order exercise any power which the said authority might have exercised.

11.7 The powers under SCA 1981 s48(2) are, by virtue of s48(3), made subject to any express limitation provided for by the statute that governs the appeal, in this case, CDA 1998. However, as can be seen from CDA 1998 s4, there is nothing that restricts the SCA 1981 s48(2) powers. Accordingly, the Crown Court has a wide jurisdiction on appeal. It is open to a defendant to appeal against either the imposition of the ASBO itself or specific terms of it.[8]

Post-conviction ASBOs

11.8 CDA 1998 s4 does not on the face of it give a right of appeal to the Crown Court against an ASBO made by the magistrates' court under s1C following conviction. However, MCA 1980 s108(1) gives a right of appeal against any sentence and MCA 1980 s108(3) defines sentence as including any order made by the magistrates' court upon conviction. This includes a post-conviction ASBO.

What are the correct procedural rules in the Crown Court?

Stand-alone ASBOs

11.9 Since 2005, Criminal Procedure Rules[9] have been introduced to regulate procedure in the criminal courts. It may have been thought, therefore, that these rules should apply to all appeals from the magistrates' court to the Crown Court. However, the position is more complicated than this.

11.10 As pointed out in earlier chapters, all stand-alone ASBOs, whether final or interim, are made by a magistrates' court sitting in its civil

8 *R (Manchester City Council) v Manchester Crown Court*, unreported, 13 October 2000, CO/1950/200, QBD.

9 2005 SI No 384. They are available on the DCA website at www.dca.gov.uk/criminal/procrules_fin/index.htm.

capacity. Section 69 of the Courts Act (CA) 2003 provides that the Criminal Procedure Rules 2005 only apply to the 'criminal courts'. CA 2003 s68(b)(ii) defines a criminal court as meaning the Crown Court or a magistrates' court 'when dealing with any criminal cause or matter'. Accordingly, the Criminal Procedure Rules do not apply in ASBO cases. Nor do the Civil Procedure Rules (CPR), because CPR 2.1 expressly states that they only apply in the county court, the High Court and the Civil Division of the Court of Appeal.[10] This means that some other procedural rules must apply to the bringing of appeals from the magistrates' courts, and indeed the relevant rules are found in the Crown Court Rules 1982.[11]

Post-conviction ASBOs

11.11 The position is equally complex in the case of a final or interim ASBO which is made following conviction under CDA 1998 ss1C or 1D. In this situation, the magistrates' court and the Crown Court are both undoubtedly sitting as criminal courts when sentencing the defendant for the criminal offence. However, given that proceedings under both s1C and 1D are classed as civil,[12] the court would not be dealing with a criminal cause or matter in so far as that order is concerned.

11.12 As mentioned in chapters 4 and 6, the Court of Appeal (Criminal Division), in *Luke Paul Wadmore and Liam Philip Foreman v R*,[13] suggested that it was not clear that the Criminal Procedure Rules applied to s1C proceedings in the Crown Court.[14] The Court was not directed to the provisions of CA 2003 to which reference has been made above, and which suggests that the Crown Court would be sitting in its civil capacity when making such an order. If anything, this would reinforce the view of the Court of Appeal in the *Wadmore* case that there is a lack of clarity as to which procedural rules apply. However, the Court of Appeal applied the Magistrates' Courts (Hearsay Evidence in Civil Proceedings) Rules 1999[15] by analogy.

11.13 Part 50.4 of the Criminal Procedure Rules creates further confusion. This expressly stipulates the prescribed form which should be completed when the Crown Court makes an ASBO under s1C. That

10 See discussion at para 6.12 on post-conviction ASBOs and the non-applicability of the Criminal Procedure Rules 2005 and the CPR.

11 SI No 1109 (although these rules are now replicated in the Criminal Procedure Rules 2005).

12 See *R (W) v Acton Youth Court* [2005] EWHC 954 (Admin) and para 6.6.

13 [2006] EWCA Crim 686.

14 [2006] EWCA Crim 686 at para 33. See discussion in chapter 6.

15 SI No 681. Reproduced in full in appendix D.

said, the identical provision, with the same prescribed form, appears in Rule 38 of the Crown Court Rules 1982 (as amended).[16]

Procedure on appeal to the Crown Court

11.14 On the basis that the appeal from the magistrates' court to the Crown Court, whether it be in relation to an ASBO under section 1 (stand-alone), section 1C (post-conviction) or section 1D (interim), is governed by the Crown Court Rules 1982,[17] criminal practitioners will be more than familiar with the procedure as it is exactly the same as for appeals against conviction and sentence in criminal cases. The most important points are as follows:

- an intention to appeal must be made in writing (rules 7(1) and 7(2));
- an appeal must be brought not later than 21 days after the day on which the decision appealed against is given (rule 7(3));
- it is possible to obtain an extension of time for appealing and this must be made in writing to the Crown Court (rule 7(6)).

Appeals against ASBOs made by the Crown Court (CDA 1998 ss1C and 1D)

11.15 As stated above, although these are made in the context of criminal proceedings, they are civil orders and do not come within the scope of the Criminal Procedure Rules. However, the Court of Appeal has held, in *R v P (Shane Tony)*,[18] that the proper route is nevertheless by way of appeal to the Court of Appeal, Criminal Division.[19] The basis for this decision was that an ASBO made by the Crown Court is a sentence within the meaning of s50 of the Criminal Appeal Act (CAA) 1968[20] and so CAA 1968 s9 gives the Court of Appeal jurisdiction to deal with the appeal.

11.16 To this, it should be added that CAA 1968 s10(3) provides that there is an appeal to the Court of Appeal (Criminal Division) against a sentence imposed by the Crown Court, which again includes the

16 See para 6.49.

17 Now contained in the Criminal Procedure Rules 2005 r63.2. See *Archbold* 2006, para 2-181.

18 [2004] EWCA Crim 287.

19 [2004] EWCA Crim 287 at para 36.

20 Because s50 defines a sentence as including any order made by a court when dealing with an offender.

making of an ASBO, when a defendant is sentenced having been committed for sentence to the Crown Court from the magistrates' court.

11.17 Because these orders are civil, and for the reasons set out above, the Criminal Procedure Rules do not apply to such appeals. However, the Criminal Appeal Rules 1968[21] remain in force and the relevant parts are in identical form to those parts of the Criminal Procedure Rules 2005 which deal with appeals against sentence.[22] An appeal against sentence has to be lodged within 28 days of the sentence being passed by way of a form NG.[23] Except where the Crown Court has granted a certificate under CAA 1968 s11(1A), appeal lies only by leave of the Court of Appeal. The power to give leave may, however, be exercised by a single judge. Reference should be made to *Archbold* and/or *Blackstones'* for these rules and the procedure to be followed.[24]

Appeals by way of case stated

From the Crown Court

11.18 SCA 1981 s28(1) provides that an appeal from the Crown Court lies to the High Court by case stated, save where the decision sought to be challenged is one of the Crown Court relating to trial on indictment (as to which see below). There is no right of appeal to the Court of Appeal (Criminal Division) against a stand-alone ASBO upheld by a Crown Court following an appeal from a magistrates' court.[25]

From the magistrates' court

11.19 There is an identical right of appeal from the magistrates' court to the High Court by virtue of MCA 1980 s111. However, if this route of appeal is chosen, the party appealing loses their right to appeal to the Crown Court.[26] Of course, this will only affect a defendant since the

21 SI No 1262.

22 Rule 2 of the 1968 Rules deals with the institution of an appeal and the corresponding provision in the Criminal Procedure Rules 2005 can be found in Part 68. Available at www.dca.gov.uk.

23 Form NG is available in the 'forms' section of the Criminal Procedure Rules 2005 (available on www.dca.gov.uk).

24 See also www.hmcourts-service.gov.uk.

25 This is specifically excluded by CAA 1968 s10(1).

26 MCA 1980 s111(4).

applying authority has no right of appeal to the Crown Court in any event.

When is appeal by way of case stated appropriate?

11.20 In both the Crown Court and the magistrates' court, this route of appeal is available to any party to the proceedings on the basis that the lower court's decision was wrong in law or in excess of jurisdiction. In essence, this means that it is necessary to show an error of law in the lower court's decision. There is no rehearing where the appeal is by way of case stated.

11.21 In broad terms, an appeal by way of case stated has two stages. First, there is the process of asking the lower court to state a case. Once the case has been stated in final form, an appeal is pursued.

11.22 In so far as obtaining a stated case from a magistrates' court or the Crown Court is concerned, the relevant procedure is as follows:[27]

(1) The application should be made in writing to the relevant court within 21 days after the date of the decision. The Crown Court has power to extend the time limit in the case of an appeal against its decision[28] but there is no extension of time available where the magistrates' court is concerned.
(2) The application should set out the basis upon which the decision is challenged.
(3) In the case of an appeal against a Crown Court decision, the applicant must send a copy of the application to the other parties in the proceedings.
(4) If the court considers that the application is frivolous, it may refuse to state a case and, if requested, shall provide the applicant with a certificate giving the reasons for the refusal.
(5) If a case is to be stated then:
    (a) in the Crown Court, the applicant has 21 days from the date of being told that the Court has agreed to state a case, to draft a case and send a copy of it to the Court and to the parties to the proceedings in the Crown Court.
    (b) in the magistrates' court, the clerk to the justices has 21 days from receipt of the application to send a draft case to the applicant and the other parties.

27 See rule 26 of the Crown Court Rules 1982 (SI No 1109) for the procedure in the Crown Court and MCA 1980 s111 and rules 76 to 81 of the Magistrates' Court Rules 1981 SI No 552 for the magistrates' court. These rules are replicated in full in the Criminal Procedure Rules 2005 Part 64.

28 See rule 26(14) of the Crown Court Rules 1982.

(6) There is then a further 21-day period when:
   (a) in the Crown Court, the other parties are permitted, if they wish to take part in the appeal, to agree to the applicant's draft or provide an alternative draft;
   (b) in the magistrates' court, the parties can make representations on the case as drafted by the clerk.

(7) The final version of the stated case is then provided within the following time limits:
   (a) in the Crown Court, within 14 days of receiving comments from the other parties, or 21 days, whichever is soonest;
   (b) in the magistrates' court, within 21 days of the parties' representations on the draft case.

11.23 In both cases, a refusal to state a case can be judicially reviewed, normally on the basis that no reasonable court could have come to the conclusion that the application to state a case was frivolous.

11.24 The next stage is the appeal. CPR Part 52 applies in general, but with the following amendments:[29]

- either party can use this route of appeal;
- the appellant must file the appellant's notice[30] at the appeal court within 10 days after he or she receives the stated case;
- the following documents must be filed with the appellant's notice: the stated case, a copy of the judgment, order or decision in respect of which the case has been stated and where the judgment, order or decision in respect of which the case has been stated was itself given or made on appeal, a copy of the original judgment, order or decision appealed from;
- the appellant must serve the appellant's notice and accompanying documents on all respondents within 4 days after they are filed at the appeal court.

11.25 Reference should be made to the discussion of Part 52 below for full details of the procedure on appeal.

11.26 Appeals by way of case stated are usually heard by a Divisional Court (that is, a court consisting of two or three judges, one of whom will normally be a judge of the Court of Appeal) but there is no reason why the appeal cannot be heard by a judge sitting alone.

11.27 Under SCA 1981 s28A(3), the High Court has the power to reverse, affirm or amend the determination in respect of which the

29 See paragraph 18.2 of the Practice Direction to Part 52. Available at www.dca.gov.uk. Reproduced at appendix H.

30 Form N161 available in the 'forms' section of the Civil Procedure Rules at www.dca.gov.uk.

case has been stated or remit the matter to the magistrates' court, or the Crown Court, with the opinion of the High Court, and may make such other order in relation to the matter (including as to costs) as it thinks fit.

Further appeals

11.28 SCA 1981 s28A(4) states that the decision of the High Court on an appeal by way of case stated is final, except as provided by s1(1)(a) of the Administration of Justice Act 1960. This permits an appeal to the House of Lords, with leave, but only in a criminal cause or matter. Since the making of an ASBO does not fall into this category, the House of Lords has no jurisdiction to entertain such an appeal. Indeed, this was the reason for rejecting the appeal of Mr Clingham in the case of *R (on the application of McCann) v Crown Court at Manchester; Clingham v K & C Royal Borough Council.*[31]

11.29 For completeness, it should be mentioned that SCA 1981 s18(1)(c) makes it clear that there is no appeal to the Court of Appeal from a decision of the High Court which is expressed to be final.

Judicial review

11.30 Although this is not strictly speaking an appeal, it is a method of challenging a lower court's decision so can be conveniently considered under this heading. Judicial review is a method by which the High Court supervises the decisions of public authorities and lower courts. It is a discretionary remedy which is governed by SCA 1981 s31 and CPR 54. Decisions can only be challenged on a limited number of grounds. These include cases where a body has acted in excess of jurisdiction or failed to follow the rules of natural justice or misapplied the law or acted unreasonably in the *Wednesbury*[32] sense (sometimes referred to as 'irrationality'). However, it is now well established that the standards of review are much more intensive where rights under the ECHR are at stake.[33] In an appropriate case, therefore, a court will

31 [2002] UKHL 39, [2002] 3 WLR 1313, [2002] 4 All ER 593, HL at para 33. For a full discussion of the judgment in *McCann* see chapter 3.

32 After the case of *Associated Provincial Picture Houses Ltd v Wednesbury Corpn* [1948] 1 KB 223.

33 See, for example, *R (Daly) v Secretary of State for the Home Department* [2001] UKHL 26 [2001] 2 AC 532 (referred to in chapter 7).

subject a decision that interferes with fundamental rights to a greater degree of scrutiny. That said, if the High Court was to find that there had been an error of law, the only remedy available would be a quashing of the ASBO. In an appropriate case the matter would then have to be reconsidered by the lower court, applying the correct test.[34]

11.31 Reference should be made to a specialist textbook for the procedure to be followed on a claim for judicial review.[35] However, the following important points can be highlighted here:

- either party can bring the challenge;
- permission is required to bring a claim for judicial review and this will normally be considered on the papers;[36]
- a claim for judicial review must be brought promptly, and in any event, within three months of the decision complained of. This means that it is possible to be out of time even when the claim is filed within three months;
- the Legal Services Commission *Funding Code*[37] and the *Judicial Review Pre-Action Protocol*[38] require that a claimant serves a letter before action on the appropriate defendant, asking for the decision to be re-considered. However, this is not usually appropriate when challenging the decision of a court as it is normally *functus officio* its original decision (in other words, the court does not have jurisdiction to reverse its own decision).

11.32 Unsuccessful parties in civil judicial review proceedings may appeal to the Court of Appeal (Civil Division) but will require permission from either the High Court or the Court of Appeal to do so.

The different types of appeal routes

11.33 It is important to consider carefully the appropriate appeal route where it is considered that an ASBO may have been wrongly made. First, where the order is one of the magistrates' court, advisers will need to analyse whether there is any factual issue in dispute or if the error relates to a matter of legal principle. If the former, then an

34 See para 11.38 below.

35 See Jonathan Manning, *Judicial Review Proceedings, a Practitioners' Guide* (2nd edn, LAG, 2004).

36 The claim form is N461 and is available on the DCA website along with notes for guidance: www.dca.gov.uk.

37 The Funding Code is available at www.legalservices.gov.uk.

38 The Civil Procedure Rules Pre-Action Protocols (www.dca.gov.uk).

appeal by way of case stated or a claim for judicial review will be of little utility, since there is no or a very limited investigation of the facts in such cases. In such a scenario, an appeal should be made to the Crown Court, which will hold an appeal by way of rehearing.

11.34 If, on the other hand, there is a point of law involved, then an appeal to the High Court by way of case stated will often be the most appropriate course. As can be seen from the case stated procedure set out above, this will involve the appellant and the court attempting to agree the facts which are relevant to the point of law which it is sought to raise. This course is particularly useful where it will be contended that no reasonable court could have come to the conclusion on the basis of the facts before that court.

11.35 In *R v Hereford Magistrates' Court ex p Rowlands*,[39] the High Court explained the difference between appealing by way of case stated and appealing to the Crown Court as follows:

> The business of magistrates' courts is in the main handled according to the highest standards, but, as in all other courts, errors may be made and procedural lapses and irregularities may occur. To protect convicted defendants against the possibility of injustice, Parliament has conferred two rights of appeal. The first, provided by section 108 of the Magistrates' Courts Act 1980, enables a convicted defendant to appeal to the Crown Court against conviction or sentence. A defendant who exercises this right of appeal within the prescribed period of 21 days is entitled to full retrial before a judge of the Crown Court sitting with justices. The burden of proving the case is on the prosecutor, as in the magistrates' court. Full evidence may be called, whether or not it had been given in the magistrates' court. A decision is reached on the case as presented in the Crown Court. This is the ordinary avenue of appeal for a defendant who complains that the magistrates' court reached a wrong decision of fact, or a wrong decision of mixed law and fact. An alternative right of appeal is conferred by section 111 of the 1980 Act on any party to proceedings before a magistrates' court who is aggrieved by a conviction, order, determination or other proceeding of the court, who may question the proceeding on the ground that it is 'wrong in law or is in excess of jurisdiction' by applying to the justices to state a case for the opinion of the High Court on the question of law or jurisdiction involved. This right also must be exercised within 21 days, and section 111 (4) provides that on the making of an application for a case to be stated any right of the applicant to appeal against the decision to the Crown Court shall cease. This is the ordinary avenue of appeal for a convicted defendant who contends that the justices erred in law: the usual question posed for the opinion of the High Court is whether on the facts which

39 [1998] QB 110.

they found the justices were entitled to convict the defendant; but sometimes the question is whether there was any evidence upon which the justices could properly convict the defendant, which has traditionally been regarded as an issue of law.[40]

11.36 Judicial review may be appropriate where a speedy remedy is required,[41] since both an appeal to the Crown Court or the High Court by way of case stated will take some time. Indeed, where more than 21 days have elapsed since the making of the lower court's decision, an appeal by way of case stated will not be available in relation to a decision of the magistrates' court, and only with an extension of time against a Crown Court decision. Furthermore, while there is a general principle that a party should exercise a right of appeal where appropriate,[42] it is clear that the High Court retains a wide supervisory jurisdiction over lower courts. Indeed, in *R v Hereford Magistrates' Court ex p Rowlands*, the High Court rejected a submission that it was deprived of jurisdiction over the magistrates' court on the basis that there was a right of appeal to the Crown Court.[43]

11.37 In *R (A) v Leeds Magistrates' Court and Leeds City Council*,[44] which was an application for judicial review of an interim ASBO, Stanley Burnton J summarised the differences between the various routes of appeal (variation and discharge; appeal to the Crown Court; appeal by way of case stated and judicial review) as follows:

11.38 Of these procedures, judicial review is the least suitable in a case such as the present, where it is not disputed that the evidence before the magistrates' court justified (although it did not necessarily require) the making of the order. In such a case, if the claimant establishes that the District Judge applied an incorrect test, the only relief this Court can grant is to quash the ASBO. In judicial review proceedings, the High Court cannot consider the evidence before the District Judge (or any evidence subsequently available) and itself decide whether, applying the correct legal test, the order should be upheld, save in cases in which no District Judge properly applying the law could have come to any conclusion other than that the order should be made. Nor can the High Court vary the terms of the ASBO so as to accommodate the contentions successfully made by the claimant. The High Court cannot substitute its discretion for that of the magistrates' court.

40 [1998] QB 110 at paras 3–4.

41 Urgent consideration including interim remedies is available in cases of exceptional urgency. See Form N463, available at www.dca.gov.uk.

42 See, for example, the comments of Sullivan J in *R (C) v Sunderland Youth Court* [2003] EWHC 2385 (Admin) at para 39.

43 [1998] QB 110 at paras 22–23.

44 [2004] EWHC 554 (Admin).

> In all of the other procedures listed above, the situation is different. On an appeal to the Crown Court, it has the wide powers conferred by section 4(2) of the 1998 Act. Moreover, both the local authority and the Claimant would have been able to adduce evidence in that Court. On an appeal by way of case stated, the High Court may 'affirm, set aside or vary' the ASBO: CPR Part 52.10(2), as well as order a new hearing. The power to affirm or to vary an order on grounds different from those relied upon by the magistrates' court will, in my judgment, be more readily exercised in the case of an ASBO, which has continuing effect and has as its object the protection of the public while it is in force. The High Court may be the more ready to make a decision which the magistrates' court might have made in a case, such as the present, where the decision below did not depend on any conflict of oral evidence.
>
> Judicial review proceedings have a further disadvantage. There is often no reliable record of the reasons given by the magistrates' court for its decision. ... Where however a case is stated, the District Judge has the opportunity to set out the facts on which he based his decision and his reasons for making the order.[45]

11.39 Where there is an appeal against the decision of the Crown Court to impose a section 1C post-conviction ASBO after a trial on indictment, the only route of appeal is to the Court of Appeal (Criminal Division) since the decision will be a matter relating to trial on indictment, and neither an appeal by way of case stated or judicial review will be available.[46]

11.40 If the Crown Court makes an ASBO following committal for sentence this will not be a decision made in relation to trial on indictment. Accordingly, an appeal by way of case stated or a claim for judicial review will be available in theory. However, unless there is something out of the ordinary, such as an allegation of procedural unfairness or bias, then the correct route of appeal will be to the Court of Appeal (Criminal Division), on the basis of the logic in *R v P (Shane Tony)*.[47]

Appeals from the county court

11.41 CPR 52 governs routes of appeal from the civil courts. This, along with the Practice Direction to that Part, and the Access to Justice Act

45 [2004] EWHC 554 (Admin) at paras 29–33.

46 See SCA 1981 s29(3).

47 [2004] EWCA Crim 287; [2004] 2 Cr App R (S) 63.

1999 (Destination of Appeals) Order 2000[48] contains a comprehensive code for pursuing appeals. The position, in so far as it is relevant for present purposes, is as follows:

- Where the principal proceedings are on the fast-track[49] in the county court, then the appeal will be to the next level of judge. Accordingly, a decision by a district judge will go to a circuit judge. Similarly, a decision by a circuit judge will go to a High Court judge.
- However, where there is a second appeal, then it will always go to the Court of Appeal. So, for example, an appeal from the decision of a circuit judge which was itself made on appeal from a district judge will go to the Court of Appeal rather than a High Court judge.
- An appeal in a multi-track case[50] will be to the Court of Appeal, regardless of whether the initial decision was made by a district judge or a circuit judge (save as stated below in respect of interim ASBOs).

11.42 There is an exception to the above scheme where the decision of the lower court is not a final decision, this being defined as including a decision granting or refusing an interim remedy.[51] Accordingly, a decision made on an application for an interim ASBO under CDA 1998 s1D will not be a final decision. In this situation, and assuming it is not a second appeal, the appeal will always to be to the next level. Where the decision of the lower court is not a final decision, which is defined as including a decision granting or refusing an interim remedy. Accordingly, a decision made on an application for an interim ASBO under CDA 1998 s1D will not be a final decision. In this situation, the appeal will always be to the next level in the judicial hierarchy, even when the case is on the multi-track. Accordingly, an appeal against the grant or refusal of an interim ASBO by a district judge will be to the circuit judge and an appeal against the same decision made by the circuit judge will be to a High Court judge.

48 SI No 1071.

49 This is the 'track' to which a case will be allocated where the trial is expected to last one day or less and has a value of between £5,000 to £15,000. See CPR 26.6(4) and (5).

50 See CPR 26.6(6). A case will be allocated to this 'track' where it does not fall within the criteria to be allocated to the fast-track, normally because the trial is expected to last more than one day. In the context of a claim for an ASBO, this will be because the principal proceedings will normally be relatively complex and relate to lengthy allegations of anti-social behaviour.

51 PD 52, para 2A.2(2).

Who can appeal?

11.43 An appeal against any decision, whether to make or refuse to make a county court ASBO, can be instituted by either party.

Procedure

11.44
- The time for bringing an appeal is 21 days from the date of the order appealed against. This can be extended or reduced on application by either party, as well as on the court's own initiative.[52]
- Permission to appeal is always needed, save for certain types of case, of which only one, a decision on committal proceedings, is relevant for present purposes. Permission will be granted where the appeal has real prospects of success or there is some other compelling reason why the appeal should be heard.[53]
- However, the test for granting permission to the Court of Appeal on a second appeal is more stringent, namely, whether the appeal raises an important point of principle or practice or there is some other compelling reason why the Court of Appeal should hear it.[54]
- An appeal will normally be by way of review of the lower court's decision.[55] The scope of this was explained by May LJ in *EI Du Pont De Nemours & Company v ST Dupont*[56] as follows:[57]

11.45 As the terms of rule 52.11(1) make clear, subject to exceptions, every appeal is limited to a review of the decision of the lower court. A review here is not to be equated with judicial review. It is closely akin to, although not conceptually identical with, the scope of an appeal to the Court of Appeal under the former Rules of the Supreme Court. The review will engage the merits of the appeal. It will accord appropriate respect to the decision of the lower court. Appropriate respect will be tempered by the nature of the lower court and its decision-making process. There will also be a spectrum of appropriate respect depending on the nature of the decision of the lower court which is challenged. At one end of the spectrum will be decisions of primary fact reached after an evaluation of oral evidence where credibility is in issue and purely discretionary decisions. Further along the spectrum will be multi-factorial decisions often dependent on inferences and an

52 See CPR 52.3(2), CPR 52.6(1) and CPR 3.1(2)(a).
53 CPR 52.3(6).
54 CPR 52.13(2).
55 CPR 52.11.
56 [2003] EWCA Civ 1368.
57 [2003] EWCA Civ 1368 at paras 94–95.

analysis of documentary material. Rule 52.11(4) expressly empowers the court to draw inferences. ... As to fresh evidence, under rule 52.11(2) on an appeal by way of review the court will not receive evidence which was not before the lower court unless it orders otherwise. There is an obligation on the parties to bring forward all the evidence on which they intend to rely before the lower court, and failure to do this does not normally result in indulgence by the appeal court. The principles on which the appeal court will admit fresh evidence under this provision are now well understood and do not require elaboration here.

- It is possible for an appeal to be by way of rehearing, but these cases will be rare.[58]

58 See May LJ in the *EI Du Pont De Nemours & Company v ST Dupont* [2003] EWCA Civ 1368 at [96].

CHAPTER 12

Costs and public funding

with Rajeev Thacker

continued

COSTS

In the magistrates' court

Stand-alone ASBOs

12.1 The power of the magistrates' court to make an order for costs in stand-alone ASBO cases is contained in MCA 1980 s64(1) which provides as follows:

> On the hearing of a complaint, a magistrates' court shall have power in its discretion to make such order as to costs –
> (a) on making the order for which the complaint is made, to be paid by the defendant to the complainant;
> (b) on dismissing the complaint, to be paid by the complainant to the defendant,
> as it thinks just and reasonable.

12.2 MCA 1980 s64(2) requires the amount of the costs to be specified in the order, or order of dismissal, as the case may be. What the court will think is just and reasonable will depend on all the relevant facts and circumstances of the case. The court may think it just and reasonable that costs follow the event but this may not necessarily be the case. The award of costs against public authorities who have acted 'honestly, reasonably and properly' is discouraged, although financial prejudice to the successful complainant is a relevant factor to be born in mind.[1]

12.3 For the purposes of the grant of public funding, proceedings for an ASBO in the magistrates' court are classified as criminal proceedings.[2] This means that there is no costs protection, as there would be in the county court (as to which, see below), and so a defendant who is unsuccessful is liable to pay the entirety of the applicant's costs without there needing to be any investigation into his or her means. This position is in stark contrast to publicly funded parties in all other civil cases.

1 *City of Bradford MDC v Booth*, 164 JP 485. See also *Stone's Justices' Manual* 2005, at para 1-644.

2 See Regulation 3(2) of the Criminal Defence Service (General) (No. 2) Regulations 2000 SI No 1437 and Access to Justice Act 1999 s12(2)(g).

In the Crown Court

On appeal against a stand-alone ASBO made in the magistrates' court

12.4 Under Rule 12 of the Crown Court Rules 1982, the Crown Court has the power to make such order for costs as it considers just. In addition, Rule 13 makes specific provision when an appeal is brought from the magistrates' court. In this situation, the Crown Court can make such order in relation to the costs in the magistrates' court as could have been made by the lower court.[3]

On appeal against a post-conviction ASBO

12.5 Costs in this scenario are governed by s16(3) of the Prosecution of Offences Act 1985. This permits the Crown Court to make a costs order in favour of the defendant when s/he appeals under MCA 1980 s108 against sentence, which includes the making of an ASBO. For a costs order to be made, the conviction must be set aside or a less severe punishment must be awarded. Accordingly, a defendant who appeals against the making of a post-conviction ASBO may obtain a costs order where:

- he or she is appealing against the conviction for the substantive offence of which s/he was found guilty in the magistrates' court, and is acquitted; or
- the post-conviction ASBO is set aside or the defendant receives a better result in relation to it, such as a relaxation of the terms or a reduction in its length.

12.6 The order will be paid out of central funds and the amount of the order is such as is reasonable to compensate a person for the expenses incurred.[4] However, there is a wide power to reduce the amount claimed in circumstances where it would be inappropriate to allow the defendant to recover the full amount.[5] There Crown Court has no power to make a Recovery of Defence Costs Order in appeals against sentence.[6]

3 These rules are replicated in the Criminal Procedure Rules 2005 Part 78.

4 Prosecution of Offences Act 1985 s16(6).

5 Ibid, s16(7).

6 See *Archbold* 2006, 6-114h.

In the High Court

On appeal by way of case stated

12.7 Since this is an appeal governed by the CPR, the CPR rules as to costs should apply. The other party to the appeal will be the applying authority and there seems to be no reason why the usual 'costs follow the event' rule should not apply.[7]

In a claim for judicial review

12.8 Costs in this type of claim are governed by the CPR, as to which see para 12.12 below. However, since the claim will be against the lower court, costs will not normally be awarded unless there has been a flagrant instance of improper behaviour or where the lower court has unreasonably declined to sign a consent order disposing of the judicial review proceedings.[8]

In the Court of Appeal (Criminal Division)

12.9 Rather incongruently, the Court of Appeal (Criminal Division) does have power to make a costs order in favour of a defendant to criminal proceedings where there is an appeal against an ASBO made by the Crown Court. This is because s16(4)(c) of the Prosecution of Offences Act 1985 permits it to make a costs order in favour of a defendant when, amongst other things, it allows an appeal against sentence. As seen above, 'sentence' within the context of an appeal to the Court of Appeal includes an order making an ASBO. However, such costs do not include the costs of representation funded by the Legal Services Commission (LSC) as part of the Criminal Defence Service (CDS).[9]

12.10 Again, the order will be paid out of central funds and the amount paid will be reasonable in relation to the expenses incurred. There remains a power to reduce the amount payable in circumstances where it would be inappropriate to allow the defendant to recover the full amount.

12.11 The Court of Appeal (Criminal Division) does have the power to make a Recovery of Defence Costs Order in relation to publicly funded

7 See para 12.12 below.

8 *Davies (No 2), R (on the application of) v HM Deputy Coroner for Birmingham* [2004] EWCA Civ 207; *R v Bristol Justices ex p Hodge* [1997] QB 974.

9 Prosecution of Offences Act 1985 s21(4A)(a).

defendants. The registrar may require an appellant to complete a statement of means and at the conclusion of the appeal the court must consider whether to make a Recovery of Defence Costs Order: Criminal Defence Service (Recovery of Defence Costs Orders) Regulations 2001.[10] Advocates therefore ought to be in a position to provide the Court with an estimate of the appellant's costs. The Court of Appeal is unlikely to make such an order when leave has been granted.

In the county court

12.12 The civil courts have a wide discretion as to costs. It is regulated by CPR 44. The fundamental principle is that costs follow the event.[11] In other words, the loser will pay the costs of the winner unless there is good reason to depart from this rule. It is becoming increasingly common to make a costs order which reflects the overall justice of the case, so that, for example, a party who has not succeeded on all the issues will only recover a proportion of his or her costs. This may be of particular importance in ASBO cases, where an applying authority may succeed to some extent in the principal proceedings, for example, by obtaining a possession order suspended on terms, but may have failed in its application for an ASBO. In such a situation, the court will have to consider the amount of time spent on each issue and make an order which reflects the overall justice of the case.

12.13 In deciding what order to make about costs, the court has to take into account the conduct of the parties, the extent to which a party has been successful and any offer to settle which has been made.[12] However, this does not mean that it should not take any other relevant matters into account and, providing that it has done so, an appellate court will not interfere with a decision on costs unless it is plainly wrong.

In the higher civil courts

12.14 Where a party brings a claim for judicial review or appeals to the Court of Appeal (Civil Division), the general rule is that costs will follow the event. This will also apply where any appeal is pursued to the House of Lords.

10 SI No 824.
11 CPR 44.3(2)(a).
12 Discussed at para 8.44.

Costs against publicly funded parties in the civil courts

12.15 Section 11(1) of the Access to Justice Act 1999 provides as follows:

> Except in prescribed circumstances, costs ordered against an individual in relation to any proceedings or part of proceedings funded for him shall not exceed the amount (if any) which is a reasonable one for him to pay having regard to all the circumstances including –
> (a) the financial resources of all the parties to the proceedings, and
> (b) their conduct in connection with the dispute to which the proceedings relate;
> and for this purpose proceedings, or a part of proceedings, are funded for an individual if services relating to the proceedings or part are funded for him by the Commission as part of the Community Legal Service.

12.16 This is referred to as 'costs protection'. It is important to note that it is only available to those funded under the Community Legal Service (CLS) scheme and does not apply in respect of those parties who are publicly funded under the Criminal Defence Service (CDS) scheme.

12.17 In practical terms, costs protection means that a party that is successful in a claim against a publicly funded party cannot recover any costs from the losing party until there has been an assessment of that losing party's means. It is open to a trial court to assess the person's means at the conclusion of the final hearing but it will nearly always be deferred until the detailed costs assessment.

12.18 In such circumstances, a party which is entitled to costs can make an application for its costs to be paid directly by the Legal Services Commission.[13] The court will make the order if it considers it just and equitable to do so. However, if the proceedings are at first instance, then the court will only make such an order if the putative receiving party can establish that it will suffer financial hardship if the order is not made. It is highly unlikely that any applying authority will be able to make this out. However, this criterion is not applicable where the costs of any appeal are sought against the LSC.

12.19 It is important to note that there is no costs protection where proceedings are funded by way of Help at Court.[14] In addition, costs protection will only apply in relation to Legal Help if the client subsequently receives full public funding in relation to the same dispute.[15]

13 Community Legal Service (Cost Protection) Regulations 2000 SI No 824, reg 5(2).

14 Community Legal Service (Cost Protection) Regulations 2000 SI No 824, reg 3(1)(a).

15 See Community Legal Service (Cost Protection) Regulations 2000 SI No 824, regs 3(1)(c) and 3(2).

PUBLIC FUNDING

The criminal courts

Stand-alone ASBOs

12.20 The Criminal Defence Service (CDS) General Criminal Contract Part A, Rule 3.2.1(b) makes allowance for public funding in relation to any proceedings under CDA 1998 ss1 and 4 (which includes interim ASBOs). The General Criminal Contract allows for the self-grant of Advocacy Assistance to an extendable upper financial limit of £1,500.[16] There are no financial criteria for the grant of Advocacy Assistance save that it must not be provided where it appears unreasonable in the particular circumstances of the case, or where the interests of justice test is not met.[17] Given that there is a real risk of imprisonment if an anti-social behaviour order is made and subsequently breached, the interests of justice test should be met.

12.21 A solicitor may self-grant Advocacy Assistance for the purposes of proceedings to vary or discharge an ASBO, and the application is to be treated as part of the same case as the original proceedings, although the additional work may be claimed by way of a supplemental claim using the same UFN as the main proceedings. If the original firm is no longer instructed, there is no reason why the new firm cannot self-grant afresh.

12.22 The LSC gives the following guidance on Advocacy Assistance rates:

> **Rates applicable**
> 12. A written application (CDS Form 3) is required for the grant of Advocacy Assistance, solicitors may instruct counsel and the magistrates' court hourly rates specified in Part E, Section 3.3 of the Contract would apply. The solicitor may not claim time spent accompanying counsel (Part B, Rule 4.8 of the Contract Specification). Although the Commission is empowered to grant representation orders, it is unlikely that it would, given that self-granted Advocacy Assistance is available. However, in certain circumstances, for example, where equality of arms is in issue, the Commission may consider granting a representation order. Applications for representation orders in these circumstances should be made to the appropriate Processing Centre on Form CDS3 and the work claimed as a non-standard fee. The Crown Court is not empowered

16 General Criminal Contract, Part B 4 and 6.3.
17 Access to Justice Act 1999 Sch 3.

to grant representation orders in relation to appeals against ASBOs. Where the Crown Court has granted a representation order in these circumstances, both the supplier and the court should be informed that the order is *ultra vires*, and the supplier should be advised to seek an ex gratia payment from the Court Service.[18]

12.23 It is common practice for Crown Courts to grant representation orders where they have no power to do so. Solicitors should correct this mistake as soon as possible as the LSC will simply refuse to pay out and lawyers are left dependent on *ex gratia* payments.

Appeals against stand-alones

12.24 Advocacy Assistance is also available for proceedings in the Crown Court in relation to an appeal against a stand-alone ASBO. The Advocacy Assistance merits test must be applied, and for proceedings in the Crown Court, this is based only on the general reasonableness test.[19]

Post-conviction ASBOs

12.25 Post-conviction ASBOs in the magistrates' court are considered incidental to the main proceedings and are funded by the LSC in terms of Part A, Rule 3.2.1(c) of the General Criminal Contract under the representation order granted in the main proceedings.

12.26 Work undertaken in relation to post-conviction ASBOs in the Crown Court, however, does not fall within the scope of the General Criminal Contract but is assessed and paid by the National Taxing Team under the Crown Court representation order. The representation order will also cover an application to vary or discharge the anti-social behaviour order.

Appeals against post-conviction ASBOs

12.27 As an appeal against a post-conviction ASBO is treated as an appeal against sentence, a representation order will fund appeals from the magistrates' court to the Crown Court. The original representation order will cover advice on appeal and the lodging of the notice of appeal but a new application form should be filled in along with the notice of appeal, as the original order will not cover representation

18 See ASBO guidance at www.legalservices.gov.uk.

19 See General Criminal Contract, Part B, Rule 4.3 and 6.3.20.

by counsel in the Crown Court. Any application for a representation order is by way of a Form A.

Court of Appeal (Criminal Division)

12.28 As explained above, only appeals against post-conviction ASBOs will be by this route. A representation order covers funding in the same way as in an appeal against sentence. The original representation order will cover counsel's advice and grounds and any work done by the solicitor in order to lodge the appeal. The appeal is lodged by way of a form NG which includes a box for an application for a representation order.[20] If leave is granted a representation order is normally granted to cover counsel's attendance alone.

Appeal by way of case stated

12.29 As ASBOs are criminal proceedings for the purpose of Access to Justice Act 1999 s12(2)(g), which defines those proceedings which are to be funded by Criminal Defence Service, appeals by way of case stated are also funded by way of a representation order. Solicitors are required to fill in a Form A. The High Court has the power to order a Recovery of Defence Costs Order but it is not its practice to do so in such appeals.

Breaches of ASBOs

12.30 A breach of an anti-social behaviour order is a criminal offence. Publicly funded representation by way of a representation order is available to anyone charged with a criminal offence, subject to the interests of justice test. A solicitor is required to fill in a Form A. In the Crown Court a means Form B must also be filled in. The Crown Court has the power to make a Recovery of Defence Costs Order in certain circumstances.[21]

The civil courts

12.31 Public funding is available to defend an application for an ASBO in the county court. It is provided by the CLS, which is that part of the

20 See www.dca.gov.uk.

21 See *Archbold* 2006, para 6-114h.

LSC which funds civil proceedings. There is no separate section in the published guidance dealing with ASBOs in the county courts. Rather, it appears that such proceedings will be treated as ancillary to the principal proceedings. Section H3.5 of the H3.5 (Housing-Financial Limits)[22] is in the following terms:

12.32 46. Twenty units (2 hours) will normally be sufficient to allow you to take full instructions and advise on possible defences, the action to be taken and to make any necessary application for funding.

> 47. The initial twenty units (2 hours) should, where the existing proceedings are the subject of a live certificate, cover any amendment to extend the certificate's scope to include the ASBO application.
>
> 48. Where the existing proceedings are not publicly funded, you should consider whether Legal Representation for the ASBO application is justified. If legal representation is not appropriate, Help at Court may be appropriate to provide mitigation for the client where the allegations are accepted.

12.33 This deals with the initial work that can be carried out by civil contract holders. However, if representation in court proceedings is required, then it will be necessary to apply for an amendment to the certificate in the principal proceedings. Paragraph 19.11 of the LSC *Funding Code* sets out the following criteria: [23]

> 12. Such cases must be the subject of an amendment where existing proceedings are already publicly funded. The amendment is likely to be granted where it is in the interests of justice that the client should defend the application.
>
> 13. If the existing proceedings, in which the ASBO is issued, are not, for whatever reason, publicly funded, certificates are likely to be issued solely for the ASBO application where it is in the interests of justice for representation to be provided. Representation will be refused if the allegations made are not sufficiently serious to justify representation, the prospects of success are poor or if mitigation at court is required and it is considered that Help at Court is more appropriate.

12.34 Where the county court ASBO is being sought against a person newly-joined to the proceedings (so that the ASBO can be sought against them) they will need a certificate to be funded for representation to resist the application.

22 *LSC Manual*, para 2D-097, available at www.legalservices.gov.uk.

23 See *LSC Manual*, para 3C-166, available at www.legalservices.gov.uk.

Appeals from civil courts

12.35 A certificate of public funding will not cover an appeal. It will accordingly be necessary to obtain an amendment to the certificate so that an appeal can be pursued. Except in the simplest of cases, the Legal Services Commission (LSC) will require an advice from counsel or an external advocate in order to support any such application. If possible, the advice should set out the proposed grounds of appeal and clearly identify the error of law which the lower court is alleged to have made. The LSC will need to be satisfied that there are reasonable prospects of success in order to grant funding.

12.36 If permission to appeal has been granted then it should not be difficult to persuade the LSC that funding should be granted. This is because there will have already been a judicial view expressed, through the grant of permission, that the appeal has prospects of success. If, however, permission has not yet been obtained, consideration should be given to requesting limited funding from the LSC on the basis that if the case does have merit, and permission is granted, the LSC will be more willing to grant further funding at the later stage.

Judicial reviews

12.37 This is dealt with in chapter 16 of the *Funding Code*.[24] Unless the case is straightforward, the LSC will grant funding in the form of Investigative Help so that initial enquiries can be carried out and a pre-action protocol letter sent to the proposed defendant. The guidance further stresses the importance of ensuring that alternative remedies are pursued where appropriate. However, where counsel or an external advocate advises that the proposed claim for judicial review has prospects of success, it is unlikely that the LSC will refuse funding, especially given that the judicial review procedure has its own filter, in the form of a permission stage, which guards against unmeritorious claims.

24 *LSC Manual*, paras 3C-136 onwards, available at www.legalservices.gov.uk.

APPENDICES

APPENDIX A

Crime and Disorder Act 1998

Crime and disorder: general

Anti-social behaviour orders

1 (1) An application for an order under this section may be made by a relevant authority if it appears to the authority that the following conditions are fulfilled with respect to any person aged 10 or over, namely –

(a) that the person has acted, since the commencement date, in an anti-social manner, that is to say, in a manner that caused or was likely to cause harassment, alarm or distress to one or more persons not of the same household as himself; and

(b) that such an order is necessary to protect relevant persons from further anti-social acts by him.

...

(1A) In this section and sections 1B, 1CA, 1E and 1F 'relevant authority' means –

(a) the council for a local government area;

(aa) in relation to England, a county council;

(b) the chief officer of police of any police force maintained for a police area;

(c) the chief constable of the British Transport Police Force; ...

(d) any person registered under section 1 of the Housing Act 1996 as a social landlord who provides or manages any houses or hostel in a local government area; or

(e) a housing action trust established by order in pursuance of section 62 of the Housing Act 1988

(1B) In this section 'relevant persons' means –

(a) in relation to a relevant authority falling within paragraph (a) of subsection (1A), persons within the local government area of that council;

(aa) in relation to a relevant authority falling within paragraph (aa) of subsection (1A), persons within the county of the county council;

(b) in relation to a relevant authority falling within paragraph (b) of that subsection, persons within the police area;

(c) in relation to a relevant authority falling within paragraph (c) of that subsection –

(i) persons who are within or likely to be within a place specified in section 31(1)(a) to (f) of the Railways and Transport Safety Act 2003 in a local government area; or

(ii) persons who are within or likely to be within such a place;

(d) in relation to a relevant authority falling within paragraph (d) or (e)of that subsection –

(i) persons who are residing in or who are otherwise on or likely to be on premises provided or managed by that authority; or

(ii) persons who are in the vicinity of or likely to be in the vicinity of such premises.

(2) ...

(3) Such an application shall be made by complaint to a magistrates' court.

(4) If, on such an application, it is proved that the conditions mentioned in subsection (1) above are fulfilled, the magistrates' court may make an order under this section (an 'anti-social behaviour order') which prohibits the defendant from doing anything described in the order.

(5) For the purpose of determining whether the condition mentioned in subsection (1)(a) above is fulfilled, the court shall disregard any act of the defendant which he shows was reasonable in the circumstances.

(6) The prohibitions that may be imposed by an anti-social behaviour order are those necessary for the purpose of protecting persons (whether relevant persons or persons elsewhere in England and Wales) from further anti-social acts by the defendant.

(7) An anti-social behaviour order shall have effect for a period (not less than two years) specified in the order or until further order.

(8) Subject to subsection (9) below, the applicant or the defendant may apply by complaint to the court which made an anti-social behaviour order for it to be varied or discharged by a further order.

(9) Except with the consent of both parties, no anti-social behaviour order shall be discharged before the end of the period of two years beginning with the date of service of the order.

(10) If without reasonable excuse a person does anything which he is prohibited from doing by an anti-social behaviour order, he is guilty of an offence and liable –

(a) on summary conviction, to imprisonment for a term not exceeding six months or to a fine not exceeding the statutory maximum, or to both; or

(b) on conviction on indictment, to imprisonment for a term not exceeding five years or to a fine, or to both.

(10A) The following may bring proceedings for an offence under subsection (10) –

(a) a council which is a relevant authority;

(b) the council for the local government area in which a person in respect of whom an anti-social behaviour order has been made resides or appears to reside.

(10B) If proceedings for an offence under subsection (10) are brought in a youth court section 47(2) of the Children and Young Persons Act 1933 has effect as if the persons entitled to be present at a sitting for the purposes of those proceedings include one person authorised to be present by a relevant authority.

(10C) In proceedings for an offence under subsection (10), a copy of the original anti-social behaviour order, certified as such by the proper officer of the court which made it, is admissible as evidence of its having been made and of its contents to the same extent that oral evidence of those things is admissible in those proceedings.

(10D) In relation to proceedings brought against a child or a young person for an offence under subsection (10) –

(a) section 49 of the Children and Young Persons Act 1933 (restrictions on reports of proceedings in which children and young persons are concerned) does not apply in respect of the child or young person against whom the proceedings are brought;

(b) section 45 of the Youth Justice and Criminal Evidence Act 1999 (power to restrict reporting of criminal proceedings involving persons under 18) does so apply.

(10E) If, in relation to any such proceedings, the court does exercise its power to give a direction under section 45 of the Youth Justice and Criminal Evidence Act 1999, it shall give its reasons for doing so.

(11) Where a person is convicted of an offence under subsection (10) above, it shall not be open to the court by or before which he is so convicted to make an order under subsection (1)(b) (conditional discharge) of section 12 of the Powers of Criminal Courts (Sentencing) Act 2000] in respect of the offence.

(12) In this section –

'British Transport Police Force' means the force of constables appointed under section 53 of the British Transport Commission Act 1949;

'child' and 'young person' shall have the same meaning as in the Children and Young Persons Act 1933;

'the commencement date' means the date of the commencement of this section;

'local government area' means –

(a) in relation to England, a district or London borough, the City of London, the Isle of Wight and the Isles of Scilly;

(b) in relation to Wales, a county or county borough.

...

Power of Secretary of State to add to relevant authorities

1A(1) The Secretary of State may by order provide that the chief officer of a body of constables maintained otherwise than by a police authority is, in such cases and circumstances as may be prescribed by the order, to be a relevant authority for the purposes of section 1 above.

(2) The Secretary of State may by order –

(a) provide that a person or body of any other description specified in the order is, in such cases and circumstances as may be prescribed by the order, to be a relevant authority for the purposes of such of sections 1 above and 1B, 1CA and 1E below as are specified in the order; and

(b) prescribe the description of persons who are to be 'relevant persons' in relation to that person or body.

Individual support orders

1AA(1) Where a court makes an anti-social behaviour order in respect of a defendant who is a child or young person when that order is made, it must consider whether the individual support conditions are fulfilled.

(2) If it is satisfied that those conditions are fulfilled, the court must make an order under this section ('an individual support order') which –

(a) requires the defendant to comply, for a period not exceeding six months, with such requirements as are specified in the order; and

(b) requires the defendant to comply with any directions given by the responsible officer with a view to the implementation of the requirements under paragraph (a) above.

(3) The individual support conditions are –

(a) that an individual support order would be desirable in the interests of preventing any repetition of the kind of behaviour which led to the making of the anti-social behaviour order;

(b) that the defendant is not already subject to an individual support order; and

(c) that the court has been notified by the Secretary of State that arrangements for implementing individual support orders are available in the area in which it appears to it that the defendant resides or will reside and the notice has not been withdrawn.

(4) If the court is not satisfied that the individual support conditions are fulfilled, it shall state in open court that it is not so satisfied and why it is not.

(5) The requirements that may be specified under subsection (2)(a) above are those that the court considers desirable in the interests of preventing any repetition of the kind of behaviour which led to the making of the anti-social behaviour order.

(6) Requirements included in an individual support order, or directions given under such an order by a responsible officer, may require the defendant to do all or any of the following things –

(a) to participate in activities specified in the requirements or directions at a time or times so specified;

(b) to present himself to a person or persons so specified at a place or places and at a time or times so specified;

(c) to comply with any arrangements for his education so specified.

(7) But requirements included in, or directions given under, such an order may not require the defendant to attend (whether at the same place or at different places) on more than two days in any week; and 'week' here means a period of seven days beginning with a Sunday.

(8) Requirements included in, and directions given under, an individual support order shall, as far as practicable, be such as to avoid –

(a) any conflict with the defendant's religious beliefs; and

(b) any interference with the times, if any, at which he normally works or attends school or any other educational establishment.

(9) Before making an individual support order, the court shall obtain from a social worker of a local authority ... or a member of a youth offending team any information which it considers necessary in order –

(a) to determine whether the individual support conditions are fulfilled, or
(b) to determine what requirements should be imposed by an individual support order if made,

and shall consider that information.

(10) In this section and section 1AB below 'responsible officer', in relation to an individual support order, means one of the following who is specified in the order, namely –
(a) a social worker of a local authority . . .;
(b) a person nominated by a person appointed as chief education officer under section 532 of the Education Act 1996 (c 56);
(c) a member of a youth offending team.

Individual support orders: explanation, breach, amendment etc

1AB(1) Before making an individual support order, the court shall explain to the defendant in ordinary language –
(a) the effect of the order and of the requirements proposed to be included in it;
(b) the consequences which may follow (under subsection (3) below) if he fails to comply with any of those requirements; and
(c) that the court has power (under subsection (6) below) to review the order on the application either of the defendant or of the responsible officer.

(2) The power of the Secretary of State under section 174(4) of the Criminal Justice Act 2003 includes power by order to –
(a) prescribe cases in which subsection (1) above does not apply; and
(b) prescribe cases in which the explanation referred to in that subsection may be made in the absence of the defendant, or may be provided in written form.

(3) If the person in respect of whom an individual support order is made fails without reasonable excuse to comply with any requirement included in the order, he is guilty of an offence and liable on summary conviction to a fine not exceeding –
(a) if he is aged 14 or over at the date of his conviction, £1,000;
(b) if he is aged under 14 then, £250.

(4) No referral order under section 16(2) or (3) of the Powers of Criminal Courts (Sentencing) Act 2000 (referral of young offenders to youth offender panels) may be made in respect of an offence under subsection (3) above.

(5) If the anti-social behaviour order as a result of which an individual support order was made ceases to have effect, the individual support order (if it has not previously ceased to have effect) ceases to have effect when the anti-social behaviour order does.

(6) On an application made by complaint by –
(a) the person subject to an individual support order, or
(b) the responsible officer,

the court which made the individual support order may vary or discharge it by a further order.

(7) If the anti-social behaviour order as a result of which an individual support

order was made is varied, the court varying the anti-social behaviour order may by a further order vary or discharge the individual support order.

Orders in county court proceedings

1B(1) This section applies to any proceedings in a county court ('the principal proceedings').

(2) If a relevant authority –

(a) is a party to the principal proceedings, and

(b) considers that a party to those proceedings is a person in relation to whom it would be reasonable for it to make an application under section 1,

it may make an application in those proceedings for an order under subsection (4).

(3) If a relevant authority –

(a) is not a party to the principal proceedings, and

(b) considers that a party to those proceedings is a person in relation to whom it would be reasonable for it to make an application under section 1,

it may make an application to be joined to those proceedings to enable it to apply for an order under subsection (4) and, if it is so joined, may apply for such an order.

(3A) Subsection (3B) applies if a relevant authority is a party to the principal proceedings and considers –

(a) that a person who is not a party to the proceedings has acted in an anti-social manner, and

(b) that the person's anti-social acts are material in relation to the principal proceedings.

(3B) The relevant authority may –

(a) make an application for the person mentioned in subsection (3A)(a) to be joined to the principal proceedings to enable an order under subsection (4) to be made in relation to that person;

(b) if that person is so joined, apply for an order under subsection (4).

(3C) But a person must not be joined to proceedings in pursuance of subsection (3B) unless his anti-social acts are material in relation to the principal proceedings.

(4) If, on an application for an order under this subsection, it is proved that the conditions mentioned in section 1(1) are fulfilled as respects that other party, the court may make an order which prohibits him from doing anything described in the order.

(5) Subject to subsection (6), the person against whom an order under this section has been made and the relevant authority on whose application that order was made may apply to the county court which made an order under this section for it to be varied or discharged by a further order.

(6) Except with the consent of the relevant authority and the person subject to the order, no order under this section shall be discharged before the end of the period of two years beginning with the date of service of the order.

(7) Subsections (5) to (7) and (10) to (12) of section 1 apply for the purposes of the making and effect of orders made under this section as they apply for the purposes of the making and effect of anti-social behaviour orders.

Orders on conviction in criminal proceedings

1C(1) This section applies where a person (the 'offender') is convicted of a relevant offence.

(2) If the court considers –

(a) that the offender has acted, at any time since the commencement date, in an anti-social manner, that is to say in a manner that caused or was likely to cause harassment, alarm or distress to one or more persons not of the same household as himself, and

(b) that an order under this section is necessary to protect persons in any place in England and Wales from further anti-social acts by him,

it may make an order which prohibits the offender from doing anything described in the order.

(3) The court may make an order under this section –

(a) if the prosecutor asks it to do so, or

(b) if the court thinks it is appropriate to do so.

(3A) For the purpose of deciding whether to make an order under this section the court may consider evidence led by the prosecution and the defence.

(3B) It is immaterial whether evidence led in pursuance of subsection (3A) would have been admissible in the proceedings in which the offender was convicted.

(4) An order under this section shall not be made except –

(a) in addition to a sentence imposed in respect of the relevant offence; or

(b) in addition to an order discharging him conditionally.

(4A) The court may adjourn any proceedings in relation to an order under this section even after sentencing the offender.

(4B) If the offender does not appear for any adjourned proceedings, the court may further adjourn the proceedings or may issue a warrant for his arrest.

(4C) But the court may not issue a warrant for the offender's arrest unless it is satisfied that he has had adequate notice of the time and place of the adjourned proceedings.

(5) An order under this section takes effect on the day on which it is made, but the court may provide in any such order that such requirements of the order as it may specify shall, during any period when the offender is detained in legal custody, be suspended until his release from that custody.

(6) . . .

(7) . . .

(8) . . .

(9) Subsections (7), (10), (10C), (10D), (10E) and (11) of section 1 apply for the purposes of the making and effect of orders made by virtue of this section as they apply for the purposes of the making and effect of anti-social behaviour orders.

(9A) The council for the local government area in which a person in respect of whom an anti-social behaviour order has been made resides or appears to reside may bring proceedings under section 1(10) (as applied by subsection (9) above) for breach of an order under subsection (2) above.

(9B) Subsection (9C) applies in relation to proceedings in which an order under subsection (2) is made against a child or young person who is convicted of an offence.

(9C) In so far as the proceedings relate to the making of the order –
(a) section 49 of the Children and Young Persons Act 1933 (c 12) (restrictions on reports of proceedings in which children and young persons are concerned) does not apply in respect of the child or young person against whom the order is made;
(b) section 39 of that Act (power to prohibit publication of certain matter) does so apply.

(10) In this section –
'child' and 'young person' have the same meaning as in the Children and Young Persons Act 1933 (c 12);
'the commencement date' has the same meaning as in section 1 above;
'the court' in relation to an offender means –
(a) the court by or before which he is convicted of the relevant offence; or
(b) if he is committed to the Crown Court to be dealt with for that offence, the Crown Court; and
'relevant offence' means an offence committed after the coming into force of section 64 of the Police Reform Act 2002 (c 30).

Variation and discharge of orders under section 1C

1CA(1) An offender subject to an order under section 1C may apply to the court which made it for it to be varied or discharged.

(2) If he does so, he must also send written notice of his application to the Director of Public Prosecutions.

(3) The Director of Public Prosecutions may apply to the court which made an order under section 1C for it to be varied or discharged.

(4) A relevant authority may also apply to the court which made an order under section 1C for it to be varied or discharged if it appears to it that –
(a) in the case of variation, the protection of relevant persons from anti-social acts by the person subject to the order would be more appropriately effected by a variation of the order;
(b) in the case of discharge, that it is no longer necessary to protect relevant persons from anti-social acts by him by means of such an order.

(5) If the Director of Public Prosecutions or a relevant authority applies for the variation or discharge of an order under section 1C, he or it must also send written notice of the application to the person subject to the order.

(6) In the case of an order under section 1C made by a magistrates' court, the references in subsections (1), (3) and (4) to the court by which the order was made include a reference to any magistrates' court acting in the same local justice area as that court.

(7) No order under section 1C shall be discharged on an application under this section before the end of the period of two years beginning with the day on which the order takes effect, unless –
(a) in the case of an application under subsection (1), the Director of Public Prosecutions consents, or
(b) in the case of an application under subsection (3) or (4), the offender consents.

Interim orders

1D(1) This section applies where –
(a) an application is made for an anti-social behaviour order;
(b) an application is made for an order under section 1B;
(c) a request is made by the prosecution for an order under section 1C; or
(d) the court is minded to make an order under section 1C of its own motion.

(2) If, before determining the application or request, or before deciding whether to make an order under section 1C of its own motion, the court considers that it is just to make an order under this section pending the determination of that application or request or before making that decision, it may make such an order.

(3) An order under this section is an order which prohibits the defendant from doing anything described in the order.

(4) An order under this section –
(a) shall be for a fixed period;
(b) may be varied, renewed or discharged;
(c) shall, if it has not previously ceased to have effect, cease to have effect on the determination of the application or request mentioned in subsection (1), or on the court's making a decision as to whether or not to make an order under section 1C of its own motion.

(5) In relation to cases to which this section applies by virtue of paragraph (a) or (b) of subsection (1), subsections (6), (8) and (10) to (12) of section 1 apply for the purposes of the making and effect of orders under this section as they apply for the purposes of the making and effect of anti-social behaviour orders.

(6) In relation to cases to which this section applies by virtue of paragraph (c) or (d) of subsection (1) –
(a) subsections (6) and (10) to (12) of section 1 apply for the purposes of the making and effect of orders under this section as they apply for the purposes of the making and effect of anti-social behaviour orders; and
(b) section 1CA applies for the purposes of the variation or discharge of an order under this section as it applies for the purposes of the variation or discharge of an order under section 1C.

Consultation requirements

1E (1) This section applies to –
(a) applications for an anti-social behaviour order; and
(b) applications for an order under section 1B.

(2) Before making an application to which this section applies, the council for a local government area shall consult the chief officer of police of the police force maintained for the police area within which that local government area lies.

(3) Before making an application to which this section applies, a chief officer of police shall consult the council for the local government area in which the person in relation to whom the application is to be made resides or appears to reside.

(4) Before making an application to which this section applies, a relevant authority other than a council for a local government area or a chief officer of police shall consult –
(a) the council for the local government area in which the person in relation to whom the application is to be made resides or appears to reside; and
(b) the chief officer of police of the police force maintained for the police area within which that local government area lies.
(5) Subsection (4)(a) does not apply if the relevant authority is a county council for a county in which there are no districts.

Contracting out of local authority functions

1F (1) The Secretary of State may by order provide that a relevant authority which is a local authority may make arrangements with a person specified (or of a description specified) in the order for the exercise of any function it has under sections 1 to 1E above –
(a) by such a person, or
(b) by an employee of his.
(2) The order may provide –
(a) that the power of the relevant authority to make the arrangements is subject to such conditions as are specified in the order;
(b) that the arrangements must be subject to such conditions as are so specified;
(c) that the arrangements may be made subject to such other conditions as the relevant authority thinks appropriate.
(3) The order may provide that the arrangements may authorise the exercise of the function –
(a) either wholly or to such extent as may be specified in the order or arrangements;
(b) either generally or in such cases or areas as may be so specified.
(4) An order may provide that the person with whom arrangements are made in pursuance of the order is to be treated as if he were a public body for the purposes of section 1 of the Local Authorities (Goods and Services) Act 1970.
(5) The Secretary of State must not make an order under this section unless he first consults –
(a) the National Assembly for Wales, if the order relates to a relevant authority in Wales;
(b) such representatives of local government as he thinks appropriate;
(c) such other persons as he thinks appropriate.
(6) Any arrangements made by a relevant authority in pursuance of an order under this section do not prevent the relevant authority from exercising the function to which the arrangements relate.
(7) The following provisions of the Deregulation and Contracting Out Act 1994 apply for the purposes of arrangements made in pursuance of an order under this section as they apply for the purposes of an authorisation to exercise functions by virtue of an order under section 70(2) of that Act –
(a) section 72 (effect of contracting out);
(b) section 73 (termination of contracting out);

(c) section 75 and Schedule 15 (provision relating to disclosure of information);

(d) paragraph 3 of Schedule 16 (authorised persons to be treated as officers of local authority).

(8) For the purposes of subsection (7), any reference in the provisions specified in paragraphs (a) to (d) to a person authorised to exercise a function must be construed as a reference to a person with whom an arrangement is made for the exercise of the function in pursuance of an order under this section.

(9) Relevant authorities and any person with whom arrangements are made in pursuance of an order under this section must have regard to any guidance issued by the Secretary of State for the purposes of this section.

(10) An order under this section may make different provision for different purposes.

(11) An order under this section may contain –

(a) such consequential, supplemental or incidental provisions (including provision modifying any enactment), or

(b) such transitional provisions or savings,

as the person making the order thinks appropriate.

(12) Each of the following is a local authority –

(a) a local authority within the meaning of section 270 of the Local Government Act 1972;

(b) the Common Council of the City of London;

(c) the Council of the Isles of Scilly.

Intervention orders

1G *(1) Thissection applies if, in relation to a person who has attained the age of 18, a relevant authority –*

(a) makes an application for an anti-social behaviour order or an order under section 1B above (the behaviour order),

(b) has obtained from an appropriately qualified person a report relating to the effect on the person's behaviour of the misuse of controlled drugs or of such other factors as the Secretary of State by order prescribes, and

(c) has engaged in consultation with such persons as the Secretary of State by order prescribes for the purpose of ascertaining that, if the report recommends that an order under this section is made, appropriate activities will be available.

(2) The relevant authority may make an application to the court which is considering the application for the behaviour order for an order under this section (an intervention order).

(3) If the court –

(a) makes the behaviour order, and

(b) is satisfied that the relevant conditions are met,

it may also make an intervention order.

(4) The relevant conditions are –

(a) that an intervention order is desirable in the interests of preventing a repetition of the behaviour which led to the behaviour order being made (trigger behaviour);

(b) that appropriate activities relating to the trigger behaviour or its cause are available for the defendant;

(c) that the defendant is not (at the time the intervention order is made) subject to another intervention order or to any other treatment relating to the trigger behaviour or its cause (whether on a voluntary basis or by virtue of a requirement imposed in pursuance of any enactment);

(d) that the court has been notified by the Secretary of State that arrangements for implementing intervention orders are available in the area in which it appears that the defendant resides or will reside and the notice has not been withdrawn.

(5) An intervention order is an order which –

(a) requires the defendant to comply, for a period not exceeding six months, with such requirements as are specified in the order, and

(b) requires the defendant to comply with any directions given by a person authorised to do so under the order with a view to the implementation of the requirements under paragraph (a) above.

(6) An intervention order or directions given under the order may require the defendant –

(a) to participate in the activities specified in the requirement or directions at a time or times so specified;

(b) to present himself to a person or persons so specified at a time or times so specified.

(7) Requirements included in, or directions given under, an intervention order must, as far as practicable, be such as to avoid –

(a) any conflict with the defendant's religious beliefs, and

(b) any interference with the times (if any) at which he normally works or attends an educational establishment.

(8) If the defendant fails to comply with a requirement included in or a direction given under an intervention order, the person responsible for the provision or supervision of appropriate activities under the order must inform the relevant authority of that fact.

(9) The person responsible for the provision or supervision of appropriate activities is a person of such description as is prescribed by order made by the Secretary of State.

(10) In this section –

'appropriate activities' means such activities, or activities of such a description, as are prescribed by order made by the Secretary of State for the purposes of this section;

'appropriately qualified person' means a person who has such qualifications or experience as the Secretary of State by order prescribes;

'controlled drug' has the same meaning as in the Misuse of Drugs Act 1971;

'relevant authority' means a relevant authority for the purposes of section 1 above.

(11) An order under this section made by the Secretary of State may make different provision for different purposes.

(12) This section and section 1H below apply to a person in respect of whom a behaviour order has been made subject to the following modifications –

(a) in subsection (1) above paragraph (a) must be ignored;

(b) in subsection (2) above, for 'is considering the application for' substitute 'made';

(c) in subsection (3) above paragraph (a), the word 'and' following it and the word 'also' must be ignored.[1]

Intervention orders: explanation, breach, amendment etc

1H *(1) Before making an intervention order the court must explain to the defendant in ordinary language –*

(a) the effect of the order and of the requirements proposed to be included in it,

(b) the consequences which may follow (under subsection (3) below) if he fails to comply with any of those requirements, and

(c) that the court has power (under subsection (5) below) to review the order on the application either of the defendant or of the relevant authority.

(2) The power of the Secretary of State under section 174(4) of the Criminal Justice Act 2003 includes power by order to –

(a) prescribe cases in which subsection (1) does not apply, and

(b) prescribe cases in which the explanation referred to in that subsection may be made in the absence of the defendant, or may be provided in written form.

(3) If a person in respect of whom an intervention order is made fails without reasonable excuse to comply with any requirement included in the order he is guilty of an offence and liable on summary conviction to a fine not exceeding level 4 on the standard scale.

(4) If the behaviour order as a result of which an intervention order is made ceases to have effect, the intervention order (if it has not previously ceased to have effect) ceases to have effect when the behaviour order does.

(5) On an application made by –

(a) a person subject to an intervention order, or

(b) the relevant authority,

the court which made the intervention order may vary or discharge it by a further order.

(6) An application under subsection (5) made to a magistrates' court must be made by complaint.

(7) If the behaviour order as a result of which an intervention order was made is varied, the court varying the behaviour order may by a further order vary or discharge the intervention order.

(8) Expressions used in this section and in section 1G have the same meaning in this section as in that section.[2]

Special measures for witnesses

1I (1) This section applies to the following proceedings –

(a) any proceedings in a magistrates' court on an application for an anti-social behaviour order,

1 In force as of 1 October 2006 by Crime and Disorder Act 1998 (Intervention Orders) Order 2006 SI No 2138.

2 In force as of 1 October 2006 by Crime and Disorder Act 1998 (Intervention Orders) Order 2006 SI No 2138.

(b) any proceedings in a magistrates' court or the Crown Court so far as relating to the issue whether to make an order under section 1C, and
(c) any proceedings in a magistrates' court so far as relating to the issue whether to make an order under section 1D.

(2) Chapter 1 of Part 2 of the Youth Justice and Criminal Evidence Act 1999 (special measures directions in the case of vulnerable and intimidated witnesses) shall apply in relation to any such proceedings as it applies in relation to criminal proceedings, but with –
(a) the omission of the provisions of that Act mentioned in subsection (3) (which make provision appropriate only in the context of criminal proceedings), and
(b) any other necessary modifications.

(3) The provisions are –
(a) section 17(4),
(b) section 21(1)(b) and (5) to (7),
(c) section 22(1)(b) and (2)(b) and (c),
(d) section 27(10), and
(e) section 32.

(4) Any rules of court made under or for the purposes of Chapter 1 of Part 2 of that Act shall apply in relation to proceedings to which this section applies –
(a) to such extent as may be provided by rules of court, and
(b) subject to such modifications as may be so provided.

(5) Section 47 of that Act (restrictions on reporting special measures directions etc) applies, with any necessary modifications, in relation to –
(a) a direction under section 19 of the Act as applied by this section, or
(b) a direction discharging or varying such a direction,
and sections 49 and 51 of that Act (offences) apply accordingly.

...

Appeals against orders

4 (1) An appeal shall lie to the Crown Court against the making by a magistrates' court of an anti-social behaviour order, an individual support order, an order under section 1D above,. . ..

(2) On such an appeal the Crown Court –
(a) may make such orders as may be necessary to give effect to its determination of the appeal; and
(b) may also make such incidental or consequential orders as appear to it to be just.

(3) Any order of the Crown Court made on an appeal under this section (other than one directing that an application be re-heard by a magistrates' court) shall, for the purposes of section 1(8), 1AB(6). . ., be treated as if it were an order of the magistrates' court from which the appeal was brought and not an order of the Crown Court.

...

Youth crime and disorder

Parenting orders

8 (1) This section applies where, in any court proceedings –

(a) a child safety order is made in respect of a child or the court determines on an application under section 12(6) below that a child has failed to comply with any requirement included in such an order;

(aa) a parental compensation order is made in relation to a child's behaviour;[3]

(b) an anti-social behaviour order or sex offender order is made in respect of a child or young person;

(c) a child or young person is convicted of an offence; or

(d) a person is convicted of an offence under section 443 (failure to comply with school attendance order) or section 444 (failure to secure regular attendance at school of registered pupil) of the Education Act 1996.

(2) Subject to subsection (3) and section 9(1) below . . ., if in the proceedings the court is satisfied that the relevant condition is fulfilled, it may make a parenting order in respect of a person who is a parent or guardian of the child or young person or, as the case may be, the person convicted of the offence under section 443 or 444 ('the parent').

(3) A court shall not make a parenting order unless it has been notified by the Secretary of State that arrangements for implementing such orders are available in the area in which it appears to the court that the parent resides or will reside and the notice has not been withdrawn.

(4) A parenting order is an order which requires the parent –

(a) to comply, for a period not exceeding twelve months, with such requirements as are specified in the order, and

(b) subject to subsection (5) below, to attend, for a concurrent period not exceeding three months, such counselling or guidance programme as may be specified in directions given by the responsible officer.

(5) A parenting order may, but need not, include such a requirement as is mentioned in subsection (4)(b) above in any case where a parenting order under this section or any other enactment has been made in respect of the parent on a previous occasion.

(6) The relevant condition is that the parenting order would be desirable in the interests of preventing –

(a) in a case falling within paragraph (a), *(aa)*[4] or (b) of subsection (1) above, any repetition of the kind of behaviour which led to the child safety order, *parental compensation order,*[5] anti-social behaviour order or sex offender order being made;

(b) in a case falling within paragraph (c) of that subsection, the commission of any further offence by the child or young person;

3 Words in italics inserted by SOCPA 2005 s144, Sch 10, Pt 1, paras 1, 3(1), (2). Not yet in force.

4 Words in italics inserted by SOCPA 2005 s144, Sch 10, Pt 1, paras 1, 3(1) , (3)(a). Not yet in force.

5 Words in italics inserted by SOCPA 2005 s144, Sch 10, Pt 1, paras 1, 3(1) , (3)(b). Not yet in force.

(c) in a case falling within paragraph (d) of that subsection, the commission of any further offence under section 443 or 444 of the Education Act 1996.

(7) The requirements that may be specified under subsection (4)(a) above are those which the court considers desirable in the interests of preventing any such repetition or, as the case may be, the commission of any such further offence.

(7A) A counselling or guidance programme which a parent is required to attend by virtue of subsection (4)(b) above may be or include a residential course but only if the court is satisfied –

(a) that the attendance of the parent at a residential course is likely to be more effective than his attendance at a non-residential course in preventing any such repetition or, as the case may be, the commission of any such further offence, and

(b) that any interference with family life which is likely to result from the attendance of the parent at a residential course is proportionate in all the circumstances.

(8) In this section and section 9 below 'responsible officer', in relation to a parenting order, means one of the following who is specified in the order, namely –

(a) an officer of a local probation board;

(b) a social worker of a local authority . . .; and

(bb) a person nominated by *a person appointed as director of children's services under section 18 of the Children Act 2004 or by*[6] a person appointed as chief education officer under section 532 of the Education Act 1996;

(c) a member of a youth offending team.

6 Words in italics inserted by the Children Act 2004, s 18(9), (10), Sch 2, para 5(1), (2). Not yet in force.

Crime and Disorder Act 1998 (Relevant Authorities and Relevant Persons) Order 2006 SI No 2137

The Secretary of State makes the following Order in exercise of the powers conferred by section 1A(2) of the Crime and Disorder Act 1998:

Citation and commencement

1 This Order may be cited as the Crime and Disorder Act 1998 (Relevant Authorities and Relevant Persons) Order 2006 and shall come into force on 1 September 2006.

Relevant authority and relevant persons: Environment Agency

2 (1) The Environment Agency is to be a relevant authority for the purposes of sections 1, 1B, 1CAand 1E of the Crime and Disorder Act 1998 in the cases and circumstances prescribed by paragraph (2).

(2) Those cases and circumstances are where a person has acted in an anti-social manner on, or in relation to, any land and the Environment Agency has a statutory function in relation to that land.

(3) The relevant persons in relation to the Environment Agency are –

(a) persons who are on, or likely to be on, the land referred to in paragraph (2); or

(b) persons who are in the vicinity of, or likely to be in the vicinity of, that land.

Relevant authority and relevant persons: Transport for London

3 (1) Transport for London is to be a relevant authority for the purposes of sections 1, 1B, 1CA and 1E of the Crime and Disorder Act 1998 in the cases and circumstances prescribed by paragraph (2).

(2) Those cases and circumstances are where a person has acted in an anti-social manner on, or in relation to, any land or vehicles used in connection with, or for the purposes of, the provision of a relevant transport service.

(3) The relevant persons in relation to Transport for London are –

(a) persons who are on, or likely to be on, any of the land or vehicles referred to in paragraph (2); or

(b) persons who are in the vicinity of, or likely to be in the vicinity of, such land or vehicles.

(4) In this article –

(a) the references to Transport for London are references to the body established by section 154 of the Greater London Authority Act 1999 ('the 1999 Act'); and

(b) 'relevant transport service' means a bus, tramway, river transport or train service provided by Transport for London or any of its subsidiaries, or by any other person, in pursuance of –

(i) an agreement entered into by Transport for London under section 156(2) or (3)(a) of the 1999 Act;

(ii) a transport subsidiary's agreement within the meaning given by section 169 of the 1999 Act; or

(iii) an agreement which was entered into by London Regional Transport under section 3(2) or (2A) of the London Regional Transport Act 1984and which, by virtue of section 300 or section 415 of the 1999 Act, has effect as if made by Transport for London.

APPENDIX B

Magistrates' Courts (Anti-social Behaviour Orders) Rules 2002

The Lord Chancellor, in exercise of the powers conferred upon him by section 144 of the Magistrates' Courts Act 1980, and after consultation with the rule committee appointed under that section, hereby makes the following Rules:

Citation, interpretation and commencement

2 (1) These Rules may be cited as the Magistrates' Courts (Anti-Social Behaviour Orders) Rules 2002 and shall come into force on 2nd December 2002.

(2) In these Rules any reference to a numbered section is a reference to the section so numbered in the Crime and Disorder Act 1998, any reference to a 'form' includes a form to like effect, and, unless otherwise stated, reference to a 'Schedule' is a reference to a Schedule hereto.

Transitional Provisions

3 After these Rules come into force, rules 6 and 7 of, and Schedules 5 and 6 to the Magistrates' Courts (Sex Offender and Anti-Social Behaviour Orders) Rules 1998 shall (notwithstanding their revocation) continue to apply to proceedings commenced prior to the commencement of these Rules.

Forms

4 (1) An application for an anti-social behaviour order [may] be in the form set out in Schedule 1.

(2) ...

(3) ...

(4) ...

(5) An application for an interim anti-social behaviour order made under section 1D [may] be in the form set out in Schedule 5.

(6) ...

Interim Orders

5 (1) An application for an interim order under section 1D, may, with leave of the justices' clerk, be made without notice being given to the defendant.

(2) The justices' clerk shall only grant leave under paragraph (1) of this rule if he is satisfied that it is necessary for the application to be made without notice being given to the defendant.

(3) If an application made under paragraph (2) is granted, then the interim order and the application for an anti-social behaviour order under section 1 (together with a summons giving a date for the defendant to attend court) shall be served on the defendant in person as soon as practicable after the making of the interim order.

(4) An interim order which is made at the hearing of an application without notice shall not take effect until it has been served on the defendant.

(5) If such an interim order made without notice is not served on the defendant within seven days of being made, then it shall cease to have effect.

(6) An interim order shall cease to have effect if the application for an anti-social behaviour order is withdrawn.

(7) Where the court refuses to make an interim order without notice being given to the defendant it may direct that the application be made on notice.

(8) If an interim order is made without notice being given to the defendant, and the defendant subsequently applies to the court for the order to be discharged or varied, his application shall not be dismissed without the opportunity for him to make oral representations to the court.

Application for variation or discharge

6 (1) This rule applies to the making of an application for the variation or discharge of an order made under section 1, 1C or, subject to rule 5(8) above, 1D.

(2) An application to which this rule applies shall be made in writing to the magistrates' court which made the order, or in the case of an application under section 1C to any magistrates' court in the same [local justice area], and shall specify the reason why the applicant for variation or discharge believes the court should vary or discharge the order, as the case may be.

(3) Subject to rule 5(8) above, where the court considers that there are no grounds upon which it might conclude that the order should be varied or discharged, as the case may be, it may determine the application without hearing representations from the applicant for variation or discharge or from any other person.

(4) Where the court considers that there are grounds upon which it might conclude that the order should be varied or discharged, as the case may be, the [designated officer for the court] shall, unless the application is withdrawn, issue a summons giving not less than 14 days' notice in writing of the date, time and place appointed for the hearing.

(5) The [designated officer] shall send with the summons under paragraph 4 above a copy of the application for variation or discharge of the anti-social behaviour order.

Service

7 (1) Subject to rule 5(3), any summons, or copy of an order or application required to be sent under these Rules to the defendant shall be either given to him in person or sent by post to the last known address, and, if so given or sent, shall be deemed to have been received by him unless he proves otherwise.

(2) Any summons, copy of an order or application required to be sent to the

defendant under these Rules shall also be sent by the [designated officer for the court] to the applicant authority, and to any relevant authority whom the applicant is required by section 1E to have consulted before making the application and, where appropriate, shall invite them to make observations and advise them of their right to be heard at the hearing.

Delegation by justices' clerk

8 (1) In this rule, 'employed as a clerk of the court' has the same meaning as in rule 2(1) of the Justices' Clerks (Qualifications of Assistants) Rules 1979.

(2) Anything authorised to be done by, to or before a justices' clerk under these Rules, may be done instead by, to or before a person employed as a clerk of the court where that person is appointed by the [Lord Chancellor] to assist him and where that person has been specifically authorised by the justices' clerk for that purpose.

(3) Any authorisation by the justices' clerk under paragraph (2) shall be recorded in writing at the time the authority is given or as soon as practicable thereafter.

SCHEDULE 1

FORM

Rule 4(1)

Application for Anti-social Behaviour Order (Crime and Disorder Act 1998 s1(1))

................................Magistrates' Court
(Code)

Date: ....
Defendant: ....
Address: ....
....
....
Applicant Authority: ....
Relevant authorities consulted: ....
And it is alleged

(a) that the defendant has acted on...................... [dates(s)] at [place(s)] in an anti-social manner, that is to say, in a manner that caused or was likely to cause harassment, alarm or distress to one or more persons not of the same household as himself; and

(b) that an anti-social behaviour order is necessary to protect relevant persons from further anti-social acts by him, and accordingly application is made for an anti-social behaviour order containing the following prohibition(s):–

Short description of acts: ....
....

The complaint of: ....
Name of Applicant Authority: ....
Address of Applicant Authority: ....
who [upon oath] states that the defendant was responsible for the acts of which particulars are given above, in respect of which this complaint is made.
Taken [and sworn] before me

Justice of the Peace
[By order of the clerk of the court]

SCHEDULE 2

[*Revoked.*]

SCHEDULE 3

[*Revoked.*]

SCHEDULE 4

[*Revoked.*]

SCHEDULE 5

FORM

Rule 4(5)

Application for an Interim Order (Crime and Disorder Act 1998 s1D)

................................Magistrates' Court
(Code)

Date: ....
Defendant: ....
Address: ....
....
....
Applicant Authority: ....
Relevant authorities consulted: ....
....
....
Reasons for applying for an interim order: ....
....
....

Do you wish this application to be heard:

[ ] without notice being given to the defendant

[ ] with notice being given to the defendant

If you wish the application to be heard without notice state reasons:–

....

....

....

The complaint of: ....

Address of Applicant Authority: ....

Who [upon oath] states that the information given above is correct.

Taken [and sworn] before me.

Justice of the Peace

[By order of the clerk of the court]

NOTE: This application must be accompanied by an application for an anti-social behaviour order (Crime and Disorder Act 1998, s1).

SCHEDULE 6

[*Revoked.*]

APPENDIX C

Civil Evidence Act 1995

Admissibility of hearsay evidence

Admissibility of hearsay evidence

1 (1) In civil proceedings evidence shall not be excluded on the ground that it is hearsay.

(2) In this Act –

(a) 'hearsay' means a statement made otherwise than by a person while giving oral evidence in the proceedings which is tendered as evidence of the matters stated; and

(b) references to hearsay include hearsay of whatever degree.

(3) Nothing in this Act affects the admissibility of evidence admissible apart from this section.

(4) The provisions of sections 2 to 6 (safeguards and supplementary provisions relating to hearsay evidence) do not apply in relation to hearsay evidence admissible apart from this section, notwithstanding that it may also be admissible by virtue of this section.

Safeguards in relation to hearsay evidence

Notice of proposal to adduce hearsay evidence

2 (1) A party proposing to adduce hearsay evidence in civil proceedings shall, subject to the following provisions of this section, give to the other party or parties to the proceedings –

(a) such notice (if any) of that fact, and

(b) on request, such particulars of or relating to the evidence,

as is reasonable and practicable in the circumstances for the purpose of enabling him or them to deal with any matters arising from its being hearsay.

(2) Provision may be made by rules of court –

(a) specifying classes of proceedings or evidence in relation to which subsection (1) does not apply, and

(b) as to the manner in which (including the time within which) the duties imposed by that subsection are to be complied with in the cases where it does apply.

(3) Subsection (1) may also be excluded by agreement of the parties; and compliance with the duty to give notice may in any case be waived by the person to whom notice is required to be given.

(4) A failure to comply with subsection (1), or with rules under subsection (2)(b), does not affect the admissibility of the evidence but may be taken into account by the court –

(a) in considering the exercise of its powers with respect to the course of proceedings and costs, and

(b) as a matter adversely affecting the weight to be given to the evidence in accordance with section 4.

Power to call witness for cross-examination on hearsay statement

3 Rules of court may provide that where a party to civil proceedings adduces hearsay evidence of a statement made by a person and does not call that person as a witness, any other party to the proceedings may, with the leave of the court, call that person as a witness and cross-examine him on the statement as if he had been called by the first-mentioned party and as if the hearsay statement were his evidence in chief.

Considerations relevant to weighing of hearsay evidence

4 (1) In estimating the weight (if any) to be given to hearsay evidence in civil proceedings the court shall have regard to any circumstances from which any inference can reasonably be drawn as to the reliability or otherwise of the evidence.

(2) Regard may be had, in particular, to the following –

(a) whether it would have been reasonable and practicable for the party by whom the evidence was adduced to have produced the maker of the original statement as a witness;

(b) whether the original statement was made contemporaneously with the occurrence or existence of the matters stated;

(c) whether the evidence involves multiple hearsay;

(d) whether any person involved had any motive to conceal or misrepresent matters;

(e) whether the original statement was an edited account, or was made in collaboration with another or for a particular purpose;

(f) whether the circumstances in which the evidence is adduced as hearsay are such as to suggest an attempt to prevent proper evaluation of its weight.

Supplementary provisions as to hearsay evidence

Competence and credibility

5 (1) Hearsay evidence shall not be admitted in civil proceedings if or to the extent that it is shown to consist of, or to be proved by means of, a statement made by a person who at the time he made the statement was not competent as a witness.

For this purpose 'not competent as a witness' means suffering from such mental or physical infirmity, or lack of understanding, as would render a person incompetent as a witness in civil proceedings; but a child shall be treated as competent as a witness if he satisfies the requirements of section 96(2)(a) and (b) of the Children Act 1989 (conditions for reception of unsworn evidence of child).

(2) Where in civil proceedings hearsay evidence is adduced and the maker of the original statement, or of any statement relied upon to prove another statement, is not called as a witness –

(a) evidence which if he had been so called would be admissible for the purpose of attacking or supporting his credibility as a witness is admissible for that purpose in the proceedings; and

(b) evidence tending to prove that, whether before or after he made the statement, he made any other statement inconsistent with it is admissible for the purpose of showing that he had contradicted himself.

Provided that evidence may not be given of any matter of which, if he had been called as a witness and had denied that matter in cross-examination, evidence could not have been adduced by the cross-examining party.

Previous statements of witnesses

6 (1) Subject as follows, the provisions of this Act as to hearsay evidence in civil proceedings apply equally (but with any necessary modifications) in relation to a previous statement made by a person called as a witness in the proceedings.

(2) A party who has called or intends to call a person as a witness in civil proceedings may not in those proceedings adduce evidence of a previous statement made by that person, except –

(a) with the leave of the court, or

(b) for the purpose of rebutting a suggestion that his evidence has been fabricated.

This shall not be construed as preventing a witness statement (that is, a written statement of oral evidence which a party to the proceedings intends to lead) from being adopted by a witness in giving evidence or treated as his evidence.

(3) Where in the case of civil proceedings section 3, 4 or 5 of the Criminal Procedure Act 1865 applies, which make provision as to –

(a) how far a witness may be discredited by the party producing him,

(b) the proof of contradictory statements made by a witness, and

(c) cross-examination as to previous statements in writing,

this Act does not authorise the adducing of evidence of a previous inconsistent or contradictory statement otherwise than in accordance with those sections.

This is without prejudice to any provision made by rules of court under section 3 above (power to call witness for cross-examination on hearsay statement).

(4) Nothing in this Act affects any of the rules of law as to the circumstances in which, where a person called as a witness in civil proceedings is cross-examined on a document used by him to refresh his memory, that document may be made evidence in the proceedings.

(5) Nothing in this section shall be construed as preventing a statement of any description referred to above from being admissible by virtue of section 1 as evidence of the matters stated.

Evidence formerly admissible at common law

7 (1) The common law rule effectively preserved by section 9(1) and (2)(a) of the Civil Evidence Act 1968 (admissibility of admissions adverse to a party) is superseded by the provisions of this Act.

(2) The common law rules effectively preserved by section 9(1) and (2)(b) to (d) of the Civil Evidence Act 1968, that is, any rule of law whereby in civil proceedings –

(a) published works dealing with matters of a public nature (for example, histories, scientific works, dictionaries and maps) are admissible as evidence of facts of a public nature stated in them,

(b) public documents (for example, public registers, and returns made under public authority with respect to matters of public interest) are admissible as evidence of facts stated in them, or

(c) records (for example, the records of certain courts, treaties, Crown grants, pardons and commissions) are admissible as evidence of facts stated in them,

shall continue to have effect.

(3) The common law rules effectively preserved by section 9(3) and (4) of the Civil Evidence Act 1968, that is, any rule of law whereby in civil proceedings –

(a) evidence of a person's reputation is admissible for the purpose of proving his good or bad character, or

(b) evidence of reputation or family tradition is admissible –

(i) for the purpose of proving or disproving pedigree or the existence of a marriage, or

(ii) for the purpose of proving or disproving the existence of any public or general right or of identifying any person or thing,

shall continue to have effect in so far as they authorise the court to treat such evidence as proving or disproving that matter.

Where any such rule applies, reputation or family tradition shall be treated for the purposes of this Act as a fact and not as a statement or multiplicity of statements about the matter in question.

(4) The words in which a rule of law mentioned in this section is described are intended only to identify the rule and shall not be construed as altering it in any way.

Proof of statements contained in documents

8 (1) Where a statement contained in a document is admissible as evidence in civil proceedings, it may be proved –

(a) by the production of that document, or

(b) whether or not that document is still in existence, by the production of a copy of that document or of the material part of it,

authenticated in such manner as the court may approve.

(2) It is immaterial for this purpose how many removes there are between a copy and the original.

Proof of records of business or public authority

9 (1) A document which is shown to form part of the records of a business or public authority may be received in evidence in civil proceedings without further proof.

(2) A document shall be taken to form part of the records of a business or public authority if there is produced to the court a certificate to that effect signed by an officer of the business or authority to which the records belong.

For this purpose –

(a) a document purporting to be a certificate signed by an officer of a business or public authority shall be deemed to have been duly given by such an officer and signed by him; and

(b) a certificate shall be treated as signed by a person if it purports to bear a facsimile of his signature.

(3) The absence of an entry in the records of a business or public authority may be proved in civil proceedings by affidavit of an officer of the business or authority to which the records belong.

(4) In this section –

'records' means records in whatever form;

'business' includes any activity regularly carried on over a period of time, whether for profit or not, by any body (whether corporate or not) or by an individual;

'officer' includes any person occupying a responsible position in relation to the relevant activities of the business or public authority or in relation to its records; and

'public authority' includes any public or statutory undertaking, any government department and any person holding office under Her Majesty.

(5) The court may, having regard to the circumstances of the case, direct that all or any of the above provisions of this section do not apply in relation to a particular document or record, or description of documents or records.

Admissibility and proof of Ogden Tables

10 *(1) The actuarial tables (together with explanatory notes) for use in personal injury and fatal accident cases issued from time to time by the Government Actuary's Department are admissible in evidence for the purpose of assessing, in an action for personal injury, the sum to be awarded as general damages for future pecuniary loss.*

(2) They may be proved by the production of a copy published by Her Majesty's Stationery Office.

(3) For the purposes of this section –

(a) 'personal injury' includes any disease and any impairment of a person's physical or mental condition; and

(b) 'action for personal injury' includes an action brought by virtue of the Law Reform (Miscellaneous Provisions) Act 1934 or the Fatal Accidents Act 1976.[1]

1 Repealed with savings by the Civil Evidence (Northern Ireland) Order 1997 SI No 2983, art 13(2), Sch 2; for savings see art 12. Not yet in force – see the Civil Evidence (Northern Ireland) Order 1997 SI 1997 No 2983 art 1(2).

General

Meaning of 'civil proceedings'

11 In this Act 'civil proceedings' means civil proceedings, before any tribunal, in relation to which the strict rules of evidence apply, whether as a matter of law or by agreement of the parties.

References to 'the court' and 'rules of court' shall be construed accordingly.

Provisions as to rules of court

12 (1) Any power to make rules of court regulating the practice or procedure of the court in relation to civil proceedings includes power to make such provision as may be necessary or expedient for carrying into effect the provisions of this Act.

(2) Any rules of court made for the purposes of this Act as it applies in relation to proceedings in the High Court apply, except in so far as their operation is excluded by agreement, to arbitration proceedings to which this Act applies, subject to such modifications as may be appropriate.

Any question arising as to what modifications are appropriate shall be determined, in default of agreement, by the arbitrator or umpire, as the case may be.

Interpretation

13 In this Act –

'civil proceedings' has the meaning given by section 11 and 'court' and 'rules of court' shall be construed in accordance with that section;

'document' means anything in which information of any description is recorded, and 'copy', in relation to a document, means anything onto which information recorded in the document has been copied, by whatever means and whether directly or indirectly;

'hearsay' shall be construed in accordance with section 1(2);

'oral evidence' includes evidence which, by reason of a defect of speech or hearing, a person called as a witness gives in writing or by signs;

'the original statement', in relation to hearsay evidence, means the underlying statement (if any) by –

(a) in the case of evidence of fact, a person having personal knowledge of that fact, or

(b) in the case of evidence of opinion, the person whose opinion it is; and

'statement' means any representation of fact or opinion, however made.

Savings

14 (1) Nothing in this Act affects the exclusion of evidence on grounds other than that it is hearsay.

This applies whether the evidence falls to be excluded in pursuance of any enactment or rule of law, for failure to comply with rules of court or an order of the court, or otherwise.

(2) Nothing in this Act affects the proof of documents by means other than those specified in section 8 or 9.

(3) Nothing in this Act affects the operation of the following enactments –

(a) section 2 of the Documentary Evidence Act 1868 (mode of proving certain official documents);

(b) section 2 of the Documentary Evidence Act 1882 (documents printed under the superintendence of Stationery Office);

(c) section 1 of the Evidence (Colonial Statutes) Act 1907 (proof of statutes of certain legislatures);

(d) section 1 of the Evidence (Foreign, Dominion and Colonial Documents) Act 1933 (proof and effect of registers and official certificates of certain countries);

(e) section 5 of the Oaths and Evidence (Overseas Authorities and Countries) Act 1963 (provision in respect of public registers of other countries).

Consequential amendments and repeals

15 (1) The enactments specified in Schedule 1 are amended in accordance with that Schedule, the amendments being consequential on the provisions of this Act.

(2) The enactments specified in Schedule 2 are repealed to the extent specified.

Short title, commencement and extent

16 (1) This Act may be cited as the Civil Evidence Act 1995.

(2) The provisions of this Act come into force on such day as the Lord Chancellor may appoint by order made by statutory instrument, and different days may be appointed for different provisions and for different purposes.

(3) Subject to subsection (3A), the provisions of this Act shall not apply in relation to proceedings begun before commencement.

(3A) Transitional provisions for the application of the provisions of this Act to proceedings begun before commencement may be made by rules of court or practice directions.

(4) This Act extends to England and Wales.

(5) *Section 10 (admissibility and proof of Ogden Tables) also extends to Northern Ireland.*

As it extends to Northern Ireland, the following shall be substituted for subsection (3)(b) –

'(b) 'action for personal injury' includes an action brought by virtue of the Law Reform (Miscellaneous Provisions) (Northern Ireland) Act 1937 or the Fatal Accidents (Northern Ireland) Order 1977.'[2]

(6) The provisions of Schedules 1 and 2 (consequential amendments and repeals) have the same extent as the enactments respectively amended or repealed.

2 Repealed with savings by the Civil Evidence (Northern Ireland) Order 1997 SI 1997 No 2983, art 13(2), Sch 2; for savings see art 12 . Not yet in force – see the Civil Evidence (Northern Ireland) Order 1997 SI 1997 No 2983 art 1(2).

SCHEDULE 1: CONSEQUENTIAL AMENDMENT

Section 15(1)

1 ...
2 ...
3 ...
4 ...
5 ...
6 ...
7 ...
8 ...
9 ...
10 ...
11 ...
12 ...
13 ...
14 ...
15 ...
16 ...
17 ...
18 ...
19 ...
20 ...

SCHEDULE 2: REPEALS

Section 15(2)

Chapter	Short title	Extent of repeal
1938 c 28	Evidence Act 1938	Sections 1 and 2
		Section 6(1) except the words from "Proceedings" to 'references'
		Section 6(2)(b)
1968 c 64	Civil Evidence Act 1968	Part I
1971 c 33	Armed Forces Act 1971	Section 26
1972 c 30	Civil Evidence Act 1972	Section 1
		Section 2(1) and (2)
		In section 2(3)(b), the words from 'by virtue of section 2' to
		In section 3(1), the words 'Part I of the Civil Evidence Act 1968 or'
		In section 6(3), the words '1 and', in both places where they occur
1975 c 63	Inheritance (Provision for Family and Dependants) Act 1975	Section 21
1979 c 2	Customs and Excise Management Act 1979	Section 75A(6)(a)
		Section 118A(6)(a)
1980 c 43	Magistrates' Courts Act 1980	In Schedule 7, paragraph 75
1984 c 28	County Courts Act 1984	In Schedule 2, paragraphs 33 and 34
1985 c 54	Finance Act 1985	Section 10(7)
1986 c 21	Armed Forces Act 1986	Section 3
1988 c 39	Finance Act 1988	Section 127(5)
1990 c 26	Gaming (Amendment) Act 1990	In the Schedule, paragraph 2(7)
1994 c 9	Finance Act 1994	Section 22(2)(a)
		In Schedule 7, paragraph 1(6)(a)
1994 c 23	Value Added Tax Act 1994	Section 96(6) and (7)
		In Schedule 11, paragraph 6(6)(a)
1995 c 4	Finance Act 1995	In Schedule 4, paragraph 38

APPENDIX D

European Convention on Human Rights Articles 5, 6, 8, 10 and 11

Article 5: Right to liberty and security

1 Everyone has the right to liberty and security of person. No one shall be deprived of his liberty save in the following cases and in accordance with a procedure prescribed by law:
   (a) the lawful detention of a person after conviction by a competent court;
   (b) the lawful arrest or detention of a person for non-compliance with the lawful order of a court or in order to secure the fulfilment of any obligation prescribed by law;
   (c) the lawful arrest or detention of a person effected for the purpose of bringing him before the competent legal authority on reasonable suspicion of having committed an offence or when it is reasonably considered necessary to prevent his committing an offence or fleeing after having done so;
   (d) the detention of a minor by lawful order for the purpose of educational supervision or his lawful detention for the purpose of bringing him before the competent legal authority;
   (e) the lawful detention of persons for the prevention of the spreading of infectious diseases, of persons of unsound mind, alcoholics or drug addicts or vagrants;
   (f) the lawful arrest or detention of a person to prevent his effecting an unauthorised entry into the country or of a person against whom action is being taken with a view to deportation or extradition.

2 Everyone who is arrested shall be informed promptly, in a language which he understands, of the reasons for his arrest and of any charge against him.

3 Everyone arrested or detained in accordance with the provisions of paragraph 1(c) of this Article shall be brought promptly before a judge or other officer authorised by law to exercise judicial power and shall be entitled to trial within a reasonable time or to release pending trial. Release may be conditioned by guarantees to appear for trial.

4 Everyone who is deprived of his liberty by arrest or detention shall be entitled to take proceedings by which the lawfulness of his detention shall be decided speedily by a court and his release ordered if the detention is not lawful.

5 Everyone who has been the victim of arrest or detention in contravention of the provisions of this Article shall have an enforceable right to compensation.

Article 6: Right to a fair trial

1 In the determination of his civil rights and obligations or of any criminal charge against him, everyone is entitled to a fair and public hearing within a reasonable time by an independent and impartial tribunal established by law. Judgment shall be pronounced publicly but the press and public may be excluded from all or part of the trial in the interest of morals, public order or national security in a democratic society, where the interests of juveniles or the protection of the private life of the parties so require, or to the extent strictly necessary in the opinion of the court in special circumstances where publicity would prejudice the interests of justice.

2 Everyone charged with a criminal offence shall be presumed innocent until proved guilty according to law.

3 Everyone charged with a criminal offence has the following minimum rights:

(a) to be informed promptly, in a language which he understands and in detail, of the nature and cause of the accusation against him;

(b) to have adequate time and facilities for the preparation of his defence;

(c) to defend himself in person or through legal assistance of his own choosing or, if he has not sufficient means to pay for legal assistance, to be given it free when the interests of justice so require;

(d) to examine or have examined witnesses against him and to obtain the attendance and examination of witnesses on his behalf under the same conditions as witnesses against him;

(e) to have the free assistance of an interpreter if he cannot understand or speak the language used in court.

Article 8: Right to respect for private and family life

1 Everyone has the right to respect for his private and family life, his home and his correspondence.

2 There shall be no interference by a public authority with the exercise of this right except such as is in accordance with the law and is necessary in a democratic society in the interests of national security, public safety or the economic well-being of the country, for the prevention of disorder or crime, for the protection of health or morals, or for the protection of the rights and freedoms of others.

Article 10: Freedom of expression

1 Everyone has the right to freedom of expression. This right shall include freedom to hold opinions and to receive and impart information and ideas without interference by public authority and regardless of frontiers. This Article shall not prevent States from requiring the licensing of broadcasting, television or cinema enterprises.

2 The exercise of these freedoms, since it carries with it duties and responsibilities, may be subject to such formalities, conditions, restrictions or penalties as are prescribed by law and are necessary in a democratic society, in the interests of national security, territorial integrity or public safety, for the prevention of disorder or crime, for the protection of health or morals, for the

protection of the reputation or rights of others, for preventing the disclosure of information received in confidence, or for maintaining the authority and impartiality of the judiciary.

Article 11: Freedom of assembly and association

1 Everyone has the right to freedom of peaceful assembly and to freedom of association with others, including the right to form and to join trade unions for the protection of his interests.

2 No restrictions shall be placed on the exercise of these rights other than such as are prescribed by law and are necessary in a democratic society in the interests of national security or public safety, for the prevention of disorder or crime, for the protection of health or morals or for the protection of the rights and freedoms of others. This Article shall not prevent the imposition of lawful restrictions on the exercise of these rights by members of the armed forces, of the police or of the administration of the State.

APPENDIX E

Magistrates' Courts (Hearsay Evidence in Civil Proceedings) Rules 1999 SI No 681

Citation and commencement

1 These Rules may be cited as the Magistrates' Courts (Hearsay Evidence in Civil Proceedings) Rules 1999 and shall come into force on 1st April 1999.

Application and interpretation

2 (1) In these Rules, the '1995 Act' means the Civil Evidence Act 1995.

(2) In these Rules –

'hearsay evidence' means evidence consisting of hearsay within the meaning of section 1(2) of the 1995 Act;

'hearsay notice' means a notice under section 2 of the 1995 Act.

(3) These Rules shall apply to hearsay evidence in civil proceedings in magistrates' courts.

Hearsay notices

3 (1) Subject to paragraphs (2) and (3), a party who desires to give hearsay evidence at the hearing must, not less than 21 days before the date fixed for the hearing, serve a hearsay notice on every other party and file a copy in the court by serving it on the justices' chief executive.

(2) Subject to paragraph (3), the court or the justices' clerk may make a direction substituting a different period of time for the service of the hearsay notice under paragraph (1) on the application of a party to the proceedings.

(3) The court may make a direction under paragraph (2) of its own motion.

(4) A hearsay notice must –

(a) state that it is a hearsay notice;

(b) identify the proceedings in which the hearsay evidence is to be given;

(c) state that the party proposes to adduce hearsay evidence;

(d) identify the hearsay evidence;

(e) identify the person who made the statement which is to be given in evidence; and

(f) state why that person will not be called to give oral evidence.

(5) A single hearsay notice may deal with the hearsay evidence of more than one witness.

Power to call witness for cross-examination on hearsay evidence

4 (1) Where a party tenders as hearsay evidence a statement made by a person but does not propose to call the person who made the statement to give evidence, the court may, on application, allow another party to call and cross-examine the person who made the statement on its contents.

(2) An application under paragraph (1) must –

(a) be served on the [justices' chief executive] with sufficient copies for all other parties;

(b) unless the court otherwise directs, be made not later than 7 days after service of the hearsay notice; and

(c) give reasons why the person who made the statement should be cross-examined on its contents.

(3) On receipt of an application under paragraph (1) –

(a) the justices' clerk must –

(i) unless the court otherwise directs, allow sufficient time for the applicant to comply with paragraph (4); and

(ii) fix the date, time and place of the hearing; and

(b) the justices' chief executive must –

(i) endorse the date, time and place of the hearing on the copies of the application filed by the applicant; and

(ii) return the copies to the applicant forthwith.

(4) Subject to paragraphs (5) and (6), on receipt of the copies from the justices' chief executive under paragraph (3)(c), the applicant must serve a copy on every other party giving not less than 3 days' notice of the hearing of the application.

(5) The court or the justices' clerk may give directions as to the manner in which service under paragraph (4) is to be effected and may, subject to [the justices' chief executive's] giving notice to the applicant, alter or dispense with the notice requirement under paragraph (4) if the court or the justices' clerk, as the case may be, considers it is in the interests of justice to do so.

(6) The court may hear an application under paragraph (1) *ex parte* if it considers it is in the interests of justice to do so.

(7) Subject to paragraphs (5) and (6), where an application under paragraph (1) is made, the applicant must file with the court a statement at or before the hearing of the application that service of a copy of the application has been effected on all other parties and the statement must indicate the manner, date, time and address at which the document was served.

(8) The court must notify all parties of its decision on an application under paragraph (1).

Credibility and previous inconsistent statements

5 (1) If –

(a) a party tenders as hearsay evidence a statement made by a person but does not call the person who made the statement to give oral evidence, and

(b) another party wishes to attack the credibility of the person who made the statement or allege that the person who made the statement made any other statement inconsistent with it,

that other party must notify the party tendering the hearsay evidence of his intention.

(2) Unless the court or the justices' clerk otherwise directs, a notice under paragraph (1) must be given not later than 7 days after service of the hearsay notice and, in addition to the requirements in paragraph (1), must be served on every other party and a copy filed in the court.

(3) If, on receipt of a notice under paragraph (1), the party referred to in paragraph (1)(a) calls the person who made the statement to be tendered as hearsay evidence to give oral evidence, he must, unless the court otherwise directs, notify the court and all other parties of his intention.

(4) Unless the court or the justices' clerk otherwise directs, a notice under paragraph (3) must be given not later than 7 days after the service of the notice under paragraph (1).

Service

6 (1) Where service of a document is required by these Rules it may be effected, unless the contrary is indicated –

(a) if the person to be served is not known by the person serving to be acting by solicitor –

(i) by delivering it to him personally, or

(ii) by delivering at, or by sending it by first-class post to, his residence or his last known residence, or

(b) if the person to be served is known by the person serving to be acting by solicitor –

(i) by delivering the document at, or sending it by first-class post to, the solicitor's address for service,

(ii) where the solicitor's address for service includes a numbered box at a document exchange, by leaving the document at that document exchange or at a document exchange which transmits documents on every business day to that document exchange, or

(iii) by sending a legible copy of the document by facsimile transmission to the solicitor's office.

(2) In this rule, 'first-class post' means first-class post which has been pre-paid or in respect of which pre-payment is not required.

(3) A document shall, unless the contrary is proved, be deemed to have been served –

(a) in the case of service by first-class post, on the second business day after posting,

(b) in the case of service in accordance with paragraph (1)(b)(ii), on the second business day after the day on which it is left at the document exchange, and

(c) in the case of service in accordance with paragraph (1)(b)(iii), where it is transmitted on a business day before 4 pm, on that day and in any other case, on the next business day.

(4) In this rule, 'business day' means any day other than –
  (a) a Saturday, Sunday, Christmas Day or Good Friday; or
  (b) a bank holiday under the Banking and Financial Dealings Act 1971, in England and Wales.

Amendment to the Justices' Clerks Rules 1970

7 The Justices' Clerks Rules 1970 shall be amended by the insertion, after paragraph 18 of the Schedule, of the following paragraph –

'**19** The giving, variation or revocation of directions in accordance with rules 3(2), 4(5), 5(2) and (4) of the Magistrates' Courts (Hearsay Evidence in Civil Proceedings) Rules 1999.'.

APPENDIX F

Post-conviction ASBO form

Anti-Social Behaviour Order made on conviction under s.1C Crime and Disorder Act 1998

(Criminal Procedure Rules, r 50.4)

. . . . Crown Court
(Code)

1 On the . . . . [date] Crown Court sitting at . . . . convicted

Name: . . . . [the defendant] of
. . . .

Address:

. . . .

. . . . of

Date of Birth:
Offence(s) . . . . [relevant offence(s)

and imposed the following sentence/conditional discharge . . . .

2 The court found that

(i) the defendant had acted in an anti-social manner which caused or was likely to cause harassment, alarm or distress to one or more persons not of the same household as himself

. . . .

. . . . [details of behaviour]

and that

(ii) an order was necessary to protect persons in England and Wales from further anti-social acts by him.

3 It is ordered that the defendant . . . . [name] is prohibited from:

. . . .

. . . .

[Where appropriate, the court must specify whether any of the requirements of the order are suspended until the defendant's release from custody] . . . .
. . . .

. . . .

Until [ ] [further order].

The Judge

NOTE: If without reasonable excuse the defendant does anything which he is prohibited from doing by this order, he shall be liable on conviction to a term of imprisonment not exceeding five years or to a fine or to both."

[Note: Formerly set out in Schedule 12 of the Crown Court Rules 1982 (as amended), relating to rule 38 of those Rules and section 1C of the Crime and Disorder Act 1998].

APPENDIX G

County Court ASBO – Form N113

Anti-social behaviour (Order under section 1B(4) of the Crime and Disorder Act 1998)

In the County Court	
Claim No.	
Claimant	
Applicant	
Defendant	

SEAL

On 20 , District Judge
sitting at

considered the application of the [claimant] [applicant] [defendant] and found that the [claimant] [defendant] has acted in an anti-social manner that caused or was likely to cause harassment, alarm or distress to one or more persons not of the same household as [himself] [herself]; **and** that this order is necessary to protect persons from further anti-social acts by the [claimant] [defendant] **and the court ordered** that the [claimant] [defendant] is forbidden from:-

until [ ] [further order]

[The [claimant] [applicant] [or] [defendant] may apply to the court for this order to be varied or discharged. Unless both parties consent, this order may not be discharged within two years of the order being served.]

To

You **must** obey this order. If, without reasonable excuse, you do anything which you are forbidden from doing by this order, you will be liable on conviction to a term of imprisonment not exceeding five years or to a fine or to both.

[Notice of further hearing [(see also note overleaf)]
The court will re-consider the application and whether the order should continue at a further hearing at

on the day of 20 at o'clock

If you do not attend at the time shown the court may make an order in your absence.]

Anti social behaviour order - Record of hearing Claim No.

On the day of 20

Before District Judge

The court was sitting at

The [claimant] [applicant]

was
- ☐ represented by counsel
- ☐ represented by a solicitor
- ☐ in person

The [claimant] [defendant]

was
- ☐ represented by counsel
- ☐ represented by a solicitor
- ☐ in person
- ☐ not given notice of this hearing

or

- ☐ did not appear having been given notice of this hearing

The court read the statements of
- ☐ the claimant
- ☐ the applicant
- ☐ the defendant

[And of]

[The court heard spoken evidence on oath from]

Signed________________________________ Dated___________________________

[**Note:** This order was made without notice being given to you. You may apply for it to be set aside, varied or stayed. If you wish to apply, do not delay. You must make your application to the court within 7 days of the date you received it. You may make your application by writing to the court or asking the court for a Form N244 Application Notice. You will have to pay a fee to make your application unless you qualify for fee exemption or remission]

APPENDIX H

Civil Procedure Rules Parts 1, 19, 31, 33, 44, 52, 54 and 65 (as relates to ASBOs)

Part 1 Overriding objective

1.1 (1) These Rules are a new procedural code with the overriding objective of enabling the court to deal with cases justly.
(2) Dealing with a case justly includes, so far as is practicable –
(a) ensuring that the parties are on an equal footing;
(b) saving expense;
(c) dealing with the case in ways which are proportionate –
(i) to the amount of money involved;
(ii) to the importance of the case;
(iii) to the complexity of the issues; and
(iv) to the financial position of each party;
(d) ensuring that it is dealt with expeditiously and fairly; and
(e) allotting to it an appropriate share of the court's resources, while taking into account the need to allot resources to other cases.

1.2 Application by the court of the overriding objective

The court must seek to give effect to the overriding objective when it –
(a) exercises any power given to it by the Rules; or
(b) interprets any rule subject to rule 76.2.

1.3 Duty of the parties

The parties are required to help the court to further the overriding objective.

1.4 Court's duty to manage cases

(1) The court must further the overriding objective by actively managing cases.
(2) Active case management includes –
(a) encouraging the parties to co-operate with each other in the conduct of the proceedings;
(b) identifying the issues at an early stage;

(c) deciding promptly which issues need full investigation and trial and accordingly disposing summarily of the others;
(d) deciding the order in which issues are to be resolved;
(e) encouraging the parties to use an alternative dispute resolution procedure if the court considers that appropriate and facilitating the use of such procedure;
(f) helping the parties to settle the whole or part of the case;
(g) fixing timetables or otherwise controlling the progress of the case;
(h) considering whether the likely benefits of taking a particular step justify the cost of taking it;
(i) dealing with as many aspects of the case as it can on the same occasion;
(j) dealing with the case without the parties needing to attend at court;
(k) making use of technology; and
(l) giving directions to ensure that the trial of a case proceeds quickly and efficiently.

Part 19
Parties and group litigation

Parties – general

19.1 Any number of claimants or defendants may be joined as parties to a claim.

I Addition and substitution of parties

Change of parties – general

19.2 (1) This rule applies where a party is to be added or substituted except where the case falls within rule 19.5 (special provisions about changing parties after the end of a relevant limitation period).

(2) The court may order a person to be added as a new party if –

(a) it is desirable to add the new party so that the court can resolve all the matters in dispute in the proceedings; or

(b) there is an issue involving the new party and an existing party which is connected to the matters in dispute in the proceedings, and it is desirable to add the new party so that the court can resolve that issue.

(3) The court may order any person to cease to be a party if it is not desirable for that person to be a party to the proceedings.

(4) The court may order a new party to be substituted for an existing one if –

(a) the existing party's interest or liability has passed to the new party; and

(b) it is desirable to substitute the new party so that the court can resolve the matters in dispute in the proceedings.

Provisions applicable where two or more persons are jointly entitled to a remedy

19.3 (1) Where a claimant claims a remedy to which some other person is jointly entitled with him, all persons jointly entitled to the remedy must be parties unless the court orders otherwise.

(2) If any person does not agree to be a claimant, he must be made a defendant, unless the court orders otherwise.

(3) This rule does not apply in probate proceedings.

Procedure for adding and substituting parties

19.4 (1) The court's permission is required to remove, add or substitute a party, unless the claim form has not been served.

(2) An application for permission under paragraph (1) may be made by –

(a) an existing party; or

(b) a person who wishes to become a party.

(3) An application for an order under rule 19.2(4) (substitution of a new party where existing party's interest or liability has passed) –

(a) may be made without notice; and

(b) must be supported by evidence.

(4) Nobody may be added or substituted as a claimant unless –
   (a) he has given his consent in writing; and
   (b) that consent has been filed with the court.

(4A) The Commissioners for HM Revenue and Customs may be added as a party to proceedings only if they consent in writing.

(5) An order for the removal, addition or substitution of a party must be served on –
   (a) all parties to the proceedings; and
   (b) any other person affected by the order.

(6) When the court makes an order for the removal, addition or substitution of a party, it may give consequential directions about –
   (a) filing and serving the claim form on any new defendant;
   (b) serving relevant documents on the new party; and
   (c) the management of the proceedings.

Human rights

19.4A Section 4 of the Human Rights Act 1998

(1) The court may not make a declaration of incompatibility in accordance with section 4 of the Human Rights Act 1998 unless 21 days' notice, or such other period of notice as the court directs, has been given to the Crown.

(2) Where notice has been given to the Crown a Minister, or other person permitted by that Act, shall be joined as a party on giving notice to the court.

(Only courts specified in section 4 of the Human Rights Act 1998 can make a declaration of incompatibility)

Section 9 of the Human Rights Act 1998

(3) Where a claim is made under that Act for damages in respect of a judicial act –
   (a) that claim must be set out in the statement of case or the appeal notice; and
   (b) notice must be given to the Crown.

(4) Where paragraph (3) applies and the appropriate person has not applied to be joined as a party within 21 days, or such other period as the court directs, after the notice is served, the court may join the appropriate person as a party.

(A practice direction makes provision for these notices)

19.5 Special provisions about adding or substituting parties after the end of a relevant limitation period

(1) This rule applies to a change of parties after the end of a period of limitation under –
   (a) the Limitation Act 1980[1];
   (b) the Foreign Limitation Periods Act 1984[2]; or

(c) any other enactment which allows such a change, or under which such a change is allowed.

(2) The court may add or substitute a party only if –

(a) the relevant limitation period was current when the proceedings were started; and

(b) the addition or substitution is necessary.

(3) The addition or substitution of a party is necessary only if the court is satisfied that –

(a) the new party is to be substituted for a party who was named in the claim form in mistake for the new party;

(b) the claim cannot properly be carried on by or against the original party unless the new party is added or substituted as claimant or defendant; or

(c) the original party has died or had a bankruptcy order made against him and his interest or liability has passed to the new party.

(4) In addition, in a claim for personal injuries the court may add or substitute a party where it directs that –

(a) (i) section 11 (special time limit for claims for personal injuries); or

(ii) section 12 (special time limit for claims under fatal accidents legislation), of the Limitation Act 1980 shall not apply to the claim by or against the new party; or

(b) the issue of whether those sections apply shall be determined at trial.

(Rule 17.4 deals with other changes after the end of a relevant limitation period)

Special rules about parties in claims for wrongful interference with goods

19.5A (1) A claimant in a claim for wrongful interference with goods must, in the particulars of claim, state the name and address of every person who, to his knowledge, has or claims an interest in the goods and who is not a party to the claim.

(2) A defendant to a claim for wrongful interference with goods may apply for a direction that another person be made a party to the claim to establish whether the other person –

(3) Where the person referred to in paragraph (2) fails to attend the hearing of the application, or comply with any directions, the court may order that he is deprived of any claim against the defendant in respect of the goods.

(Rule 3.1(3) provides that the court may make an order subject to conditions)

(4) The application notice must be served on all parties and on the person referred to in paragraph (2).

[Part 19, sections II and III not reproduced]

Practice Direction: Part 19

Addition and substitution of parties

This Practice Direction supplements CPR Part 19

A party applying for an amendment will usually be responsible for the costs of and arising from the amendment.

Change of parties

General

1.1 Parties may be removed, added or substituted in existing proceedings either on the court's own initiative or on the application of either an existing party or a person who wishes to become a party.

1.2 The application may be dealt with without a hearing where all the existing parties and the proposed new party are in agreement.

1.3 The application to add or substitute a new party should be supported by evidence setting out the proposed new party's interest in or connection with the claim.

1.4 The application notice should be filed in accordance with rule 23.3 and, unless the application is made under rule 19.2(4),[1] be served in accordance with rule 23.4.

1.5 An order giving permission to amend will, unless the court orders otherwise, be drawn up. It will be served by the court unless the parties wish to serve it or the court orders them to do so.

Addition or substitution of claimant

2.1 Where an application is made to the court to add or to substitute a new party to the proceedings as claimant, the party applying must file:

(1) the application notice,

(2) the proposed amended claim form and particulars of claim, and

(3) the signed, written consent of the new claimant to be so added or substituted.

2.2 Where the court makes an order adding or substituting a party as claimant but the signed, written consent of the new claimant has not been filed:

(1) the order, and

(2) the addition or substitution of the new party as claimant, will not take effect until the signed, written consent of the new claimant is filed.

2.3 Where the court has made an order adding or substituting a new claimant, the court may direct:

(1) a copy of the order to be served on every party to the proceedings and any other person affected by the order,

(2) copies of the statements of case and of documents referred to in any statement of case to be served on the new party,

(3) the party who made the application to file within 14 days an amended claim form and particulars of claim.

1 See rule 19.4(3)(a).

Addition or substitution of defendant

3.1 The Civil Procedure Rules apply to a new defendant who has been added or substituted as they apply to any other defendant (see in particular the provisions of Parts 9, 10, 11 and 15).

3.2 Where the court has made an order adding or substituting a defendant whether on its own initiative or on an application, the court may direct:

(1) the claimant to file with the court within 14 days (or as ordered) an amended claim form and particulars of claim for the court file,

(2) a copy of the order to be served on all parties to the proceedings and any other person affected by it,

(3) the amended claim form and particulars of claim, forms for admitting, defending and acknowledging the claim and copies of the statements of case and any other documents referred to in any statement of case to be served on the new defendant.

(4) unless the court orders otherwise, the amended claim form and particulars of claim to be served on any other defendants.

3.3 A new defendant does not become a party to the proceedings until the amended claim form has been served on him.[2]

Removal of party

4 Where the court makes an order for the removal of a party from the proceedings:

(1) the claimant must file with the court an amended claim form and particulars of claim, and

(2) a copy of the order must be served on every party to the proceedings and on any other person affected by the order.

Transfer of interest or liability

5.1 Where the interest or liability of an existing party has passed to some other person, application should be made to the court to add or substitute that person.[3]

5.2 The application must be supported by evidence showing the stage the proceedings have reached and what change has occurred to cause the transfer of interest or liability.

(For information about making amendments generally, see the practice direction supplementing Part 17.)

Human Rights, joining the Crown

Section 4 of the Human Rights Act 1998

6.1 Where a party has included in his statement of case –

(1) a claim for a declaration of incompatibility in accordance with section 4 of the Human Rights Act 1998, or

(2) an issue for the court to decide which may lead to the court considering

2 *Kettleman v Hansel Properties Ltd* (1987) AC 189, HL.

3 See rule 19.2(4).

making a declaration, then the court may at any time consider whether notice should be given to the Crown as required by that Act and give directions for the content and service of the notice. The rule allows a period of 21 days before the court will make the declaration but the court may vary this period of time.

6.2 The court will normally consider the issues and give the directions referred to in paragraph 6.1 at the case management conference.

6.3 Where a party amends his statement of case to include any matter referred to in paragraph 6.1, then the court will consider whether notice should be given to the Crown and give directions for the content and service of the notice.

(The practice direction to CPR Part 16 requires a party to include issues under the Human Rights Act 1998 in his statement of case)

6.4 (1) The notice given under rule 19.4A must be served on the person named in the list published under section 17 of the Crown Proceedings Act 1947. (The list, made by the Minister for the Civil Service, is annexed to the practice direction to Part 66)

(2) The notice will be in the form directed by the court but will normally include the directions given by the court and all the statements of case in the claim. The notice will also be served on all the parties.

(3) The court may require the parties to assist in the preparation of the notice. (4) In the circumstances described in the National Assembly for Wales (Transfer of Functions)(No 2) Order 2000 the notice must also be served on the National Assembly for Wales.

(Section 5(3) of the Human Rights Act 1998 provides that the Crown may give notice that it intends to become a party at any stage in the proceedings once notice has been given)

6.5 Unless the court orders otherwise, the Minister or other person permitted by the Human Rights Act 1998 to be joined as a party must, if he wishes to be joined, give notice of his intention to be joined as a party to the court and every other party. Where the Minister has nominated a person to be joined as a party the notice must be accompanied by the written nomination.

(Section 5(2)(a) of the Human Rights Act 1998 permits a person nominated by a Minister of the Crown to be joined as a party. The nomination may be signed on behalf of the Minister) Section 9 of the Human Rights Act 1998.)

6.6 (1) The procedure in paragraphs 6.1 to 6.5 also applies where a claim is made under sections 7(1)(a) and 9(3) of the Human Rights Act 1998 for damages in respect of a judicial act.

(2) Notice must be given to the Lord Chancellor and should be served on the Treasury Solicitor on his behalf, except where the judicial act is of a Court-Martial when the appropriate person is the Secretary of State for Defence and the notice must be served on the Treasury Solicitor on his behalf.

(3) The notice will also give details of the judicial act, which is the subject of the claim for damages, and of the court or tribunal that made it.

(Section 9(4) of the Human Rights Act 1998 provides that no award of damages may be made against the Crown as provided for in section 9(3) unless the appropriate person is joined in the proceedings. The appropriate person is the Minister responsible for the court concerned or a person or department nominated by him (section 9(5) of the Act))

[*Practice Direction B not reproduced here.*]

Part 31
Disclosure and inspection of documents

Scope of this Part

31.1 (1) This Part sets out rules about the disclosure and inspection of documents.

(2) This Part applies to all claims except a claim on the small claims track.

Meaning of disclosure

31.2 A party discloses a document by stating that the document exists or has existed.

Right of inspection of a disclosed document

31.3 (1) A party to whom a document has been disclosed has a right to inspect that document except where –

(a) the document is no longer in the control of the party who disclosed it;

(b) the party disclosing the document has a right or a duty to withhold inspection of it; or

(c) paragraph (2) applies.

(Rule 31.8 sets out when a document is in the control of a party)

(Rule 31.19 sets out the procedure for claiming a right or duty to withhold inspection)

(2) Where a party considers that it would be disproportionate to the issues in the case to permit inspection of documents within a category or class of document disclosed under rule 31.6(b) –

(a) he is not required to permit inspection of documents within that category or class; but

(b) he must state in his disclosure statement that inspection of those documents will not be permitted on the grounds that to do so would be disproportionate.

(Rule 31.6 provides for standard disclosure)

(Rule 31.10 makes provision for a disclosure statement)

(Rule 31.12 provides for a party to apply for an order for specific inspection of documents)

Meaning of document

31.4 In this Part –

'document' means anything in which information of any description is recorded; and

'copy', in relation to a document, means anything onto which information recorded in the document has been copied, by whatever means and whether directly or indirectly.

Disclosure limited to standard disclosure

31.5 (1) An order to give disclosure is an order to give standard disclosure unless the court directs otherwise.

(2) The court may dispense with or limit standard disclosure.

(3) The parties may agree in writing to dispense with or to limit standard disclosure.

(The court may make an order requiring standard disclosure under rule 28.3 which deals with directions in relation to cases on the fast track and under rule 29.2 which deals with case management in relation to cases on the multi-track)

Standard disclosure – what documents are to be disclosed

31.6 Standard disclosure requires a party to disclose only –

(a) the documents on which he relies; and

(b) the documents which –

(i) adversely affect his own case;

(ii) adversely affect another party's case; or

(iii) support another party's case; and

(c) the documents which he is required to disclose by a relevant practice direction.

Duty of search

31.7 (1) When giving standard disclosure, a party is required to make a reasonable search for documents falling within rule 31.6(b) or (c).

(2) The factors relevant in deciding the reasonableness of a search include the following –

(a) the number of documents involved;

(b) the nature and complexity of the proceedings;

(c) the ease and expense of retrieval of any particular document; and

(d) the significance of any document which is likely to be located during the search.

(3) Where a party has not searched for a category or class of document on the grounds that to do so would be unreasonable, he must state this in his disclosure statement and identify the category or class of document.

(Rule 31.10 makes provision for a disclosure statement)

Duty of disclosure limited to documents which are or have been in a party's control

31.8 (1) A party's duty to disclose documents is limited to documents which are or have been in his control.

(2) For this purpose a party has or has had a document in his control if –

(a) it is or was in his physical possession;

(b) he has or has had a right to possession of it; or

(c) he has or has had a right to inspect or take copies of it.

Disclosure of copies

31.9 (1) A party need not disclose more than one copy of a document.

(2) A copy of a document that contains a modification, obliteration or other marking or feature –

(a) on which a party intends to rely; or

(b) which adversely affects his own case or another party's case or supports another party's case; shall be treated as a separate document.

(Rule 31.4 sets out the meaning of a copy of a document)

Procedure for standard disclosure

31.10 (1) The procedure for standard disclosure is as follows.

(2) Each party must make and serve on every other party, a list of documents in the relevant practice form.

(3) The list must identify the documents in a convenient order and manner and as concisely as possible.

(4) The list must indicate –

(a) those documents in respect of which the party claims a right or duty to withhold inspection; and

(b) (i) those documents which are no longer in the party's control; and

(ii) what has happened to those documents.

(Rule 31.19 (3) and (4) require a statement in the list of documents relating to any documents inspection of which a person claims he has a right or duty to withhold)

(5) The list must include a disclosure statement.

(6) A disclosure statement is a statement made by the party disclosing the documents –

(a) setting out the extent of the search that has been made to locate documents which he is required to disclose;

(b) certifying that he understands the duty to disclose documents; and

(c) certifying that to the best of his knowledge he has carried out that duty.

(7) Where the party making the disclosure statement is a company, firm, association or other organisation, the statement must also –

(a) identify the person making the statement; and

(b) explain why he is considered an appropriate person to make the statement.

(8) The parties may agree in writing –

(a) to disclose documents without making a list; and

(b) to disclose documents without the disclosing party making a disclosure statement.

(9) A disclosure statement may be made by a person who is not a party where this is permitted by a relevant practice direction.

Duty of disclosure continues during proceedings

31.11 (1) Any duty of disclosure continues until the proceedings are concluded.

(2) If documents to which that duty extends come to a party's notice at any

time during the proceedings, he must immediately notify every other party.

Specific disclosure or inspection

31.12 (1) The court may make an order for specific disclosure or specific inspection.

(2) An order for specific disclosure is an order that a party must do one or more of the following things –

(a) disclose documents or classes of documents specified in the order;

(b) carry out a search to the extent stated in the order;

(c) disclose any documents located as a result of that search.

(3) An order for specific inspection is an order that a party permit inspection of a document referred to in rule 31.3(2).

(Rule 31.3(2) allows a party to state in his disclosure statement that he will not permit inspection of a document on the grounds that it would be disproportionate to do so)

Disclosure in stages

31.13 The parties may agree in writing, or the court may direct, that disclosure or inspection or both shall take place in stages.

Documents referred to in statements of case etc

31.14 (1) A party may inspect a document mentioned in –

(a) a statement of case;

(b) a witness statement;

(c) a witness summary; or

(d) an affidavit.

(e) Revoked.

(2) Subject to rule 35.10(4), a party may apply for an order for inspection of any document mentioned in an expert's report which has not already been disclosed in the proceedings.

(Rule 35.10(4) makes provision in relation to instructions referred to in an expert's report)

Inspection and copying of documents

31.15 Where a party has a right to inspect a document –

(a) that party must give the party who disclosed the document written notice of his wish to inspect it;

(b) the party who disclosed the document must permit inspection not more than 7 days after the date on which he received the notice; and

(c) that party may request a copy of the document and, if he also undertakes to pay reasonable copying costs, the party who disclosed the document must supply him with a copy not more than 7 days after the date on which he received the request.

(Rule 31.3 and 31.14 deal with the right of a party to inspect a document)

Disclosure before proceedings start

31.16 (1) This rule applies where an application is made to the court under any Act for disclosure before proceedings have started.[4]

(2) The application must be supported by evidence.

(3) The court may make an order under this rule only where –

(a) the respondent is likely to be a party to subsequent proceedings;

(b) the applicant is also likely to be a party to those proceedings;

(c) if proceedings had started, the respondent's duty by way of standard disclosure, set out in rule 31.6, would extend to the documents or classes of documents of which the applicant seeks disclosure; and

(d) disclosure before proceedings have started is desirable in order to –

(i) dispose fairly of the anticipated proceedings;

(ii) assist the dispute to be resolved without proceedings; or

(iii) save costs.

(4) An order under this rule must –

(a) specify the documents or the classes of documents which the respondent must disclose; and

(b) require him, when making disclosure, to specify any of those documents –

(i) which are no longer in his control; or

(ii) in respect of which he claims a right or duty to withhold inspection.

(5) Such an order may –

(a) require the respondent to indicate what has happened to any documents which are no longer in his control; and

(b) specify the time and place for disclosure and inspection.

Orders for disclosure against a person not a party

31.17 (1) This rule applies where an application is made to the court under any Act for disclosure by a person who is not a party to the proceedings.[5]

(2) The application must be supported by evidence.

(3) The court may make an order under this rule only where – (a) the documents of which disclosure is sought are likely to support the case of the applicant or adversely affect the case of one of the other parties to the proceedings; and (b) disclosure is necessary in order to dispose fairly of the claim or to save costs.

(4) An order under this rule must –

(a) specify the documents or the classes of documents which the respondent must disclose; and

4 An application for disclosure before proceedings have started is permitted under section 33 of the Supreme Court Act 1981 or section 52 of the County Courts Act 1984.

5 An application for disclosure against a person who is not a party to proceedings is permitted under section 34 of the Supreme Court Act 1981 or section 53 of the County Courts Act 1984.

(b) require the respondent, when making disclosure, to specify any of those documents –

(i) which are no longer in his control; or

(ii) in respect of which he claims a right or duty to withhold inspection.

(5) Such an order may –

(a) require the respondent to indicate what has happened to any documents which are no longer in his control; and

(b) specify the time and place for disclosure and inspection.

Rules not to limit other powers of the court to order disclosure

1.18 Rules 31.16 and 31.17 do not limit any other power which the court may have to order –

(a) disclosure before proceedings have started; and

(b) disclosure against a person who is not a party to proceedings.

Claim to withhold inspection or disclosure of a document

1.19 (1) A person may apply, without notice, for an order permitting him to withhold disclosure of a document on the ground that disclosure would damage the public interest.

(2) Unless the court orders otherwise, an order of the court under paragraph (1) –

(a) must not be served on any other person; and

(b) must not be open to inspection by any person.

(3) A person who wishes to claim that he has a right or a duty to withhold inspection of a document, or part of a document, must state in writing –

(a) that he has such a right or duty; and

(b) the grounds on which he claims that right or duty.

(4) The statement referred to in paragraph (3) must be made –

(a) in the list in which the document is disclosed; or

(b) if there is no list, to the person wishing to inspect the document.

(5) A party may apply to the court to decide whether a claim made under paragraph (3) should be upheld.

(6) For the purpose of deciding an application under paragraph (1) (application to withhold disclosure) or paragraph (3) (claim to withhold inspection) the court may –

(a) require the person seeking to withhold disclosure or inspection of a document to produce that document to the court; and

(b) invite any person, whether or not a party, to make representations.

(7) An application under paragraph (1) or paragraph (5) must be supported by evidence.

(8) This Part does not affect any rule of law which permits or requires a document to be withheld from disclosure or inspection on the ground that its disclosure or inspection would damage the public interest.

Restriction on use of a privileged document inspection of which has been inadvertently allowed

31.20 Where a party inadvertently allows a privileged document to be inspected, the party who has inspected the document may use it or its contents only with the permission of the court.

Consequence of failure to disclose documents or permit inspection

31.21 A party may not rely on any document which he fails to disclose or in respect of which he fails to permit inspection unless the court gives permission.

Subsequent use of disclosed documents

31.22 (1) A party to whom a document has been disclosed may use the document only for the purpose of the proceedings in which it is disclosed, except where –

(a) the document has been read to or by the court, or referred to, at a hearing which has been held in public;

(b) the court gives permission; or

(c) the party who disclosed the document and the person to whom the document belongs agree.

(2) The court may make an order restricting or prohibiting the use of a document which has been disclosed, even where the document has been read to or by the court, or referred to, at a hearing which has been held in public.

(3) An application for such an order may be made –

(a) by a party; or

(b) by any person to whom the document belongs.

False disclosure statements

31.23 (1) Proceedings for contempt of court may be brought against a person if he makes, or causes to be made, a false disclosure statement, without an honest belief in its truth.

(2) Proceedings under this rule may be brought only –

(a) by the Attorney General; or

(b) with the permission of the court.

Practice Direction: Part 31

Disclosure and inspection

General

1.1 The normal order for disclosure will be an order that the parties give standard disclosure.

1.2 In order to give standard disclosure the disclosing party must make a reasonable search for documents falling within the paragraphs of rule 31.6.

1.3 Having made the search the disclosing party must (unless rule 31.10(8) applies) make a list of the documents of whose existence the party is aware that fall within those paragraphs and which are or have been in the party's control (see rule 31.8).

1.4 The obligations imposed by an order for standard disclosure may be dispensed with or limited either by the court or by written agreement between the parties. Any such written agreement should be lodged with the court.

The search

2 The extent of the search which must be made will depend upon the circumstances of the case including, in particular, the factors referred to in rule 31.7(2). The parties should bear in mind the overriding principle of proportionality (see rule 1.1(2)(c)). It may, for example, be reasonable to decide not to search for documents coming into existence before some particular date, or to limit the search to documents in some particular place or places, or to documents falling into particular categories.

Electronic disclosure

2A.1 Rule 31.4 contains a broad definition of a document. This extends to electronic documents, including e-mail and other electronic communications, word processed documents and databases. In addition to documents that are readily accessible from computer systems and other electronic devices and media, the definition covers those documents that are stored on servers and back-up systems and electronic documents that have been 'deleted'. It also extends to additional information stored and associated with electronic documents known as metadata.

2A.2 The parties should, prior to the first Case Management Conference, discuss any issues that may arise regarding searches for and the preservation of electronic documents. This may involve the parties providing information about the categories of electronic documents within their control, the computer systems, electronic devices and media on which any relevant documents may be held, the storage systems maintained by the parties and their document retention policies. In the case of difficulty or disagreement, the matter should be referred to a judge for directions at the earliest practical date, if possible at the first Case Management Conference.

2A.3 The parties should co-operate at an early stage as to the format in which electronic copy documents are to be provided on inspection. In the case of difficulty or disagreement, the matter should be referred to a Judge for directions at the earliest practical date, if possible at the first Case Management Conference.

2A.4 The existence of electronic documents impacts upon the extent of the reasonable search required by Rule 31.7 for the purposes of standard disclosure. The factors that may be relevant in deciding the reasonableness of a search for electronic documents include (but are not limited to) the following:–

(a) The number of documents involved.

(b) The nature and complexity of the proceedings.

(c) The ease and expense of retrieval of any particular document. This includes:

(i) The accessibility of electronic documents or data including e-mail communications on computer systems, servers, back-up systems and other electronic devices or media that may contain such documents taking into account alterations or developments in hardware or software systems used by the disclosing party and/or available to enable access to such documents.

(ii) The location of relevant electronic documents, data, computer systems, servers, back-up systems and other electronic devices or media that may contain such documents.

(iii) The likelihood of locating relevant data.

(iv) The cost of recovering any electronic documents.

(v) The cost of disclosing and providing inspection of any relevant electronic documents.

(vi) The likelihood that electronic documents will be materially altered in the course of recovery, disclosure or inspection.

(d) The significance of any document which is likely to be located during the search.

2A.5 It may be reasonable to search some or all of the parties' electronic storage systems. In some circumstances, it may be reasonable to search for electronic documents by means of keyword searches (agreed as far as possible between the parties) even where a full review of each and every document would be unreasonable. There may be other forms of electronic search that may be appropriate in particular circumstances.

The list

3.1 The list should be in Form N265.

3.2 In order to comply with rule 31.10(3) it will normally be necessary to list the documents in date order, to number them consecutively and to give each a concise description (e.g. letter, claimant to defendant). Where there is a large number of documents all falling into a particular category the disclosing party may list those documents as a category rather than individually e.g. 50 bank statements relating to account number _ at _ Bank, _20_ to _20_; or, 35 letters passing between _ and _ between _20_ and _20_.

3.3 The obligations imposed by an order for disclosure will continue until the proceedings come to an end. If, after a list of documents has been prepared and served, the existence of further documents to which the order applies comes to the attention of the disclosing party, the party must prepare and serve a supplemental list.

Disclosure statement

4.1 A list of documents must (unless rule 31.10(8)(b) applies) contain a disclosure statement complying with rule 31.10. The form of disclosure statement is set out in the Annex to this practice direction.

4.2 The disclosure statement should:

(1) expressly state that the disclosing party believes the extent of the search to have been reasonable in all the circumstances, and

(2) in setting out the extent of the search (see rule 31.10(6)) draw attention to any particular limitations on the extent of the search which were adopted for proportionality reasons and give the reasons why the limitations were adopted, eg the difficulty or expense that a search not subject to those limitations would have entailed or the marginal relevance of categories of documents omitted from the search.

4.3 Where rule 31.10(7) applies, the details given in the disclosure statement about the person making the statement must include his name and address and the office or position he holds in the disclosing party or the basis upon which he makes the statement on behalf of the party.

4.4 If the disclosing party has a legal representative acting for him, the legal representative must endeavour to ensure that the person making the disclosure statement (whether the disclosing party or, in a case to which rule 31.10(7) applies, some other person) understands the duty of disclosure under Part 31.

4.5 If the disclosing party wishes to claim that he has a right or duty to withhold a document, or part of a document, in his list of documents from inspection (see rule 31.19(3)), he must state in writing:

(1) that he has such a right or duty, and

(2) the grounds on which he claims that right or duty.

4.6 The statement referred to in paragraph 4.5 above should normally be included in the disclosure statement and must indicate the document, or part of a document, to which the claim relates.

4.7 An insurer or the Motor Insurers' Bureau may sign a disclosure statement on behalf of a party where the insurer or the Motor Insurers' Bureau has a financial interest in the result of proceedings brought wholly or partially by or against that party. Rule 31.10(7) and paragraph 4.3 above shall apply to the insurer or the Motor Insurers' Bureau making such a statement.

Specific disclosure

5.1 If a party believes that the disclosure of documents given by a disclosing party is inadequate he may make an application for an order for specific disclosure (see rule 31.12).

5.2 The application notice must specify the order that the applicant intends to ask the court to make and must be supported by evidence (see rule 31.12(2) which describes the orders the court may make).

5.3 The grounds on which the order is sought may be set out in the application notice itself but if not there set out must be set out in the evidence filed in support of the application.

5.4 In deciding whether or not to make an order for specific disclosure the court will take into account all the circumstances of the case and, in particular, the overriding objective described in Part 1. But if the court concludes that the party from whom specific disclosure is sought has failed adequately to comply with the obligations imposed by an order for disclosure (whether by failing to make a sufficient search for documents or otherwise) the court will usually make such order as is necessary to ensure that those obligations are properly complied with.

5.5 An order for specific disclosure may in an appropriate case direct a party to –

(1) carry out a search for any documents which it is reasonable to suppose may contain information which may – (a) enable the party applying for disclosure either to advance his own case or to damage that of the party giving disclosure; or (b) lead to a train of enquiry which has either of those consequences; and

(2) disclose any documents found as a result of that search.

Claims to withhold disclosure or inspection of a document

6.1 A claim to withhold inspection of a document, or part of a document, disclosed in a list of documents does not require an application to the court. Where such a claim has been made, a party who wishes to challenge it must apply to the court (see rule 31.19(5)).

6.2 Rule 31.19(1) and (6) provide a procedure enabling a party to apply for an order permitting disclosure of the existence of a document to be withheld.

Inspection of documents mentioned in expert's report (rule 31.14(2))

7.1 If a party wishes to inspect documents referred to in the expert report of another party, before issuing an application he should request inspection of the documents informally, and inspection should be provided by agreement unless the request is unreasonable.

7.2 Where an expert report refers to a large number or volume of documents and it would be burdensome to copy or collate them, the court will only order inspection of such documents if it is satisfied that it is necessary for the just disposal of the proceedings and the party cannot reasonably obtain the documents from another source.

False disclosure statement

8 Attention is drawn to rule 31.23 which sets out the consequences of making a false disclosure statement without an honest belief in its truth, and to the procedures set out in paragraphs 28.1 – 28.3 of the practice direction supplementing Part 32.

Annex

Disclosure statement

I, the above named claimant [or defendant] [if party making disclosure is a company, firm or other organisation identify here who the person making the disclosure statement is and why he is the appropriate person to make it] state that I have carried out a reasonable and proportionate search to locate all the documents which I am required to disclose under the order made by the court on day of

I did not search:

(1) for documents predating ,

(2) (for documents located elsewhere than ,

(3) for documents in categories other than .

(4) for electronic documents

I carried out a search for electronic documents contained on or created by the following: [list what was searched and extent of search]

I did not search for the following:

(1) documents created before,

(2) documents contained on or created by the Claimant's/Defendant's PCs/portable data storage media/databases/servers/back-up tapes/off-site storage/mobile phones/laptops/notebooks/ handheld devices/PDA devices (delete as appropriate),

(3) documents contained on or created by the Claimant's/Defendant's mail files/document files/ calendar files/spreadsheet files/graphic and presentation files/web-based applications (delete as appropriate),

(4) documents other than by reference to the following keyword(s)/concepts (delete if your search was not confined to specific keywords or concepts). I certify that I understand the duty of disclosure and to the best of my knowledge I have carried out that duty. I certify that the list above is a complete list of all documents which are or have been in my control and which I am obliged under the said order to disclose.

Part 44
General rules about costs

44.1 Scope of this Part

This Part contains general rules about costs and entitlement to costs.

(The definitions contained in Part 43 are relevant to this Part)

44.2 Solicitor's duty to notify client

Where –

(a) the court makes a costs order against a legally represented party; and

(b) the party is not present when the order is made,

the party's solicitor must notify his client in writing of the costs order no later than 7 days after the solicitor receives notice of the order.

44.3 Court's discretion and circumstances to be taken into account when exercising its discretion as to costs

(1) The court has discretion as to –
   (a) whether costs are payable by one party to another;
   (b) the amount of those costs; and
   (c) when they are to be paid.

(2) If the court decides to make an order about costs –
   (a) the general rule is that the unsuccessful party will be ordered to pay the costs of the successful party; but
   (b) the court may make a different order.

(3) The general rule does not apply to the following proceedings –
   (a) proceedings in the Court of Appeal on an application or appeal made in connection with proceedings in the Family Division; or
   (b) proceedings in the Court of Appeal from a judgment, direction, decision or order given or made in probate proceedings or family proceedings.

(4) In deciding what order (if any) to make about costs, the court must have regard to all the circumstances, including –
   (a) the conduct of all the parties;
   (b) whether a party has succeeded on part of his case, even if he has not been wholly successful; and
   (c) any payment into court or admissible offer to settle made by a party which is drawn to the court's attention (whether or not made in accordance with Part 36).

(Part 36 contains further provisions about how the court's discretion is to be exercised where a payment into court or an offer to settle is made under that Part)

(5) The conduct of the parties includes –
   (a) conduct before, as well as during, the proceedings and in particular the extent to which the parties followed any relevant pre-action protocol;

(b) whether it was reasonable for a party to raise, pursue or contest a particular allegation or issue;
(c) the manner in which a party has pursued or defended his case or a particular allegation or issue; and
(d) whether a claimant who has succeeded in his claim, in whole or in part, exaggerated his claim.

(6) The orders which the court may make under this rule include an order that a party must pay –
(a) a proportion of another party's costs;
(b) a stated amount in respect of another party's costs;
(c) costs from or until a certain date only;
(d) costs incurred before proceedings have begun;
(e) costs relating to particular steps taken in the proceedings;
(f) costs relating only to a distinct part of the proceedings; and
(g) interest on costs from or until a certain date, including a date before judgment.

(7) Where the court would otherwise consider making an order under paragraph (6) (f), it must instead, if practicable, make an order under paragraph (6)(a) or (c).

(8) Where the court has ordered a party to pay costs, it may order an amount to be paid on account before the costs are assessed.

(9) Where a party entitled to costs is also liable to pay costs the court may assess the costs which that party is liable to pay and either –
(a) set off the amount assessed against the amount the party is entitled to be paid and direct him to pay any balance; or
(b) delay the issue of a certificate for the costs to which the party is entitled until he has paid the amount which he is liable to pay.

44.3A Costs orders relating to funding arrangements

(1) The court will not assess any additional liability until the conclusion of the proceedings, or the part of the proceedings, to which the funding arrangement relates.

('Funding arrangement' and 'additional liability' are defined in rule 43.2)

(2) At the conclusion of the proceedings, or the part of the proceedings, to which the funding arrangement relates the court may –
(a) make a summary assessment of all the costs, including any additional liability;
(b) make an order for detailed assessment of the additional liability but make a summary assessment of the other costs; or
(c) make an order for detailed assessment of all the costs.

(Part 47 sets out the procedure for the detailed assessment of costs)

44.3B Limits on recovery under funding arrangements

(1) A party may not recover as an additional liability –
(a) any proportion of the percentage increase relating to the cost to the legal representative of the postponement of the payment of his fees and expenses;

(b) any provision made by a membership organisation which exceeds the likely cost to that party of the premium of an insurance policy against the risk of incurring a liability to pay the costs of other parties to the proceedings;

(c) any additional liability for any period in the proceedings during which he failed to provide information about a funding arrangement in accordance with a rule, practice direction or court order;

(d) any percentage increase where a party has failed to comply with –

(i) a requirement in the costs practice direction; or

(ii) a court order,

to disclose in any assessment proceedings the reasons for setting the percentage increase at the level stated in the conditional fee agreement.

(2) This rule does not apply in an assessment under rule 48.9 (assessment of a solicitor's bill to his client).

(Rule 3.9 sets out the circumstances the court will consider on an application for relief from a sanction for failure to comply with any rule, practice direction or court order)

44.4 Basis of assessment

(1) Where the court is to assess the amount of costs (whether by summary or detailed assessment) it will assess those costs –

(a) on the standard basis; or

(b) on the indemnity basis,

but the court will not in either case allow costs which have been unreasonably incurred or are unreasonable in amount.

(Rule 48.3 sets out how the court decides the amount of costs payable under a contract)

(2) Where the amount of costs is to be assessed on the standard basis, the court will –

(a) only allow costs which are proportionate to the matters in issue; and

(b) resolve any doubt which it may have as to whether costs were reasonably incurred or reasonable and proportionate in amount in favour of the paying party.

(Factors which the court may take into account are set out in rule 44.5)

(3) Where the amount of costs is to be assessed on the indemnity basis, the court will resolve any doubt which it may have as to whether costs were reasonably incurred or were reasonable in amount in favour of the receiving party.

(4) Where –

(a) the court makes an order about costs without indicating the basis on which the costs are to be assessed; or

(b) the court makes an order for costs to be assessed on a basis other than the standard basis or the indemnity basis, the costs will be assessed on the standard basis.

(5) Omitted.

(6) Where the amount of a solicitor's remuneration in respect of non-contentious business is regulated by any general orders made under the Solicitors Act 1974, the amount of the costs to be allowed in respect of any such business which falls to be assessed by the court will be decided in accordance with those general orders rather than this rule and rule 44.5.

44.5 Factors to be taken into account in deciding the amount of costs

(1) The court is to have regard to all the circumstances in deciding whether costs were –
  (a) if it is assessing costs on the standard basis –
    (i) proportionately and reasonably incurred; or
    (ii) were proportionate and reasonable in amount, or
  (b) if it is assessing costs on the indemnity basis –
    (i) unreasonably incurred; or
    (ii) unreasonable in amount.

(2) In particular the court must give effect to any orders which have already been made.

(3) The court must also have regard to –
  (a) the conduct of all the parties, including in particular –
    (i) conduct before, as well as during, the proceedings; and
    (ii) the efforts made, if any, before and during the proceedings in order to try to resolve the dispute;
  (b) the amount or value of any money or property involved;
  (c) the importance of the matter to all the parties;
  (d) the particular complexity of the matter or the difficulty or novelty of the questions raised;
  (e) the skill, effort, specialised knowledge and responsibility involved;
  (f) the time spent on the case; and
  (g) the place where and the circumstances in which work or any part of it was done.

(Rule 35.4(4) gives the court power to limit the amount that a party may recover with regard to the fees and expenses of an expert)

44.6 Fixed costs

A party may recover the fixed costs specified in Part 45 in accordance with that Part.

44.7 Procedure for assessing costs

Where the court orders a party to pay costs to another party (other than fixed costs) it may either –

(a) make a summary assessment of the costs; or
(b) order detailed assessment of the costs by a costs officer, unless any rule, practice direction or other enactment provides otherwise.

(The costs practice direction sets out the factors which will affect the court's decision under this rule)

44.8 Time for complying with an order for costs

A party must comply with an order for the payment of costs within 14 days of –

(a) the date of the judgment or order if it states the amount of those costs;
(b) if the amount of those costs (or part of them) is decided later in accordance with Part 47, the date of the certificate which states the amount; or
(c) in either case, such later date as the court may specify.

(Part 47 sets out the procedure for detailed assessment of costs)

44.9–44.17

[Not reproduced here.]

Part 52
Appeals

I General rules about appeals

52.1 Scope and interpretation

(1) The rules in this Part apply to appeals to –
 (a) the civil division of the Court of Appeal;
 (b) the High Court; and
 (c) a county court.

(2) This Part does not apply to an appeal in detailed assessment proceedings against a decision of an authorised court officer.

(Rules 47.20 to 47.23 deal with appeals against a decision of an authorised court officer in detailed assessment proceedings)

(3) In this Part –
 (a) 'appeal' includes an appeal by way of case stated;
 (b) 'appeal court' means the court to which an appeal is made;
 (c) 'lower court' means the court, tribunal or other person or body from whose decision an appeal is brought;
 (d) 'appellant' means a person who brings or seeks to bring an appeal;
 (e) 'respondent' means –
  (i) a person other than the appellant who was a party to the proceedings in the lower court and who is affected by the appeal; and
  (ii) a person who is permitted by the appeal court to be a party to the appeal; and
 (f) 'appeal notice' means an appellant's or respondent's notice.

(4) This Part is subject to any rule, enactment or practice direction which sets out special provisions with regard to any particular category of appeal.

52.2 Parties to comply with the practice direction

All parties to an appeal must comply with the relevant practice direction.

52.3 Permission

(1) An appellant or respondent requires permission to appeal –
 (a) where the appeal is from a decision of a judge in a county court or the High Court, except where the appeal is against –
  (i) a committal order;
  (ii) a refusal to grant habeas corpus; or
  (iii) a secure accommodation order made under section 25 of the Children Act 1989; or
 (b) as provided by the relevant practice direction.

(Other enactments may provide that permission is required for particular appeals)

(2) An application for permission to appeal may be made –

(a) to the lower court at the hearing at which the decision to be appealed was made; or

(b) to the appeal court in an appeal notice.

(Rule 52.4 sets out the time limits for filing an appellant's notice at the appeal court. Rule 52.5 sets out the time limits for filing a respondent's notice at the appeal court. Any application for permission to appeal to the appeal court must be made in the appeal notice (see rules 52.4(1) and 52.5(3))

(Rule 52.13(1) provides that permission is required from the Court of Appeal for all appeals to that court from a decision of a county court or the High Court which was itself made on appeal)

(3) Where the lower court refuses an application for permission to appeal, a further application for permission to appeal may be made to the appeal court.

(4) *Subject to paragraph (4A)*[6] where the appeal court, without a hearing, refuses permission to appeal, the person seeking permission may request the decision to be reconsidered at a hearing.

(4A) Where the Court of Appeal refuses permission to appeal without a hearing, it may, if it considers that the application is totally without merit, make an order that the person seeking permission may not request the decision to be reconsidered at a hearing. The court may not make such an order in family proceedings.

('Family proceedings' is defined by section 32 of the Matrimonial and Family Proceedings Act 1984)

(4B) Rule 3.3(5) will not apply to an order that the person seeking permission may not request the decision to be reconsidered at a hearing made under paragraph (4A).[7]

(5) A request under paragraph (4) must be filed within 7 days after service of the notice that permission has been refused.

(6) Permission to appeal may be given only where –

(a) the court considers that the appeal would have a real prospect of success; or

(b) there is some other compelling reason why the appeal should be heard.

(7) An order giving permission may –

(a) limit the issues to be heard; and

(b) be made subject to conditions.

(Rule 3.1(3) also provides that the court may make an order subject to conditions)

(Rule 25.15 provides for the court to order security for costs of an appeal)

52.4 Appellant's notice

(1) Where the appellant seeks permission from the appeal court it must be requested in the appellant's notice.

6 Inserted by the Civil Procedure (Amendment) Rules 2006 SI No 1689 r7(1)(a). In force as of 2 October 2006.

7 Inserted by the Civil Procedure (Amendment) Rules 2006 SI No 1689 r7(1)(b). In force as of 2 October 2006.

(2) The appellant must file the appellant's notice at the appeal court within –
  (a) such period as may be directed by the lower court (which may be longer or shorter than the period referred to in sub-paragraph (b)); or
  (b) where the court makes no such direction, 21 days after the date of the decision of the lower court that the appellant wishes to appeal.

(3) Unless the appeal court orders otherwise, an appellant's notice must be served on each respondent –
  (a) as soon as practicable; and
  (b) in any event not later than 7 days, after it is filed.

52.5 Respondent's notice

(1) A respondent may file and serve a respondent's notice.

(2) A respondent who –
  (a) is seeking permission to appeal from the appeal court; or
  (b) wishes to ask the appeal court to uphold the order of the lower court for reasons different from or additional to those given by the lower court, must file a respondent's notice.

(3) Where the respondent seeks permission from the appeal court it must be requested in the respondent's notice.

(4) A respondent's notice must be filed within –
  (a) such period as may be directed by the lower court; or
  (b) where the court makes no such direction, 14 days after the date in paragraph (5).

(5) The date referred to in paragraph (4) is –
  (a) the date the respondent is served with the appellant's notice where –
    (i) permission to appeal was given by the lower court; or
    (ii) permission to appeal is not required;
  (b) the date the respondent is served with notification that the appeal court has given the appellant permission to appeal; or
  (c) the date the respondent is served with notification that the application for permission to appeal and the appeal itself are to be heard together.

(6) Unless the appeal court orders otherwise a respondent's notice must be served on the appellant and any other respondent –
  (a) as soon as practicable; and
  (b) in any event not later than 7 days, after it is filed.

52.6 Variation of time

(1) An application to vary the time limit for filing an appeal notice must be made to the appeal court.

(2) The parties may not agree to extend any date or time limit set by –
  (a) these Rules;
  (b) the relevant practice direction; or
  (c) an order of the appeal court or the lower court.

(Rule 3.1(2)(a) provides that the court may extend or shorten the time for compliance with any rule, practice direction or court order (even if an application for extension is made after the time for compliance has expired))

(Rule 3.1(2)(b) provides that the court may adjourn or bring forward a hearing)

52.7 Stay

Unless –

(a) the appeal court or the lower court orders otherwise; or

(b) the appeal is from the [Immigration Appeal Tribunal] *Asylum and Immigration Tribunal*[8],

an appeal shall not operate as a stay of any order or decision of the lower court.

52.8 Amendment of appeal notice

An appeal notice may not be amended without the permission of the appeal court.

52.9 Striking out appeal notices and setting aside or imposing conditions on permission to appeal

(1) The appeal court may –
   (a) strike out the whole or part of an appeal notice;
   (b) set aside permission to appeal in whole or in part;
   (c) impose or vary conditions upon which an appeal may be brought.

(2) The court will only exercise its powers under paragraph (1) where there is a compelling reason for doing so.

(3) Where a party was present at the hearing at which permission was given he may not subsequently apply for an order that the court exercise its powers under sub-paragraphs (1)(b) or (1)(c).

52.10 Appeal court's powers

(1) In relation to an appeal the appeal court has all the powers of the lower court.

(Rule 52.1(4) provides that this Part is subject to any enactment that sets out special provisions with regard to any particular category of appeal – where such an enactment gives a statutory power to a tribunal, person or other body it may be the case that the appeal court may not exercise that power on an appeal)

(2) The appeal court has power to –
   (a) affirm, set aside or vary any order or judgment made or given by the lower court;
   (b) refer any claim or issue for determination by the lower court;
   (c) order a new trial or hearing;
   (d) make orders for the payment of interest;

8 Words in square brackets replaced and words in italics inserted by the Civil Procedure (Amendment) Rules 2006 SI No 1689 r7(1). In force as of 2 October 2006.

(e) make a costs order.

(3) In an appeal from a claim tried with a jury the Court of Appeal may, instead of ordering a new trial –

(a) make an order for damages; or

(b) vary an award of damages made by the jury.

(4) The appeal court may exercise its powers in relation to the whole or part of an order of the lower court.

(Part 3 contains general rules about the court's case management powers)

(5) If the appeal court –

(a) refuses an application for permission to appeal;

(b) strikes out an appellant's notice; or

(c) dismisses an appeal, and it considers that the application, the appellant's notice or the appeal is totally without merit, the provisions of paragraph (6) must be complied with.

(6) Where paragraph (5) applies –

(a) the court's order must record the fact that it considers the application, the appellant's notice or the appeal to be totally without merit; and

(b) the court must at the same time consider whether it is appropriate to make a civil restraint order.

52.11 Hearing of appeals

(1) Every appeal will be limited to a review of the decision of the lower court unless –

(a) a practice direction makes different provision for a particular category of appeal; or

(b) the court considers that in the circumstances of an individual appeal it would be in the interests of justice to hold a re-hearing.

(2) Unless it orders otherwise, the appeal court will not receive –

(a) oral evidence; or

(b) evidence which was not before the lower court.

(3) The appeal court will allow an appeal where the decision of the lower court was –

(a) wrong; or

(b) unjust because of a serious procedural or other irregularity in the proceedings in the lower court.

(4) The appeal court may draw any inference of fact which it considers justified on the evidence.

(5) At the hearing of the appeal a party may not rely on a matter not contained in his appeal notice unless the appeal court gives permission.

52.12 Non-disclosure of Part 36 offers and payments

(1) The fact that a Part 36 offer or Part 36 payment has been made must not be disclosed to any judge of the appeal court who is to hear or determine –

(a) an application for permission to appeal; or

(b) an appeal, until all questions (other than costs) have been determined.

(2) Paragraph (1) does not apply if the Part 36 offer or Part 36 payment is relevant to the substance of the appeal.

(3) Paragraph (1) does not prevent disclosure in any application in the appeal proceedings if disclosure of the fact that a Part 36 offer or Part 36 payment has been made is properly relevant to the matter to be decided.

II Special provisions applying to the Court of Appeal

52.13 Second appeals to the court

(1) Permission is required from the Court of Appeal for any appeal to that court from a decision of a county court or the High Court which was itself made on appeal.

(2) The Court of Appeal will not give permission unless it considers that –

(a) the appeal would raise an important point of principle or practice; or

(b) there is some other compelling reason for the Court of Appeal to hear it.

52.14 Assignment of appeals to the Court of Appeal

(1) Where the court from or to which an appeal is made or from which permission to appeal is sought ('the relevant court') considers that –

(a) an appeal which is to be heard by a county court or the High Court would raise an important point of principle or practice; or

(b) there is some other compelling reason for the Court of Appeal to hear it,

the relevant court may order the appeal to be transferred to the Court of Appeal.

(The Master of the Rolls has the power to direct that an appeal which would be heard by a county court or the High Court should be heard instead by the Court of Appeal – see section 57 of the Access to Justice Act 1999.)

(2) The Master of the Rolls or the Court of Appeal may remit an appeal to the court in which the original appeal was or would have been brought.

52.15 Judicial review appeals

(1) Where permission to apply for judicial review has been refused at a hearing in the High Court, the person seeking that permission may apply to the Court of Appeal for permission to appeal.

(2) An application in accordance with paragraph (1) must be made within 7 days of the decision of the High Court to refuse to give permission to apply for judicial review.

(3) On an application under paragraph (1), the Court of Appeal may, instead of giving permission to appeal, give permission to apply for judicial review.

(4) Where the Court of Appeal gives permission to apply for judicial review in accordance with paragraph (3), the case will proceed in the High Court unless the Court of Appeal orders otherwise.

52.16 Who may exercise the powers of the Court of Appeal

(1) A court officer assigned to the Civil Appeals Office who is –
(a) a barrister; or
(b) a solicitor
may exercise the jurisdiction of the Court of Appeal with regard to the matters set out in paragraph (2) with the consent of the Master of the Rolls.

(2) The matters referred to in paragraph (1) are –
(a) any matter incidental to any proceedings in the Court of Appeal;
(b) any other matter where there is no substantial dispute between the parties; and
(c) the dismissal of an appeal or application where a party has failed to comply with any order, rule or practice direction.

(3) A court officer may not decide an application for –
(a) permission to appeal;
(b) bail pending an appeal;
(c) an injunction;
(d) a stay of any proceedings, other than a temporary stay of any order or decision of the lower court over a period when the Court of Appeal is not sitting or cannot conveniently be convened.

(4) Decisions of a court officer may be made without a hearing.

(5) A party may request any decision of a court officer to be reviewed by the Court of Appeal.

(6) At the request of a party, a hearing will be held to reconsider a decision of –
(a) a single judge; or
(b) a court officer,
made without a hearing.

(6A) A request under paragraph (5) or (6) must be filed within 7 days after the party is served with notice of the decision.

(7) A single judge may refer any matter for a decision by a court consisting of two or more judges.

(Section 54(6) of the Supreme Court Act 1981[9] provides that there is no appeal from the decision of a single judge on an application for permission to appeal)

(Section 58(2) of the Supreme Court Act 1981[10] provides that there is no appeal to the House of Lords from decisions of the Court of Appeal that –
(a) are taken by a single judge or any officer or member of staff of that court in proceedings incidental to any cause or matter pending before the civil division of that court; and
(b) do not involve the determination of an appeal or of an application for permission to appeal, and which may be called into question by rules of court. Rules 52.16(5) and (6) provide the procedure for the calling into question of such decisions)

9 Section 54 was amended by section 59 of the Access to Justice Act 1999.
10 Section 58 was amended by section 60 of the Access to Justice Act 1999.

III Provisions about reopening appeals

52.17 Reopening of final appeals

(1) The Court of Appeal or the High Court will not reopen a final determination of any appeal unless –
  (a) it is necessary to do so in order to avoid real injustice;
  (b) the circumstances are exceptional and make it appropriate to reopen the appeal; and
  (c) there is no alternative effective remedy.

(2) In paragraphs (1), (3), (4) and (6), 'appeal' includes an application for permission to appeal.

(3) This rule does not apply to appeals to a county court.

(4) Permission is needed to make an application under this rule to reopen a final determination of an appeal even in cases where under rule 52.3(1) permission was not needed for the original appeal.

(5) There is no right to an oral hearing of an application for permission unless, exceptionally, the judge so directs.

(6) The judge will not grant permission without directing the application to be served on the other party to the original appeal and giving him an opportunity to make representations.

(7) There is no right of appeal or review from the decision of the judge on the application for permission, which is final.

(8) The procedure for making an application for permission is set out in the practice direction.

Practice Direction: Part 52

Contents of this practice direction

1.1 This Practice Direction is divided into four sections:
- Section I – General provisions about appeals
- Section II – General provisions about statutory appeals and appeals by way of case stated
- Section III – Provisions about specific appeals [*not reproduced here.*]
- Section IV – Provisions about reopening appeals

Section I – general provisions about appeals

2.1 This practice direction applies to all appeals to which Part 52 applies except where specific provision is made for appeals to the Court of Appeal.

2.2 For the purpose only of appeals to the Court of Appeal from cases in family proceedings this Practice Direction will apply with such modifications as may be required.

Routes of appeal

2A.1 The court or judge to which an appeal is to be made (subject to obtaining any necessary permission) is set out in the tables below:

Table 1[11] addresses appeals in cases other than insolvency proceedings and those cases to which Table 3 applies;
Table 2 addresses insolvency proceedings; and
Table 3 addresses certain family cases to which CPR Part 52 may apply.

The tables do not include so-called 'leap frog' appeals either to the Court of Appeal pursuant to section 57 of the Access to Justice Act 1999 or to the House of Lords pursuant to section 13 of the Administration of Justice Act 1969.

(An interactive routes of appeal guide can be found on the Court of Appeal's website at http://www.hmcourts-service.gov.uk/infoabout/coa_civil/routes_app/index.htm)

11 Table 1 reproduced with the permission of Tottel publishing.

Table 1

In this Table references to a 'Circuit judge' include a recorder or a district judge who is exercising the jurisdiction of a circuit judge with the permission of the designated civil judge in respect of that case (see: Practice Direction 2B, paragraph 11.1(d)).

For the meaning of 'final decision' for the purposes of this table see paragraphs 2A.2 and 2A.3 below.

Court	Track/nature of claim	Judge who made decision	Nature of decision	Decision
County	Unallocated Small fast	District judge	Any	Circuit judge in county court
County	CPR Pt 8 (if not allocated to any track or if simply treated as allocated to the multi-track under CPR 8.9(c))	District judge	Final	Circuit judge in county court
County	County CPR Pt 8 (if not allocated to any track or if simply treated as allocated to the multi-track under CPR 8.9(c))	District judge	Final	Circuit judge in county court
County	Multi-track	District judge	Any decision other than a final decision	Circuit judge in county court
County	Multi-track	District judge	Final decision	Court of Appeal
County	Multi-track	District judge	Final decision	Court of Appeal

Court	Track/nature of claim	Judge who made decision	Nature of decision	Decision
County	Specialist Proceedings (under the Companies Acts 1985 or 1989 or to which sections I, II or III of Part 57 or any of Parts 59, 60, 62 or 63 apply)	District judge	Any decision other than a final decision	Circuit judge in county court
County	Specialist Proceedings (under the Companies Acts 1985 or 1989 or to which sections I, II or III Part 57 or any of Parts 59, 60, 62 or 63 apply)	District judge	Final decision	Court of Appeal
County	Unallocated Small Fast	Circuit judge	Any (except final decision in specialist proceedings; see below)	Single judge of the High Court
County	Multi-track	Circuit judge	Any decision other than a final decision	Single judge of the High Court
County	CPR Pt 8 (if not allocated to any track or if simply treated as allocated to the multi-track under CPR 8.9(c))	Circuit judge	Final	Single judge of the High Court
County	Specialist Proceedings (under the Companies Acts 1985 or 1989 or to which sections I, II or III of Part 57 or any of Parts 59, 60, 62 or 63 apply)	Circuit judge	Final	Court of Appeal

Court	Track/nature of claim	Judge who made decision	Nature of decision	Decision
County	Multi-track	Circuit judge	Final decision	Court of Appeal
High Court	Multi-track	Master or district judge sitting in a District Registry	Any decision other than a final decision	Single judge of the High Court
High Court	CPR Pt 8 (if not allocated to any track or if simply treated as allocated to the multi-track under CPR 8.9(c))	Master or district judge sitting in a District Registry	Final	Single judge of the High Court
High Court	Multi-track	Master or district judge sitting in a District Registry	Final	Court of Appeal
High Court	Specialist Proceedings (under the Companies Acts 1985 or 1989 or to which sections I, II or III of Part 57 or any of Parts 58 to 63 apply)	Master or district judge sitting in a District Registry	Any decision other than a final decision	High Court
High Court	Specialist Proceedings (under the Companies Acts 1985 or 1989 orto which sections I, II or III of art 57 or any of Parts 58 to 63 apply)	Master or district judge sitting in a District Registry	Final decision	Court of Appeal
High Court	Any	High Court judge	Any	Court of Appeal

Table 2

[*Not reproduced here.*]

Table 3

[*Not reproduced here.*]

2A.2 A 'final decision' is a decision of a court that would finally determine (subject to any possible appeal or detailed assessment of costs) the entire proceedings whichever way the court decided the issues before it. Decisions made on an application to strike-out or for summary judgment are not final decisions for the purpose of determining the appropriate route of appeal (Access to Justice Act 1999 (Destination of Appeals) Order 2000, art 1). Accordingly:

(1) a case management decision;
(2) the grant or refusal of interim relief;
(3) a summary judgment;
(4) a striking out,

are not final decisions for this purpose.

2A.3 A decision of a court is to be treated as a final decision for routes of appeal purposes where it:

(1) is made at the conclusion of part of a hearing or trial which has been split into parts; and
(2) would, if it had been made at the conclusion of that hearing or trial, have been a final decision.

Accordingly, a judgment on liability at the end of a split trial is a 'final decision' for this purpose and the judgment at the conclusion of the assessment of damages following a judgment on liability is also a 'final decision' for this purpose.

2A.4 An order made:

(1) on a summary or detailed assessment of costs; or
(2) on an application to enforce a final decision,

is not a 'final decision' and any appeal from such an order will follow the routes of appeal set out in the tables above.

(Section 16(1) of the Supreme Court Act 1981 (as amended); section 77(1) of the County Courts Act 1984 (as amended); and the Access to Justice Act 1999 (Destination of Appeals) Order 2000 set out the provisions governing routes of appeal).

2A.5 (1) Where an applicant attempts to file an appellant's notice and the appeal court does not have jurisdiction to issue the notice, a court officer may notify the applicant in writing that the appeal court does not have jurisdiction in respect of the notice.

(2) Before notifying a person under paragraph (1) the court officer must confer –
  (a) with a judge of the appeal court; or,
  (b) where the Court of Appeal, Civil Division is the appeal court, with a court officer who exercises the jurisdiction of that Court under rule 52.16.

(3) Where a court officer in the Court of Appeal, Civil Division notifies a person under paragraph (1), rule 52.16(5) shall not apply.

Grounds for appeal

3.1 Rule 52.11(3) (a) and (b) sets out the circumstances in which the appeal court will allow an appeal.

3.2 The grounds of appeal should –

(1) set out clearly the reasons why rule 52.11(3)(a) or (b) is said to apply; and

(2) specify, in respect of each ground, whether the ground raises an appeal on a point of law or is an appeal against a finding of fact.

Permission to appeal

4.1 Rule 52.3 sets out the circumstances when permission to appeal is required.

4.2 The permission of –

(1) the Court of Appeal; or

(2) where the lower court's rules allow, the lower court,

is required for all appeals to the Court of Appeal except as provided for by statute or rule 52.3.

(The requirement of permission to appeal may be imposed by a practice direction – see rule 52.3(b))

4.3 Where the lower court is not required to give permission to appeal, it may give an indication of its opinion as to whether permission should be given.

(Rule 52.1(3)(c) defines 'lower court')

4.3A (1) This paragraph applies where a party applies for permission to appeal against a decision at the hearing at which the decision was made.

(2) Where this paragraph applies, the judge making the decision shall state –

(a) whether or not the judgment or order is final;

(b) whether an appeal lies from the judgment or order and, if so, to which appeal court;

(c) whether the court gives permission to appeal; and

(d) if not, the appropriate appeal court to which any further application for permission may bemade.

(Rule 40.2(4) contains requirements as to the contents of the judgment or order in these circumstances.)

4.3B Where no application for permission to appeal has been made in accordance with rule 52.3(2)(a) but a party requests further time to make such an application, the court may adjourn the hearing to give that party the opportunity to do so.

Appeals from case management decisions

4.4 Case management decisions include decisions made under rule 3.1(2) and decisions about:

(1) disclosure

(2) filing of witness statements or experts reports

(3) directions about the timetable of the claim
(4) adding a party to a claim
(5) security for costs.

4.5 Where the application is for permission to appeal from a case management decision, the court dealing with the application may take into account whether:
(1) the issue is of sufficient significance to justify the costs of an appeal;
(2) the procedural consequences of an appeal (e.g. loss of trial date) outweigh the significance of the case management decision;
(3) it would be more convenient to determine the issue at or after trial.

Court to which permission to appeal application should be made

4.6 An application for permission should be made orally at the hearing at which the decision to be appealed against is made.

4.7 Where:
(a) no application for permission to appeal is made at the hearing; or
(b) the lower court refuses permission to appeal,
an application for permission to appeal may be made to the appeal court in accordance with rules 52.3(2) and (3).

4.8 There is no appeal from a decision of the appeal court to allow or refuse permission to appeal to that court (although where the appeal court, without a hearing, refuses permission to appeal, the person seeking permission may request that decision to be reconsidered at a hearing). See section 54(4) of the Access to Justice Act and rule 52.3(2), (3), (4) and (5).

Second appeals

4.9 An application for permission to appeal from a decision of the High Court or a county court which was itself made on appeal must be made to the Court of Appeal.

4.10 If permission to appeal is granted the appeal will be heard by the Court of Appeal.

Consideration of permission without a hearing

4.11 Applications for permission to appeal may be considered by the appeal court without a hearing.

4.12 If permission is granted without a hearing the parties will be notified of that decision and the procedure in paragraphs 6.1 to 6.6 will then apply.

4.13 If permission is refused without a hearing the parties will be notified of that decision with the reasons for it. The decision is subject to the appellant's right to have it reconsidered at an oral hearing. This may be before the same judge.

4.14 A request for the decision to be reconsidered at an oral hearing must be filed at the appeal court within 7 days after service of the notice that permission has been refused. A copy of the request must be served by the appellant on the respondent at the same time.

Permission hearing

4.14A (1) This paragraph applies where an appellant, who is represented, makes a request for a decision to be reconsidered at an oral hearing.

(2) The appellant's advocate must, at least 4 days before the hearing, in a brief written statement –

(a) inform the court and the respondent of the points which he proposes to raise at the hearing;

(b) set out his reasons why permission should be granted notwithstanding the reasons given for the refusal of permission; and

(c) confirm, where applicable, that the requirements of paragraph 4.17 have been complied with (appellant in receipt of services funded by the Legal Services Commission).

4.15 Notice of a permission hearing will be given to the respondent but he is not required to attend unless the court requests him to do so.

4.16 If the court requests the respondent's attendance at the permission hearing, the appellant must supply the respondent with a copy of the appeal bundle (see paragraph 5.6A) within 7 days of being notified of the request, or such other period as the court may direct. The costs of providing that bundle shall be borne by the appellant initially, but will form part of the costs of the permission application.

Appellants in receipt of services funded by the Legal Services Commission applying for permission to appeal

4.17 Where the appellant is in receipt of services funded by the Legal Services Commission (or legally aided) and permission to appeal has been refused by the appeal court without a hearing, the appellant must send a copy of the reasons the appeal court gave for refusing permission to the relevant office of the Legal Services Commission as soon as it has been received from the court. The court will require confirmation that this has been done if a hearing is requested to re-consider the question of permission.

Limited permission

4.18 Where a court under rule 52.3(7) gives permission to appeal on some issues only, it will –

(1) refuse permission on any remaining issues; or

(2) reserve the question of permission to appeal on any remaining issues to the court hearing the appeal.

4.19 If the court reserves the question of permission under paragraph 4.18(2), the appellant must, within 14 days after service of the court's order, inform the appeal court and the respondent in writing whether he intends to pursue the reserved issues. If the appellant does intend to pursue the reserved issues, the parties must include in any time estimate for the appeal hearing, their time estimate for the reserved issues.

4.20 If the appeal court refuses permission to appeal on the remaining issues without a hearing and the applicant wishes to have that decision reconsidered at an oral hearing, the time limit in rule 52.3(5) shall apply. Any application for an extension of this time limit should be made promptly. The court hearing the appeal on the issues for which permission has been granted will not normally grant, at the appeal hearing, an application to extend the time limit in rule 52.3(5) for the remaining issues.

4.21 If the appeal court refuses permission to appeal on remaining issues at or after an oral hearing, the application for permission to appeal on those issues cannot be renewed at the appeal hearing. See section 54(4) of the Access to Justice Act 1999.

Respondents' costs of permission applications

4.22 In most cases, applications for permission to appeal will be determined without the court requesting –
(1) submissions from, or
(2) if there is an oral hearing, attendance by the respondent.

4.23 Where the court does not request submissions from or attendance by the respondent, costs will not normally be allowed to a respondent who volunteers submissions or attendance.

4.24 Where the court does request –
(1) submissions from; or
(2) attendance by the respondent,
the court will normally allow the respondent his costs if permission is refused.

Appellant's notice

5.1 An appellant's notice must be filed and served in all cases. Where an application for permission to appeal is made to the appeal court it must be applied for in the appellant's notice.

Human rights

5.1A (1) This paragraph applies where the appellant seeks –
(a) to rely on any issue under the Human Rights Act 1998; or
(b) a remedy available under that Act,
for the first time in an appeal.
(2) The appellant must include in his appeal notice the information required by paragraph 15.1 of the practice direction supplementing Part 16.
(3) Paragraph 15.2 of the practice direction supplementing Part 16 applies as if references to a statement of case were to the appeal notice.

5.1B CPR rule 19.4A and the practice direction supplementing it shall apply as if references to the case management conference were to the application for permission to appeal.
(The practice direction to Part 19 provides for notice to be given and parties joined in certain circumstances to which this paragraph applies)

Extension of time for filing appellant's notice

5.2 Where the time for filing an appellant's notice has expired, the appellant must –
(a) file the appellant's notice; and
(b) include in that appellant's notice an application for an extension of time.

The appellant's notice should state the reason for the delay and the steps taken prior to the application being made.

5.3 Where the appellant's notice includes an application for an extension of time and permission to appeal has been given or is not required the respondent has the right to be heard on that application. He must be served with a copy of the appeal bundle (see paragraph 5.6A). However, a respondent who unreasonably opposes an extension of time runs the risk of being ordered to pay the appellant's costs of that application.

5.4 If an extension of time is given following such an application the procedure at paragraphs 6.1 to 6.6 applies.

Applications

5.5 Notice of an application to be made to the appeal court for a remedy incidental to the appeal (eg an interim remedy under rule 25.1 or an order for security for costs) may be included in the appeal notice or in a Part 23 application notice.

(Rule 25.15 deals with security for costs of an appeal)

(Paragraph 11 of this practice direction contains other provisions relating to applications)

Documents

5.6 (1) This paragraph applies to every case except where the appeal –
- (a) relates to a claim allocated to the small claims track; and
- (b) is being heard in a county court or the High Court.

(Paragraph 5.8 applies where this paragraph does not apply)

(2) The appellant must file the following documents together with an appeal bundle (see paragraph 5.6A) with his appellant's notice –
- (a) two additional copies of the appellant's notice for the appeal court; and
- (b) one copy of the appellant's notice for each of the respondents;
- (c) one copy of his skeleton argument for each copy of the appellant's notice that is filed (see paragraph 5.9);
- (d) a sealed copy of the order being appealed;
- (e) a copy of any order giving or refusing permission to appeal, together with a copy of the judge's reasons for allowing or refusing permission to appeal;
- (f) any witness statements or affidavits in support of any application included in the appellant's notice.
- (g) a copy of the order allocating a case to a track (if any).

5.6A (1) An appellant must include in his appeal bundle the following documents:
- (a) a sealed copy of the appellant's notice;
- (b) a sealed copy of the order being appealed;
- (c) a copy of any order giving or refusing permission to appeal, together with a copy of the judge's reasons for allowing or refusing permission to appeal;

(d) any affidavit or witness statement filed in support of any application included in the appellant's notice;
(e) a copy of his skeleton argument;
(f) a transcript or note of judgment (see paragraph 5.12), and in cases where permission to appeal was given by the lower court or is not required those parts of any transcript of evidence which are directly relevant to any question at issue on the appeal;
(g) the claim form and statements of case (where relevant to the subject of the appeal);
(h) any application notice (or case management documentation) relevant to the subject of the appeal;
(i) in cases where the decision appealed was itself made on appeal (eg from district judge to circuit judge), the first order, the reasons given and the appellant's notice used to appeal from that order;
(j) in the case of judicial review or a statutory appeal, the original decision which was the subject of the application to the lower court;
(k) in cases where the appeal is from a Tribunal, a copy of the Tribunal's reasons for the decision, a copy of the decision reviewed by the Tribunal and the reasons for the original decision and any document filed with the Tribunal setting out the grounds of appeal from that decision;
(l) any other documents which the appellant reasonably considers necessary to enable the appeal court to reach its decision on the hearing of the application or appeal; and
(m) such other documents as the court may direct.

(2) All documents that are extraneous to the issues to be considered on the application or the appeal must be excluded. The appeal bundle may include affidavits, witness statements, summaries, experts' reports and exhibits but only where these are directly relevant to the subject matter of the appeal.

(3) Where the appellant is represented, the appeal bundle must contain a certificate signed by his solicitor, counsel or other representative to the effect that he has read and understood paragraph (2) above and that the composition of the appeal bundle complies with it.

5.7 Where it is not possible to file all the above documents, the appellant must indicate which documents have not yet been filed and the reasons why they are not currently available. The appellant must then provide a reasonable estimate of when the missing document or documents can be filed and file them as soon as reasonably practicable.

Small claims

5.8 (1) This paragraph applies where –
(a) the appeal relates to a claim allocated to the small claims track; and
(b) the appeal is being heard in a county court or the High Court.

(1A) An appellant's notice must be filed and served in Form N164.

(2) The appellant must file the following documents with his appellant's notice –

(a) a sealed copy of the order being appealed; and

(b) any order giving or refusing permission to appeal, together with a copy of the reasons for that decision.

(3) The appellant may, if relevant to the issues to be determined on the appeal, file any other document listed in paragraph 5.6 or 5.6A in addition to the documents referred to in subparagraph (2).

(4) The appellant need not file a record of the reasons for judgment of the lower court with his appellant's notice unless sub-paragraph (5) applies.

(5) The court may order a suitable record of the reasons for judgment of the lower court (see paragraph 5.12) to be filed –

(a) to enable it to decide if permission should be granted; or

(b) if permission is granted to enable it to decide the appeal.

Skeleton arguments

5.9 (1) The appellant's notice must, subject to (2) and (3) below, be accompanied by a skeleton argument. Alternatively the skeleton argument may be included in the appellant's notice. Where the skeleton argument is so included it will not form part of the notice for the purposes of rule 52.8.

(2) Where it is impracticable for the appellant's skeleton argument to accompany the appellant's notice it must be filed and served on all respondents within 14 days of filing the notice.

(3) An appellant who is not represented need not file a skeleton argument but is encouraged to do so since this will be helpful to the court.

Content of skeleton arguments

5.10 (1) A skeleton argument must contain a numbered list of the points which the party wishes to make. These should both define and confine the areas of controversy. Each point should be stated as concisely as the nature of the case allows.

(2) A numbered point must be followed by a reference to any document on which the party wishes to rely.

(3) A skeleton argument must state, in respect of each authority cited –

(a) the proposition of law that the authority demonstrates; and

(b) the parts of the authority (identified by page or paragraph references) that support the proposition.

(4) If more than one authority is cited in support of a given proposition, the skeleton argument must briefly state the reason for taking that course.

(5) The statement referred to in sub-paragraph (4) should not materially add to the length of the skeleton argument but should be sufficient to demonstrate, in the context of the argument –

(a) the relevance of the authority or authorities to that argument; and

(b) that the citation is necessary for a proper presentation of that argument.

(6) The cost of preparing a skeleton argument which –

(a) does not comply with the requirements set out in this paragraph; or

(b) was not filed within the time limits provided by this Practice Direction (or any further time granted by the court), will not be allowed on assessment except to the extent that the court otherwise directs.

(7) A skeleton argument filed in the Court of Appeal, Civil Division on behalf of the appellant should contain in paragraph 1 the advocate's time estimate for the hearing of the appeal. [12]

5.11 The appellant should consider what other information the appeal court will need. This may include a list of persons who feature in the case or glossaries of technical terms. A chronology of relevant events will be necessary in most appeals.

Suitable record of the judgment

5.12 Where the judgment to be appealed has been officially recorded by the court, an approved transcript of that record should accompany the appellant's notice. Photocopies will not be accepted for this purpose. However, where there is no officially recorded judgment, the following documents will be acceptable:

Written judgments

(1) Where the judgment was made in writing a copy of that judgment endorsed with the judge's signature.

Note of judgment

(2) When judgment was not officially recorded or made in writing a note of the judgment (agreed between the appellant's and respondent's advocates) should be submitted for approval to the judge whose decision is being appealed. If the parties cannot agree on a single note of the judgment, both versions should be provided to that judge with an explanatory letter. For the purpose of an application for permission to appeal the note need not be approved by the respondent or the lower court judge.

Advocates' notes of judgments where the appellant is unrepresented

(3) When the appellant was unrepresented in the lower court it is the duty of any advocate for the respondent to make his/her note of judgment promptly available, free of charge to the appellant where there is no officially recorded judgment or if the court so directs. Where the appellant was represented in the lower court it is the duty of his/her own former advocate to make his/her note available in these circumstances. The appellant should submit the note of judgment to the appeal court.

Reasons for judgment in tribunal cases

(4) A sealed copy of the Tribunal's reasons for the decision.

5.13 An appellant may not be able to obtain an official transcript or other suitable record of the lower court's decision within the time within which the appellant's notice must be filed. In such cases the appellant's notice must still be completed to the best of the appellant's ability on the basis of the documentation available. However it may be amended subsequently with the permission of the appeal court.

12 Words in italics inserted by the 42nd update to the Civil Procedures Rules. In force 2 October 2006. See www.dca.gov.uk.

Advocates' notes of judgments

5.14 Advocates' brief (or, where appropriate, refresher) fee includes:
(1) remuneration for taking a note of the judgment of the court;
(2) having the note transcribed accurately;
(3) attempting to agree the note with the other side if represented;
(4) submitting the note to the judge for approval where appropriate;
(5) revising it if so requested by the judge,
(6) providing any copies required for the appeal court, instructing solicitors and lay client; and
(7) providing a copy of his note to an unrepresented appellant.

Transcripts or notes of evidence

5.15 When the evidence is relevant to the appeal an official transcript of the relevant evidence must be obtained. Transcripts or notes of evidence are generally not needed for the purpose of determining an application for permission to appeal.

Notes of evidence

5.16 If evidence relevant to the appeal was not officially recorded, a typed version of the judge's notes of evidence must be obtained.

Transcripts at public expense

5.17 Where the lower court or the appeal court is satisfied that –
(1) an unrepresented appellant; or
(2) an appellant whose legal representation is provided free of charge to the appellant and not funded by the Community Legal Service;
is in such poor financial circumstances that the cost of a transcript would be an excessive burden the court may certify that the cost of obtaining one official transcript should be borne at public expense.

5.18 In the case of a request for an official transcript of evidence or proceedings to be paid for at public expense, the court must also be satisfied that there are reasonable grounds for appeal. Whenever possible a request for a transcript at public expense should be made to the lower court when asking for permission to appeal.

Filing and service of appellant's notice

5.19 Rule 52.4 sets out the procedure and time limits for filing and serving an appellant's notice. The appellant must file the appellant's notice at the appeal court within such period as may be directed by the lower court which should not normally exceed 28 days or, where the lower court directs no such period, within 14 days of the date of the decision that the appellant wishes to appeal.
(Rule 52.15 sets out the time limit for filing an application for permission to appeal against the refusal of the High Court to grant permission to apply for judicial review)

5.19 *Rule 52.4 sets out the procedure and time limits for filing and serving an appellant's notice. The appellant must file the appellant's notice at the appeal court* *within such period as may be directed by the lower court which should not normally exceed 35 days or, where the lower court directs no such period, within 21 days of the date of the decision that the appellant wishes to appeal. (Rule 52.15 sets out the time limit for filing an application for permission to appeal against the refusal of the High Court to grant permission to apply for judicial review).*[13]

5.20 Where the lower court judge announces his decision and reserves the reasons for his judgment or order until a later date, he should, in the exercise of powers under rule 52.4(2)(a), fix a period for filing the appellant's notice at the appeal court that takes this into account.

5.21 (1) Except where the appeal court orders otherwise a sealed copy of the appellant's notice, including any skeleton arguments must be served on all respondents in accordance with the timetable prescribed by rule 52.4(3) except where this requirement is modified by paragraph 5.9(2) in which case the skeleton argument should be served as soon as it is filed.

(2) The appellant must, as soon as practicable, file a certificate of service of the documents referred to in paragraph (1).

5.22 Unless the court otherwise directs a respondent need not take any action when served with an appellant's notice until such time as notification is given to him that permission to appeal has been given.

5.23 The court may dispense with the requirement for service of the notice on a respondent. Any application notice seeking an order under rule 6.9 to dispense with service should set out the reasons relied on and be verified by a statement of truth.

5.24 (1) Where the appellant is applying for permission to appeal in his appellant's notice, he must serve on the respondents his appellant's notice and skeleton argument (but not the appeal bundle), unless the appeal court directs otherwise.

(2) Where permission to appeal –

(a) has been given by the lower court; or

(b) is not required,

the appellant must serve the appeal bundle on the respondents with the appellant's notice.

Amendment of appeal notice

5.25 An appeal notice may be amended with permission. Such an application to amend and any application in opposition will normally be dealt with at the hearing unless that course would cause unnecessary expense or delay in which case a request should be made for the application to amend to be heard in advance.

Procedure after permission is obtained

6.1 This paragraph sets out the procedure where:

(1) permission to appeal is given by the appeal court; or

(2) the appellant's notice is filed in the appeal court and –

13 Para 5.19 replaced by the words in italics by the 42nd update to the Civil Procedure Rules. In force 2 October 2006. See www.dca.gov.uk.

(a) permission was given by the lower court; or
(b) permission is not required.

6.2 If the appeal court gives permission to appeal, the appeal bundle must be served on each of the respondents within 7 days of receiving the order giving permission to appeal.

(Part 6 (service of documents) provides rules on service)

6.3 The appeal court will send the parties –

(1) notification of –
   (a) the date of the hearing or the period of time (the 'listing window') during which the appeal is likely to be heard; and
   (b) in the Court of Appeal, the date by which the appeal will be heard (the 'hear by date');
(2) where permission is granted by the appeal court a copy of the order giving permission to appeal; and
(3) any other directions given by the court.

6.3A (1) Where the appeal court grants permission to appeal, the appellant must add the following documents to the appeal bundle –
   (a) the respondent's notice and skeleton argument (if any);
   (b) those parts of the transcripts of evidence which are directly relevant to any question at issue on the appeal;
   (c) the order granting permission to appeal and, where permission to appeal was granted at an oral hearing, the transcript (or note) of any judgment which was given; and
   (d) any document which the appellant and respondent have agreed to add to the appeal bundle in accordance with paragraph 7.11.

(2) Where permission to appeal has been refused on a particular issue, the appellant must remove from the appeal bundle all documents that are relevant only to that issue.

Appeal Questionnaire in the Court of Appeal

6.4 The Court of Appeal will send an Appeal Questionnaire to the appellant when it notifies him of the matters referred to in paragraph 6.3.

6.5 The appellant must complete and file the Appeal Questionnaire within 14 days of the date of the letter of notification of the matters in paragraph 6.3. The Appeal Questionnaire must contain:

(1) if the appellant is legally represented, the advocate's time estimate for the hearing of the appeal;
(2) where a transcript of evidence is relevant to the appeal, confirmation as to what parts of a transcript of evidence have been ordered where this is not already in the bundle of documents;
(3) confirmation that copies of the appeal bundle are being prepared and will be held ready for the use of the Court of Appeal and an undertaking that they will be supplied to the court on request. For the purpose of these bundles photocopies of the transcripts will be accepted;
(4) confirmation that copies of the Appeal Questionnaire and the appeal bundle have been served on the respondents and the date of that service.

Time estimates

6.6 The time estimate included in an Appeal Questionnaire must be that of the advocate who will argue the appeal. It should exclude the time required by the court to give judgment. If the respondent disagrees with the time estimate, the respondent must inform the court within 7 days of receipt of the Appeal Questionnaire. In the absence of such notification the respondent will be deemed to have accepted the estimate proposed on behalf of the appellant.

Respondent

7.1 A respondent who wishes to ask the appeal court to vary the order of the lower court in any way must appeal and permission will be required on the same basis as for an appellant.

(Paragraph 3.2 applies to grounds of appeal by a respondent.)

7.2 A respondent who wishes only to request that the appeal court upholds the judgment or order of the lower court whether for the reasons given in the lower court or otherwise does not make an appeal and does not therefore require permission to appeal in accordance with rule 52.3(1).

(Paragraph 7.6 requires a respondent to file a skeleton argument where he wishes to address the appeal court)

7.3 (1) A respondent who wishes to appeal or who wishes to ask the appeal court to uphold the order of the lower court for reasons different from or additional to those given by the lower court must file a respondent's notice.

(2) If the respondent does not file a respondent's notice, he will not be entitled, except with the permission of the court, to rely on any reason not relied on in the lower court.

.3A Paragraphs 5.1A, 5.1B and 5.2 of this practice direction (Human Rights and extension for time for filing appellant's notice) also apply to a respondent and a respondent's notice.

Time limits

7.4 The time limits for filing a respondent's notice are set out in rule 52.5 (4) and (5).

7.5 Where an extension of time is required the extension must be requested in the respondent's notice and the reasons why the respondent failed to act within the specified time must be included.

7.6 Except where paragraph 7.7A applies, the respondent must file a skeleton argument for the court in all cases where he proposes to address arguments to the court. The respondent's skeleton argument may be included within a respondent's notice. Where a skeleton argument is included within a respondent's notice it will not form part of the notice for the purposes of rule 52.8.

7.7 (1) A respondent who –

(a) files a respondent's notice; but

(b) does not include his skeleton argument within that notice,

must file and serve his skeleton argument within 14 days of filing the notice.

(2) A respondent who does not file a respondent's notice but who files a skeleton argument must file and serve that skeleton argument at least 7 days before the appeal hearing.

(Rule 52.5(4) sets out the period for filing and serving a respondent's notice)

7.7A (1) Where the appeal relates to a claim allocated to the small claims track and is being heard in a county court or the High Court, the respondent may file a skeleton argument but is not required to do so.

(2) A respondent who is not represented need not file a skeleton argument but is encouraged to do so in order to assist the court.

7.7B The respondent must –

(1) serve his skeleton argument on –

(a) the appellant; and

(b) any other respondent,

at the same time as he files it at the court; and

(2) file a certificate of service.

Content of skeleton arguments

7.8 A respondent's skeleton argument must conform to the directions at paragraphs 5.10 and 5.11 with any necessary modifications. It should, where appropriate, answer the arguments set out in the appellant's skeleton argument.

Applications within respondent's notices

7.9 A respondent may include an application within a respondent's notice in accordance with paragraph 5.5 above.

Filing respondent's notices and skeleton arguments

7.10 (1) The respondent must file the following documents with his respondent's notice in every case:

(a) two additional copies of the respondent's notice for the appeal court; and

(b) one copy each for the appellant and any other respondents.

(2) The respondent may file a skeleton argument with his respondent's notice and –

(a) where he does so he must file two copies; and

(b) where he does not do so he must comply with paragraph 7.7.

7.11 If the respondent wishes to rely on any documents which he reasonably considers necessary to enable the appeal court to reach its decision on the appeal in addition to those filed by the appellant, he must make every effort to agree amendments to the appeal bundle with the appellant.

7.12 (1) If the representatives for the parties are unable to reach agreement, the respondent may prepare a supplemental bundle.

(2) If the respondent prepares a supplemental bundle he must file it, together with the requisite number of copies for the appeal court, at the appeal court –

(a) with the respondent's notice; or
(b) if a respondent's notice is not filed, within 21 days after he is served with the appeal bundle.

7.13 The respondent must serve –
(1) the respondent's notice;
(2) his skeleton argument (if any); and
(3) the supplemental bundle (if any), on –
(a) the appellant; and
(b) any other respondent,
at the same time as he files them at the court.

Appeals to the High Court

Application

8.1 This paragraph applies where an appeal lies to a High Court judge from the decision of a county court or a district judge of the High Court.

8.2 The following table sets out the following venues for each circuit –
(a) Appeal centres – court centres where appeals to which this paragraph applies may be filed, managed and heard. Paragraphs 8.6 to 8.8 provide for special arrangements in relation to the South Eastern Circuit.
(b) Hearing only centres – court centres where appeals to which this paragraph applies may be heard by order made at an appeal centre (see paragraph 8.10).

Circuit	Appeal centres	Hearing-only centres
Midland Circuit	Birmingham Nottingham	Lincoln Leicester Northampton Stafford
North-Eastern Circuit	Leeds Newcastle Sheffield	Teeside
Northern Circuit	Manchester Liverpool Preston	Carlisle
Wales and Chester Circuit	Cardiff Swansea Chester	
Western Circuit	Bristol Exeter Winchester	Truro Plymouth

South Eastern Circuit	Royal Courts of Justice Lewes Luton Norwich Reading Chelmsford St Albans Maidstone Oxford

Venue for appeals and filing of notices on circuits other than the South Eastern Circuit

8.3 Paragraphs 8.4 and 8.5 apply where the lower court is situated on a circuit other than the South Eastern Circuit.

8.4 The appellant's notice must be filed at an appeal centre on the circuit in which the lower court is situated. The appeal will be managed and heard at that appeal centre unless the appeal court orders otherwise.

8.5 A respondent's notice must be filed at the appeal centre where the appellant's notice was filed unless the appeal has been transferred to another appeal centre, in which case it must be filed at that appeal centre.

Venue for appeals and filing of notices on the South Eastern Circuit

8.6 Paragraphs 8.7 and 8.8 apply where the lower court is situated on the South Eastern Circuit.

8.7 The appellant's notice must be filed at an appeal centre on the South Eastern Circuit. The appeal will be managed and heard at the Royal Courts of Justice unless the appeal court orders otherwise. An order that an appeal is to be managed or heard at another appeal centre may not be made unless the consent of the Presiding Judge of the circuit in charge of civil matters has been obtained.

8.8 A respondent's notice must be filed at the Royal Courts of Justice unless the appeal has been transferred to another appeal centre, in which case it must be filed at that appeal centre.

General provisions

8.9 The appeal court may transfer an appeal to another appeal centre (whether or not on the same circuit). In deciding whether to do so the court will have regard to the criteria in rule 30.3 (criteria for a transfer order). The appeal court may do so either on application by a party or of its own initiative. Where an appeal is transferred under this paragraph, notice of transfer must be served on every person on whom the appellant's notice has been served. An appeal may not be transferred to an appeal centre on another circuit, either for management or hearing, unless the consent of the Presiding Judge of that circuit in charge of civil matters has been obtained.

8.10 Directions may be given for –

(a) an appeal to be heard at a hearing only centre; or

(b) an application in an appeal to be heard at any other venue, instead of at the appeal centre managing the appeal.

8.11 Unless a direction has been made under 8.10, any application in the appeal must be made at the appeal centre where the appeal is being managed.

8.12 The appeal court may adopt all or any part of the procedure set out in paragraphs 6.4 to 6.6.

8.13 Where the lower court is a county court:

(1) subject to paragraph (1A), appeals and applications for permission to appeal will be heard by a High Court Judge or by a person authorised under paragraphs (1), (2) or (4) of the Table in section 9(1) of the Supreme Court Act 1981 to act as a judge of the High Court;

(1A) an appeal or application for permission to appeal from the decision of a Recorder in the county court may be heard by a Designated Civil Judge who is authorised under paragraph (5) of the Table in section 9(1) of the Supreme Court Act 1981 to act as a judge of the High Court; and

(2) other applications in the appeal may be heard and directions in the appeal may be given either by a High Court Judge or by any person authorised under section 9 of the Supreme Court Act 1981 to act as a judge of the High Court.

8.14 In the case of appeals from Masters or district judges of the High Court, appeals, applications for permission and any other applications in the appeal may be heard and directions in the appeal may be given by a High Court Judge or by any person authorised under section 9 of the Supreme Court Act 1981 to act as a judge of the High Court.

Appeals to a judge of a county court from a District judge

8A.1 The Designated Civil Judge in consultation with his Presiding Judges has responsibility for allocating appeals from decisions of district judges to circuit judges.

Re-hearings

9.1 The hearing of an appeal will be a re-hearing (as opposed to a review of the decision of the lower court) if the appeal is from the decision of a minister, person or other body and the minister, person or other body –

(1) did not hold a hearing to come to that decision; or

(2) held a hearing to come to that decision, but the procedure adopted did not provide for the consideration of evidence.

Appeals transferred to the Court of Appeal

10.1 Where an appeal is transferred to the Court of Appeal under rule 52.14 the Court of Appeal may give such additional directions as are considered appropriate.

Applications

11.1 Where a party to an appeal makes an application whether in an appeal notice or by Part 23 application notice, the provisions of Part 23 will apply.

11.2 The applicant must file the following documents with the notice

(1) one additional copy of the application notice for the appeal court and one copy for each of the respondents;

(2) where applicable a sealed copy of the order which is the subject of the main appeal;
(3) a bundle of documents in support which should include:
  (a) the Part 23 application notice; and
  (b) any witness statements and affidavits filed in support of the application notice.

Disposing of applications or appeals by consent

Dismissal of applications or appeals by consent

12.1 These paragraphs do not apply where any party to the proceedings is a child or patient.

12.2 Where an appellant does not wish to pursue an application or an appeal, he may request the appeal court for an order that his application or appeal be dismissed. Such a request must contain a statement that the appellant is not a child or patient. If such a request is granted it will usually be on the basis that the appellant pays the costs of the application or appeal.

12.3 If the appellant wishes to have the application or appeal dismissed without costs, his request must be accompanied by a consent signed by the respondent or his legal representative stating that the respondent is not a child or patient and consents to the dismissal of the application or appeal without costs.

12.4 Where a settlement has been reached disposing of the application or appeal, the parties may make a joint request to the court stating that none of them is a child or patient, and asking that the application or appeal be dismissed by consent. If the request is granted the application or appeal will be dismissed.

Allowing unopposed appeals or applications on paper

13.1 The appeal court will not normally make an order allowing an appeal unless satisfied that the decision of the lower court was wrong, but the appeal court may set aside or vary the order the lower court with consent and without determining the merits of the appeal, if it is satisfied that there are good and sufficient reasons for doing so. Where the appeal court is requested all parties to allow an application or an appeal the court may consider the request on the papers. The request should state that none of the parties is a child or patient and set out the relevant history of the proceedings and the matters relied on as justifying the proposed order and be accompanied by a copy of the proposed order.

Procedure for consent orders and agreements to pay periodical payments involving a child or patient

13.2 Where one of the parties is a child or patient –
(1) a settlement relating to an appeal or application; or
(2) in a personal injury claim for damages for future pecuniary loss, an agreement reached at the appeal stage to pay periodical payments, requires the court's approval.

Child

13.3 In cases involving a child a copy of the proposed order signed by the parties' solicitors should be sent to the appeal court, together with an opinion from the advocate acting on behalf of child.

Patient

13.4 Where a party is a patient the same procedure will be adopted, but the documents filed should also include any relevant reports prepared for the Court of Protection and a document evidencing formal approval by that court where required.

Periodical payments

13.5 Where periodical payments for future pecuniary loss have been negotiated in a personal injury case which is under appeal, the documents filed should include those which would be required in the case of a personal injury claim for damages for future pecuniary loss dealt with at first instance. Details can be found in the Practice Direction which supplements Part 21.

Summary assessment of costs

14.1 Costs are likely to be assessed by way of summary assessment at the following hearings:

(1) contested directions hearings;

(2) applications for permission to appeal at which the respondent is present;

(3) dismissal list hearings in the Court of Appeal at which the respondent is present;

(4) appeals from case management decisions; and

(5) appeals listed for one day or less.

14.2 Parties attending any of the hearings referred to in paragraph 14.1 should be prepared to deal with the summary assessment.

Other special provisions regarding the Court of Appeal

Filing of Documents

15.1 (1) The documents relevant to proceedings in the Court of Appeal, Civil Division must be filed in the Civil Appeals Office Registry, Room E307, Royal Courts of Justice, Strand, London, WC2A 2LL.

(2) The Civil Appeals Office will not serve documents and where service is required by the CPR or this practice direction it must be effected by the parties.

15.1A (1) A party may file by email –

(a) an appellant's notice;

(b) a respondent's notice;

(c) an application notice,

in the Court of Appeal, Civil Division, using the email account +specified in the 'Guidelines for filing by Email' which appear on the Court of Appeal, Civil Division website at www.civilappeals.gov.uk.

(2) A party may only file a notice in accordance with paragraph (1) where he is permitted to do so by the 'Guidelines for filing by Email'.

15.1B *(1) A party to an appeal in the Court of Appeal, Civil Division may file –*

(a) an appellant's notice;

(b) a respondent's notice; or

(c) an application notice,

electronically using the online forms service on the Court of Appeal, Civil Division website at www.civilappeals.gov.uk.

(2) A party may only file a notice in accordance with paragraph (1) where he is permitted to so do by the 'Guidelines for filing electronically'. The Guidelines for filing electronically may be found on the Court of Appeal, Civil Division website.

(3) The online forms service will assist the user in completing a document accurately but the user is responsible for ensuring that the rules and practice directions relating to the document have been complied with. Transmission by the service does not guarantee that the document will be accepted by the Court of Appeal, Civil Division.

(4) A party using the online forms service in accordance with this paragraph is responsible for ensuring that the transmission or any document attached to it is filed within any relevant time limits.

(5) Parties are advised not to transmit electronically any correspondence or documents of a confidential or sensitive nature, as security cannot be guaranteed.

(6) Where a party wishes to file a document containing a statement of truth electronically, that party should retain the document containing the original signature and file with the court a version of the document on which the name of the person who has signed the statement of truth is typed underneath the statement.[14]

Core bundles

15.2 In cases where the appeal bundle comprises more than 500 pages, exclusive of transcripts, the appellant's solicitors must, after consultation with the respondent's solicitors, also prepare and file with the court, in addition to copies of the appeal bundle (as amended in accordance with paragraph 7.11) the requisite number of copies of a core bundle.

15.3 (1) The core bundle must be filed within 28 days of receipt of the order giving permission to appeal or, where permission to appeal was granted by the lower court or is not required, within 28 days of the date of service of the appellant's notice on the respondent.

(2) The core bundle –

(a) must contain the documents which are central to the appeal; and

(b) must not exceed 150 pages.

Preparation of bundles

15.4 The provisions of this paragraph apply to the preparation of appeal bundles,

14 Para 15(1)B inserted by the 42nd update to the Civil Procedure Rules. In force as of 2 October 2006. See www.dca.gov.uk.

supplemental respondents' bundles where the parties are unable to agree amendments to the appeal bundle, and core bundles.

(1) **Rejection of bundles.** Where documents are copied unnecessarily or bundled incompletely, costs may be disallowed. Where the provisions of this Practice Direction as to the preparation or delivery of bundles are not followed the bundle may be rejected by the court or be made the subject of a special costs order.

(2) **Avoidance of duplication.** No more than one copy of any document should be included unless there is a good reason for doing otherwise (such as the use of a separate core bundle – see paragraph 15.2).

(3) **Pagination**

(a) Bundles must be paginated, each page being numbered individually and consecutively. The pagination used at trial must also be indicated. Letters and other documents should normally be included in chronological order. (An exception to consecutive page numbering arises in the case of core bundles where it may be preferable to retain the original numbering).

(b) Page numbers should be inserted in bold figures at the bottom of the page and in a form that can be clearly distinguished from any other pagination on the document.

(4) **Format and presentation**

(a) Where possible the documents should be in A4 format. Where a document has to be read across rather than down the page, it should be so placed in the bundle as to ensure that the text starts nearest the spine.

(b) Where any marking or writing in colour on a document is important, the document must be copied in colour or marked up correctly in colour.

(c) Documents which are not easily legible should be transcribed and the transcription marked and placed adjacent to the document transcribed.

(d) Documents in a foreign language should be translated and the translation marked and placed adjacent to the document translated. The translation should be agreed or, if it cannot be agreed, each party's proposed translation should be included.

(e) The size of any bundle should be tailored to its contents. A large lever arch file should not be used for just a few pages nor should files of whatever size be overloaded.

(f) Where it will assist the Court of Appeal, different sections of the file may be separated by cardboard or other tabbed dividers so long as these are clearly indexed. Where, for example, a document is awaited when the appeal bundle is filed, a single sheet of paper can be inserted after a divider, indicating the nature of the document awaited. For example, 'Transcript of evidence of Mr J Smith (to follow)'.

(5) **Binding**

(a) All documents, with the exception of transcripts, must be bound together. This may be in a lever arch file, ring binder or plastic folder.

Plastic sleeves containing loose documents must not be used. Binders and files must be strong enough to withstand heavy use.

(b) Large documents such as plans should be placed in an easily accessible file. Large documents which will need to be opened up frequently should be inserted in a file larger than A4 size.

(6) Indices and labels

(a) An index must be included at the front of the bundle listing all the documents and providing the page references for each. In the case of documents such as letters, invoices or bank statements, they may be given a general description.

(b) Where the bundles consist of more than one file, an index to all the files should be included in the first file and an index included for each file. Indices should, if possible, be on a single sheet. The full name of the case should not be inserted on the index if this would waste space.

Documents should be identified briefly but properly.

(7) Identification

(a) Every bundle must be clearly identified, on the spine and on the front cover, with the name of the case and the Court of Appeal's reference. Where the bundle consists of more than one file, each file must be numbered on the spine, the front cover and the inside of the front cover.

(b) Outer labels should use large lettering eg ' Appeal Bundle A' or 'Core Bundle'. The full title of the appeal and solicitors' names and addresses should be omitted. A label should be used on the front as well as on the spine.

(8) Staples etc. All staples, heavy metal clips etc, must be removed.

(9) Statements of case

(a) Statements of case should be assembled in 'chapter' form – i.e claim followed by particulars of claim, followed by further information, irrespective of date.

(b) Redundant documents, eg particulars of claim overtaken by amendments, requests for further information recited in the answers given, should generally be excluded.

(10) New Documents

(a) Before a new document is introduced into bundles which have already been delivered to the court, steps should be taken to ensure that it carries an appropriate bundle/page number so that it can be added to the court documents. It should not be stapled and it should be prepared with punch holes for immediate inclusion in the binders in use.

(b) If it is expected that a large number of miscellaneous new documents will from time to time be introduced, there should be a special tabbed empty loose-leaf file for that purpose. An index should be produced for this file, updated as necessary.

(11) Inter-solicitor correspondence. Since inter-solicitor correspondence is unlikely to be required for the purposes of an appeal, only those letters which will need to be referred to should be copied.

(12) **Sanctions for non-compliance.** If the appellant fails to comply with the requirements as to the provision of bundles of documents, the application or appeal will be referred for consideration to be given as to why it should not be dismissed for failure to so comply.

Master in the Court of Appeal, Civil Division

15.5 When the Head of the Civil Appeals Office acts in a judicial capacity pursuant to rule 52.16, he shall be known as Master. Other eligible officers may also be designated by the Master of the Rolls to exercise judicial authority under rule 52.16 and shall then be known as Deputy Masters.

Respondent to notify Civil Appeals Office whether he intends to file respondent's notice

15.6 A respondent must, no later than 21 days after the date he is served with notification that –

(1) permission to appeal has been granted; or

(2) the application for permission to appeal and the appeal are to be heard together, inform the Civil Appeals Office and the appellant in writing whether –

(a) he proposes to file a respondent's notice appealing the order or seeking to uphold the order for reasons different from, or additional to, those given by the lower court; or

(b) he proposes to rely on the reasons given by the lower court for its decision.

(Paragraph 15.11B requires all documents needed for an appeal hearing, including a respondent's skeleton argument, to be filed at least 7 days before the hearing)

Listing and hear-by dates

15.7 The management of the list will be dealt with by the listing officer under the direction of the Master.

15.8 The Civil Appeals List of the Court of Appeal is divided as follows:

- *The applications list* – applications for permission to appeal and other applications.
- *The appeals list* – appeals where permission to appeal has been given or where an appeal lies without permission being required where a hearing date is fixed in advance. (Appeals in this list which require special listing arrangements will be assigned to the special fixtures list)
- *The expedited list* – appeals or applications where the Court of Appeal has directed an expedited hearing. The current practice of the Court of Appeal is summarised in *Unilever plc v Chefaro Proprietaries Ltd (Practice Note)* [1995]1 WLR 243.
- *The stand-out list* – Appeals or applications which, for good reason, are not at present ready to proceed and have been stood out by judicial direction.
- *The second fixtures list* – [see paragraph 15.9A(1) below].
- *The second fixtures list* – if an appeal is designated as a 'second fixture' it

means that a hearing date is arranged in advance on the express basis that the list is fully booked for the period in question and therefore the case will be heard only if a suitable gap occurs in the list.

- *The short-warned list* – appeals which the court considers may be prepared for the hearing by an advocate other than the one originally instructed with a half day's notice, or such other period as the court may direct.

Special provisions relating to the short-warned list

15.9 (1) Where an appeal is assigned to the short-warned list, the Civil Appeals Office will notify the parties' solicitors in writing. The court may abridge the time for filing any outstanding bundles in an appeal assigned to this list.

(2) The solicitors for the parties must notify their advocate and their client as soon as the Civil Appeals Office notifies them that the appeal has been assigned to the short-warned list.

(3) The appellant may apply in writing for the appeal to be removed from the short-warned list within 14 days of notification of its assignment. The application will be decided by a Lord Justice, or the Master, and will only be granted for the most compelling reasons.

(4) The Civil Appeals Listing Officer may place an appeal from the short-warned list 'on call' from a given date and will inform the parties' advocates accordingly.

(5) An appeal which is 'on call' may be listed for hearing on half a day's notice or such longer period as the court may direct.

(6) Once an appeal is listed for hearing from the short warned list it becomes the immediate professional duty of the advocate instructed in the appeal, if he is unable to appear at the hearing, to take all practicable measures to ensure that his lay client is represented at the hearing by an advocate who is fully instructed and able to argue the appeal.

Special provisions relating to the special fixtures list

15.9A (1) The special fixtures list is a sub-division of the appeals list and is used to deal with appeals that may require special listing arrangements, such as the need to list a number of cases before the same constitution, in a particular order, during a particular period or at a given location.

(2) The Civil Appeals Office will notify the parties' representatives, or the parties if acting in person, of the particular arrangements that will apply. The notice –

(a) will give details of the specific period during which a case is scheduled to be heard; and

(b) may give directions in relation to the filing of any outstanding documents.

(3) The listing officer will notify the parties' representatives of the precise hearing date as soon as practicable. While every effort will be made to accommodate the availability of counsel, the requirements of the court will prevail.

Requests for directions

15.10 To ensure that all requests for directions are centrally monitored and correctly allocated, all requests for directions or rulings (whether relating to listing or any other matters) should be made to the Civil Appeals Office. Those seeking directions or rulings must not approach the supervising Lord Justice either directly, or via his or her clerk.

Bundles of authorities

15.11 (1) Once the parties have been notified of the date fixed for the hearing, the appellant's advocate must, after consultation with his opponent, file a bundle containing photocopies of the authorities upon which each side will rely at the hearing.

(2) The bundle of authorities should, in general –

(a) have the relevant passages of the authorities marked;

(b) not include authorities for propositions not in dispute; and

(c) not contain more than 10 authorities unless the scale of the appeal warrants more extensive citation.

(3) The bundle of authorities must be filed –

(a) at least 7 days before the hearing; or

(b) where the period of notice of the hearing is less than 7 days, immediately.

(4) If, through some oversight, a party intends, during the hearing, to refer to other authorities the parties may agree a second agreed bundle. The appellant's advocate must file this bundle at least 48 hours before the hearing commences.

(5) A bundle of authorities must bear a certification by the advocates responsible for arguing the case that the requirements of sub-paragraphs (3) to (5) of paragraph 5.10 have been complied with in respect of each authority included.

Supplementary skeleton arguments

15.11A (1) A supplementary skeleton argument on which the appellant wishes to rely must be filed at least 14 days before the hearing.

(2) A supplementary skeleton argument on which the respondent wishes to rely must be filed at least 7 days before the hearing.

(3) All supplementary skeleton arguments must comply with the requirements set out in paragraph 5.10.

(4) At the hearing the court may refuse to hear argument from a party not contained in a skeletonargument filed within the relevant time limit set out in this paragraph.

Papers for the appeal hearing

15.11B (1) All the documents which are needed for the appeal hearing must be filed at least 7 days before the hearing. Where a document has not been filed 10 days before the hearing a reminder will be sent by the Civil Appeals Office.

(2) Any party who fails to comply with the provisions of paragraph (1) may be required to attend before the Presiding Lord Justice to seek permission to proceed with, or to oppose, the appeal.

Disposal of bundles of documents

15.11C (1) Where the court has determined a case, the official transcriber will retain one set of papers. The Civil Appeals Office will destroy any remaining sets of papers not collected within 21 days of –

(a) where one or more parties attend the hearing, the date of the court's decision;

(b) where there is no attendance, the date of the notification of court's decision.

(2) The parties should ensure that bundles of papers supplied to the court do not contain original documents (other than transcripts). The parties must ensure that they –

(a) bring any necessary original documents to the hearing; and

(b) retrieve any original documents handed up to the court before leaving the court.

(3) The court will retain application bundles where permission to appeal has been granted. Where permission is refused the arrangements in sub-paragraph (1) will apply.

(4) Where a single Lord Justice has refused permission to appeal on paper, application bundles will not be destroyed until after the time limit for seeking a hearing has expired.

Availability of Reserved judgments before hand down

15.12 This section applies where the presiding Lord Justice is satisfied that the result of the appeal will attract no special degree of confidentiality or sensitivity.

15.13 A copy of the written judgment will be made available to the parties' legal advisers by 4 pm on the second working day before judgment is due to be pronounced or such other period as the court may direct. This can be shown, in confidence, to the parties but only for the purpose of obtaining instructions and on the strict understanding that the judgment, or its effect, is not to be disclosed to any other person. A working day is any day on which the Civil Appeals Office is open for business.

15.14 The appeal will be listed for judgment in the cause list and the judgment handed down at the appropriate time.

Attendance of advocates on the handing down of a reserved judgment

15.15 Where any consequential orders are agreed, the parties' advocates need not attend on the handing down of a reserved judgment. Where an advocate does attend the court may, if it considers such attendance unnecessary, disallow the costs of the attendance. If the parties do not indicate that they intend to attend, the judgment may be handed down by a single member of the court.

Agreed orders following judgment

15.16 The parties must, in respect of any draft agreed orders –

(a) fax a copy to the clerk to the presiding Lord Justice; and
(b) file four copies in the Civil Appeals Office,

no later than 12 noon on the working day before the judgment is handed down.

15.17 A copy of a draft order must bear the Court of Appeal case reference, the date the judgment is to be handed down and the name of the presiding Lord Justice.

Corrections to the draft judgment

15.18 Any proposed correction to the draft judgment should be sent to the clerk to the judge who prepared the draft with a copy to any other party.

Application for leave to appeal

15.19 Where a party wishes to apply for leave to appeal to the House of Lords under section 1 of the Administration of Justice (Appeals) Act 1934 the court may deal with the application on the basis of written submissions.

15.20 A party must, in relation to his submission –

(a) fax a copy to the clerk to the presiding Lord Justice; and
(b) file four copies in the Civil Appeals Office,

no later than 12 noon on the working day before the judgment is handed down.

15.21 A copy of a submission must bear the Court of Appeal case reference, the date the judgment is to be handed down and the name of the presiding Lord Justice.

Section II – general provisions about statutory appeals and appeals by way of case stated

16.1 This section of this practice direction contains general provisions about statutory appeals (paragraphs 17.1–17.6) and appeals by way of case stated (paragraphs 18.1–18.20).

16.2 Where any of the provisions in this section provide for documents to be filed at the appeal court, these documents are in addition to any documents required under Part 52 or section I of this practice direction.

Statutory appeals

17.1 This part of this section –

(1) applies where under any enactment an appeal (other than by way of case stated) lies to the court from a Minister of State, government department, tribunal or other person ('statutory appeals'); and
(2) is subject to any provision about a specific category of appeal in any enactment or Section III of this practice direction.

Part 52

17.2 Part 52 applies to statutory appeals with the following amendments:

Filing of appellant's notice

17.3 The appellant must file the appellant's notice at the appeal court within 28 days after the date of the decision of the lower court he wishes to appeal.

17.4 Where a statement of the reasons for a decision is given later than the notice of that decision, the period for filing the appellant's notice is calculated from the date on which the statement is received by the appellant.

Service of appellant's notice

17.5 In addition to the respondents to the appeal, the appellant must serve the appellant's notice in accordance with rule 52.4(3) on the chairman of the tribunal, Minister of State, government department or other person from whose decision the appeal is brought.

Right of minister, etc to be heard on the appeal

17.6 Where the appeal is from an order or decision of a Minister of State or government department, the Minister or department, as the case may be, is entitled to attend the hearing and to make representations to the court.

Appeals by way of case stated

18.1 This part of this section –

(1) applies where under any enactment –

   (a) an appeal lies to the court by way of case stated; or

   (b) a question of law may be referred to the court by way of case stated; and

(2) is subject to any provision about to a specific category of appeal in any enactment or Section III of this practice direction.

Part 52

18.2 Part 52 applies to appeals by way of case stated subject to the following amendments.

Case stated by Crown Court or Magistrates' Court
Application to state a case

18.3 The procedure for applying to the Crown Court or a Magistrates' Court to have a case stated for the opinion of the High Court is set out in the Crown Court Rules 1982 and the Magistrates' Courts Rules 1981 respectively.

Filing of appellant's notice

18.4 The appellant must file the appellant's notice at the appeal court within 10 days after he receives the stated case.

Documents to be lodged

The appellant must lodge the following documents with his appellant's notice:

(1) the stated case;

(2) a copy of the judgment, order or decision in respect of which the case has been stated; and

(3) where the judgment, order or decision in respect of which the case has been stated was itself given or made on appeal, a copy of the judgment, order or decision appealed from.

Service of appellant's notice

18.6 The appellant must serve the appellant's notice and accompanying documents on all respondents within 4 days after they are filed or lodged at the appeal court.

Case stated by Minister, government department, tribunal or other person

Application to state a case

18.7 The procedure for applying to a Minister, government department, tribunal or other person ('Minister or tribunal etc.') to have a case stated for the opinion of the court may be set out in –

(1) the enactment which provides for the right of appeal; or

(2) any rules of procedure relating to the Minister or tribunal etc.

Signing of stated case by Minister or tribunal etc

18.8 A case stated by a tribunal must be signed by the chairman or president of the tribunal. A case stated by any other person must be signed by that person or by a person authorised to do so.

Service of stated case by Minister or tribunal etc

18.9 The Minister or tribunal etc. must serve the stated case on –

(1) the party who requests the case to be stated; or

(2) the party as a result of whose application to the court, the case was stated.

18.10 Where an enactment provides that a Minister or tribunal etc. may state a case or refer a question of law to the court by way of case stated without a request being made, the Minister or tribunal etc must –

(1) serve the stated case on those parties that the Minister or tribunal etc. considers appropriate; and

(2) give notice to every other party to the proceedings that the stated case has been served on the party named and on the date specified in the notice.

Filing and service of appellant's notice

18.11 The party on whom the stated case was served must file the appellant's notice and the stated case at the appeal court and serve copies of the notice and stated case on –

(1) the Minister or tribunal etc. who stated the case; and

(2) every party to the proceedings to which the stated case relates,

within 14 days after the stated case was served on him.

18.12 Where paragraph 18.10 applies the Minister or tribunal etc. must –

(1) file an appellant's notice and the stated case at the appeal court; and

(2) serve copies of those documents on the persons served under paragraph 18.10 within 14 days after stating the case.

18.13 Where –

(1) a stated case has been served by the Minister or tribunal etc. in accordance with paragraph 18.9; and

(2) the party on whom the stated case was served does not file an appellant's notice in accordance with paragraph 18.11, any other party may file an appellant's notice with the stated case at the appeal court and serve a copy of the notice and the case on the persons listed in paragraph 18.11 within the period of time set out in paragraph 18.14.

18.14 The period of time referred to in paragraph 18.13 is 14 days from the last day on which the party on whom the stated case was served may file an appellant's notice in accordance with paragraph 18.11.

Amendment of stated case

18.15 The court may amend the stated case or order it to be returned to the Minister or tribunal etc. for amendment and may draw inferences of fact from the facts stated in the case.

Right of Minister etc. to be heard on the appeal

18.16 Where the case is stated by a Minister or government department, that Minister or department, as the case may be, is entitled to appear on the appeal and to make representations to the court.

Application for order to state a case

18.17 An application to the court for an order requiring a minister or tribunal etc. to state a case for the decision of the court, or to refer a question of law to the court by way of case stated must be made to the court which would be the appeal court if the case were stated.

18.18 An application to the court for an order directing a Minister or tribunal etc. to –

(1) state a case for determination by the court; or

(2) refer a question of law to the court by way of case stated, must be made in accordance with

18.19 The application notice must contain –

(1) the grounds of the application;

(2) the question of law on which it is sought to have the case stated; and

(3) any reasons given by the minister or tribunal etc. for his or its refusal to state a case.

18.20 The application notice must be filed at the appeal court and served on –

(1) the minister, department, secretary of the tribunal or other person as the case may be; and

(2) every party to the proceedings to which the application relates,

within 14 days after the appellant receives notice of the refusal of his request to state a case.

Section III: provisions about specific appeals

[*Not reproduced here.*]

Section IV – provisions about reopening appeals

Reopening of final appeals

25.1 This paragraph applies to applications under rule 52.17 for permission to reopen a final determination of an appeal.

25.2 In this paragraph, 'appeal' includes an application for permission to appeal.

25.3 Permission must be sought from the court whose decision the applicant wishes to reopen.

25.4 The application for permission must be made by application notice and supported by written evidence, verified by a statement of truth.

25.5 A copy of the application for permission must not be served on any other party to the original appeal unless the court so directs.

25.6 Where the court directs that the application for permission is to be served on another party, that party may within 14 days of the service on him of the copy of the application file and serve a written statement either supporting or opposing the application.

25.7 The application for permission, and any written statements supporting or opposing it, will be considered on paper by a single judge, and will be allowed to proceed only if the judge so directs.

Part 54
Judicial review and statutory review

I Judicial review

54.1 Scope and interpretation

(1) This Section of this Part contains rules about judicial review.
(2) In this Section –
  (a) a 'claim for judicial review' means a claim to review the lawfulness of –
    (i) an enactment; or
    (ii) a decision, action or failure to act in relation to the exercise of a public function.
  (b) revoked
  (c) revoked
  (d) revoked
  (e) 'the judicial review procedure' means the Part 8 procedure as modified by this Section;
  (f) 'interested party' means any person (other than the claimant and defendant) who is directly affected by the claim; and
  (g) 'court' means the High Court, unless otherwise stated.

(Rule 8.1(6)(b) provides that a rule or practice direction may, in relation to a specified type of proceedings, disapply or modify any of the rules set out in Part 8 as they apply to those proceedings)

54.2 When this section must be used

The judicial review procedure must be used in a claim for judicial review where the claimant is seeking –
(a) a mandatory order;
(b) a prohibiting order;
(c) a quashing order; or
(d) an injunction under section 30 of the Supreme Court Act 1981 (restraining a person from acting in any office in which he is not entitled to act).

54.3 When this section may be used

(1) The judicial review procedure may be used in a claim for judicial review where the claimant is seeking –
  (a) a declaration; or
  (b) an injunction.

(Section 31(2) of the Supreme Court Act 1981 sets out the circumstances in which the court may grant a declaration or injunction in a claim for judicial review)

(Where the claimant is seeking a declaration or injunction in addition to one of the remedies listed in rule 54.2, the judicial review procedure must be used)

(2) A claim for judicial review may include a claim for damages, restitution or the recovery of a sum due but may not seek such a remedy alone.

(Section 31(4) of the Supreme Court Act sets out the circumstances in which the court may award damages, restitution or the recovery of a sum due on a claim for judicial review)

54.4 Permission required

The court's permission to proceed is required in a claim for judicial review whether started under this Section or transferred to the Administrative Court.

54.5 Time limit for filing claim form

(1) The claim form must be filed –
    (a) promptly; and
    (b) in any event not later than 3 months after the grounds to make the claim first arose.
(2) The time limit in this rule may not be extended by agreement between the parties.
(3) This rule does not apply when any other enactment specifies a shorter time limit for making the claim for judicial review.

54.6 Claim form

(1) In addition to the matters set out in rule 8.2 (contents of the claim form) the claimant must also state –
    (a) the name and address of any person he considers to be an interested party;
    (b) that he is requesting permission to proceed with a claim for judicial review; and
    (c) any remedy (including any interim remedy) he is claiming.

(Part 25 sets out how to apply for an interim remedy)

(2) The claim form must be accompanied by the documents required by the relevant practice direction.

54.7 Service of claim form

The claim form must be served on –
(a) the defendant; and
(b) unless the court otherwise directs, any person the claimant considers to be an interested party, within 7 days after the date of issue.

54.8 Acknowledgment of service

(1) Any person served with the claim form who wishes to take part in the judicial review must file an acknowledgment of service in the relevant practice form in accordance with the following provisions of this rule.
(2) Any acknowledgment of service must be –
    (a) filed not more than 21 days after service of the claim form; and
    (b) served on –
        (i) the claimant; and

(ii) subject to any direction under rule 54.7(b), any other person named in the claim form, as soon as practicable and, in any event, not later than 7 days after it is filed.

(3) The time limits under this rule may not be extended by agreement between the parties.

(4) The acknowledgment of service –

(a) must –

(i) where the person filing it intends to contest the claim, set out a summary of his grounds for doing so; and

(ii) state the name and address of any person the person filing it considers to be an interested party; and

(b) may include or be accompanied by an application for directions.

(5) Rule 10.3(2) does not apply.

54.9 Failure to file acknowledgment of service

(1) Where a person served with the claim form has failed to file an acknowledgment of service in accordance with rule 54.8, he –

(a) may not take part in a hearing to decide whether permission should be given unless the court allows him to do so; but

(b) provided he complies with rule 54.14 or any other direction of the court regarding the filing and service of –

(i) detailed grounds for contesting the claim or supporting it on additional grounds; and

(ii) any written evidence,

may take part in the hearing of the judicial review.

(2) Where that person takes part in the hearing of the judicial review, the court may take his failure to file an acknowledgment of service into account when deciding what order to make about costs.

(3) Rule 8.4 does not apply.

54.10 Permission given

(1) Where permission to proceed is given the court may also give directions.

(2) Directions under paragraph (1) may include a stay(GL) of proceedings to which the claim relates.

(Rule 3.7 provides a sanction for the non-payment of the fee payable when permission to proceed has been given)

54.11 Service of order giving or refusing permission

The court will serve –

(a) the order giving or refusing permission; and

(b) any directions,

on –

(i) the claimant;

(ii) the defendant; and

(iii) any other person who filed an acknowledgment of service.

54.12 Permission decision without a hearing

(1) This rule applies where the court, without a hearing –
   (a) refuses permission to proceed; or
   (b) gives permission to proceed –
      (i) subject to conditions; or
      (ii) on certain grounds only.

(2) The court will serve its reasons for making the decision when it serves the order giving or refusing permission in accordance with rule 54.11.

(3) The claimant may not appeal but may request the decision to be reconsidered at a hearing.

(4) A request under paragraph (3) must be filed within 7 days after service of the reasons under paragraph (2).

(5) The claimant, defendant and any other person who has filed an acknowledgment of service will be given at least 2 days' notice of the hearing date.

54.13 Defendant etc may not apply to set aside

Neither the defendant nor any other person served with the claim form may apply to set aside an order giving permission to proceed.

54.14 Response

(1) A defendant and any other person served with the claim form who wishes to contest the claim or support it on additional grounds must file and serve –
   (a) detailed grounds for contesting the claim or supporting it on additional grounds; and
   (b) any written evidence,

   within 35 days after service of the order giving permission.

(2) The following rules do not apply –
   (a) rule 8.5 (3) and 8.5 (4)(defendant to file and serve written evidence at the same time as acknowledgment of service); and
   (b) rule 8.5 (5) and 8.5(6) (claimant to file and serve any reply within 14 days).

54.15 Where claimant seeks to rely on additional grounds

The court's permission is required if a claimant seeks to rely on grounds other than those for which he has been given permission to proceed.

54.16 Evidence

(1) Rule 8.6 (1) does not apply.

(2) No written evidence may be relied on unless –
   (a) it has been served in accordance with any –
      (i) rule under this Section; or
      (ii) direction of the court; or
   (b) the court gives permission.

54.17 Court's powers to hear any person

(1) Any person may apply for permission –
   (a) to file evidence; or
   (b) make representations at the hearing of the judicial review.
(2) An application under paragraph (1) should be made promptly.

54.18 Judicial review may be decided without a hearing

The court may decide the claim for judicial review without a hearing where all the parties agree.

54.19 Court's powers in respect of quashing orders

(1) This rule applies where the court makes a quashing order in respect of the decision to which the claim relates.
(2) The court may –
   (a) remit the matter to the decision-maker; and
   (b) direct it to reconsider the matter and reach a decision in accordance with the judgment of the court.
(3) Where the court considers that there is no purpose to be served in remitting the matter to the decision-maker it may, subject to any statutory provision, take the decision itself.

(Where a statutory power is given to a tribunal, person or other body it may be the case that the court cannot take the decision itself)

54.20 Transfer

The court may
(a) order a claim to continue as if it had not been started under this Section; and
(b) where it does so, give directions about the future management of the claim.

(Part 30 (transfer) applies to transfers to and from the Administrative Court)

II Statutory review under the Nationality, Immigration and Asylum Act 2002

[*Not reproduced here.*]

III Applications for statutory review under section 103a of the Nationality, Immigration and Asylum Act 2002

[*Not reproduced here.*]

Practice direction: Part 54

Judicial review

This Practice Direction supplements Part 54

1.1 In addition to Part 54 and this practice direction attention is drawn to:

- section 31 of the Supreme Court Act 1981; and
- the Human Rights Act 1998

The court

2.1 Part 54 claims for judicial review are dealt with in the Administrative Court.

2.2 Where the claim is proceeding in the Administrative Court in London, documents must be filed at the Administrative Court Office, the Royal Courts of Justice, Strand, London, WC2A 2LL.

2.3 Where the claim is proceeding in the Administrative Court in Wales (see paragraph 3.1), documents must be filed at the Civil Justice Centre, 2 Park Street, Cardiff, CF10 1ET.

Urgent applications

2.4 Where urgency makes it necessary for the claim for judicial review to be made outside London or Cardiff, the Administrative Court Office in London should be consulted (if necessary, by telephone) prior to filing the claim form.

Judicial review claims in Wales

3.1 A claim for judicial review may be brought in the Administrative Court in Wales where the claim or any remedy sought involves:

(1) a devolution issue arising out of the Government of Wales Act 1998; or

(2) an issue concerning the National Assembly for Wales, the Welsh executive, or any Welsh public body (including a Welsh local authority) (whether or not it involves a devolution issue).

3.2 Such claims may also be brought in the Administrative Court at the Royal Courts of Justice.

Rule 54.5 – Time limit for filing claim form

4.1 Where the claim is for a quashing order in respect of a judgment, order or conviction, the date when the grounds to make the claim first arose, for the purposes of rule 54.5(1)(b), is the date of that judgment, order or conviction.

Rule 54.6 – claim form

Interested parties

5.1 Where the claim for judicial review relates to proceedings in a court or tribunal, any other parties to those proceedings must be named in the claim form as interested parties under rule 54.6(1)(a) (and therefore served with the claim form under rule 54.7(b)).

5.2 For example, in a claim by a defendant in a criminal case in the Magistrates or Crown Court for judicial review of a decision in that case, the prosecution must always be named as an interested party.

Human rights

5.3 Where the claimant is seeking to raise any issue under the Human Rights Act 1998, or seeks a remedy available under that Act, the claim form must include the information required by paragraph 15 of the practice direction supplementing Part 16.

Devolution issues

5.4 Where the claimant intends to raise a devolution issue, the claim form must:

(1) specify that the applicant wishes to raise a devolution issue and identify the relevant provisions of the Government of Wales Act 1998, the Northern Ireland Act 1998 or the Scotland Act 1998; and

(2) contain a summary of the facts, circumstances and points of law on the basis of which it is alleged that a devolution issue arises.

5.5 In this practice direction 'devolution issue' has the same meaning as in paragraph 1, schedule 8 to the Government of Wales Act 1998; paragraph 1, schedule 10 to the Northern Ireland Act 1998; and paragraph 1, schedule 6 of the Scotland Act 1998.

Claim form

5.6 The claim form must include or be accompanied by –

(1) a detailed statement of the claimant's grounds for bringing the claim for judicial review;

(2) a statement of the facts relied on;

(3) any application to extend the time limit for filing the claim form;

(4) any application for directions.

5.7 In addition, the claim form must be accompanied by

(1) any written evidence in support of the claim or application to extend time;

(2) a copy of any order that the claimant seeks to have quashed;

(3) where the claim for judicial review relates to a decision of a court or tribunal, an approved copy of the reasons for reaching that decision;

(4) copies of any documents on which the claimant proposes to rely;

(5) copies of any relevant statutory material; and

(6) a list of essential documents for advance reading by the court (with page references to the passages relied on).

5.8 Where it is not possible to file all the above documents, the claimant must indicate which documents have not been filed and the reasons why they are not currently available.

Bundle of documents

5.9 The claimant must file two copies of a paginated and indexed bundle containing all the documents referred to in paragraphs 5.6 and 5.7.

5.10 Attention is drawn to rules 8.5(1) and 8.5(7).

Rule 54.7 – service of claim form

6.1 Except as required by rules 54.11 or 54.12(2), the Administrative Court will not serve documents and service must be effected by the parties.

Rule 54.8 – acknowledgment of service

7.1 Attention is drawn to rule 8.3(2) and the relevant practice direction and to rule 10.5.

Rule 54.10 – permission given

Directions

8.1 Case management directions under rule 54.10(1) may include directions about serving the claim form and any evidence on other persons.

8.2 Where a claim is made under the Human Rights Act 1998, a direction may be made for giving notice to the Crown or joining the Crown as a party. Attention is drawn to rule 19.4A and paragraph 6 of the Practice Direction supplementing Section I of Part 19.

8.3 A direction may be made for the hearing of the claim for judicial review to be held outside London or Cardiff. Before making any such direction the judge will consult the judge in charge of the Administrative Court as to its feasibility.

Permission without a hearing

8.4 The court will generally, in the first instance, consider the question of permission without a hearing.

Permission hearing

8.5 Neither the defendant nor any other interested party need attend a hearing on the question of permission unless the court directs otherwise.

8.6 Where the defendant or any party does attend a hearing, the court will not generally make an order for costs against the claimant.

Rule 54.11 – service of order giving or refusing permission

9.1 An order refusing permission or giving it subject to conditions or on certain grounds only must set out or be accompanied by the court's reasons for coming to that decision.

Rule 54.14 – response

10.1 Where the party filing the detailed grounds intends to rely on documents not already filed, he must file a paginated bundle of those documents when he files the detailed grounds.

Rule 54.15 – where claimant seeks to rely on additional grounds

11.1 Where the claimant intends to apply to rely on additional grounds at the hearing of the claim for judicial review, he must give notice to the court and to any other person served with the claim form no later than 7 clear days before the hearing (or the warned date where appropriate).

Rule 54.16 – evidence

12.1 Disclosure is not required unless the court orders otherwise.

Rule 54.17 – court's powers to hear any person

13.1 Where all the parties consent, the court may deal with an application under rule 54.17 without a hearing.

13.2 Where the court gives permission for a person to file evidence or make representations at the hearing of the claim for judicial review, it may do so on conditions and may give case management directions.

13.3 An application for permission should be made by letter to the Administrative Court office, identifying the claim, explaining who the applicant is and indicating why and in what form the applicant wants to participate in the hearing.

13.4 If the applicant is seeking a prospective order as to costs, the letter should say what kind of order and on what grounds.

13.5 Applications to intervene must be made at the earliest reasonable opportunity, since it will usually be essential not to delay the hearing.

Rule 54.20 – transfer

14.1 Attention is drawn to rule 30.5.

14.2 In deciding whether a claim is suitable for transfer to the Administrative Court, the court will consider whether it raises issues of public law to which Part 54 should apply.

Skeleton arguments

15.1 The claimant must file and serve a skeleton argument not less than 21 working days before the date of the hearing of the judicial review (or the warned date).

15.2 The defendant and any other party wishing to make representations at the hearing of the judicial review must file and serve a skeleton argument not less than 14 working days before the date of the hearing of the judicial review (or the warned date).

15.3 Skeleton arguments must contain:

(1) a time estimate for the complete hearing, including delivery of judgment;

(2) a list of issues;

(3) a list of the legal points to be taken (together with any relevant authorities with page references to the passages relied on);

(4) a chronology of events (with page references to the bundle of documents (see paragraph 16.1);
(5) a list of essential documents for the advance reading of the court (with page references to the passages relied on) (if different from that filed with the claim form) and a time estimate for that reading; and
(6) a list of persons referred to.

Bundle of documents to be filed

16.1 The claimant must file a paginated and indexed bundle of all relevant documents required for the hearing of the judicial review when he files his skeleton argument.

16.2 The bundle must also include those documents required by the defendant and any other party who is to make representations at the hearing.

Agreed final order

17.1 If the parties agree about the final order to be made in a claim for judicial review, the claimant must file at the court a document (with 2 copies) signed by all the parties setting out the terms of the proposed agreed order together with a short statement of the matters relied on as justifying the proposed agreed order and copies of any authorities or statutory provisions relied on.

17.2 The court will consider the documents referred to in paragraph 17.1 and will make the order if satisfied that the order should be made.

17.3 If the court is not satisfied that the order should be made, a hearing date will be set.

17.4 Where the agreement relates to an order for costs only, the parties need only file a document signed by all the parties setting out the terms of the proposed order.

[*Practice Direction 54B not reproduced here.*]

Practice direction: Part 54C

References by the Legal Services Commission

1.1 This Practice Direction applies where the Legal Services Commission ('the Commission) refers to the High Court a question that arises on a review of a decision about an individual's financial eligibility for a representation order in criminal proceedings under the Criminal Defence Service (Financial Eligibility) Regulations 2006.

1.2 A reference of a question by the Legal Services Commission must be made to the Administrative Court.

1.3 Part 52 does not apply to a review under this paragraph.

1.4 The Commission must-

(a) file at the court –

(i) the individual's applications for a representation order and for a review, and any supporting documents;

(ii) a copy of the question on which the court's decision is sought; and

(iii) a statement of the Commission's observations on the question; and

(b) serve a copy of the question and the statement on the individual.

1.5 The individual may file representations on the question at the court within 7 days after service on him of the copy of the question and the statement.

1.6 The question will be decided without a hearing unless the court directs otherwise.

Part 65
Proceedings relating to anti-social behaviour and harassment

65.1 Scope of this Part

This Part contains rules –

(a) in Section I, about injunctions under the Housing Act 1996;

(b) in Section II, about applications by local authorities under section 91(3) of the Anti-social Behaviour Act 2003 for a power of arrest to be attached to an injunction;

(c) in Section III, about claims for demotion orders under the Housing Act 1985 and Housing Act 1988 and proceedings relating to demoted tenancies;

(d) in Section IV, about anti-social behaviour orders under the Crime and Disorder Act 1998;

(e) in Section V, about claims under section 3 of the Protection from Harassment Act 1997 .

I Housing Act 1996 injunctions

65.2 Scope of this section and interpretation

(1) This Section applies to applications for an injunction and other related proceedings under Chapter III of Part V of the Housing Act 1996 (injunctions against anti-social behaviour).

(2) In this Section 'the 1996 Act' means the Housing Act 1996.

65.3 Applications for an injunction

(1) An application for an injunction under Chapter III of Part V of the 1996 Act shall be subject to the Part 8 procedure as modified by this rule and the relevant practice direction.

(2) The application must be –

  (a) made by a claim form in accordance with the relevant practice direction;

  (b) commenced in the court for the district in which the defendant resides or the conduct complained of occurred; and

  (c) supported by a witness statement which must be filed with the claim form.

(3) The claim form must state –

  (a) the matters required by rule 8.2; and

  (b) the terms of the injunction applied for.

(4) An application under this rule may be made without notice and where such an application without notice is made –

  (a) the witness statement in support of the application must state the reasons why notice has not been given; and

  (b) the following rules do not apply –

    (i) 8.3;

(ii) 8.4;
(iii) 8.5(2) to (6);
(iv) 8.6(1);
(v) 8.7; and
(vi) 8.8.

(5) In every application made on notice, the application notice must be served, together with a copy of the witness statement, by the claimant on the defendant personally.

(6) An application made on notice may be listed for hearing before the expiry of the time for the defendant to file an acknowledgement of service under rule 8.3, and in such a case –

(a) the claimant must serve the application notice and witness statement on the defendant not less than two days before the hearing; and

(b) the defendant may take part in the hearing whether or not he has filed an acknowledgment of service.

65.4 Injunction containing provisions to which a power of arrest is attached

(1) In this rule 'relevant provision' means a provision of an injunction to which a power of arrest is attached.

(Sections 153C(3) and 153D(4) of the 1996 Act confer powers to attach a power of arrest to an injunction)

(2) Where an injunction contains one or more relevant provisions –

(a) each relevant provision must be set out in a separate paragraph of the injunction; and

(b) subject to paragraph (3), the claimant must deliver a copy of the relevant provisions to any police station for the area where the conduct occurred.

(3) Where the injunction has been granted without notice, the claimant must not deliver a copy of the relevant provisions to any police station for the area where the conduct occurred before the defendant has been served with the injunction containing the relevant provisions.

(4) Where an order is made varying or discharging any relevant provision, the claimant must –

(a) immediately inform the police station to which a copy of the relevant provisions was delivered under paragraph (2)(b); and

(b) deliver a copy of the order to any police station so informed.

65.5 Application for warrant of arrest under section 155(3) of the 1996 Act

(1) An application for a warrant of arrest under section 155(3) of the 1996 Act must be made in accordance with Part 23 and may be made without notice.

(2) An applicant for a warrant of arrest under section 155(3) of the 1996 Act must –

(a) file an affidavit setting out grounds for the application with the application notice; or

(b) give oral evidence as to the grounds for the application at the hearing.

65.6 Proceedings following arrest

(1) This rule applies where a person is arrested pursuant to –
  (a) a power of arrest attached to a provision of an injunction; or
  (b) a warrant of arrest.

(2) The judge before whom a person is brought following his arrest may –
  (a) deal with the matter; or
  (b) adjourn the proceedings.

(3) Where the proceedings are adjourned the judge may remand the arrested person in accordance with section 155(2)(b) or (5) of the 1996 Act.

(4) Where the proceedings are adjourned and the arrested person is released –
  (a) the matter must be dealt with (whether by the same or another judge) within 28 days of the date on which the arrested person appears in court; and
  (b) the arrested person must be given not less than 2 days' notice of the hearing.

(5) An application notice seeking the committal for contempt of court of the arrested person may be issued even if the arrested person is not dealt with within the period mentioned in paragraph (4)(a).

(6) CCR Order 29, rule 1 shall apply where an application is made in a county court to commit a person for breach of an injunction, as if references in that rule to the judge included references to a district judge.

(For applications in the High Court for the discharge of a person committed to prison for contempt of court see RSC Order 52, rule 8. For such applications in the county court see CCR Order 29, rule 3.)

65.7 Recognizance

(1) Where, in accordance with paragraph 2(2)(b) of Schedule 15 to the 1996 Act, the court fixes the amount of any recognizance with a view to it being taken subsequently, the recognizance may be taken by –
  (a) a judge;
  (b) a justice of the peace;
  (c) a justices' clerk;
  (d) a police officer of the rank of inspector or above or in charge of a police station; or
  (e) where the arrested person is in his custody, the governor or keeper of a prison, with the same consequences as if it had been entered into before the court.

(2) The person having custody of an applicant for bail must release him if satisfied that the required recognizances have been taken.

II Applications by local authorities for power of arrest to be attached to an injunction

65.8 Scope of this section and interpretation

(1) This Section applies to applications by local authorities under section 91(3) of the Anti-social Behaviour Act 2003 for a power of arrest to be attached to an injunction.

(Section 91 of the 2003 Act applies to proceedings in which a local authority is a party by virtue of section 222 of the Local Government Act 1972 (power of local authority to bring, defend or appear in proceedings for the promotion or protection of the interests of inhabitants in their area)

(2) In this Section 'the 2003 Act' means the Anti-social Behaviour Act 2003.

65.9 Applications under section 91(3) of the 2003 Act for a power of arrest to be attached to any provision of an injunction

(1) An application under section 91(3) of the 2003 Act for a power of arrest to be attached to any provision of an injunction must be made in the proceedings seeking the injunction by –

(a) the claim form;

(b) the acknowledgment of service;

(c) the defence or counterclaim in a Part 7 claim; or

(d) application under Part 23.

(2) Every application must be supported by written evidence.

(3) Every application made on notice must be served personally, together with a copy of the written evidence, by the local authority on the person against whom the injunction is sought not less than 2 days before the hearing.

(Attention is drawn to rule 25.3(3) – applications without notice)

65.10 Injunction containing provisions to which a power of arrest is attached

(1) Where a power of arrest is attached to a provision of an injunction on the application of a local authority under section 91(3) of the 2003 Act, the following rules in Section I of this Part shall apply –

(a) rule 65.4; and

(b) paragraphs (1), (2), (4) and (5) of rule 65.6.

(2) CCR Order 29, rule 1 shall apply where an application is made in a county court to commit a person for breach of an injunction.

III Demotion claims, proceedings related to demoted tenancies and applications to suspend the right to buy

65.11 Scope of this section and interpretation

(1) This Section applies to –

(a) claims by a landlord for an order under section 82A of the Housing Act 1985 or under section 6A of the Housing Act 1988 ('a demotion order');

(aa) claims by a landlord for an order under section 121A of the Housing Act 1985 ('a suspension order'); and

(b) proceedings relating to a tenancy created by virtue of a demotion order.

(2) In this Section –

(a) 'a demotion claim' means a claim made by a landlord for a demotion order;

(b) 'a demoted tenancy' means a tenancy created by virtue of a demotion order;

(c) 'suspension claim' means a claim made by a landlord for a suspension order; and
(d) 'suspension period' means the period during which the suspension order suspends the right to buy in relation to the dwelling house.

65.12 Demotion claims or suspension claims made in the alternative to possession claims

Where a demotion order or suspension order (or both) is claimed in the alternative to a possession order, the claimant must use the Part 55 procedure and Section I of Part 55 applies, except that the claim must be made in the county court for the district in which the property to which the claim relates is situated.

65.13 Other demotion or suspension claims

Where a demotion claim or suspension claim (or both) is made other than in a possession claim, rules 65.14 to 65.19 apply.

65.14 Starting a demotion or suspension claim

(1) The claim must be made in the county court for the district in which the property to which the claim relates is situated.
(2) The claim form and form of defence sent with it must be in the forms set out in the relevant practice direction.

(The relevant practice direction and Part 16 provide details about the contents of the particulars of claim)

65.15 Particulars of claim

The particulars of claim must be filed and served with the claim form.

65.16 Hearing date

(1) The court will fix a date for the hearing when it issues the claim form.
(2) The hearing date will be not less than 28 days from the date of issue of the claim form.
(3) The standard period between the issue of the claim form and the hearing will be not more than 8 weeks.
(4) The defendant must be served with the claim form and the particulars of claim not less than 21 days before the hearing date.

(Rule 3.1(2)(a) provides that the court may extend or shorten the time for compliance with any rule and rule 3.1(2)(b) provides that the court may adjourn or bring forward a hearing)

65.17 Defendant's response

(1) An acknowledgement of service is not required and Part 10 does not apply.
(2) Where the defendant does not file a defence within the time specified in rule 15.4 he may take part in any hearing but the court may take his failure to do so into account when deciding what order to make about costs.
(3) Part 12 (default judgment) does not apply.

65.18 The hearing

(1) At the hearing fixed in accordance with rule 65.16(1) or at any adjournment of that hearing the court may –
   (a) decide the claim; or
   (b) give case management directions.

(2) Where the claim is genuinely disputed on grounds which appear to be substantial, case management directions given under paragraph (1)(b) will include the allocation of the claim to a track or directions to enable it to be allocated.

(3) Except where –
   (a) the claim is allocated to the fast track or the multi-track; or
   (b) the court directs otherwise,

   any fact that needs to be proved by the evidence of witnesses at a hearing referred to in paragraph (1) may be proved by evidence in writing.

(Rule 32.2(1) sets out the general rule about evidence. Rule 32.2(2) provides that rule 32.2(1) is subject to any provision to the contrary)

(4) All witness statements must be filed and served at least two days before the hearing.

(5) Where the claimant serves the claim form and particulars of claim, he must produce at the hearing a certificate of service of those documents and rule 6.14(2)(a) does not apply.

65.19 Allocation

When the court decides the track for the claim, the matters to which it shall have regard include –

(a) the matters set out in rule 26.8; and
(b) the nature and extent of the conduct alleged.

65.20 Proceedings relating to demoted tenancies

A practice direction may make provision about proceedings relating to demoted tenancies.

IV Anti-social behaviour orders under the Crime and Disorder Act 1998

65.21 Scope of this Section and interpretation

(1) This Section applies to applications in proceedings in a county court under sub-sections (2), (3) or (3B) of section 1B of the Crime and Disorder Act 1998 by a relevant authority, and to applications for interim orders under section 1D of that Act.

(2) In this Section –
   (a) 'the 1998 Act' means the Crime and Disorder Act 1998;
   (b) 'relevant authority' has the same meaning as in section 1(1A) of the 1998 Act; and
   (c) 'the principal proceedings' means any proceedings in a county court.

65.22 Application where the relevant authority is a party in principal proceedings

(1) Subject to paragraph (2) –

(a) where the relevant authority is the claimant in the principal proceedings, an application under section 1B(2) of the 1998 Act for an order under section 1B(4) of the 1998 Act must be made in the claim form; and

(b) where the relevant authority is a defendant in the principal proceedings, an application for an order must be made by application notice which must be filed with the defence.

(2) Where the relevant authority becomes aware of the circumstances that lead it to apply for an order after its claim is issued or its defence filed, the application must be made by application notce as soon as possible thereafter.

(3) Where the application is made by application notice, it should normally be made on notice to the person against whom the order is sought.

65.23 Application by a relevant authority to join a person to the principal proceedings

(1) An application under section 1B(3B) of the 1998 Act by a relevant authority which is a party to the principal proceedings to join a person to the principal proceedings must be made –

(a) in accordance with Section I of Part 19;

(b) in the same application notice as the application for an order under section 1B(4) of the 1998 Act against the person; and

(c) as soon as possible after the relevant authority considers that the criteria in section 1B(3A) of the 1998 Act are met.

(2) The application notice must contain –

(a) the relevant authority's reasons for claiming that the person's anti-social acts are material in relation to the principal proceedings; and

(b) details of the anti-social acts alleged.

(3) The application should normally be made on notice to the person against whom the order is sought.

65.24 Application where the relevant authority is not party in principal proceedings

(1) Where the relevant authority is not a party to the principal proceedings –

(a) an application under section 1B(3) of the 1998 Act to be made a party must be made in accordance with Section I of Part 19; and

(b) the application to be made a party and the application for an order under section 1B(4) of the 1998 Act must be made in the same application notice.

(2) The applications –

(a) must be made as soon as possible after the authority becomes aware of the principal proceedings; and

(b) should normally be made on notice to the person against whom the order is sought.

65.25 Evidence

An application for an order under section 1B(4) of the 1998 Act must be accompanied by written evidence, which must include evidence that section 1E of the 1998 Act has been complied with.

65.26 Application for an interim order

(1) An application for an interim order under section 1D of the 1998 Act must be made in accordance with Part 25.

(2) The application should normally be made –

(a) in the claim form or application notice seeking the order; and

(b) on notice to the person against whom the order is sought.

V Proceedings under the Protection from Harassment Act 1997

65.27 Scope of this section

This section applies to proceedings under section 3 of the Protection from Harassment Act 1997 ('the 1997 Act').

65.28 Claims under section 3 of the 1997 Act

A claim under section 3 of the 1997 Act –

(a) shall be subject to the Part 8 procedure; and

(b) must be commenced –

(i) if in the High Court, in the Queen's Bench Division;

(ii) if in the county court, in the court for the district in which the defendant resides or carries on business or the court for the district in which the claimant resides or carries on business.

65.29 Applications for issue of a warrant of arrest under section 3(3) of the 1997 Act

(1) An application for a warrant of arrest under section 3(3) of the 1997 Act –

(a) must be made in accordance with Part 23; and

(b) may be made without notice.

(2) The application notice must be supported by affidavit evidence which must –

(a) set out the grounds for the application;

(b) state whether the claimant has informed the police of the conduct of the defendant as described in the affidavit; and

(c) state whether, to the claimant's knowledge, criminal proceedings are being pursued.

65.30 Proceedings following arrest

(1) The judge before whom a person is brought following his arrest may –

(a) deal with the matter; or

(b) adjourn the proceedings.

(2) Where the proceedings are adjourned and the arrested person is released –

(a) the matter must be dealt with (whether by the same or another judge) within 28 days of the date on which the arrested person appears in court; and

(b) the arrested person must be given not less than 2 days' notice of the hearing.

Practice direction: Part 65 Anti-social behaviour and harassment

This Practice Direction supplements CPR Part 65

Section I – Housing Act 1996 injunctions

Issuing the claim

1.1 An application for an injunction under section Chapter III of Part V of the 1996 Act must be made by form N16A and for the purposes of applying the practice direction that supplements Part 8 to applications under Section I of Part 65, form N16A shall be treated as the Part 8 claim form.

Warrant of arrest on an application under section 155(3) of the 1996 Act

2.1 In accordance with section 155(4) of the 1996 Act, a warrant of arrest on an application under section 155(3) of that Act shall not be issued unless –

(1) the application is substantiated on oath; and

(2) the judge has reasonable grounds for believing that the defendant has failed to comply with the injunction.

Application for bail

3.1 An application for bail by a person arrested under –

(1) a power of arrest attached to an injunction under Chapter III of Part V of the 1996 Act; or

(2) a warrant of arrest issued on an application under section 155(3) of that Act,may be made either orally or in an application notice.

3.2 An application notice seeking bail must contain –

(1) the full name of the person making the application;

(2) the address of the place where the person making the application is detained at the time when the application is made;

(3) the address where the person making the application would reside if he were to be granted bail;

(4) the amount of the recognizance in which he would agree to be bound; and

(5) the grounds on which the application is made and, where previous application has been refused, full details of any change in circumstances which has occurred since that refusal.

3.3 A copy of the application notice must be served on the person who obtained the injunction.

Remand for medical examination and report

4.1 Section 156(4) of the 1996 Act provides that the judge has power to make an order under section 35 of the Mental Health Act 1983 in certain circumstances. If he does so attention is drawn to section 35(8) of that Act, which provides that a person remanded to hospital under that section may obtain at his own expense an independent report on his mental condition from a registered medical practitioner chosen by him and apply to the court on the basis of it for his remand to be terminated under section 35(7).

Section III – demotion or suspension claims

(Suspension claims may be made in England, but may not be made in Wales).

Demotion claims made in the alternative to possession claims

5.1 If the claim relates to residential property let on a tenancy and if the claim includes a demotion claim, the particulars of claim must –

(1) state whether the demotion claim is a claim under section 82A(2) of the 1985 Act or under section 6A(2) of the 1988 Act;

(2) state whether the claimant is a local housing authority, a housing action trust or a registered social landlord;

(3) provide details of any statement of express terms of the tenancy served on the tenant under section 82A(7) of the 1985 Act or under section 6A(10) of the 1988 Act, as applicable; and

(4) state details of the conduct alleged.

Suspension claims made in the alternative to possession claims

5A.1 If the claim relates to a residential property let on a tenancy and if the claim includes a suspension claim, the particulars of claim must –

(1) state that the suspension claim is a claim under section 121A of the 1985 Act;

(2) state which of the bodies the claimant's interest belongs to in order to comply with the landlord condition under section 80 of the 1985 Act;

(3) state details of the conduct alleged; and

(4) explain why it is reasonable to make the suspension order, having regard in particular to the factors set out in section 121A(4) of the 1985 Act.

Other demotion or suspension claims

6.1 Demotion or suspension claims, other than those made in the alternative to possession claims, must be made in the county court for the district in which the property to which the claim relates is situated.

6.2 The claimant must use the appropriate claim form and particulars of claim form set out in Table 1 to the Part 4 practice direction. The defence must be in form N11D as appropriate.

6.3 The claimant's evidence should include details of the conduct alleged, and any other matters relied upon.

Particulars of claim

7.1 In a demotion claim the particulars of claim must –

(1) state whether the demotion claim in a claim under section 82A(2) of the 1985 Act or under section 6A(2) of the 1988 Act;

(2) state whether the claimant is a local housing authority, a housing action trust or a registered social landlord;

(3) identify the property to which the claim relates;
(4) provide the following details about the tenancy to which the demotion claim relates –
  (a) the parties to the tenancy;
  (b) the period of the tenancy;
  (c) the amount of the rent;
  (d) the dates on which the rent is payable; and
  (e) any statement of express terms of the tenancy served on the tenant under section 82A(7) of the 1985 Act or under section 6A(10) of the 1988 Act, as applicable; and
(5) state details of the conduct alleged.

7.2 In a suspension claim, the particulars of claim must –
(1) state that the suspension claim is a claim under section 121A of the 1985 Act;
(2) state which of the bodies the claimant's interest belongs to in order to comply with the landlord condition under section 80 of the 1985 Act;
(3) identify the property to which the claim relates;
(4) state details of the conduct alleged; and
(5) explain why it is reasonable to make the order, having regard in particular to the factors set out in section 121A(4) of the 1985 Act.

Hearing date

8.1 The court may use its powers under rules 3.1(2)(a) and (b) to shorten the time periods set out in rules 65.16(2), (3) and (4).

8.2 Particular consideration should be given to the exercise of this power if –
(1) the defendant, or a person for whom the defendant is responsible, has assaulted or threatened to assault –
  (a) the claimant;
  (b) a member of the claimant's staff; or
  (c) another resident in the locality;
(2) there are reasonable grounds for fearing such an assault; or
(3) the defendant, or a person for whom the defendant is responsible, has caused serious damage or threatened to cause serious damage to the property or to the home or property of another resident in the locality.

8.3 Where paragraph 8.2 applies but the case cannot be determined at the first hearing fixed under rule 65.16, the court will consider what steps are needed to finally determine the case as quickly as reasonably practicable.

The hearing

9.1 Attention is drawn to rule 65.18(3). Each party should wherever possible include all the evidence he wishes to present in his statement of case, verified by a statement of truth.

9.2 The claimant's evidence should include details of the conduct to which section 153A or 153B of the 1996 Act applies and in respect of which the claim is made.

9.3 If –

(1) the maker of a witness statement does not attend a hearing; and

(2) the other party disputes material evidence contained in the statement,

the court will normally adjourn the hearing so that oral evidence can be given.

Section III – proceedings relating to demoted tenancies

Proceedings for the possession of a demoted tenancy

10.1 Proceedings against a tenant of a demoted tenancy for possession must be brought under the procedure in Part 55 (Possession Claims).

Proceedings in relation to a written statement of demoted tenancy terms

11.1 Proceedings as to whether a statement supplied in pursuance to section 143M(4)(b) of the 1996 Act (written statement of certain terms of tenancy) is accurate must be brought under the procedure in Part 8.

Recovery of costs

12.1 Attention is drawn to section 143N(4) of the 1996 Act which provides that if a person takes proceedings under Chapter 1A of the 1996 Act in the High Court which he could have taken in the county court, he is not entitled to recover any costs.

Section IV – Anti-social behaviour orders under the Crime and Disorder Act 1998

Service of an order under sections 1B(4) or 1D of the 1998 Act

13.1 An order under section 1B(4) or an interim order under section 1D of the 1998 Act must be served personally on the defendant.

Application to join a person to the principal proceedings

13.2 Except as provided in paragraph 13.3, an application by a relevant authority under section 1B(3B) of the 1998 Act to join a person to the principal proceedings may only be made against a person aged 18 or over.

Pilot scheme : application to join a child to the principal proceedings

13.3 (1) A pilot scheme shall operate from 1st October 2004 to 30th September 2006 in the county courts specified below, under which a relevant authority may –

(a) apply under section 1B(3B) of the 1998 Act to join a child to the principal proceedings; and

(b) if that child is so joined, apply for an order under section 1B(4) of the 1998 Act against him.

(2) In this paragraph, 'child' means a person aged under 18.

(3) The county courts in which the pilot scheme shall operate are Bristol, Central London, Clerkenwell, Dewsbury, Huddersfield, Leicester, Manchester, Oxford, Tameside, Wigan and Wrexham.

(4) Attention is drawn to the provisions of Part 21 and its practice direction: in particular as to the requirement for a child to have a litigation friend unless the court makes an order under rule 21.2(3), and as to the procedure for appointment of a litigation friend. The Official Solicitor may be invited to act as litigation friend where there is no other willing and suitable person.

(5) Rule 21.3(2)(b) shall not apply to an application under the pilot scheme, and sub-paragraph (6) shall apply instead.

(6) A relevant authority may not, without the permission of the court, take any step in an application to join a child to the principal proceedings, except –

(a) filing and serving its application notice; and

(b) applying for the appointment of a litigation friend under rule 21.6,

unless the child has a litigation friend.

Section V – proceedings under the Protection from Harassment Act 1997

Warrant of arrest on application under section 3(3) of the 1997 Act

14.1 In accordance with section 3(5) of the 1997 Act, a warrant of arrest on an application under section 3(3) of that Act may only be issued if –

(1) the application is substantiated on oath; and

(2) the judge has reasonable grounds for believing that the defendant has done anything which he is prohibited from doing by the injunction.

APPENDIX I

Practitioner checklist

Preparation for the ASBO hearing

Before the hearing, which determines whether or not an ASBO should be imposed, practitioners should consider whether they have dealt with each of the issues raised below, as appropriate.

- Have you applied for the correct form of public funding?
- Is the applicant body a 'relevant authority' within the meaning of CDA 1998?
- Is the application for an ASBO a late one and if so, have you considered applying to strike it out? (county court only)
- Has the applicant body complied with its statutory duty to consult? (stand-alone and county court ASBOs only)
- Has your client got any current mental health needs? Is there any history of mental illness? If so, has the local authority complied with any statutory obligations it may have towards your client? Have you obtained a psychiatric report?
- Has the applicant body complied with its disclosure obligations?
- Is it appropriate to seek disclosure of the consultation process itself?
- Have alternatives to ASBOs been considered? (particularly important when an ASBO is sought against a child or young person)
- If your client is a 'child' or 'young person'? if so, is s/he 'in need'? Has the local authority carried out an assessment of her/his needs?
- If your client is a 'looked after" child or young person, has the applicant body followed the guidance given in *R (M) v Sheffield Magistrates' Court and Sheffield City Council*[1]?
- Is there an interim order in place? Have you obtained a copy?
- Have you taken detailed instructions on the effects of the interim ASBO on your client? Have their been any breaches or alleged breaches?
- Have you taken detailed instructions on the proposed ASBO and the impact of its terms on your client?
- Have you taken witness statements from your client's family and friends who support her/ his account of why the proposed prohibitions interfere with his right to family life?

1 [2004] EWHC 1830 (Admin). See chapter 10.

- Have you taken witness statements from your client's social worker, hostel worker, probation officer, drugs worker, etc outlining his/her support needs as well as where they are geographically located? Are they within or outside of any proposed exclusion zone?
- Has the applicant body / CPS specified the particular anti-social acts relied upon? If not, have you written to request that it does (in the county court, by way of a Part 18 request for further information)?
- Have you taken detailed instructions from your client on each alleged anti-social act?
- Have you considered whether the anti-social acts are 'out of time' or took place pre- 1 April 1999 and therefore potentially irrelevant to the first limb of the test? Are they at all relevant to the second limb?
- Should any of the acts be disregarded because they were reasonable in the circumstances? (stand-alone and county court ASBOs only)
- Has the applicant body / CPS served hearsay notices in relation to the evidence it seeks to rely upon?
- Has it complied with the hearsay rules / CPR?
- Do you require the witness to attend live? Have you complied with the relevant rules in reply?
- Do you wish to serve any witness statements as hearsay? Have you served a hearsay notice?
- Have you considered whether the evidence disclosed is capable of satisfying the first limb of the statutory test to the criminal standard of proof?
- Have you considered CEA 1995 s4 and submissions on the weight, if any, the court should give to any hearsay evidence relied upon by the applicant body?
- If the first limb of the test is satisfied, have you considered whether each of the proposed terms is necessary and proportionate?
- Have you drafted a skeleton argument to hand up to the court if necessary? (highly recommended)

APPENDIX J

Resources

Governmental organisations

Together Campaign: Tackling Anti-Social Behaviour
www.together.gov.uk
Useful links to a wide variety of information and government policy. The 2006 Home Office *Guide to Anti-Social Behaviour Orders* can also be downloaded from this site.

Respect Campaign
www.respect.gov.uk

Home Office:
www.homeoffice.gov.uk/anti-social behaviour

Crime Reduction website
www.crimereduction.gov.uk
Site run by Home Office Crime Reduction Centre 'providing information and resources for people working to reduce crime in their local area'.

Crime Reduction Toolkits
www.crimereduction.gov.uk/toolkits/
Part of the Crime Reduction website, contains crime reduction "toolkits" on issues including anti-social behaviour.

Home Office: Community Safety
www.homeoffice.gov.uk/crime-victims/reducing-crime/crime/community-safety/
Main Home Office area for information on Crime & Disorder Reduction Partnerships, Community Safety Officers, and Neighbourhood Wardens

The Youth Justice Board for England and Wales
www.youth-justice-board.gov.uk
The YJB comprises Youth Offending Teams (YOTs), the police, youth courts and the institutions in which young people are held in custody.

Non-governmental organisations

ASBOconcern
www.asboconcern.org.uk
Asbo Concern is a campaigning alliance of organisations and individuals who are concerned about the use ASBOs.

Statewatch
www.statewatch.org
Very useful links to other organisations, publications, statistics, media coverage.

Young people

Action on Rights for Children
www.arch-ed.org

Barnardos
www.barnardos.org.uk

Children Express
www.childrens-express.org

Children's Legal Centre
www.childrenslegalcentre.com

Children's Rights Alliance
www.crae.org.uk

Howard League for Penal Reform
www.howardleague.org

Inquest
www.inquest.org.uk

National Association for Youth Justice
www.nayj.org.uk

NCH Action for Children
www.nch.org.uk/

Mental Health and learning disabilities

Mind
www.mind.org.uk
The leading mental health charity in England and Wales, working to create a better life for everyone with experience of mental distress

Young Minds
www.youngminds.org.uk

British Institute for Brain Injured Children
www.bibic.org.uk

Attention Deficit and Hyperactivity Disorder
www.adhdinsuffolk.org

Housing

Department for Communities & Local Government
www.communities.gov.uk

Housing Law Practitioners Association
www.hlpa.org.uk

Housing Ombudsman Service
www.ihos.org.uk
Deals with disputes between landlords and tenants in England

Local Government Ombudsman
www.lgo.org.uk

Public Register of Social Landlords
www.housingcorp.gov.uk/resources/register
List of all registered social landlords in England from the housing corporation.

Shelter
www.shelter.org.uk
National organisation working with the homeless and badly housed people

Legal

Department for Constitutional Affairs (DCA)
www.dca.gov.uk
Public funding, Civil Procedure Rules, Criminal Procedure Rules, Court Forms

Judicial Studies Board
www.jsboard.gov.uk
Links to the Adult and Youth Court Bench Books

Sentencing Guidelines website
www.sentencing-guidelines.gov.uk
Produced by the Sentencing Advisory Panel and the Sentencing Guidelines Council to provide sentencing guidelines for particular offences or categories of offences.

BAILII: British and Irish Legal Institute
www.bailii.org
Free access to case law

Statistics

Home Office RDS: research into anti-social behaviour
www.homeoffice.gov.uk/rds/index.htm

Joseph Rowntree Foundation
www.jrf.org.uk
The UK's largest independent social research and development charity

National Statistics
www.statistics.gov.uk

Index

IN and numeral refers to Introduction and page number